Home
Learning
Year by Year

HOME LEARNING YEAR BY YEAR

How to Design a
Homeschool Curriculum
from Preschool
Through High School

REBECCA RUPP

THREE RIVERS PRESS • NEW YORK

Published by Three Rivers Press, New York, New York.
Member of the Crown Publishing Group.

Random House, Inc. New York, Toronto, London, Sydney, Auckland
www.randomhouse.com

THREE RIVERS PRESS is a registered trademark and the Three Rivers Press colophon is a trademark of Random House, Inc.

Printed in the United States of America

Design by Meryl Sussman Levavi/Digitext

Library of Congress Cataloging-in-Publication Data
Rupp, Rebecca.
    Home learning year by year : how to design a homeschool curriculum from preschool through high school / Rebecca Rupp.—1st ed.
        p. cm.
        Includes bibliographical references.
        1. Home schooling—United States—Curricula—Handbooks, manuals, etc.   2. Curriculum planning—United States—Handbooks, manuals, etc.   I. Title.
    LC40.R89   2000
    371.04′2—dc21   00-023312

ISBN 0-609-80585-1 (pbk.)

10 9 8 7 6

CONTENTS

ACKNOWLEDGMENTS

Many thanks to all who helped in the making of this book. A special thanks to my editors at Three Rivers Press, Ayesha Pande, Lane Eastland, and Rachel Kahan, for their encouragement and near-infinite patience, and to all the homeschooling friends and acquaintances who provided help and support. Most of all, as always, thanks to my sons, Joshua, Ethan, and Caleb, who are kind-hearted and understanding about deadlines, and to my husband, Randy, who makes me feel brave, competent, and beautiful.

HOME
LEARNING
YEAR BY YEAR

THE TRUTH ABOUT CURRICULA

Or, There Is No Such Thing as a First-Grader

Don't panic.

THE HITCHHIKER'S GUIDE TO THE GALAXY

Kids, as any parent knows, are determinedly individual. Interests, learning styles, attention spans, growth rates, developmental progress, and food preferences vary wildly from child to child. One learns to read at five, another at seven, a third at ten. One is a natural athlete; another falls flat while walking across a room. One is fascinated by rockets, a second by insects, a third by Greek mythology. One thinks math is cool; another loathes the very sight of a number. So where do standardized curricula fit in here? What course of study can possibly fit all?

The answer is a resounding *none*. There is no effective one-size-fits-all mode of education. The public school system, which has to cope with some fifty million school-age children annually, does the best it can to meet the needs of the many, targeting its content and goals at a hypothetical average child. On a large scale, it's unfeasible, inefficient, and downright impossible to create curricula tailored to meet the needs of fifty million idiosyncratic individuals.

1

In large-scale education, therefore, kids have to adapt to the decreed norm.

One of the primary advantages of homeschooling is the ability to bypass the decreed norm. Homeschoolers can design their own curricula, assembling resources and using approaches that best suit their own children's needs. Your child is enthralled by marine biology? Invent a curriculum that builds upon this interest. Read books, fiction and nonfiction, about the oceans; play ocean-related games; collect seashells; conduct experiments on water pressure, temperature, and salinity; visit an aquarium; adopt a whale. Your child is fascinated by ancient Egypt? Read ancient Egyptian myths; build a model pyramid; experiment with hieroglyphics; locate Egypt on the map; visit a museum to view ancient Egyptian artifacts. Find out how to make a mummy; read a biography of archaeologist Howard Carter; learn about the Rosetta stone.

When it comes to curricula, kids should always come first. It's not what teachers teach that's important; it's what children learn—and what children learn best is what interests them, what they want and need to know. This, in a nutshell, is the prime source of discord among teachers, children, and standardized curricula. The curriculum says Johnny should be studying long division; Johnny doesn't want to. Now what?

Homeschoolers, given this situation, have a wide range of options. No curriculum is written in stone. Perhaps an alternative math program will do the trick—or math games and manipulatives rather than workbooks; a computer software program; or real-world math exercises involving cooking, carpentry, and other hands-on projects. Perhaps the best course is to drop math altogether for the time being and concentrate on something that sparks Johnny's interest—say, space travel, rock collecting, or raising tropical fish—all of which, willy-nilly, eventually involve math. Our long experience in homeschooling has shown, time and again, that an intense interest in anything inevitably leads everywhere.

On the other hand, almost all homeschoolers, at some point or another, run into the puzzling question of sequence. Where do we start? How do we assure that our kids have an adequate grounding in the basics? What *are* the basics? What comes first? What should we tackle next? While public school curricula vary somewhat from state to state, all have similarities in that they attempt to present an appropriate developmental sequence of skills. Kids learn the letters of the alphabet first, then letter sounds, then the art of blending letter sounds into whole words. Addition and subtraction precede multiplication and division; studies of holidays and famous people prepare beginners for more structured studies of world and American history. Invented spelling precedes conventional spelling and grammar; basic algebra is a prerequisite for chemistry and physics.

Many states require that homeschoolers keep step with the public school curricula and demand proof—in the form of written assessments or tests—to ensure that they are indeed doing so. Colleges, though increasingly enthusiastic about accepting homeschooled students, often require a specific battery of high school background courses. For all of these reasons, it's to homeschoolers' advantage to be familiar with the general course of the standardized educational curriculum. The basic curriculum, however, should be used as a reference point and a guideline rather than a set of predetermined assignments. In many cases, there are equivalents and alternatives to the courses described here; and parents should adjust and adapt to best meet the needs of their own children.

Finally, no parent should view the standardized curriculum as cause for worry. Children vary, and homeschoolers inevitably will find that their more-or-less first-grader isn't quite standard. He or she may be reading at an advanced level but lagging in such essentials as arithmetic, time-telling, and the competent tying of shoes. Or, alternatively, he or she may have whizzed confidently ahead in math but be struggling with the awful process of grouping letters into words. As needed, move forward or back in the curriculum for lists of concepts and suggestions. The standardized curriculum can indicate academic areas in which kids need extra help and support—or creative substitutes and alternatives, or stress-reducing periods of being left alone. Variation, though, is normal, and our many individual differences are what make the world the interesting place it is. Kids are natural learners, and each will find his or her own best way to learn. There are many roads to an educational Rome.

STATE STANDARDS IN PUBLIC EDUCATION

Public-school standards categorized by state, subject, and grade level; Web site: www.putnamvalleyschools.org/Standards.html.

STATE STANDARDS

Click on a state to access information on standards and assessment methods, plus related lesson plans and resources; Web site: www.statestandards.com.

STATE EDUCATION DEPARTMENTS

Links to every state department of education; Web site: promise. cahs.colostate.edu/Project/DOE.html or www.harcourt.com/ educators/education_depts.html.

THE BEST STATE STANDARDS

Which state has the best standards? This site explains the rating process and includes the texts of the very best. The winners: Massachusetts (English), Colorado (geography), California (math), Indiana (science), and Virginia (history); Web site: www.edexcellence.net.

NATIONAL STANDARDS IN PUBLIC EDUCATION

A summary of the national curriculum standards in all academic subjects. The complete standards are available in book form or on CD-ROM; see *Content Knowledge: A Compendium of Standards and Benchmarks for K-12 Education* (John S. Kendall and Robert J. Marzano; McREL, 1997); Web site: www.mcrel.org.

EDUCATION WORLD: NATIONAL STANDARDS

National standards for the fine arts, language arts, mathematics, physical education and health, science, and social sciences; Web site: www.education-world.com/standards/national/index.shtml.

U.S. DEPARTMENT OF EDUCATION

The U.S. Department of Education web site provides a wealth of information about the state of national education, including the "Nation's Report Card," an annual assessment of the academic performance of the nation's fourth-, eighth-, and twelfth-graders, and a summary of national education goals and standards; Web site: www.ed.gov.

NATIONAL COUNCIL OF TEACHERS OF ENGLISH (NCTE)

The Web site includes a summary of the national language arts standards, a standards discussion forum, and a list of publications on standards. For more information, contact NCTE, 1111 W. Kenyon Rd., Urbana, IL 61801-1096; (800) 369-6283; Web site: www.ncte.org.

NATIONAL COUNCIL OF TEACHERS OF MATHEMATICS (NCTM)

The Web site includes an overview of the national mathematics standards. Published in book form as *Principles and Standards for School Mathematics* (NCTM, 2000), with accompanying CD-ROM. For more information, contact NCTM, 1906 Association Dr., Reston, VA 20191-9988; (703) 620-9820; Web site: www.nctm.org.

NATIONAL COUNCIL FOR THE SOCIAL STUDIES (NCSS)

The Web site includes a summary of the national curriculum standards for social studies, with grade-appropriate examples of lessons. A more detailed explanation is available in book form: see *Expectations of Excellence: Curriculum Standards for Social Studies* (NCSS, 1994), available from NCSS Publications, Box 2067, Waldorf, MD 20604-2067; (800) 683-0812. For more information, contact NCSS, 3501 Newark St. NW, Washington, D.C. 20016; (202) 966-7840; Web site: www.ncss.org.

NATIONAL SCIENCE TEACHERS ASSOCIATION (NSTA)

Information on the site includes detailed coverage of the national science education standards. Also available in book form: see *National Science Education Standards* (National Academy Press, 1995). For more information, contact NSTA, 1840 Wilson Blvd., Arlington, VA 22201-3000; (703) 243-7100; Web site: www.nsta.org.

NATIONAL K-12 FOREIGN LANGUAGE RESOURCE CENTER

Information and publications on national foreign language standards and assessment; Web site: www.educ.iastate.edu/nflrc. For more information, contact the National Foreign Language Resource Center, N131 Lagomarcino Hall, Iowa State University, Ames, IA 50011; (515) 294-6699; or the American Council on the

Teaching of Foreign Languages, 6 Executive Plaza, Yonkers, NY 10701; (914) 963-8830; www.actfl.org.

NATIONAL STANDARDS FOR ARTS EDUCATION

A discussion and summary of national standards of dance, music, theater, and visual arts; Web site: artsedge.kennedy-center.org/professional_resources/standards/natstandards/index.html. Also see *The National Standards for Arts Education: What Every Young American Should Know and Be Able to Do in the Arts* (Consortium of National Arts Education Associations, MENC, 1995), available from MENC Publication Sales, 1806 Robert Fulton Dr., Reston, VA 20191; (800) 828-0229. For more information contact the National Art Education Association (NAEA), 1916 Association Dr., Reston, VA 20191-1590; (703) 860-8200; www.naea.org; and the Music Educators National Conference (MENC), 1806 Robert Fulton Dr., Reston, VA 20191; (800) 336-3768; www.menc.org.

NATIONAL STANDARDS FOR HEALTH EDUCATION

A brief explanation of the purposes of health instruction, a list of proposed national standards and essential curriculum content areas, and a bibliography; Web site: www.ed.gov/databases/ERIC_Digests/ed387483.html.

NATIONAL STANDARDS FOR PHYSICAL EDUCATION

Information and publications on educational standards, strategies, and research from the American Alliance for Health, Physical Education, Recreation, and Dance (AAHPERD). The AAHPERD is composed of several related organizations, among them the National Association for Sport and Physical Education (NASPE), devoted to the development of quality sport and physical fitness programs. For more information, contact AAHPERD, 1900 Association Dr., Reston, VA 20191; (800) 213-7193; Web site: www.aahperd.org.

The following curriculum was compiled from a synthesis of the public school curricula of all fifty states, as well as curriculum proposals from private sources and innovative educators. Some limited resources are suggested for most academic subjects and subject categories; for a more complete listing, see *The Complete Home Learning Source Book* (Rebecca Rupp; Three Rivers Press, 1998).

PRESCHOOL

Babies are such a nice way to start people.

DON HEROLD

"What curriculum did you use with your toddlers?" a nervous parent asks; and I have to admit that we used no curriculum at all when our kids were toddlers, and furthermore never dreamed of doing such a thing. We didn't need one. For all children, phenomenal amounts of learning take place in the course of daily living—and never more so than in their very early years.

What to do with your preschoolers? Cuddle them. Talk to them. Answer their questions. Play games. Read picture books. Let them help bake bread, sort socks, and plant the garden. Make play dough. Sing silly songs. Feed the birds. Scribble with crayons and sidewalk chalks. Experiment with finger paint. And just watch: Amazingly, as they grow from infants to toddlers, from age two to three to four, they will acquire an ever-expanding vocabulary and amass an astonishing fund of knowledge. In comfortable everyday fashion, they'll learn to count to ten, absorb the names of shapes and colors, memorize nursery rhymes, the words to "Twinkle,

Twinkle, Little Star," and the alphabet, and figure out how to pedal a tricycle, turn a somersault, and—at least in our experience—to disassemble the toilet, crib, and clock radio, operate the telephone answering machine, coffee grinder, and computer, write their names (both backward and forward) on the wallpaper, and drop the entire contents of the silverware drawer down the radiator. Generally—within limits of safety and parental sanity—preschoolers should be given the freedom to explore. Chances are they'll learn more in an afternoon spent making mud in the sandbox than they will from even the best-designed curriculum.

Most sources agree that by four years of age (or so), kids should know the alphabet. They should also (more or less) share cooperatively with friends and siblings, get dressed by themselves (except for complicated things like snowsuits), recite simple rhymes, songs, and fingerplays, follow one- or two-step directions, and have enough hand-eye coordination to build block towers and string big beads. Most preschoolers can count at least to seven (though not always in correct order), know the names of colors and shapes, and can catch and bounce a ball. All this comes naturally. Letters and numbers are easily learned in the context of everyday activities: Point out the letters on Stop signs; count the spoons on the breakfast table.

Kids grow up fast. Cherish these early years while you've got them. Henry David Thoreau could have been speaking to the parents of small children when he touted the beauties of daily living and the importance of taking time to pay heed to the marvels taking place about you. "It is a great art," Thoreau once wrote, "to saunter." Such is my advice for the preschool curriculum: Saunter. Hold hands and giggle while you're doing it, and bring some bread along to feed the ducks.

EARLY CHILDHOOD RESOURCES

Catalogs

Recommended toys for preschoolers include simple manipulatives: blocks, puzzles, shape-sorting boxes, and bead-threading sets. As kids grow older, add crayons and paper (big sheets of it), sewing cards, and simple board games. Laminated board books—which are durable and tough—are a good choice for toddlers. A lot of the best toys for the very young come straight out of the kitchen cupboards: Among the best is a collection of plastic measuring cups and spoons in varied sizes. For an even better learning experience, add water.

GW SCHOOL SUPPLY EARLY LEARNING CATALOG

Resources and materials for kids aged 0–5. The company also publishes a homeschool catalog. GW School Supply, 1220 Oak St. #E, Bakersfield, CA 93304; (800) 234-1065; www.gwschool.com.

LAKESHORE LEARNING MATERIALS

Resources and materials for preschool and early elementary students, including games, toys, manipulatives, and arts and crafts supplies. Lakeshore Learning Materials, 2695 E. Dominguez St., Carson, CA 90749; (800) 421-5354; www.lakeshorelearning.com.

MICHAEL OLAF'S ESSENTIAL MONTESSORI

The company publishes two catalogs of informative text and product listings: *The Joyful Child,* for children aged 0–3; and *Child of the World* for kids aged 3–18. Each $5, from Michael Olaf's Essential Montessori, 65 Ericson Ct., Arcata, CA 95521; (888) 880-9235; www.michaelolaf.net.

NASCO HOMESCHOOL INTERNET CATALOG: EARLY CHILDHOOD

Art, math, and reading readiness materials for under-fives. Web site: www.homeschoolnasco.com.

MAGAZINES FOR PARENTS

Early Childhood Education Today

Early childhood curricula, activities, and general information. Eight issues per year. Scholastic, Inc., 555 Broadway, New York, NY 10012; (800) 544-2917; www.teacher.scholastic.com/products/ect.htm.

Parent and Child

Described as "the learning link between home and school." The magazine includes articles on health, nutrition, behavior, and educational activities for parents of preschoolers. Six issues per year. Scholastic, Inc., 555 Broadway, New York, NY 10022; (800) 544-2917; place.scholastic.com/parentandchild/.

Totline Magazine
Ideas for active learning for preschoolers. Six issues per year. (800) 609-1724; www.frankshaffer.com/totnews.html.

MAGAZINES FOR PRESCHOOLERS

Babybug
A magazine in board-book format for kids aged 6 months– 2 years. Nine issues per year. The Cricket Magazine Group, Box 7434, Red Oak, IA 51591-4434; (800) 827-0227; www. cricketmag.com.

Ladybug
Simple stories and activites for kids aged 2–6, from the publishers of the acclaimed children's literary magazine *Cricket.* Twelve issues per year. The Cricket Magazine Group, Box 7434, Red Oak, IA 51591-4434; (800) 827-0227; www.cricketmag.com.

Sesame Street Magazine
Stories, games, and activities for Big Bird fans aged 2–5, plus an insert of helpful information for parents. Ten issues per year. Children's Television Workshop; www.ctw.org.

Turtle
Stories, poems, and puzzles on health- and nutrition-related issues for kids aged 2–5. *Turtle,* Box 587, Indianapolis, IN 46206-0567; (317) 636-8881.

Your Big Backyard
Stories, science, games, and puzzles about nature and the environment for kids aged 3–5. Twelve issues per year. National Wildlife Foundation, 8925 Leesburg Pike, Vienna, VA 22184; (800) 588-1650; www.nwf.org.

Books for Parents

The Absolute Best Play Days
Pamela Waterman; Sourcebooks, Inc., 1999
> A theme for each week of the year, Brown Paper Preschool Series with accompanying activities for kids aged 2–6. Topics include dinosaurs, pirates, nursery rhymes, and clocks.

The Complete Idiot's Guide to Parenting a Preschooler and Toddler, Too
Kenneth Boyd and Kevin Osborn; Macmillan, 1997
> Over 350 pages of essential information and instructions on everything from toilet training to television. Along the same lines, also see *Parenting for Dummies* by Sandra and Dan Gookin (IDG Books Worldwide, 1995).

The Complete Resource Book: An Early Childhood Curriculum with Over 2000 Activities and Ideas
Pamela Schiller and Kay Hastings; Gryphon House, 1998
> The title says it all.

The Early Childhood Almanac
Dana Newmann; Prentice Hall, 1997
> Many creative learning ideas and activities for each month of the year for kids aged 3–7. For kids aged 6–12, see *The Complete Teachers Almanac* by the same author (1977).

Great Explorations: 100 Creative Play Ideas for Parents and Preschoolers from Playspace
Amy Nolan; Pocket Books, 1997
> Terrific projects from the Boston Children's Museum. Each is preceded by a description of the skills that the activity helps kids learn.

Miseducation: Preschoolers at Risk
David Elkind; Alfred A. Knopf, 1988
> No matter how bright your preschooler is, beware of too much too soon. Elkind argues forcefully against the early introduction of formal academics.

More Than Magnets: Exploring the Wonders of Science in Preschool and Kindergarten
Sally Moomaw and Brenda Hieronymus; Gryphon House, 1997
> Scientific background information and related hands-on activities for kids aged 3–6. Projects incorporate math, literature, art, music,

cooking, and motor development. Other books in the same format include *More Than Singing: Discovering Music in Preschool and Kindergarten* (Redleaf Press, 1997) and *More Than Painting: Exploring the Wonders of Art in Preschool and Kindergarten* (Redleaf Press, 1999).

Not! The Same Old Activities for Early Childhood
Moira D. Green; Delmar Publishing, 1997

An extra-creative collection of activities for kids aged 3–6, incorporating science, math, social studies, art, and music. Chapter titles include "Feather Frenzy," "Woodworkers" (great for preschool carpenters), "Waxworks," "Sound Makers," and "Seed-Sational."

The Parents' and Teachers' Guide to Helping Young Children Learn
Betty Farber, ed.; Preschool Publications, 1997

Articles from thirty-five contributors on the joys of learning through everyday experience, with suggestions for choosing toys, sharing books, nurturing the imagination, taking neighborhood field trips, introducing math, and discovering the computer.

Positive Discipline for Preschoolers
Jane Nelsen, Rosalyn Duffy, and Cheryl Erwin; Prima Publishing, 1998

Information on the normal emotional and social developmental process and detailed discussions of effective disciplinary skills. Chapters include "Don't Talk to Me in That Tone of Voice!" and "You Can't Come to My Birthday Party!" Other titles in the series include *Positive Discipline: The First Three Years* (1998) and *Positive Discipline A–Z: From Toddlers to Teens* (1999).

BOOKS AND RESOURCES FOR KIDS

ABC Drive!: A Car Trip Alphabet
Naomi Howland; Clarion Books, 1994

There are many wonderful alphabet books, but this one exemplifies how learning takes place naturally in the course of daily life. Here a small boy accompanies his mother on a drive around San Francisco, identifying letter-related features as they travel, beginning with *A* (for Ambulance) and *B* (for Bus).

Alphabet Art: With A to Z Animal Art and Fingerplays
Judy Press; Williamson Publishing, 1997

Many creative ways to learn to alphabet (and much more) for kids aged 2–6.

Brain Quest Series

Workman Publishing

Question-and-answer games for kids from preschool through grade 7 in the form of color-illustrated decks of hinged cards. *My First Brain Quest,* for children aged 2–3, includes "400 questions to build your toddler's vocabulary." *Brain Quest for Threes,* for ages 3–4, includes letter and number quizzes, matching puzzles, and shadow pictures. *Brain Quest for Preschool,* for ages 4–5, contains 300 illustrated questions and activities, including alphabet and number quizzes, Mother Goose challenges, and mix-and-match puzzles. Brain Quest/Workman Publishing; (800) 722-7202; www.brainquest.com.

Everybody Has a Body: Science from Head to Toe
Robert E. Rockwell, Robert A. Williams, and Elizabeth A. Sherwood; Gryphon House, 1992

Science activities for kids aged 3–6, all centering around the workings of their very own bodies.

The Little Hands Art Book
Judy Press; Williamson Publishing, 1994

Over seventy art projects in a wide range of media for kids aged 2–6. In the same format, see *The Little Hands Nature Book: Earth, Sky, Critters, and More* (Nancy Fusco Castaldo, 1997).

Math Counts Series

Henry Pluckrose; Children's Press, 1995

A mathematical series for young children, creatively illustrated with color photographs. First titles include *Pattern, Shape,* and *Size.* In *Pattern,* for example, kids identify patterns in checkerboards, leaves, peacock feathers, zebra stripes, honeycombs, Persian carpets, and wallpaper. Subsequent titles include *Sorting, Counting,* and *Numbers.*

Math Play!

Diane McGowan and Mark Schrooten; Williamson Publishing, 1997

"80 Ways to Count and Learn" for kids aged 2–6. Games and activities cover counting, sequencing, pattern formation, and shapes.

Science Play!

Jil Frankel Hauser; Williamson Publishing, 1998

Simple, varied, and mind-expanding science activities for kids aged 2–6.

Wee Sing Series

Price Stern Sloan Publishing

Many titles, among them *Wee Sing for Baby, Wee Sing Nursery Rhymes and Lullabies,* and *Wee Sing Children's Songs and Fingerplays.* Each includes a musical cassette and illustrated booklet.

BEST READING

Recommended books for toddlers and preschoolers include *Pat the Bunny* by Dorothy Kunhardt, *Goodnight Moon* by Margaret Wise Brown, *Where's Spot?* by Eric Hill (as well as Spot's many sequels), *Brown Bear, Brown Bear, What do You See?* by Bill Martin, Jr., *The Carrot Seed* by Ruth Krauss, *The Snowy Day* by Ezra Jack Keats, and *The Very Hungry Caterpillar* by Eric Carle. Read nursery rhymes, new and old, and enrich the experience with songs and fingerplays. Read childhood classics: the tales of Goldilocks and the Three Bears, and the Big Bad Wolf and the Three Little Pigs, the adventures of Little Red Riding Hood, the stories of Cinderella, Sleeping Beauty, Snow White, and Jack and his magical beanstalk.

Add some challenge to the mix. Kids can enjoy a wide range of literature, including works beyond their present vocabulary levels. If they're interested—believe me—they'll sit still, enthralled, and listen; and their command of vocabulary will advance by leaps and bounds. A flip through my homeschool journals for the year our sons—Caleb, Ethan, and Josh—were respectively four, six, and seven shows that we read not only stacks of early elementary-level picture books but a good selection of longer fare as well. Lists include Eric Hill's *Spot's Birthday Party,* Laura J. Numeroff's *If You Give a Mouse a Cookie,* Leo Lionni's *Inch by Inch,* and P. D. Eastman's *Sam and the Firefly,* along with Rudyard Kipling's *Just-So Stories,* Beverly Cleary's *Ramona the Pest,* Norton Juster's *The Phantom Tollbooth,* everything we could find by Edward Eager, and Walter R. Brooks's *Freddy the Detective.* I wrote down some of the questions the boys asked while reading *Freddy.* "What's *incriminate*?" "What's *indict*?" "What's *degrade*?" "What's a *verdict*?" "What's a *sentence*?" "What's a *gavel*?" And from Ethan, the mechanically minded child: "How does a magnifying glass work? How come it makes things look bigger?" You can't do better than that in the way of curriculum. Kids in the preschool and early elementary years are unquenchable sources of questions. All you have to do is answer all of them.

ALSO SEE:

Best Books for Beginning Readers
Thomas Gunning; Allyn & Bacon, 1998
   A large annotated collection of best books for young children preschool–grade 2.

Eentsy Weentsy Spider: Fingerplays and Action Rhymes
Joanna Cole; Mulberry Books, 1991
   A picture book of thirty-eight classic childhood rhymes with associated games and fingerplays, including the "Eentsy Weentsy Spider" and "I'm a Little Teapot."

My Very First Mother Goose
Iona Opie, ed.; Candlewick Press, 1996
   A beautifully illustrated 100-plus-page collection of nursery rhymes, assembled under the auspices of famed folklorist Iona Opie. Also see the sequel *Here Comes Mother Goose* (1999).

The Read-Aloud Treasury
Joanna Cole, ed.; Doubleday, 1988
   An excellent illustrated anthology of classic and modern nursery rhymes, poems, and stories for kids aged 1–5.

BOOK LISTS

Books listed by age group, including a "Toddler's Library" and collections recommended for kids aged 3–4, 5, and 6–7. Web site: members.aol.com/ivonavon/booklis.htm.

GREAT BOOK LISTS

Book lists by age and subject. Included are "Nonfiction Books for Preschoolers" and "Books for the Young and Restless" (toddlers). Web site: www.buffalolib.org/kc.books.html.

PRESCHOOL PICTURE BOOKS BY THEME

Books for preschoolers listed by topic, among them animals, the alphabet, counting, feelings, and teddy bears. Web site: www. preschoolrainbow.org/book-themes.htm.

READ ME A BOOK: READING LISTS

Recommended reading lists for babies, toddlers, and preschoolers aged 3–4. Web site: readmeabook.com/lists.htm.

COMPUTER SOFTWARE

Blue's ABC Time Activities

Blue's 123 Time Activities

Clever and varied activities for kids aged 3–6, starring a floppy-eared blue dog. Humongous Entertainment; (800) 499-8386; www.humongous.com.

Jumpstart Toddlers

Jumpstart Preschool

Jumpstart Preschool–Kindergarten

Multifaceted activities and experiences for a year's worth of learning skills. *Toddlers,* for kids aged 18 months–3 years, covers computer-mouse skills, letters and numbers, simple words, and music; *Preschool,* for ages 2–4, covers mouse skills, letters and numbers, phonics and beginning vocabulary, and music; *Preschool–Kindergarten,* for ages 3–5, covers letter order and phonics, vocabulary, counting, simple problem-solving, "social rules," and music. Knowledge Adventure, Inc.; (800) 545-7677; www.jumpstart.com or www.knowledgeadvenure.com.

Living Books: Dr. Seuss's ABC
An animated interactive version of Seuss's popular alphabet book for kids aged 3–7. Also see other titles in the Living Books series. Mattel Interactive; (800) 395-0277; www.mattelinteractive.com.

Reader Rabbit Preschool
Sixty interactive activities comprising a full year of learning skills for kids aged 3–5, accessible at four different levels. Included are sing-alongs, letter and phonics exercises, numbers and counting, matching and sequencing puzzles, pattern identification and classification games, and simple arithmetic. Mattel Interactive; (800) 395-0277; www.mattelinteractive.com.

Sesame Street Baby and Me
Sesame Street Toddler
Sesame Street: Elmo's Preschool
Baby and Me, for kids aged 1–3, covers colors, shapes, letters, and animals; Toddler, for kids aged 2–4, includes activities involving letters, numbers, counting, shapes, and rhyming. Elmo's Preschool, for ages 3–5, includes forty varied activities covering letters, phonics, shapes and colors, numbers and counting, and following directions. Mattel Interactive; (800) 395-0277; www.mattelinteractive.com.

WEB SITES

EARLY CHILDHOOD EDUCATORS
Links to information on all aspects of early childhood education, including developmental stages, teaching methods, arts and crafts, learning disabilities, curricula, and lesson plans. Web site: www.earlychildhood.about.com.

ENCHANTED LEARNING PRESCHOOL ACTIVITIES
Craft projects, coloring books, nursery rhymes, a multilingual picture dictionary, and many mind-expanding games for preschoolers; Web site: www.EnchantedLearning.com.

HOMESCHOOLING PRESCHOOL

The preschool page includes games and activities, educational resources, and many suggestions for encouraging your toddler's love of learning; Web site: www.homeschooling.about.com.

INTERACTIVE PARENT

Developmental information and age-appropriate activities for infants, toddlers, preschoolers, elementary school students, and teens. Web site: interactiveparent.com.

INTERNET GAMES FOR KIDS: PRESCHOOL

A long list of interactive games for kids aged 2–5. Players learn letters and numbers, solve contect-the-dots puzzles, experiment with color-mixing, access an audio picture dictionary, and much more; Web site: kidsnetgames.about.com.

NATIONAL NETWORK FOR CHILD CARE: AGES AND STAGES

Detailed information on the physical, intellectual, social, and emotional development of children, listed by age, newborn–12. Web site: www.nncc.org/Child.Dev/child.dev.page.html.

PARENTSOUP

Information, discussion groups, and resources for parents of babies, toddlers and preschoolers, school-aged children, and teenagers. Web site: www.parentsoup.com.

PRESCHOOL AND KINDERGARTEN LINKS

Many annotated links, categorized by age. Everything from alphabet and number games to coloring pages, recipes for play dough, and interactive stories in Spanish; Web site: www.geocities.com/Athens/Aegean/3446/preschool.htm.

PRESCHOOL EDUCATION

Many educational activities for preschoolers in a wide range of categories; Web site: www.preschooleducation.com.

ZERO TO THREE

Information, developmental milestones, and a substantial resource list for the parents of children aged 0–3. Web site: www.zerotothree.org.

KINDERGARTEN

There must be a beginning of any great matter, but the continuing unto the end until it be thoroughly finished yields the true glory.

SIR FRANCIS DRAKE

LANGUAGE ARTS

READING

Kindergartners generally are considered to be prereaders—that is, they're trembling on the brink but they're not quite there yet. In most public school programs, kindergartners concentrate on a battery of readiness skills, designed to prepare them for the upcoming (in first grade) plunge into literature. They therefore learn the letters of the alphabet, the sounds of the letters (phonemes), and—using both—begin to translate simple three-letter groups (*cat*) into spoken words. In the accepted scheme of things, reading proceeds in logical and incremental fashion, from the memorization of letters to the mastering of phonemes, then to the decoding of words, and finally to the stringing of words into sentences and the comprehension of their meaning.

"Dear parent," write the authors of one reading program, "conventional wisdom says that if you teach children the alphabet, buy them picture books, and read to them every night, they will magically start to read. Conventional wisdom is wrong." Wrong or no, I remain firmly convinced that at least two of our children learned to read in just this fashion, though precisely what combination of rudimentary phonics skills, visual and verbal memory, and inspired guess went on behind the scenes is conjecture. Joshua, I suspect, learned to read by poring over *Calvin and Hobbes* comic strips. Caleb learned to read via the homemade adventures of Bad Bob, a ravenous, ill-behaved, and slightly cross-eyed sheep.

Ethan learned phonics.

PHONICS, DECODING, AND WORD RECOGNITION

1. Know the upper- and lower-case letters of the alphabet, both in and out of sequence. There are many excellent alphabet picture books for young letter-learners; a list appears below. Another popular resource for kids at this stage is a set of magnetic letters for display (at kid level) on the family refrigerator. These are available in both upper- and lower-case sets and can be obtained from most toy and game stores.

Kids of kindergarten age learn best through hands-on activities. Try making letter posters for each letter of the alphabet—say, a big *A* made of construction-paper apples—or making play-dough letters or baking letter-shaped cookies.

Learning Letters Through All Five Senses
Lois McCue; Gryphon House, 1983

Suggestions for multifaceted projects for each letter of the alphabet. Under *P*, for example, kids push boxes, sniff perfume, sing "Polly Put the Kettle On," and make play-dough *P*s.

PARTICULARLY INTERESTING ALPHABET BOOKS

The Absolutely Awful Alphabet
Mordicai Gerstein; Harcourt Brace, 1999

A is an awfully arrogant amphibian; *D* a pack of dreadfully dangerous drooling demons. Each letter in this collection of alliterative monsters looks worse than the last, and all behave badly too.

The Accidental Zucchini: An Unexpected Alphabet
Max Grover; Harcourt Brace, 1997
Bright paintings illustrate such unexpected sights as an apple auto, fork fence, and vegetable volcano.

Animalia
Graeme Base; Harry N. Abrams, 1997
Fantastic and fascinating. Twenty-six spectacular illustrations cover the alphabet from the "Armored Armadillo Avoiding an Angry Alligator" to the "Zany Zebras Zigzagging in Zinc Zeppelins."

Chicka Chicka Boom Boom
John Archambault; Simon & Schuster, 1991
The alphabet in irresistible rhyme. "A told B and B told C, 'I'll meet you at the top of the coconut tree.'" As more and more letters make the climb, the coconuts begin to fall, with the sound "Chicka Chicka Boom Boom."

Curious George Learns the Alphabet
H. A. Rey; Houghton Mifflin, 1973
Curious George learns all his letters, both upper- and lower-case. The book is a clever visual mnemonic: The letters are incorporated into pictures showing appropriate objects or animals. *P,* for example, is a penguin. Also see *Curious George: ABC Adventure,* an interactive series of letter and phonics activities on CD-ROM for kids aged 3–6. Houghton Mifflin; (800) 733-2828; www.eduplace.com.

The Disappearing Alphabet
Richard Wilbur; Harcourt Brace, 1998
Twenty-six clever poems show what would happen if the letters of the alphabet began to disappear. (Without *S,* we'd have nothing but hissless "erpent" and "nake.")

Dr. Seuss's ABC
Dr. Seuss; Random House, 1963
A zany classic of upper- and lower-case letters, from Aunt Annie's alligator to the Zizzer-zazzer-zuzz.

Eating the Alphabet: Fruits and Vegetables from A to Z
Lois Ehlert; Harcourt Brace, 1993
Not just apple, but endive, jicama, papaya, xigua, and yam.

Q Is for Duck
Mary Elting; Houghton Mifflin, 1980

An entertaining alphabet of riddles. *Q* is for *Duck* because ducks Quack. So why is *A* for *Zoo*? *B* for *Dog*?

A World of Words: An ABC of Quotations
Tobi Tobias; Lothrop, Lee & Shepard, 1998

Enchanting paintings and wonderful quotations from everything from Inuit folklore to Shakespeare illustrate single alphabetical words. A William Blake quote accompanies *moon*, Lewis Carroll is paired with *unicorn*, and J. R. R. Tolkien with *dream*.

2. Know letter sounds for all the consonants and the short vowels (a, e, i, o, and u). Given a letter sound, kids should be able to come up with the correct letter (the process of *encoding*); alternatively, given a letter, kids should know the correct letter sound (*decoding*).

3. Know that letters are linked together to form words. Kids should recognize that letters are grouped to form words; and words are linked to form sentences. They should also know that—in English—words are decoded from left to right; and that reading proceeds from left to right, and from top to bottom on a page. Left-to-right sequencing is an essential skill for readers. Kids should practice tracking short sequences of phonemes in proper order, such as *s-m-b* or *th-j-d*.

4. Be able to blend short sequences of phonemes to form words. Kids should be able to blend *onsets*—beginning consonants—with *rimes* (a vowel plus any ending consonant) to form words (c + at = cat). They should be able to extend this process to form rhyming families of words: Having decoded *cat,* for example, they should be able to come up with *bat, fat, hat, mat,* and *sat.*

Kindergartners should also be able to combine isolated phonemes to form short words, blending *p, i,* and *g,* for example, to produce a complete *pig.* Once this technique is mastered, kids should be able to read any three-letter CVC (consonant-vowel-consonant) word.

5. Understand syllabication. Kids should be able to count the number of syllables in words and the number of sounds in syllables. Kids should recognize that such words as *Pooh* and *Roo* contain only a single syllable, while *Piglet* and *Kanga* contain two, and *Christopher,* three. To reinforce this concept, kids are encouraged to repeat words while clapping: *Pig* (clap) *let* (clap).

6. Know simple VCC, CVCC, and CCVC words. Once kids are comfortable with a written vocabulary of simple CVC words, add common VCC (vowel-consonant-consonant), CVCC, and CCVC words—such as *ant* and *art* (VCC), *milk* (CVCC), and *frog* (CCVC).

7. Kids should be able to recognize their own names in print. They should also be encouraged to identify and recognize words in everyday contexts: the STOP on stop signs, for example. (See *ABC Drive!*, page 12.)

8. Know age-appropriate sight words. "Sight words" are generally defined as those irregular misfits that do not follow the logical rules of phonics and thus must be memorized. The category also includes very frequently used words that readers, for purposes of speed and fluency, should be able to recognize at a glance. Various (and slightly different) compilations of these words are available, listed by grade. A popular example is the Dolch Word List, which recommends that kindergartners assimilate about thirty simple words, including *a, and, I, the, is, it, we,* and *said.*

> DOLCH WORD LIST
>
> Lists of required sight words, categorized by grade, for learners in preschool through grade 3; Web site: www.geminischool.org/sheppard/reading/dolch.html.

READING COMPREHENSION

1. Be able to order pictures in proper sequence for telling a story. For example, *first* Jack's mother threw the bean seeds out the window, *then* the beanstalk grew, and *then* Jack climbed up the stalk and met the giant.

2. Listen and respond to a variety of age-appropriate texts, including fiction and nonfiction books, myths and legends, fables and folktales, and poetry. Parents should discuss books with kids after (or during) reading—a process that encourages critical thinking and builds vocabulary skills. (It also leads to a lot of impassioned debate over the relative merits of Pooh and Piglet; and turns up some startling revelations about the ethics of that destructive trespasser, Goldilocks.) Kids should also be encouraged to retell stories that they've heard, an exercise that is not only fun but also encourages narrative skills, vocabulary development, self-confidence, and self-expression.

Suggestions for best books for five-year-olds include:

Bedtime for Frances (Russell Hoban; HarperTrophy, 1995)
Blueberries for Sal (Robert McCloskey; Viking Press, 1976)
Caps for Sale (Esphyr Slobodkina; HarperTrophy, 1987)
The Little Engine That Could (Watty Piper; Grosset & Dunlap, 1978)
Mike Mulligan and His Steam Shovel (Virginia Lee Burton; Houghton Mifflin, 1977)
Millions of Cats (Wanda Gag; Paper Star, 1996)
The Runaway Bunny (Margaret Wise Brown; HarperCollins, 1974)
Stone Soup (Marcia Brown; Atheneum, 1989)
The Story About Ping (Marjorie Flack; Viking Press, 1977)
The Story of Ferdinand (Munro Leaf; Viking Press, 1977)
Tikki Tikki Tembo (Arlene Mosel; Henry Holt, 1988)
The Very Hungry Caterpillar (Eric Carle; Putnam, 1984)

Also see:

A Treasury of Stories for Five-Year-Olds
Edward and Nancy Blishen, eds.; Kingfisher Books, 1992
A collection of traditional and modern stories by many different authors, carefully selected for their appeal for five-year-olds. Each takes about ten minutes to read aloud. Titles in the same series include *A Treasury of Stories for Six-Year-Olds* and *A Treasury of Stories for Seven-Year-Olds*.

See Book Lists, pages 400–402, and Great Books Read-Aloud Program, page 59.

3. Know the definitions of *title, author,* and *illustrator.* Age-appropriate picture books about the process of writing a book and the persons who contribute to it include:

From Pictures to Words: A Book About Making a Book
Janet Stevens; Holiday House, 1995

How a Book Is Made
Aliki; HarperTrophy, 1988

RESOURCES FOR READING: BOOKS

Bob Books

Bobby Lynn Maslen; Scholastic
Bright-covered booklets for just-beginning readers, available in three sets, at increasing levels of difficulty. Set 1 includes twelve small books, which manage to be funny with a very, very limited vocabulary. Sample sentence: "Sam sat." Scholastic, Inc.; (800) 724-6527; www.scholastic.com.

Brand New Readers

A series of books for absolute beginners from Candlewick Press, available in four-book packets. Each book is eight pages long, with very simple sentences, helpful illustrations, and a gentle sense of humor. Many titles, among them *Monkey Trouble* (David Martin), *Winnie Plays Ball* (Leda Schubert), and *Here Comes Tabby Cat* (Phyllis Root).

School Zone Start-to-Read Books

Short illustrated paperbacks for beginners, available in three levels. Level 1 books manage to have a humorous plot with only a few simple words. *Jog, Frog, Jog,* for example, centers on a clever frog, an aggressive dog, and a nicely placed log. School Zone Publishing Co.; (800) 253-0564; www.schoolzone.com.

RESOURCES FOR READING: CATALOGS

Sources for early reading materials, including alphabet tiles, flash cards, letter stamps, beginner books, and phonics and early reading games include:

EDUCATIONAL INSIGHTS

16941 Keagan Ave., Carson, CA 90746; (800) 995-4436; www.edin.com.

INSTRUCTIONAL FAIR

Box 1650, Grand Rapids, MI 49501; (800) 443-2976; www.instructionalfair.com.

LAKESHORE LEARNING MATERIALS

2695 E. Dominguez St., Carson, CA 90749; (800) 421-5354; www.lakeshorelearning.com.

WRITING

Kindergartners, along with their beginning reading skills, are generally just learning how to write—or rather to print, a penmanship technique formally known as "manuscript handwriting." According to most public school curricula, kindergartners are expected to master the writing of the alphabet and to begin writing assorted simple words. Kindergartners generally write on paper with a wide three-quarter-inch horizonal ruling, with a red baseline and broken midline for extra guidance in the formation of letters.

HANDWRITING WITHOUT TEARS

A developmentally based program created by an occupational therapist and handwriting specialist for kids in preschool through grade 4. The recommended workbook for beginners is "My Printing Book." Handwriting Without Tears, 8802 Quiet Stream Ct., Potomac, MD 20854; (301) 983-8409; www.hwtears.com.

ZANER-BLOSER

A source for handwriting and spelling programs, ruled paper in all sizes, student writing journals, and other educational supplies. Zaner-Bloser, 2200 W. Fifth Ave., Box 16764, Columbus, OH 43216-6764; www.zaner-bloser.com.

Also see *Handwriting Worksheets*, page 27, and *Draw Write Now*, page 61.

1. **Know proper methods of holding and positioning writing materials.** Right-handed kids should slant their paper to the left; left-handed kids should slant to the right. Beginning writers often have an easier time using oversize pencils, which are easier to hang on to, or using an attached pencil grip, a rubber holder that fits over the barrel of a standard-size pencil and is shaped to encourage proper finger-gripping position.

2. **Be able to print all the letters of the alphabet, both upper- and lower-case.** Kids vary considerably in rate of fine-motor development and coordination. Of our three, one—at age five or six—wrote in staggering capitals with no relationship to any kind of baseline or midline; another wrote in tight, precise, and tiny lower-case letters, approximately on the lines; and the third fell somewhere in between. (This all worked out eventually.)

My ABC Journal
A beginning learn-to-write book with a single letter on each page (upper- and lower-case) along with a related literary activity. Zaner-Bloser (see page 26).

HANDWRITING WORKSHEETS
Handwriting worksheets in a choice of fonts, including manuscript, cursive, and italic; exercises cover the alphabet, numbers, and words. The site includes downloadable samples of blank lined paper in various sizes. Web site: rozalski.tripod.com/handwriting.html.

3. **Be able to write simple words, messages, descriptions, and stories, using basic knowledge of phonics and invented spelling.** The emphasis in early writing projects should be on creativity and the joy of personal expression rather than the niceties of grammar.

Games for Writing
Peggy Kaye; HarperCollins, 1995
A large collection of creative writing games, projects, and activities for kids aged 4 and up, from beginning prehandwriting exercises to family journals.

GNYS AT WRK
Glenda Bissex; Harvard University Press, 1980

So how does writing happen? *GNYS AT WRK* (read "Genius At Work") is a detailed account of one five-year-old's progress, from simple invented spelling to comfortable competence (by age 11).

Also see *The Creative Journal for Children* and *Rainbow Writing,* page 62.

LISTENING AND SPEAKING SKILLS

1. Follow simple oral one- and two-step directions.

2. Retell familiar stories. The process of assimilating, synthesizing, and repeating back information is a highly effective learning technique. Innovative nineteenth-century educator Charlotte Mason advocated such "narration" for kids of all ages in all subjects of the academic curriculum as a means of enhancing listening and organizational skills. Mason recommended that parents or teachers spend a ten-minute period reading a passage or story aloud, after which kids are asked to repeat in their own words what they've just heard.

3. Invent and tell fantasy stories or recount stories about real-life happenings. For our boys, we made a pair of "storytelling boxes"—small plastic boxes filled with index cards—one devoted to imaginative storytelling, the other to reminiscence and real-life descriptions. These quickly evolved into favorite games. Players, in turn, would choose a card from the box and tell a story. Sample cards from the imagination box read, "You've just built a time machine. Where do you go and what happens?" and "One of the eggs in the chicken coop turns out to be a dragon's egg. What does it look like? What happens?" Sample cards from the real-life box encouraged the kids to tell stories about a favorite pet, a vacation trip, a storm, a grandparent, a picnic.

STORYTIME CARDS
Big, bright, color-coded cards in several categories (Characters, Places, Goodies, Activities) designed to serve as story starters or storytelling props for kids aged 3–8. Available in several different sets, along with a booklet, "101 Fun Ways to Use StoryTime Cards." From game stores or Learning Passport, Co., 7104 Loch

Lomond Dr., Bethesda, MD 20817-4760; (800) U-LEARN-2; www.learningpassport.com.

TABLETALK CARDS

Conversation-promoting cards for persons of all ages. Each card poses a thought-provoking discussion question. There are many different TableTalk card sets, among them AnimalTalk, ScienceTalk, MusicTalk, ArtTalk, BibleTalk, and TravelTalk. TableTalk, 1230 Macklind Ave., St. Louis, MO 63110; (800) 444-0435; www.tbltalk.com.

4. Memorize and recite short poems and rhymes. Suggestions for kindergartners include traditional nursery rhymes, such as "Jack and Jill," "Hey Diddle Diddle," and "Humpty-Dumpty."

STUDY SKILLS

Teaching "study skills" to preschoolers and kindergartners generally means introducing kids to the many uses of the public library. Children should know the basics of library etiquette (how to check books out, how to replace books on the shelves) and should know the several different areas of the library (children's room, reading room, reference room, and so on).

Check It Out: The Book About Libraries
Gail Gibbons; Harcourt Brace, 1988
A picture-book introduction to the library for kids aged 4–8.

American Library Association
A wealth of useful information on books and libraries, including—under "Tips for Parents"—"10 Ways Kids Connect @ the Library" and "How to Raise a Reader"; Web site: www.ala.org.

MATHEMATICS

The name of the game in early mathematics studies is *manipulatives*—that is, any collection of concrete objects that can be used to physically represent mathematical concepts. Manipulatives include such countables as beans, blocks, Popsicle sticks, and teeny plastic pigs; base 10 blocks and tiles; measuring tools and containers;

pattern blocks; and hands-on mathematical puzzles. Kids should be encouraged to play, investigate, and experiment with these in the course of their mathematical learning.

Some general resources for kindergarten math include:

CUISENAIRE RODS

Attractive wooden or plastic rods in ten color-coded sizes (units to 10s), which can be used to demonstrate all the basic principles of mathematics (pattern formation, counting, arithmetical operations, fractions). Numerous activity books and lesson-plan books are available to accompany the rods. Excellent multipurpose manipulatives. ETA/Cuisenaire, 500 Greenview Ct., Vernon Hills, IL 60061; (800) 445-5985; www.etauniverse.com or www.cuisenaire.com.

Family Math for Young Children
Grace Davila Coates and Jean Kerr Stenmark; Lawrence Hall of Science, 1997
How to create a mathematical environment for your children. Many math-enhancing games, activities, and investigations (all instructions and patterns are included in the book), plus a discussion of math assessment methods. For more information, see EQUALS Programs, Lawrence Hall of Science, University of CA, Berkeley, CA 94720-5200; (800) 897-5036; equals.lhs.berkeley.edu.

Janice Van Cleave's Play and Find Out About Math
Janice Van Cleave; John Wiley & Sons, 1998
The basics of math for kids aged 4–7 through playful activities and simple explanations.

Mathematics Their Way
Mary Baratta-Lorton; Addison-Wesley, 1995
An activity-centered math program for kids in grades K–2, with detailed lesson plans and reproducible student worksheets. Kids learn math through hands-on experiments and investigations.

Picturing Math: Using Picture Books in the Math Curriculum Prekindergarten Through Second Grade
Carol Otis Hurst and Rebecca Otis; SRA/McGraw Hill, 1996
Projects and suggestions for learning math concepts using children's picture books. Concepts discussed include patterns, numeration, geometry, measurement, time, money, data gathering and analysis, and computation. Fifty picture books are discussed

in detail; an annotated bibliography categorizes 200 additional selections by math concept.

Also see *Math Play!*, page 14, Everyday Mathematics Series, page 68, Math at About.com, page 328, Textbooks, page 393, and Lesson Plans, page 397.

PATTERNS AND CLASSIFICATION

1. Be able to group objects into sets. Kids should understand that a *set* is a group of elements with common properties (of size, shape, color, and so on), and should be able to identify elements in sets that don't belong.

> SET
>
> An award-winning card game for persons aged 5 and up in which players are challenged to identify three-item sets based on such features as shape, shading, and color. Can be played by several players of all ages, all at the same time. Tricky, fun, and mathematically mind-expanding. From game stores or Set Enterprises, 15402 E. Verbena Dr., Fountain Hills, AZ 85268; (800) 351-7765; www.sctgame.com.

2. Identify and continue simple repeating patterns. Given *red block-blue block-green block-red block-blue block* . . . , for example, kids should be able to figure out what comes next.

NUMBERS AND NUMBER THEORY

1. Be able to count from 1 to 31. Kids should be able to recognize and write the numerals 1–31. They should also be able to count backwards from 10 to 1; by 2s to 10; and by 5s and 10s to 50.

The Cheerios Counting Book
Barbara Barbieri McGrath; Scholastic, 1998
> Counting concepts using manipulatives that practically everybody has in the kitchen cupboard.

Two Ways to Count to Ten
Ruby Dee; Henry Holt, 1990
> A Liberian folktale in which King Leopard's throne will go to whoever can throw a spear high enough to count to ten before it lands. (But there's more than one way to count to ten.)

2. Understand one-to-one correspondence. In other words, kids should be able to compare groups of concrete objects or symbols, variously determining whether one group is equal to (the same as), greater than, or less than another. They should be able to count the number of items in a set (to 10) and write the corresponding numeral.

3. Identify ordinal positions from first to fifth. In mathematical language, *ordinal* numbers indicate position in sequence (first, second, third, etc.), while *cardinal* numbers indicate amount or quantity (one, two, three, etc.).

4. Given a number, be able to identify one more or one less. This is a good time to introduce kids to simple number lines. These are easy to make: Just draw a line ten inches long on a sheet of paper, mark it off in inch lengths, and label it from 0 to 10. Number line patterns can also be found in *Family Math for Young Children* (see page 30).

LINE JUMPER

An on-line number line game playable at four different levels from Easy to Superbrain. The easy-level number line runs from 0 to 10; the medium level from 0 to 20. Web site: www.funbrain.com/linejump.

5. Understand the concept of one half. This is easy to introduce in the context of daily life, especially if you have two children.

Give Me Half!
Stuart J. Murphy; HarperTrophy, 1996
A little boy has a whole pizza—until his sister comes home and he has to give her half. An exercise in sharing and fractions for beginners, with a friendly rhyming text.

OPERATIONS

1. Be able to add and subtract numbers from 1 to 10. Kids should experiment with simple addition and subtraction problems using manipulatives.

Domino Addition
Lynette Long; Charlesbridge, 1996
An introduction to simple addition using pictures of big black-and-white dominoes.

2. Know the meaning of the plus (+) and minus (−) signs.

3. Invent and solve simple story problems. Encourage kids to write (and illustrate) their own. Josh at age 5: "There were six enormous dragons. A wizard with a wand turned two of the dragons into beetles. How many dragons were left?"
See Math Stories, page 69.

4. Make and interpret simple pictorial graphs. These are exercises in data collection, classification, and organization. Data should be obtained as much as possible from real-life situations. For example: What kind of pets do your friends have? How many have cats? Dogs? Goldfish?

EXPLORING DATA

Data for graph makers, lesson plans, and related Web sites categorized by grade level (K–4, 5–8, and 9–12). Web site: forum.swarthmore.edu/workshops/usi/dataproject. Also see *The Best Vacation Ever* and *Counting: Ourselves and Our Families* (see page 73).

Money and Measurement

1. Identify pennies, nickels, dimes, quarters, and dollar bills; recognize dollar and cent signs. A useful resource here, suitable for any number of buying, selling, and counting games, is a set of play money (plastic coins and paper bills), available from most toy and game stores.

Benny's Pennies
Pat Drisson; Yearling Books, 1995
Benny has five shiny new pennies and five ideas for spending them. Finally he comes up with a clever solution.

2. Experiment with measurements of length, weight, and capacity. Kids should be able to compare measures of length (longer than, taller than, shorter than), capacity (more full, less full), and weight (heavier than, lighter than), using a variety of measuring instruments, including rulers, scales, and measuring cups and containers.

They should investigate length and weight using both nonstandard and standard measures. Nonstandard measures involve such comparisons as "How many Popsicle sticks does it take to reach all the way across the kitchen table?" or "How many red Cuisenaire rods weigh the same as one pencil?" (Be inventive; this is fun.) They should be able to use a standard ruler to measure lengths in inches.

Math Counts Series
Henry Pluckrose; Children's Press, 1995
> A series of short thought-provoking math books for young children, attractively illustrated with color photographs. Titles to enhance measurement skills include *Length, Weight, Capacity,* and *Time*.

3. Know what a thermometer is and what it measures; be able to make simple hotter than/colder than comparisons.

4. Compare lengths of time that it takes to complete various activities. For example: Does it take longer to eat a sandwich or to take a bath?

5. Tell time to the hour. An excellent resource for beginners is the Judy Clock, a classic bright-yellow timepiece with red knobbed hands (for ease of turning) that has been helping kids learn to tell time since 1952. Now available with a digital inset and accompanying instruction book from Judy/Instructo, (800) 421-5565; www. frankschaffer.com.

6. Know the days of the week in order; recognize names of the months of the year. Kids should also understand the meaning of the terms *yesterday* and *tomorrow*, and *morning* and *afternoon*.

Day by Day a Week Goes Round

Month by Month a Year Goes Round
Carol Diggory Shields; Dutton, 1998
> Brightly illustrated rhyming tours of the days of the week and the months of the year.

Dog Days: Rhymes Around the Year
Jack Prelutsky; Alfred A. Knopf, 1999
> A delightful illustrated collection of short funny dog poems, one for each month of the year.

GEOMETRY

1. Identify right and left hands; be able to use terms of position and orientation such as closed/open, over/under, in front/in back, above/below, and so on. Games to teach positional words can be as simple as sitting on the living room floor with a handful of different-colored blocks. Take turns arranging the blocks in rows. Ask questions. "What color block is behind the green block?" "Which block is on top of the blue block?" "Which color block is on the bottom?"

2. Recognize and identify the basic two-dimensional (plane) figures: square, rectangle, triangle, and circle. Kids should be able to identify basic shapes in common objects and to compare sizes of basic plane figures. Try identifying shapes around the house. Go on a "treasure hunt" to find circles, triangles, or squares.

One useful resource here is a set of *Colorforms,* a now-classic toy that has been around since 1951. The set includes a spiral-bound book of shiny black or white playing boards and a collection of bright-colored flexible geometric shapes (squares, circles, triangles, and rectangles) that can be stuck to the boards to make a variety of pictures and patterns. Available from toy and game stores.

Bear in a Square
Stella Blackstone; Barefoot Books, 1998
> Shapes and numbers for beginners, through bright illustrations and interactive rhymes.

Discovering Shapes Series
Benchmark Books, 1997
> Titles include *Triangles* and *Circles* by Sandy Riggs, and *Rectangles* and *Polygons* by David L. Stienecker. All are picture-book introductions to simply geometry: kids discover triangles in sailboat sails, circles at archery practice, and rectangles at the ball game.

Shapes, Shapes, Shapes
Tana Hoban; Mulberry Books, 1996
> Great color photographs of familiar objects (chairs, manhole covers) that demonstrate a variety of basic shapes.

HISTORY AND GEOGRAPHY

History and geography in the public schools are often grouped under the broader category of "social studies," a combination discipline that includes American and world history, geography, civics, economics, and cultural anthropology. According to the traditional curriculum of "expanding horizons," kids are first introduced to these through the familiar and the close at hand, initially studying home and family (kindergarten), then neighborhood and community (first grade), and gradually enlarging their scope to take in state, country, continent, and world.

This approach, strictly adhered to, often sacrifices interest and appeal for relevance. While children are certainly fascinated by the goings-on around them ("What does a firefighter do?" "What's under the sidewalk?"), they are equally enthralled by history's wonderful stories and by tales of the exotic and faraway: stories of pharaohs and mummies, of Aztec kings in cloaks of quetzal feathers, of mammoth hunters, pueblo dwellers, and Spanish conquistadors, of Pocahontas, the Pilgrims, Paul Revere's exciting midnight ride.

Social studies curricula are necessarily arbitrary; as in all other academic fields, parents should tailor them to suit their own children's skills, learning pace, and interests. While some fields do proceed more smoothly in sequence—addition before multiplication; printing before cursive; *cat* and *mat* before *catastrophe* and *mobilization*—there's no set time at which children absolutely have to learn about pyramids, the Great Depression, or the Minutemen.

A synthesis of more substantive history curricula suggests several themes for kindergarten-level social studies. These include a brief overview of early American history, touching on the historical significance of national holidays; a survey of family life around the world, with exposure to a range of different cultures; and a basic introduction to geography. History and geography should be approached from a number of different angles, using a variety of print materials (fiction and nonfiction books, myths and legends, poetry, and biographies), hands-on projects and activities, art and music, and field trips.

Social Studies Through Children's Literature
Anthony D. Fredericks; Teacher Ideas Press, 1991

A creative and integrated approach to social studies through thirty-two popular children's picture books, including discussion questions, activities and projects, and supplementary reading lists. For kids aged 5–10. From Libraries Unlimited; (800) 237-6124; www.lu.com/tips.

AMERICAN HISTORY

1. American Indian culture. Kindergartners might be introduced to American history through a study of American Indians, perhaps in conjunction with Native American History Month in September. Topics to cover include traditional lifestyles (homes, food, clothing, occupations), religion, legends, and Indian life today.

There are many excellent picture-book versions of traditional American Indian legends. Suggestions for this age group include *The Legend of the Indian Paintbrush* by Tomie de Paola (Paper Star, 1996), *Iktomi and the Boulder* by Paul Goble (Orchard Books, 1988), *The First Strawberries* by Joseph Bruchac (Dial Books, 1993), and the Native American Legends Series by Terri Cohlene (see page 85).

Corn Is Maize
Aliki; HarperTrophy, 1986

A delightful picture-book history of corn ("the gift of the Indians"), with simple activities.

More Than Moccasins
Laurie Carlson; Chicago Review Press, 1996

A creative activity book of Native American projects, games, songs, dances, and recipes for kids aged 3–9.

2. Early exploration and settlement. Topics to cover include the landmark voyage of Columbus in 1492 (and his mistaken belief that he had reached the "Indies") and the arrival of the Pilgrims in 1620.

A Picture Book of Columbus
David A. Adler; Holiday House, 1991

A simple first biography of Columbus.

See Picture Book Biography Series, page 38.

In 1492
Jean Marzollo; Scholastic, 1991

A rhyming account of Columbus's voyage, beginning with the unforgettable "In fourteen hundred ninety-two/Columbus sailed the ocean blue."

3. The Revolutionary War. Topics to cover include the significance of the Fourth of July/Independence Day; and the stories of important events and people of the Revolutionary period, such as Paul Revere, Betsy Ross, Ethan Allen, Benjamin Franklin, George Washington, and Thomas Jefferson.

Colonial Times from A to Z
Bobbie Kalman; Crabtree Publishing, 1997

An alphabet book of colonial life filled with interesting information for young readers. *A* is for *Apothecary; B,* for *Bootmaker.*

George the Drummer Boy

Sam the Minuteman
Nathaniel Benchley; HarperTrophy, 1987

Two different views of the Battle of Lexington and Concord in I Can Read format for beginners.

If You Lived at the Time of the American Revolution
Kay Moore; Scholastic, 1998

What was life like for children during the Revolutionary War? Appealing information presented in a friendly question-and-answer format that invites discussion from listeners.

Picture Book Biography Series
David A. Adler; Holiday House, 1991

A series of short, simple, illustrated biographies for kids aged 4–8. Over twenty-five titles, among them *A Picture Book of George Washington, A Picture Book of Thomas Jefferson,* and *A Picture Book of Paul Revere.*

Also see *If You Lived in Colonial Times* and *Colonial Kids: An Activity Guide to Life in the New World,* page 86.

4. Famous Americans. Kindergartners should know what the president of the United States does, who the current president is and how he/she is elected. They should also be introduced to stories of famous past presidents: for example, George Washington, Thomas Jefferson, Abraham Lincoln, and Teddy Roosevelt.

If I Were President
Catherine Stier; Albert Whitman, 1999
> A picture-book introduction to the presidency, covering the enactment of laws and veto power, the command of the armed forces, the cabinet, the Secret Service, and the lighting of the national Christmas tree.

5. National symbols. Kids should recognize and know the significance of the flag, the Pledge of Allegiance, the national anthem, the Statue of Liberty, and the White House.

The Story of the White House
Kate Waters; Scholastic, 1992
> A short history of the president's residence for readers aged 5–9, illustrated with maps, photographs, and drawings.

Also see New True Books: American Symbols Series, page 83.

WORLD HISTORY

1. Learn about families and family life in different times and places around the world. Kids should be introduced to different ways of life in different places through a variety of materials, including fiction and nonfiction books, hands-on projects and activities, art and music. World history studies should be correlated to geography (see below).

Children Just Like Us
Barnabas and Anabel Kindersley; Dorling Kindersley, 1995
> A superb photographic tour of the globe, featuring kids from thirty countries. Each child is shown in native dress, with accompanying photos of his/her family, home, school, pets, food, clothing, and everyday life.

Hands Around the World
Susan Milord; Williamson, 1992
> Interesting background information and 356 multicultural projects and activities for kids in grades K–6. Includes illustrations and complete instructions.

GEOGRAPHY

Kindergartners should be encouraged to use maps and globes frequently, to play geographical games, and to associate activities in other academic disciplines with geography. When reading multicultural legends, for example, they might find the location of the country of origin on the map; or they might connect geographic locations to storybook characters, native animals, or historical events. A useful—if not essential—resource for the early elementary years is a world map, posted in some readily accessible location. Ours, a twenty-five-cent book sale find, spent many years tacked to the dining-room wall, at adult knee level.

1. Be familiar with the use of maps and globes. Kids should understand what maps and globes represent. They should be able to locate the United States and their own home state on a world map or globe, as well as the Atlantic and Pacific Oceans, and the North and South Poles.

They should also know their own address (street, city, and state) and telephone number.

As the Crow Flies: A First Book of Maps
Gail Hartman; Aladdin, 1993
> A beginner's book of maps, in which kids follow the paths of a flying crow, hopping rabbit, trotting horse, and soaring gull. A sequel in the same format is *As the Roadrunner Runs* (Aladdin, 1994).

Me on the Map
Joan Sweeney; Dragonfly, 1998
> A small girl is introduced to maps, beginning with a map of her bedroom—then of her house, street, town, country, and the whole world, and back again. Colorful illustrations and diagrams and an easy-to-read text.

2. Draw simple maps of known areas, such as their bedrooms, the rooms in their house, their yards or neighborhoods.
See *Me on the Map*, above.

3. Know names and locations of the seven continents of the world. Locate Asia, Europe, Africa, North and South America,

Australia, and Antarctica on the world map and globe. Kids should know some basic information about each.

Colors of the World Series

Various authors; Carolrhoda

Count Your Way Series

Jim Haskins; Carolrhoda

Both are excellent series of world geography picture books for kids aged 4–8. Titles in the Colors of the World Series include *Colors of Mexico* (Lynn Ainsworth Olawsky), *Colors of Japan* (Holly Littlefield), and *Colors of Australia* (Lynn Ainsworth Olawsky); in each, different colors are related to interesting facts about the featured region's geography, history, and culture. There are nearly twenty titles in the Count Your Way Series, including *Count Your Way Through China, Count Your Way Through Africa,* and *Count Your Way Through the Arab World.* In each, kids learn to count to 10 in the featured foreign language, while learning geographical, historical, and cultural facts.

Also see Geography resources, pages 91–92.

SCIENCE

Early science studies should involve direct observation, and hands-on explorations and investigations. From the beginning, kids should understand that science is a process—an active means of answering questions—rather than a to-be-memorized body of facts. One possibility for homeschool science: Encourage kids to keep an ongoing nature journal, which, at kindergarten age, might include simple maps of field trips, labeled drawings, weather records, and short (dictated) accounts of experiments and observations.

Kids should also approach science through fiction and nonfiction books, poems, biographies, and multidisciplinary projects.

Books

Apples, Bubbles, Crystals: Your Science ABC's
American Chemical Society; McGraw-Hill, 1996

A brightly illustrated alphabetical rhyming introduction to science for kids in grades K–2, with accompanying creative activities.

Backyard Scientist Series

Jane Hoffman; Backyard Scientist

A series of easy-to-use science experiment books for kids aged 4 and up. Kids learn about concentrated solutions with Kool-Aid and discover how to propel paper boats with a drop of soap. Backyard Scientist, Box 16966, Irvine, CA 92623; www.backyardscientistcom.

Janice Van Cleave's Play and Find Out Series

Janice Van Cleave; John Wiley & Sons

Science activities for kids aged 4–7. The illustrated books include complete instructions and simple explanations. Titles include *Let's Play and Find Out About Nature, Let's Play and Find Out About Science,* and *Let's Play and Find Out About the Human Body.*

Sandbox Scientist: Real Science Activities for Little Kids

Michael E. Ross; Chicago Review Press, 1995

Hands-on science activities for kids aged 2–7 in a range of different fields. For example, kids build boats, marble ramps, and megaphones.

Science Play

Jill Frankel Hauser; Williamson, 1998

An illustrated collection of simple experiments and activities on air, water, plants, weather, sound, and motion for kids aged 3–6.

Science Through Children's Literature

Carol M. Butzow and John W. Butzow; Teacher Ideas Press, 1988

Science activities, projects, and experiments to accompany thirty popular picture books for kids in grades K–3. Libraries Unlimited; (800) 237-6124; www.lu.com/tips.

Wild Days: Creating Discovery Journals

Karen Skidmore Rackliffe; Sun Rise Publishing, 1998

Many ideas for keeping natural journals for kids of all ages, with examples from the journals of Rackliffe's seven homeschooled children. Karen Skidmore Rackliffe; (801) 269-1997; e-mail: rackliffe@mindspring.com.

ETA/CUISENAIRE

Science kits and materials of all kinds for grades K–6. ETA/Cuisenaire, 500 Greenview Ct., Vernon Hills, IL 60061; (800) 445-5985; www.etauniverse.com or www.cuisenaire.com.

DELTA SCIENCE NUTSHELL KITS

Comprehensive science activity kits for kids in grades K–8. Each includes detailed step-by-step instructions and all necessary materials. Topics for early elementary students include magnets, seeds, weather, the human body, simple machines, and rocks and minerals. The catalog includes many creative science materials. Delta Education, Box 3000, Nashua, NH 03061-3000; (800) 442-5444; www.delta-ed.com.

Physical Science

1. Be able to sort objects into groups according to physical characteristics. Kids should be able to classify objects by a range of basic physical properties. Which are light and which are heavy? Which float and which sink? Which are hot and which cold?

They should also be introduced to the idea that physical properties can be measured; and should conduct simple experiments using nonstandard measures (see Kindergarten Mathematics, pages 33–34).

2. Experiment with magnets. Classify objects according to whether or not they are attracted by magnets. Magnets in many shapes and sizes, including the popular bar and horseshoe, are available from most science and educational supply companies.

Also see grade 1 Science resources, page 94.

3. Experiment with light and shadow. Kids should make predictions and perform simple experiments to discover what causes shadows, and attempt to identify different objects by the shapes of their shadows.

The Little Book of Hand Shadows
Phila H. Webb and Jane Corby; Running Press, 1990
> Shadow creatures for all ages, and all you need is a light, a blank wall, and hands.

Shadow Games: A Book of Hand and Puppet Shows
Bill Mayer; Klutz, 1995
> All the necessities for putting on your own shadow show, including a flashlight and a selection of die-cut shadow figures.

Shadow Story
Nancy Willard; Harcourt Brace, 1999
> A wonderful literature connection for shadows. In this picture-book tale for kids aged 5–10, Holly Go Lolly tricks an evil ogre, the Ooboo, with her clever shadow pictures.

Also see *What Makes a Shadow?*, page 102.

LIFE SCIENCE

1. Be able to discuss differences between living and nonliving things. Kids should know that living things grow and reproduce, and require food, water, and air.

2. Become familiar with plants: beginning botany. Topics to cover include what plants require to grow, the basic parts of a plant, the process of photosynthesis (that is, plants make their own food), and the difference between *deciduous* and *evergreen* plants.

Kids should observe and discuss different kinds of plants and participate in hands-on plant projects.

All About Seeds
Melvin Berger; Scholastic, 1994
> An introduction to the different kinds of seeds, what they need to grow into plants, and suggestions for seed-related activities.

From Seed to Plant
Gail Gibbons; Holiday House, 1991
> A simple pictue-book account of how seeds develop into plants, plus a grow-your-own-bean-plant project.

Also see TOPS Radishes (page 95).

3. Become familiar with animals: beginning zoology. Topics to cover include the basic needs of animals, the different kinds of animal babies and their need for parental care, and pets.

ANIMAL FAMILIES
An animal card game for kids aged 5 and up, in which players learn the names of animal groups (a pride of lions, a pod of whales) and of male, female, and baby animals. ("What do you call a baby horse?") Aristoplay, 8122 Main St., Dexter, MI 48130; (800) 634-7738; www.aristoplay.com.

See *Your Big Backyard*, page 10.

4. The human body: Know the five senses and their associated body parts. If your kindergartner is interested in studies of the human body, there are many creative resources available.

Your Five Senses
Aliki; HarperTrophy, 1990
All about your five senses (sight, smell, hearing, touch, and taste) and the organs associated with them.

Also see *Everybody Has a Body,* page 13, Let's-Read-and-Find-Out Science Series: *The Human Body,* page 98, *SomeBody,* page 138, and *Watch Me Grow,* page 138.

EARTH/SPACE SCIENCE

1. Be able to describe the basic composition of the earth. Kids should understand the makeup of the earth at the most basic level: soil, rocks, water, and air. Hands-on activities might involve collecting rocks and sorting them according to various physical characteristics.
See Delta Science Nutshell Kits, page 43.

2. Know the names and features of the four seasons. Try making your own illustrated summer, fall, winter, and spring booklets; or making "season posters" with representative pictures cut from magazines.

SEASON MYSTERY KIT

The kit includes a simple rhyming science book and a pack of illustrated cards showing how people and animals change their coats through the seasons of the year. Learning Passport Co., 7104 Loch Lomond Dr., Bethesda, MD 20817; (800) U-LEARN-2; www.learningpassport.com.

3. Be familiar with different types of weather. Kids should make observations and keep simple weather records. They should understand the concept of *temperature* and the use of thermometers.

Topics to cover include clouds, rain and thunderstorms, snow and blizzards, and the sun.

The Cloud Book
Tomie de Paola; Holiday House, 1985
A charmingly illustrated introduction to cloud types, plus a very silly cloud story.

Puddle Jumpers
Jennifer Storey Gillis; Storey Communications, 1996
Weather-related projects for early elementary students.

FOREIGN LANGUAGE

While foreign language instruction in the public schools traditionally doesn't begin until the middle or high school years, in foreign language learning, the key seems to be starting young. Some schools, public and private, have begun to institute foreign language programs for early elementary students; many homeschoolers do the same at home. Beginners in this age group learn through listening and speaking, first acquiring simple words and phrases, including greetings, the names of the numbers from one to ten, the names of colors, and other everyday expressions. Many beginning language programs include songs: Music is an excellent memory-enhancing device for language learners of all ages. (It has been many years since my high school French lessons: I've forgotten the fine points of irregular verb conjugation, but I still know all the words to "Au Clair de la Lune.")

There are many elementary-level foreign language programs available commercially.

AUDIO-FORUM

An excellent source of foreign language programs of all kinds for learners of all ages. Audio-Forum, 96 Broad St., Guilford, CT 06437; (800) 243-1234; www.agoralang.com/audioforum.html.

POWER-GLIDE LANGUAGE COURSES

Foreign language courses for kids in kindergarten through college. Elementary-level programs include audiocassettes, illustrated workbooks, and parents' reference guide. Power-Glide, 1682 West 820 North, Provo, UT 84601; (800) 596-0910; www.power-glide.com.

TEACH ME TAPES

Foreign languages through music for kids aged 2–12. Programs include interactive coloring books and audiocassettes. Available in many languages. Teach Me Tapes, Inc., 9900 Bren Rd. E, B1–100, Minnetonka, MN 55343-9664; (800) 456-4656; www.teachmetapes.com.

ART

Art, for kids of all ages, should be a multifaceted experience, incorporating hands-on projects and activities, art theory, art appreciation, and art history. Art should be approached through a range of print materials, including fiction and nonfiction books and biographies of artists. Kids should also be acquainted with the art of different cultures. Try incorporating art into history and geography studies.

If possible, art education should include field trips to artists' studios, museums, art galleries, and exhibitions.

1. Be able to name and describe colors, shapes, and lines and to identify these in works of art. Kids should know the names of the colors (red, yellow, blue, green, orange, violet, black, brown, white, and gray); the basic shapes (square, rectangle, triangle, circle); and lines (thick, thin, straight, curved, wavy, zigzag, broken). They should also be familiar with the concepts of *texture* and *pattern*.

The Art of Shapes
Margaret Steele and Cindy Estes; Fotofolio, 1997

Kids are introduced to colors, shapes, and the parts of the body (including the ever-amusing behind) through famous works by modern artists.

2. Observe and discuss famous works of art by a variety of artists from a range of historical periods.

I Spy Series

Lucy Micklethwait; Greenwillow

An excellent introduction to art for kids aged 4–8. Titles in the series include *I Spy: An Alphabet in Art; I Spy Two Eyes: Numbers in Art; I Spy a Lion: Animals in Art;* and *I Spy a Freight Train: Transportation in Art.* In each, kids are encouraged to explore and study a wide selection of great artworks.

How to Use Child-Size Masterpieces for Art Appreciation
Aline Wolf; Parent Child Press, 1996

An art appreciation program for kids aged 3–12, using postcard-size reproductions of famous paintings. The program includes instructions and suggestions for a wide range of activities, beginning with simple matching games. As kids advance, they learn the names of famous artists and artworks, compare the characteristics of various schools of art, and order artworks on a timeline. Parent Child Press, Box 675, Hollidaysburg, PA 16648-0675; (814) 696-7512; www.nb.net/~pcp.

3. Experiment with a range of art techniques and media.
Encourage kids to try drawing, painting, and simple sculpture, and to experiment with fiber arts, collages, printmaking, mosaics, pottery, and mobiles.

Art Through Children's Literature
Debi Englebaugh; Teacher Ideas Press, 1994

Many creative activities emphasizing the basic elements of art (color, shape, texture, line), all based on award-winning children's picture books. For kids aged 5–12. Libraries Unlimited; (800) 237-6124; www.lu.com/tips.

Kids Create! Art and Craft Experiences for 3- to 9-Year-Olds
Laurie Carlson; Williamson, 1990.
> Over a hundred varied arts and crafts projects for kids, variously categorized under "Paper and Paste," "Clay and Dough," "Printmaking," "Sculpture," and more.

Also see *Drawing With Children*, page 103.

MUSIC

At all age levels, a music program should combine active participation (both vocal and instrumental) with music theory, music appreciation, and music history. Kids should use a range of print materials, including fiction and nonfiction books about music, musical legends and folktales, and simple biographies of famous composers. They should be acquainted with the work of classical composers, as well as a range of modern musical styles and the music of different cultures.

See Rabbit-Man Music Books and Alfred Publishing, page 143.

1. Be familiar with such basic elements of music as rhythm, melody, and harmony. Kids should respond to a steady beat in musical pieces—practice clapping in rhythm—and should participate in a variety of group and solo singing activities.

Kids Make Music: Clapping and Tapping to Bach and Rock
Avery Hart and Paul Mantell; Williamson, 1993
> All kinds of musical activities and projects, from rhythm games to performing your own opera.

Wee Sing Series
Price Stern Sloan Publishing
> A popular series of cassette tapes and accompanying songbooks for kids aged 3–9. Many titles, among them *Wee Sing Around the World* and *Wee Sing Fun and Folk Songs*. Also available on video.

2. Listen and respond to a range of different musical selections, both classical and multicultural. Always popular for young beginners is Serge Prokofiev's *Peter and the Wolf,* an enchanting musical tale in which each character is represented by a different orchestral instrument. (Our kids' favorite: the grandfather, a bassoon.)

3. Recognize instruments by sight and sound. Kids at this level should be able to recognize and name the guitar, violin, piano, trumpet, flute, and drum.

What Instrument Is This?
Rosemarie Hausherr; Scholastic, 1992
> A picture-book introduction to the instruments, illustrated with photographs.

HEALTH AND PHYSICAL EDUCATION

1. Know the importance of exercise, cleanliness, good nutrition, and sleep. This generally comes with the territory of normal parenting. For supportive resources, see the Berenstain Bear series by Jan and Stan Berenstain (Random House), in which Brother and Sister Bear learn about visiting the doctor and dentist, sticking to a healthy diet, developing good manners, telling the truth, resisting peer pressure, and more.
See Grade 1 Health and Physical Education, page 105, and *Turtle* magazine (Preschool), page 10.

2. Participate in age-appropriate athletic activities. Kids should exhibit such basic *locomotor movements* as running, hopping, jumping, and skipping; and such *nonlocomotor movements* as bending and straightening, curling, stretching, and twisting. They should be able to throw, catch, and kick a ball.

Fit Kids! The Complete Shape-Up Program from Birth Through High School
Kenneth H. Cooper; Broadman & Holman, 1999
> Exercise and nutritional programs for each stage of development, along with suggestions for dealing with obesity, eating disorders, superactive athletes, and vegetarians.

Home School Family Fitness: A Complete Curriculum Guide
Bruce C. Whitney; Home School Family Fitness Institute, 1995

A complete program for kids aged 4–18, with instructions, lesson plans, record charts, games and activities, and resource suggestions. Home School Family Fitness Institute, 159 Oakwood Dr., New Brighton, MN 55112; (612) 636-7738; www.tc.umn.edu/~whiten0031.

Physical Education Unit Plans for Preschool–Kindergarten: Learning Experiences in Games, Gymnastics, and Dance
Bette J. Logsdon, Ruann M. Alleman, Sue Ann Straits, David E. Belka, and Dawn Clark; Human Kinetics, 1996

Over 100 sequentially arranged units for enhancing fitness and motor skills. Sections include "Ball Handling," "Preschool Gymnastics," "Preschool Dance," "Kindergarten Games," "Kindergarten Gymnastics," and "Kindergarten Dance."

YOGA KIT FOR KIDS

Instructions, a tape of classical and instrumental music, and a pack of color-illustrated cards showing children in a range of yoga poses. Kids can be a waterfall, a squirrel, a mouse, a bird, a frog, and many more. For kids aged 4–8. Imaginazium; (800) 800-7008; www.imaginazium.com.

GENERAL KINDERGARTEN RESOURCES

BOOKS

Homeschooling: The Early Years
Linda Dobson; Prima Publishing, 1999

A chatty and comprehensive guide to homeschooling kids aged 3–8.

Kindergarten at Home
Cheryl Gorder; Blue Bird Publishing, 1997

Educational activities for kindergartners, with instructions and explanations of the learning skills involved.

Ramona the Pest
Beverly Cleary; Camelot, 1996

Ramona Quimby, aged 5, sets off to kindergarten. A delightful chapter book about the trials and tribulations of life as a five-year-old.

What Your Kindergartner Needs to Know
E. D. Hirsch, ed.; Delta, 1997

A curriculum outline for kindergartners based on the Core Knowledge Sequence, with suggestions and reading selections for language arts, math, art, music, history and geography, and science. For more information on the Core Knowledge Sequence, contact the Core Knowledge Foundation, 801 East High St., Charlottesville, VA 22902; (800) 238-3233; www.coreknowledge.org.

COMPUTER SOFTWARE

Dr. Seuss Kindergarten

A full year of early math and reading lessons hosted by a battery of zany Dr. Seuss characters, with accompanying animations and songs. A tracking feature allows parents to chart their children's progress. Mattel Interactive; (800) 395-0277; www.matelinteractive.com.

Fisher-Price Kindergarten

Interactive lessons in early reading and math, with accompanying songs and printable activity booklets. Topics covered include following directions, beginning addition and subtraction, sorting and classification, safety, health, and manners, and words and sentences. Mattel Interactive; (800) 395-0277; www.mattelinteractive.com.

Jumpstart Kindergarten

A year's worth of education for kids aged 5–6, with the help of Mr. Hopsalot, an animated rabbit, on hybrid (Win/Mac) CD-ROM. Topics covered include the alphabet (both upper- and lower-case), letter combinations, counting, comparisons, sequencing, simple problem-solving skills, shapes and colors, and telling time. Knowledge Adventure, Inc.; (800) 545-7677; www.jumpstart.com or www.knowledgeadventure.com.

PROGRAMS AND OTHER RESOURCES

BRAIN QUEST KINDERGARTEN

A hinged pack of laminated cards with 300 questions, puzzles, quizzes, and mix-and-match challenges for kids aged 5–6, covering reading and math readiness, logic, and thinking skills. Brain Quest; (800) 722-7202; www.brainquest.com.

Copycat Magazine

A bimonthly magazine of ideas and activities for K–3 teachers, with patterns, reproducibles, and pullout color calendars. Copycat Magazine, Box 08146, Racine, WI 53408-1546; (414) 634-0146; www.copycatpress.com.

CALVERT SCHOOL KINDERGARTEN

A complete kindergarten curriculum by correspondence, available at either a traditional kindergarten level or as "Kindergarten II," for more advanced students. The program covers reading and literature, spelling, vocabulary, writing, math, science, music, art, and geography. All workbooks, texts, and supplementary materials (art supplies, song tapes, flash cards) are provided. Calvert School, Dept. 2NET, 105 Tuscany Rd., Baltimore, MD 21210-3098; (410) 243-6030; www.calvertschool.org.

For more along these lines, see Distance Learning, pages 403–408.

FIVE IN A ROW

A literature-based unit study curriculum for kids aged 4–8. Multidisciplinary lessons center around a long list of great classic picture books, among them Virginia Lee Burton's *Mike Mulligan and His Steam Shovel,* Barbara Cooney's *Miss Rumphius,* and Robert McCloskey's *Make Way for Ducklings.* Kids cover language arts, social studies, art, applied math, and science. Five in a Row, Box 707, Grandview, MO 64030-0707; (816) 331-5769; www.fiveinarow.com.

Teaching PreK–8 Magazine

Ideas, activities, and lesson plans in a wide range of academic subjects for preK–8 classes. Teaching PreK–8 Magazine, 40 Richards Ave., Norwalk, CT 06854; (800) 249-9363; www.carolhurst.com/products/teaching.html.

GRADE ONE

At about ten o'clock on an evening late in February the
entire pattern of our collective lives was violently altered.
My husband and I, sitting in the kind of companionable stu-
por that sets in when all children are in bed and presumably
asleep, were startled at hearing a sudden astonished "Oh!"
from Sally's room. As we half rose, looking at one another,
her voice lifted in the greatest, most jubilant shout I have
ever heard: "I can READ! I can READ!"

SHIRLEY JACKSON

RAISING DEMONS

LANGUAGE ARTS

READING

Now armed with the principles of phonics, the hurdle for the average first-grader is developing the ability to decode rapidly and fluently, translating letters into letter sounds, letter sounds into
words, and words into sentences. Reading often seems a mysteri-
ous and near-miraculous accomplishment—Why, after all, does
one six-year-old suddenly blossom into literacy while another
struggles interminably with the opacities of *c-a-t* and *m-a-t*? In
many cases, the answer may be developmental. Some kids read at
four; some read at eight. Of our three sons, Josh was reading by the

time he was six-and-a-half; Caleb learned to read at five; and Ethan, though he understood the mechanics, didn't read comfortably until he was nine.

Books for Teaching Reading

99 Ways to Get Kids to Love Reading
Mary Leonhardt; Three Rivers Press, 1997
Useful suggestions to encourage readers of all ages.

Games for Reading
Peggy Kaye; Pantheon Books, 1984
Creative do-it-yourself games and hands-on projects for teaching sight vocabulary, phonics skills, and reading comprehension.

LEARNING LANGUAGE ARTS THROUGH LITERATURE
A grammar, reading, and writing skills series for grades 1–12. The first-grade reading program, *The Blue Book,* teaches phonics and early reading skills, beginning spelling and grammar, and handwriting through classic children's picture books, among them Margaret Wise Brown's *The Runaway Bunny,* Russell Hoban's *Bedtime for Frances,* and Beatrix Potter's *Peter Rabbit.* The series is Christian, but generally can be adapted for those of other philosophies. Common Sense Press; 8786 Highway 21, Melrose, FL 32666; (352) 475-5757; www.cspress.com.

Also see Five in a Row, page 53.

Let's Read Together! A Parent's Guide to Beginning Reading
Ellen Gordon and Eileen Zweig; Operation Bookworm, 2000
Many interactive reading games for young children, variously centered around sight vocabulary, storytelling, sequencing, and reading comprehension.

Teach Your Child to Read in 100 Easy Lessons
Siegfried Englemann, Phyllis Haddox, and Elaine Bruner; Simon & Schuster, 1983
A sequential phonics-based approach to reading, starting at the very beginning (Lesson One introduces kids to *m* and *s* sounds). By the completion of the program, kids should be reading at a second-grade level. The book includes detailed instructions for parents. For additional information, see www.startreading.com.

Brand New Readers

Candlewick Press

Books for first-time readers, packaged in sets of four. Each color-illustrated book in a set is eight pages long and features a humorous story in very simple vocabulary. Many titles, among them *Monkey Trouble* (David Martin), *Winnie Plays Ball* (Leda Schubert), and *Here Comes Tabby Cat* (Phyllis Root).

Get Ready, Get Set, Read! A Phonetic Approach to Reading

Gina Erikson; Barron's Juveniles, 1999

A set of seven phonetic readers for kids aged 4–7. Titles include *The Bug Club, A Mop for Pop,* and *Find Nat.*

Hello Reader! Funny Tale Phonics Series

Judith Bauer Stamper; Cartwheel Books

Short phonics-based picture books. Titles include *The Red Hen, Space Race, The Three Wishes,* and *Boom! Zoom!*

Schoolzone Start to Read Series

Short, cleverly illustrated phonics-based readers, available for kids at three different skill levels. Level One titles include *The Gum on the Drum, The Cat That Sat, Beep, Beep,* and *Jog, Frog, Jog.* Schoolzone Publishing Company, Box 777, Grand Haven, MI 49417; (800) 253-0564; www.schoolzone.com.

COMPUTER SOFTWARE

Curious George Learns Phonics

Six circus-themed games teach letter sounds and beginning reading skills on CD-ROM for Win/Mac. Houghton Mifflin; (800) 733-2828; www.eduplace.com.

Kid Phonics 1

A phonics and early reading skills program on Win/Mac CD-ROM for learners aged 4–7. Kids learn letter sounds and word families through an interactive series of songs, nursery rhymes, puzzles, and games. Knowledge Adventure, Inc.; (800) 545-7677; www.knowledgeadventure.com.

Reader Rabbit's Interactive Reading Journey

A complete learn-to-read program for kids aged 4–7, including 100 interactive phonics lessons, 40 electronic storybooks, and a "Record and Playback" feature that allows kids to listen to themselves reading aloud. Mattel Interactive; (800) 395-0277; www.mattelinteractive.com.

WEB SITES

BOOKS ON READING INSTRUCTION

A long annotated list of books on the theory and practice of reading instruction. Web site: learninfreedom.org/readbook.html.

MRS. ALPHABET

Everything you ever wanted to know about teaching phonics, plus alphabet games of all kinds and a creative "Alphabet Newsletter," filled with activities and interesting links for every letter. Web site: www.mrsalphabet.com.

THE PHONICS ROOM

Activities, songs and poems, book suggestions, and kid-friendly links for every letter of the alphabet. Web site: members.aol.com/phonicsrm/.

Do you need a packaged reading program for your first-grader? I'd say no. While many commercial reading programs are certainly attractive and reportedly effective, most are quite expensive for what you get. Common components are early readers and workbooks, flash cards, and simple phonics games; some also include instructional video- and audiocassettes, and CD-ROMs. Generally you can assemble a comparable program of your own—with a greater chance of suiting your child's personal learning style and interests—for much less money; and in fact, with a library card, a couple of packs of index cards, and a little ingenuity, you can devise one for practically nothing.

See Books for Teaching Reading, page 55.

1. **Review and reinforce phonemes.** Kids should know the sounds of all the consonants and both long and short vowel sounds. They should also know the common *digraphs*—double-letter combinations that represent single sounds, such as *th, ch, sh, qu,* and *wh*—and common consonant *blends,* such as *bl* and *br, sp, st,* and *sw,* and *dr* and *tr.*

They should be familiar enough with these to substitute initial consonant sounds to create rhyming "word families," such as *dog, fog, log, hog, bog.*

2. **Expand upon the ability to decode one-syllable words.** Kids should be able to "sound out" one-syllable words, converting individual letters to phonemes and blending these into recognizable words. This essential skill—decoding—is a primary means by which kids decipher unfamiliar written words.

3. **Be able to identify root words and to identify common inflectional endings: *s, es, ed, er, est,* and *ing.*** Kids should be able to read not only the word *look,* for example, but *looks, looked,* and *looking.*

4. **Know age-appropriate sight words.** According to the Dolch Word List (see page 23), there are some thirty-odd words that first-graders are expected to recognize, among them *a, an, could, from, has, her, of, once, thank, the, then, walk,* and *were.*

5. **Identify and use contractions.** Kids should be able to recognize and use such contractions as *aren't, wasn't, isn't,* and *I'm,* and to convert them to their alternative longer forms (e.g., *are not, was not*).

READING COMPREHENSION

1. **Be able to read and understand grade-level-appropriate material.** By the end of first grade, kids should be able to read aloud reasonably fluently, in a manner that approximates natural speech.

Best Books for Beginning Readers
Thomas G. Gunning; Allyn & Bacon, 1997
A large annotated bibliography of books for very early readers, preschool to grade 2.

Hundreds of in-depth book guides for kids in grades K–12. Web site: www.beyondbasals.com.

Also see Kindergarten, pages 15–16, and Book Lists, pages 400–402.

Spider

An illustrated monthly literary magazine for kids aged 6–9. Each issue includes fiction and nonfiction stories, multicultural folktales and legends, poems, games, and puzzles Annual subscription (12 issues). Cricket Magazine Group, Box 7434, Red Oak, IA 51591-4434; (800) 827-0227; www.cricketmag.com.

2. Be able to answer who, what, when, where, and why questions—the "five Ws"—about material they have read. Give accurate oral accounts of fiction and nonfiction works that they have read themselves or heard read aloud.

Ask kids to recount stories or summarize short books that they've read themselves or heard read aloud during group reading sessions. If a child can retell a story or summarize a nonfiction account accurately, chances are that he or she has assimilated and understood it. Such narrations are a superb learning tool, reinforcing memory and enhancing analytical thinking and attention.

Also see *Bookworm,* a literary board game of retelling and remembering, pages 113–114.

GREAT BOOKS READ-ALOUD PROGRAM

The Great Books program is an excellent reading and discussion program for persons of all ages, from "emerging readers" to adults. Reading selections are accompanied by thought-provoking questions for discussion and debate. There are four series in the Read-Aloud program, designed for kids who are not yet reading fluently by themselves. Selections include an African folktale, "Guinea Fowl and Rabbit Get Justice," Beatrix Potter's "The Tale of Johnny Town-Mouse," "The Shoemaker and the Elves" from the Brothers Grimm, the Native American tale "Coyote Rides the Sun," and many more. The program includes student books and a teacher's guide. Great Books Foundation, 35 E. Wacker Dr., Suite 2300, Chicago, IL 60601-2298; (800) 222-5870; www. greatbooks.org.

3. **Know the literary terms** *plot, setting, characters, hero,* and *heroine,* **and be able to identify all in their readings.**

4. **Enjoy a wide range of literature read aloud, including fiction and nonfiction books, multicultural folktales and legends, fairy tales, fables, and poems.** Listening to literature selections read aloud is an important—perhaps *the* most important—activity for kids in this age group. The shared experience is warm and wonderful, and it gives young listeners a chance to imagine, visualize, empathize, accumulate factual information, and ask questions. When our children were of early elementary age, the crux of our homeschooling program was such shared reading and discussion. After reading a collection of Norse myths, for example, the boys, fascinated, exploded with questions. "What's mead? How do you make it?" "What's a thrall?" "Did Viking kids have swords too?" "Did the Vikings use bows and arrows?" "What part of those horn cups did they drink out of? How did they put them down?" "Are Viking runes the same as our alphabet? Can I learn the alphabet in runes?"

The shared reading experience can also be expanded upon with book-related projects and activities. Encourage kids to make their own thematic bookmarks for favorite books. Plant beans to accompany "Jack and the Beanstalk"; bake blueberry muffins with *Blueberries for Sal.*

LEARNING LINKS
Book-based study guides for kids in grades K–12, each including vocabulary enhancers, reading comprehension questions, cross-curricular activities, book-related writing projects, and more. Sample guides for first-graders cover such books as Russell Hoban's *A Bargain for Frances,* Else Homelund Minarik's *Little Bear,* and Arnold Lobel's *Frog and Toad Together.* Learning Links, 2300 Marcus Ave., New Hyde Park, NY 11042; (800) 724-2616; www.learninglinks.com.

NOVEL UNITS
Literature guides and activity books to accompany many well-known books for readers in grades 1–12. ECS Learning Systems,

Box 791439, San Antonio, TX 78279-1610; (800) 688-3224; www.educyberstor.com.

The RIF Guide to Encouraging Young Readers
Ruth Graves; Doubleday, 1987
> Many activities to enhance the reading experiences of kids aged 1–11, along with an annotated book list.

Story S-t-r-e-t-c-h-e-r-s
Shirley C. Raines and Robert J. Canady; Gryphon House, 1989
> Contains 450 multidisciplinary projects and activities to accompany ninety favorite picture books for kids aged 5–9. Several sequels.

5. **Be able to define and use a book's *table of contents*.**

WRITING

First-graders print. Formally this is called "manuscript handwriting" and it takes place on wide-ruled paper tailor-made for this age group. Writing paper generally recommended for first-graders has a five-eighths-inch horizontal ruling, with a broken line marking the midpoint, such that kids have some guidance in where to put the middle crosspieces of capital letters *E*, *F*, and *H* and help in sizing lower-case letters.

Draw Write Now Series
Marie Hablitzel and Kim Stitzer; Barker Creek Publishing
> A drawing and handwriting course for kids aged 4–8 in which they learn to print and draw simple shapes while developing fine-motor skills. There are seven books in the series, each centering around science, nature, history, and geography themes. Book One, for example, teaches kids to draw farm animals and storybook characters; Book Two features Christopher Columbus and the weather; Book Three, the American Indians and the Pilgrims. Barker Creek Publishing, Box 2610, Poulsbo, WA 98370; (800) 692-5833; www.barkercreek.com.

Also see Handwriting Without Tears and Zaner-Bloser, page 26 and Handwriting Worksheets, page 27.

1. Print all upper- and lower-case letters legibly, using proper spacing. Kids should participate in regular penmanship practice, continuing to hone and develop their writing skills. They should write in the correct direction—that is, left to right, and top to bottom—and should hold pens or pencils correctly.

2. Write words and sentences, using proper spacing, capitalization and punctuation. First-graders should experiment with a wide range of writing activities: journal keeping, stories, descriptions, autobiographical narratives, poems, and the like. Kids should know that sentences begin with capital letters and end with punctuation marks (period, question mark, or exclamation point). They should also know that proper names begin with capital letters, that the pronoun *I* is capitalized, and that the plural form of a regular noun is made by adding an *s* to the end of the word. On the other hand, the emphasis in first-grade writing should be on expression and creativity rather than form and mechanics.

The Creative Journal for Children
Lucia Capacchione; Shambhala, 1989
An idea-packed guide to journal keeping for kids aged 4 and up.

Rainbow Writing
Mary Euretig and Darlene Kreisberg; Dream Tree Press, 1992
A fill-in-the-blank journal on rainbow-colored paper for just-beginning journal writers. From bookstores or Dream Tree Press, 3836 Thornwood Dr., Sacramento, CA 95821; (800) 769-9029.

Also see *Write From the Edge*, page 111.

3. Be able to identify *nouns*, *verbs*, and *adjectives*.

A is for Angry: An Animal and Adjective Alphabet
Sandra Boynton; Workman, 1987
An illustrated introduction of adjectives for kids aged 4–7. There's an animal and an accompanying adjective for each letter of the alphabet.

Kites Sail High: A Book About Verbs

Many Luscious Lollipops: A Book About Adjectives

Merry-Go-Round: A Book About Nouns

Ruth Heller; Paper Star, 1998

Beautifully illustrated introductions to the parts of speech, in memory-catching rhyme.

Slither, Swoop, Swing

Alex Ayliffe; Viking, 1993

A picture-book explanation of verbs for kids aged 4–8.

4. Be able to spell simple three- and four-letter words from dictation using phonics skills. Know spelling of first grade–level sight words. Don't panic if your first-grader uses *dge* for *doggie* and *skwrl* for *squirrel*. Not only does this show comfortable self-confidence on the part of the writer, but it's a natural part of the process of learning how to spell. As kids progress through the maddening intricacies of the English language, they first enter the *semiphonetic* stage of spelling development, in which they have just begun to grasp letter-sound correspondence; writing at this stage may turn out sentences that only a parent can translate, often using single letters to represent words, such as *n* for *and* or *in*. Next comes the *phonetic* stage in which kids have solidified their grasp of phonics and thus spell logically, according to letter sound. Their writing thus includes such perfectly sensible spellings as *enuf* for *enough;* this is the sort of approach Ben Franklin touted in his (sadly failed) eighteenth-century attempt to standardize and simplify English spelling. Kids next enter the *transitional* stage, in which their writing shows an increasing understanding of the structure of words. Finally they enter the *correct* stage, by which time they can cope competently with prefixes and suffixes, silent *e*s, irregularly spelled words (of which English has many), and the like. For a more complete explanation of how children learn to spell, see Glenda Bissex's *GNYS AT WRK*, page 28.

A personal confession: None of our kids ever used a spelling program or formally studied spelling. Instead, they learned by doing—reading and writing—which in our experience works quite well. Today two of them are excellent spellers and one of them is an expert in the use of the dictionary and the spell check function on the computer.

ASSESSMENT TOOLS

On-line tests and instructions for assessing your child's knowledge of phonics, and determining his or her reading, writing, and math levels. Web site: intranet.cps.k12.il.us/Assessments/kg-PrimaryTools/kg-primarytools.html.

Everyday Spelling Series

Spelling programs for grades 1–8. Illustrated books include exercises, activities, and cross-curricular lessons correlated to a range of learning styles. Scott Foresman-Addison Wesley; (800) 552-2259; www.everydayspelling.com.

Spectrum Spelling Series

Complete spelling programs for grades 1–6. Illustrated workbooks use a variety of approaches. McGraw-Hill; (800) 305-5571; www.mhkids.com.

Spelling Power Series

Student books for grades 1–8 with practice exercises and creative writing activities. Curriculum Associates; (800) 225-0248; www.curriculumassociates.com.

SRA Spelling Series

Multifaceted workbooks for grades K–6. Basic lessons are supplemented with cross-curricular activities, creative writing, and dictionary exercises. SRA Language Arts; (888) SRA-4543; www.sra4kids.com.

Mrs. ABC Spelling and Phonics Curriculum

A free on-line interactive program for kids aged 7–9. Exercises cover the alphabet sequence, spelling, phonics, beginning grammar, and more; Web site: www.mrsabc.com.

5. Be able to identify *synonyms, antonyms,* and *homonyms.* Synonyms are words that have the same—or approximately the same—meaning, as in *fast* and *rapid;* antonyms are words with opposite meanings, as in *fast* and *slow;* and homonyms are words that sound the same but have different spellings and meanings, as in *blue* and *blew.*

Exactly the Opposite
Tana Hoban; Mulberry Books, 1997
Wordless full-page color photographs demonstrate opposites.

A High, Low, Near, Far, Loud, Quiet Story
Nina Crews; Greenwillow, 1999
Color photographs of a brother and sister illustrate many opposites over the course of a day.

The King Who Rained
Fred Gwynne; Aladdin, 1988
A wonderful picture-book romp through homonyms, including the king who rained (rather than reigned).

Wet Foot, Dry Foot, High Foot, Low Foot
Linda Hayward; Random House, 1996
An activity-laden Dr. Seuss Beginner Fun Book that introduces kids to opposites.

LISTENING AND SPEAKING SKILLS

First-graders should be able to listen and respond appropriately to spoken information and instructions, and should be able to communicate information orally in an organized and appropriate fashion.

1. Listen to, restate, and follow two-step directions.

2. Be able to retell a story in proper sequence.

3. Participate in short dramatizations: charades, pantomimes, plays. Reenact favorite stories, create puppet shows, or participate in dramatic games. All these activities enhance expression skills, promote comprehension and sequencing abilities, and develop imagination.

KIDS ON STAGE
A board game of creative charades for kids aged 3–8: Draw a card and be a rabbit, a duck, or an airplane. From game stores or contact University Games, 1633 Adrian Rd., Burlingame, CA 94010; (415) 692-2770; www.universitygames.com.

Plays Around the Year
Liza Schafer; Scholastic, 1995
> Over twenty simple plays on a range of topics, from Chinese New Year to Martin Luther King Jr., for kids in grades 1–3.

Princess, Cowboy, Pirate, Elf
Liz Boyd; Hyperion, 1995
> Very short two-person plays for kids aged 4–8.

READER'S THEATRE

A superb tool for developing children's reading comprehension skills. "Reader's Theatre" involves dramatizing and reenacting stories, folktales, and other works of fiction and nonfiction—in other words, encouraging kids' love of "playing pretend." An excellent course for Reader's Theatre materials is Teacher Ideas Press, which has published many titles for readers/actors of all ages, among them *Reader's Theatre for Beginning Readers, Multicultural Folktales,* and *Fifty Fabulous Fables.* For a complete list, contact Libraries Unlimited; (800) 237-6124; www.lu.com/tips.

Also see "Storytelling, Drama, Creative Dramatics, Puppetry, & Reader's Theatre for Children & Young Adults," on-line at falcon.jmu.edu/~ramseyil/drama.htm for a long list of activities, resources, and printable scripts.

4. Memorize and recite short poems and rhymes.

STUDY SKILLS

A major aim of a good education is to ensure that the teacher becomes obsolete. The acquisition of study skills shouldn't be an empty exercise centered around the efficient completion of homework; instead, these are the tools that kids will use to pursue a lifetime of independent learning. They'll need to know how to follow directions, how to conduct research, how to keep usable records, and where to look things up.

Clever Kids Study Skills
World Book, Inc.; 1996
> Activities to teach kids aged 5–7 early study skills, including how to listen and follow directions.

1. **Know the uses of a dictionary, encyclopedia, and card catalog.** There are many dictionaries specifically targeted at children in this age group; kids might also try making their own illustrated versions.

The Kingfisher First Dictionary
John Grisewood, ed.; Kingfisher Books, 1995
  Many illustrations, simple definitions, and activity suggestions for enhancing dictionary skills.

My Very Own Big Dictionary
Pamela Cote; Houghton Mifflin, 1996

The Sesame Street Dictionary
Linda Hayward; Random House, 1980

2. **Be able to put words in alphabetical order according to first letter.** Try making a series of index cards with a single word printed on each. Have the kids arrange the cards in alphabetical order. (This is good preparation for volunteering at your local library.)

MATHEMATICS

First-graders should practice math daily—like piano-playing, it's a skill that improves with repetition—and should be encouraged to relate their academic experience to the mathematics of daily life. There are near-infinite mathematical possibilities in everyday activities and objects: the bathroom scale, the kitchen measuring cups, the thermometer on the back porch, the speedometer on the family car.

What's important when it comes to first-grade math? As they explore the mathematical world around them, kids should be encouraged to understand that there are many ways of approaching and solving mathematical problems. They can use hands-on experiments, pictures and diagrams, representative objects, and estimation skills (a.k.a. educated guesses). Or they may come up with a creative method all their own. Let them go for it.

Some general resources for first-grade math include:

Everyday Mathematics Series

A highly recommended activity-based K–6 mathematics program. Includes texts, math journals, activity books, instructions for cross-curricular projects, and assorted reference materials. Everyday Learning Corporation, 2 Prudential Plaza, Suite 2200, Chicago, IL 60601; (800) 382-7670; www.everydaylearning.com.

Math 1

Nancy Larson; Saxon Publishers, 1994

The home-study kit comes with a detailed teacher's manual (130 lesson plans) and two student workbooks; families will also need to purchase a kit of manipulatives. Saxon Publishers, 2450 John Saxon Blvd., Norman, OK 73071; (800) 284-7019; www.saxonpub.com.

Miquon Math Series

Innovative math workbooks for kids in the early elementary grades that stress problem-solving skills and creative thinking. All the basics, plus. Generally appropriate for first-graders are the Orange and Red books. Key Curriculum Press, Box 2304, Berkeley, CA 94702-0304; (800) 995-MATH; www.keypress.com.

SRA Math: Explorations and Applications Series

Stephen S. Willoughby; SRA/McGraw-Hill

An excellent, well-integrated, and comprehensive series for kids in grades K–6 centered around games and manipulatives. The program introduces higher math concepts in the early years, which promotes problem-solving and creative thinking skills. SRA Math; (888) SRA-4543; www.sra4kids.com.

SUPPLEMENTS

Anno's Math Games

Mitsumasa Anno; Paper Star, 1997

A creative and thought-provoking book of mathematical puzzles, problems, activities, and explanations for early elementary students. Sequels include *Anno's Math Games II* and *Anno's Math Games III*.

BIG CALCULATOR

A big, colorful calculator on-line, with accompanying math exercises for kids in grades 1 and up. Web site: www.zeeks.com.

Also see Big Friendly Calculator, a free Mac download designed to help kids learn how to use a calculator. (Your choice of color and key order.) Download sites include www.scet.com and www.kidsdomain.com.

A Collection of Math Lessons From Grades 1 through 3
Marilyn Burns and Bonnie Tank; Cuisenaire, 1993

An excellent introduction to the process of hands-on mathematical discovery for early elementary-age children, with many examples of creative and successful lessons.

MATH MATE

A calculator specifically designed for early elementary students, with large-size color-coded keys and an oversize display screen. Texas Instruments; (800) TI-CARES; www.ti.com.

MATH STORIES

Thousands of story problems of all kinds for kids in grades 1–8. Many based on popular children's books. Web site: www.math-stories.com.

Also see Math at About.com, page 328, Textbooks, page 393, Lesson Plans, page 397, Distance Learning, page 403, and Kindergarten Mathematics resources, pages 29–35.

NUMBER THEORY

1. Recognize and write the numbers 0 to 100. An invaluable aid for learning about numbers and number relationships is the *hundred chart.* The chart is a cross-hatched 10 × 10 square—for a total of 100 squares—labeled with the numbers 1–100 in horizontal rows. Thus the first row of the chart consists of 10 squares containing the numbers 1–10, the second row contains the numbers 11–20, and so on.

Experiment. What do you do on the chart to add 1 to a number? To subtract 1? To add 10?

MATHWORK

Create and print your own hundred charts. The site also includes drill exercises in arithmetic facts, time-telling fractions, graphing, and measurement; Web site: www.coastlink.com/users/sbryce/mathwork.

Counting books of various kinds are also an excellent resource for first-graders.

100 Days of School
Trudy Harris; Millbrook Press, 1999

A clever presentation of addition, subtraction, and counting to 100 with everything from blackberry pie to centipedes.

From One to One Hundred
Teri Sloat; Puffin, 1995

Counting from 1 to 10, and then—by 10s—to 100, with varied and creative illustrations. The number 30, for example, includes 30 dinosaur bones (arranged in the shape of the numeral 30), 30 dinosaurs, 30 dinosaur eggs, and the like.

LET'S CELEBRATE 100 DAYS!

Creative suggestions for incorporating math into daily life, culminating on Day 100 with a special celebration. Count off the days on a number line or write each day's number on a craft stick, bundling the sticks together each time you complete a group of ten. Keep a 100-day journal. Make a string of 100 Cheerios; make a Hundred Crown by gluing 100 items to a cardboard crown cutout; read "hundreds" books, such as Dr. Seuss's *The 500 Hats of Bartholomew Cubbins*. Web site: MathCentral.uregina.ca/RR/database/RR.09.95/danylczuk1.html.

One Potato: A Counting Book of Potato Prints
Diane Pomeroy; Harcourt Brace, 1996

Count from 1 (potato) to 100 (sunflower seeds), using colorful potato-print illustrations; instructions are included for making potato prints of your own.

2. Be able to count to 100 by 2s, 5s, and 10s.

98, 99, 100! Ready or Not, Here I Come!
Teddy Slater; Cartwheel Books, 1999

Four little girls playing hide-and-seek come up with a number of creative ways to count to 100, including by 5s, 10s, and 20s.

The Crayon Counting Book
Pam Munoz Ryan and Jerry Pallotta; Charlesbridge, 1996
Count 24 crayons by 2s, using both odd and even numbers. The book has a cheerful rhyming text and a lot of truly bizarre-colored crayons, including "emerald boa."

The King's Commissioners
Aileen Friedman; Scholastic, 1995
The King wants to know how many commissioners he has appointed. His confused advisers attempt to solve the problem by counting by 2s and 5s; but his clever daughter gets the answer first, counting by 10s.

3. Use tallies for counting. Remember using tally marks for keeping score? Four lines + a diagonal cross = a group of five. To find your total, you'll need to count by 5s.

4. Identify ordinal positions from first through twelfth. *Anno's Math Games* (see page 68) includes "Numbers in Order," a thought-provoking introduction to ordinal numbers and sequencing.

5. Compare and order numbers 0 to 100 using the terms *greater than, lesser than,* and *equal to*.

6. Understand place values for 1s, 10s, and 100s. An understanding of place value is essential to mathematical operations involving *regrouping*—that is, carrying (in addition) and borrowing (in subtraction). One excellent way of developing this ability is through simple tile-trading games. A home-style version requires a pair of dice and a set of base 10 blocks, which are available in plastic in a range of splashy colors or in cardboard, which is cheaper. Base 10 blocks include units, "longs" (10 strips), and "flats" (100 squares). On each turn, kids roll the dice to win a certain number of units, which can eventually be traded in for 10 bars and 100 squares. An alternative version uses money: Try trading pennies for dimes, and dimes for dollars.

To relate base 10 manipulatives to written numbers, try place value mats. Though commercial printed mats are available, all you need to make your own is a sheet of paper, a pencil, and a ruler. Divide the sheet into thirds: the far-right third for units, the middle section for 10s, the far left for 100s.

BASE TEN BLOCKS

PLACE VALUE MATS
ETA/Cuisenaire, 500 Greenview Ct., Vernon Hills, IL 60061; (800) 445-5985; www.etauniverse.com or www.cuisenaire.com.

Math By All Means: Place Value, Grades 1–2
Marilyn Burns; Marilyn Burns Education Association, 1994
Innovative lesson plans, games, explorations, and activities to help early elementary students learn about place value and related topics.

See Dino Math Tracks, page 117.

7. Identify halves, thirds, and fourths. Reinforce fraction concepts in everyday life—a practice that can be as simple as cutting lunchtime peanut-butter sandwiches into halves and quarters.

Eating Fractions
Bruce McMillan; Scholastic, 1991
Everybody loves food. Kids learn about halves, thirds, and fourths by dividing a banana, a roll, and a pizza.

Fraction Action
Loreen Leedy; Holiday House, 1996
A classroom of bright-colored little animals learns all about fractions, dividing geometric shapes, sets of objects, pieces of fruit, and money. Clear explanations illustrated with simple diagrams.

8. Make and interpret simple picture and bar graphs. Kids should participate in sorting and classification exercises. How, for example, to sort a collection of small objects such as pasta, dried beans, buttons, and pebbles? A bag of multicolored jelly beans?

They should also experiment with collecting data from real-life situations and organizing the results on charts and graphs. For example, do the kids in your play group wear shoes with laces or without laces? How many of each? Collect data on a trip to the park or the shopping mall. How many people are wearing hats? Caps? Nothing on their heads?

The Best Vacation Ever
Stuart J. Murphy; HarperCollins, 1997
> How to have the best vacation ever? A little girl collects opinions from all the members of her family—"Should they go someplace cold or someplace hot?" "Take the cat along or leave Fluffer at home?"—and then charts the results.

Counting: Ourselves and Our Families
Antonia Stone and Susan Jo Russell; Dale Seymour Publications, 1991
> An introduction to collecting and analyzing data through a range of kid-friendly mathematical projects. Kids set out to answer mathematical questions—such as "How many people in my friends' families?"—and organize the answers in simple graphs.

Also see Exploring Data, page 33.

OPERATIONS

1. Experiment with the addition and subtraction of whole numbers through 20 using manipulatives and number lines.
Number lines are available from most educational supply companies—or you can make your own. Cut a strip of paper about ½ inch wide and 10½ inches long. Mark it off in one-half-inch increments and number it in order from 0 to 20. For a longer-lasting number line, laminate it.
Also see Line Jumper, page 32.

2. Know the definitions of *sum* and *difference* and the names and use of the + (plus) and – (minus) signs.

3. Know basic addition facts through 10 + 10 and corresponding basic subtraction facts. A major attainment of first grade—and a skill that will be reviewed and reinforced in second grade—is the acquisition of basic addition and subtraction facts. A number of games and materials—among them double-nine dominoes and the ubiquitous flash cards—are available for helping beginners assimilate these essential facts, a ready knowledge of which is necessary for more complex math.

ADDITION SONGS/SUBTRACTION SONGS

Melody, rhythm, and rhyme are excellent memory aids for kids of all ages. There are many sources for musical math facts; the above programs include cassette tapes of either ten addition songs, covering addition facts from 1+1 to 9+9; or twelve subtraction songs, covering facts from 1–1 to 20–12. Audio Memory Publishing, 501 Cliff Dr., Newport Beach, CA 92663; (800) 365-SING; www.audiomemory.com.

PRE-MATH-IT

Memorize-and-practice games for teaching basic addition facts using double-nine dominoes. The Sycamore Tree, 2179 Meyer Pl., Costa Mesa, CA 92627; (800) 779-6750; www.sycamoretree.com.

Also see Quick Pix Math, page 119, and Math Smart, page 121.

4. Understand the commutative property of addition: that is, numbers can be added in any order. In plain terms, this means, for example, that $3 + 2$ is exactly the same as $2 + 3$.

5. Successfully solve simple equations and word problems. First-graders should be able to solve both horizontal and vertical fill-in-the-blank problems on the order of:

$$6 + \underline{\quad} = 8 \quad \text{and} \quad \begin{array}{r} 9 \\ -6 \\ \hline \end{array}$$

A sample first-grade word problem might read "Katie had twelve cookies. She gave two of them to her friend Sam. How many cookies did Katie have left?" (See Math Stories, page 69.)

Encourage your kids to invent their own word problems. Our homeschooled sons preferred our own to standard first-grade fare: In lieu of cookies, we added and subtracted with submarines, space aliens, plummeting asteroids, and extremely hungry sharks.

Money and Measurement

1. Recognize pennies, nickels, dimes, and quarters.

Math By All Means: Money, Grades 1–2
Jane Crawford; Marilyn Burns Education Association, 1996
> A creative hands-on program in which kids learn all about the mathematics of money through games, activities, and appealing lesson plans.

2. Be able to determine the value of a given set of coins up to 25 cents.
First-graders should understand that different combinations of coins can equal the same amount of money—two dimes, for example, is the same as four nickels or twenty pennies.

3. Recognize dollar and cent signs; be able to use decimals in writing money amounts.

Alexander Who Used to Be Rich Last Sunday
Judith Viorst; Aladdin, 1980
> A sad, but very funny, financial tale in which Alexander blows his only dollar in a series of disastrous trades and purchases.

ALLOWANCE KIT JUNIOR: A MONEY SYSTEM FOR LITTLE KIDS
Michael J. Searls; Summit Financial Products, 1997
> A complete money management kit for early-elementary-aged kids, complete with savings bank, instruction book, stickers, and chore sheets. Available from bookstores or on-line from www.kidsmoney.org or www.amazon.com.

The Go-Around Dollar
Barbara Adams; Simon & Schuster, 1992
> The story of a single dollar bill.

One of our favorite games when our children were of early elementary age was a homemade buying and selling game in which, for small amounts of cash, the kids could buy or sell imaginative items drawn on index cards. Each boy started out with a predetermined amount of money and bought those items he most wanted and could afford, making change as he made his purchases. Most purchases were great deals: Players could buy a leopard, a rocket ship, a robot, or the moon, all for under fifty cents.

Also see resources, pages 122–123.

4. Use calendars to identify days, weeks, and months. Try making your own illustrated monthly calendars.

CALENDARS

A blank printable monthly calendar, with optional moon phases. Web site: www.timeanddate/calendar.

Creative information about calendars, including make-your-own versions. Web site: www.calendarhome.com.

5. Be able to tell time to the hour and half hour on a standard clock. Understand the difference between A.M. and P.M.

One Hand at a Time
Patricia Smith; Dale Seymour, 1997

A time-telling activity book for kids in the early elementary grades. Students learn to decipher the mysteries of the clock face (one hand at a time) and expand their understanding of time through many hands-on projects, among them making a sundial, a water clock, and a bean clock.

STUDENT CLOCKS

Small plastic or cardboard clocks with movable hands are available from most educational supply companies, as are clock-face rubber stamps (both blank and numbered). See ETA/Cuisenaire; (800) 445-5985; www.etauniverse.com or www.cuisenaire.com; and Delta Education; (800) 442-5444; www.delta-ed.com.

6. Be familiar with the uses of common measuring instruments, such as a scale (weight), ruler (length), and thermometer (temperature).

7. Compare and order objects by length, weight, and volume using both standard and nonstandard measures. Standard measures involve determining quantities using formal systems of measurement, such as the English or metric systems. Nonstandard measures involve more eclectic comparisons, such as "How many paper clips does it take to equal the length of the kitchen table?"

How Big Is a Foot?
Rolf Myller; Young Yearling Books, 1991

A delightful explanation of the importance of standard measurements, through the tale of an unfortunate apprentice who made the queen's birthday bed much too small.

Inch by Inch
Leo Lionni; Mulberry Books, 1995
An endearing inchworm measures everything in sight (and manages to measure himself out of the reach of a hungry bird).

Twelve Snails to One Lizard
Susan Hightower; Simon & Schuster, 1997
A storybook math lesson in which Milo, a beaver, needs a yard-long branch to plug the hole in his dam. A friendly frog suggests several methods of measuring—line up thirty-six inch-long snails, three foot-long iguanas, or one yard-long snake—and then finally produce a yardstick.

GEOMETRY

Recommended materials for beginning geometry studies include pattern blocks, pattern-forming games, and geoboards: pegged plastic or wooden boards upon which kids can build geometric shapes with stretched rubber bands.

Math By All Means: Geometry, Grades 1–2
Chris Confer; Marilyn Burns Education Association, 1994
A creative hands-on program for teaching geometry to early elementary students. Kids learn the mathematics of shapes and patterns through games, activities, and notably kid-friendly lesson plans.

1. Identify and draw common two-dimensional shapes: circle, triangle, rectangle, and square.

A Cloak for the Dreamer
Aileen Friedman; Scholastic, 1995
A delightful geometric fairy tale in which a tailor asks each of his three sons to make a cloak. The first stitches a cloak of rectangles; the second, a cloak of triangles; and the third—the dreamer—makes a cloak of circles.

The Shapes Game
Paul Rogers; Henry Holt, 1989

A bright-colored introduction to circles, triangles, rectangles, squares (and more) with a catchy rhyming text.

2. Identify figures that have lines of symmetry. Symmetrical figures can be folded down the middle—along their "lines of symmetry"—to form two mirror-image objects. Valentine hearts, gingerbread men, and equilateral triangles are symmetrical. Encourage kids to investigate symmetry in hands-on fashion, using paper-folding or pattern blocks.

M Is for Mirror
Duncan Birmingham; Parkwest Publications, 1989

Hands-on investigations in symmetry. Using the mirror card that comes in the front of the book, kids try to find the "hidden picture" in each of the book's colorful illustrations. Position the mirror along a concealed line of symmetry and suddenly a whole new picture springs into view.

3. Correctly use position words to describe location: right, left, above, below, inside, outside, in front, in back, over, under, and so on.

Which Way, Ben Bunny?
Mavis Smith; Cartwheel Books, 1996

Distinguishing between right and left becomes easier as kids follow the travels of Ben Bunny, hot on the trail of the villain who stole his carrot. At the behest of a friendly crow, Ben turns left, then right, then left: Readers figure out which direction he should turn and lift flaps on the sides of the pages to see what happens next.

HISTORY AND GEOGRAPHY

"Begin at the beginning," the King said gravely. "Go on until you come to the end: then stop."

LEWIS CARROLL

ALICE'S ADVENTURES IN WONDERLAND

What about chronology? History generally is taught in sequential time-related chunks. An overview of American history, for example, generally begins with the arrival of the first prehistoric peoples and continues roughly through the development of early civilizations, the arrival of the European settlers, colonization, the Revolutionary War, the Civil War, and the events of the twentieth century. The Core Knowledge Curriculum, developed by E. D. Hirsch Jr. and colleagues, which recommends introducing children to both world and American history and geography from kindergarten on, suggests chronological overviews of historical periods, fleshed out with children's biographies, fiction and nonfiction books, myths, legends, folktales, and hands-on activities.

History also—in education, as in the real world—repeats itself. Kids generally encounter the same topics several times in the course of their primary and secondary programs, learning through picture books and simple projects in the early years, investigating in greater depth using comprehensive texts and primary source materials in later years. Jessie Wise and Susan Wise Bauer, in *The Well-Trained Mind: A Guide to Classical Education at Home* (W. W. Norton, 1999), suggest a four-year reiteration of history studies, in which kids study ancient history in grades 1, 5, and 9; medieval and Renaissance history in grades 2, 6, and 10; late Renaissance to early modern history (1600–1850) in grades 3, 7, and 11; and modern history in grades 4, 8, and 12. Thus, in four-year blocks, kids cover world history chronologically from ancient times to the present.

The Classical Curriculum

Grades 1, 5, and 9	Ancient history (5000 B.C.E. to A.D. 400)
Grades 2, 6, and 10	Medieval history (400 to 1600)
Grades 3, 7, and 11	Renaissance to early modern history (1600–1850)
Grades 4, 8, and 12	Modern history (1850–present)

The Not-So-Classical Curriculum

Kindergarten	American history from the pre-Columbian period to the Revolutionary War
	Introduction to world cultures
Grade 1	Early American history from the pre-Columbian period to the early exploration of the West
	Introduction to ancient civilizations
Grade 2	American history from the Constitutional Convention to the late nineteenth century
	Introduction to the medieval period in western Europe
	Survey of the history of ancient China, India, and Japan
Grade 3	The early explorations of America to the establishment of the thirteen colonies
	The Renaissance to the early nineteenth century in western Europe
	Survey of the history of Russia through the reign of Catherine the Great
Grade 4	American history from the colonial period to the early nineteenth century
	Survey of the history of Africa
	Survey of Central and South American history
Grade 5	American history from the pre–Civil War period through Reconstruction
	Ancient history from prehistory to the fall of Rome

Grade 6	American history from the post–Civil War period to the early twentieth century
	World history from A.D. 400 to the Renaissance
Grade 7	American history from the early twentieth century to post–World War II
	World history from the Renaissance to the early twentieth century
Grade 8	American history from post–World War II to the present
	Modern world history
Grade 9	World history from the beginning of civilization to A.D. 1000
Grade 10	World history from A.D. 1000 to the present
Grade 11	American history
Grade 12	American government

In homeschool, approaches and emphasis will inevitably vary with the interests of the students. The Middle Ages or the American Civil War period, for example, may occupy kids for several months, while other time periods get considerably less attention. A science-oriented child may be happier approaching history from a scientific standpoint, concentrating on the medieval alchemists, the astronomical discoveries of Copernicus and Galileo, and the inventions of Leonardo da Vinci; a young artist may prefer to study gargoyles and Gothic arches, Giotto's frescoes, and Michelangelo's sculptures and struggles with the Sistine ceiling. Adapt to suit their interests and learning styles. A curriculum is a general guideline, a series of best-guess suggestions. You're supposed to fool around with it. It's written on paper, not stone.

AMERICAN HISTORY: GENERAL

1. Study and compare family life, past and present. Kids should read books about families now and long ago, discussing changing customs and lifestyles. Try making illustrated timelines; research a personal family tree.

The Hundred Penny Box
Sharon Bell Mathis; Puffin, 1986

Michael's great-great-aunt has a special box of 100 pennies, one for each year of her long life. As Michael listens, she tells stories of long ago, beginning with the penny dated 1874, the year she was born.

The Quilt Story
Tony Johnston; Paper Star, 1996

A homemade quilt, passed down from generation to generation, comforts two little girls, one moving west in a covered wagon, one moving to a new town in modern times.

They Were Strong and Good
Robert Lawson; Viking Press, 1994

A gentle story of a family, told in the first person. One grandfather was a sea captain who brought home a wife from Spain; another was a soldier who fought in the Civil War.

2. Study the lives and accomplishments of famous Americans.
First-graders should learn about the lives and deeds of a variety of prominent Americans. Examples might include George Washington, Thomas Jefferson, Benjamin Franklin, George Washington Carver, Sojourner Truth, Abraham Lincoln, and Susan B. Anthony. Try presenting information through a range of books, nonfiction and fictionalized, poems, and hands-on activities.

Lives of the Presidents: Fame, Shame (and What the Neighbors Thought)
Kathleen Krull; Harcourt Brace, 1998

Short witty biographies of the presidents, with illustrations, unusual facts, and anecdotes.

My Fellow Americans: A Family Album
Alice Provensen; Browndeer Press, 1995

A marvelous picture-book collection of famous Americans throughout history, from "Pilgrims and Puritans" to "Radical Reformers" to "Scoundrels and Thieves." Fun, fascinating, and irresistible.

Also see Picture Book Biography Series, page 38.

3. Know the people and events associated with famous national holidays. First-graders should know the stories behind major national holidays such as Martin Luther King's Birthday, Presidents' Day, Independence Day, Memorial Day, and Thanksgiving. Again, the information should be presented through a mix of picture books, poems, songs, and hands-on activities.

Happy Birthday, Grandma Moses!
Claire Bonfanti Braham and Maria Bonfanti Esche; Chicago Review Press, 1995

> A month-by-month list of over 100 "special days," including national and multicultural holidays and birthdays of famous people, with accompanying activities, games, recipes, and reading lists.

Also see *The Early Childhood Almanac,* page 11.

4. Know the meaning of *democracy,* the duties of the president of the United States, and the importance of such national symbols as the flag, the Liberty Bell, the American eagle, and the Statue of Liberty.

New True Books: American Symbols Series
Patricia Ryon Quiri; Children's Press, 1998

> A series of simple large-print books on national symbols, illustrated with color photographs. Titles include *The American Flag, The Bald Eagle, Ellis Island, The National Anthem,* and *The Statue of Liberty.*

5. Be familiar with traditional American folktales, stories, and songs. Kids should know the stories of such American tall-tale figures as Paul Bunyan, Pecos Bill, John Henry, and Brer Rabbit—and of historical individuals whose life stories became legendary, such as Davy Crockett, Annie Oakley, and Johnny Appleseed. There are many excellent picture-book versions of these stories.

From Sea to Shining Sea: A Treasury of American Folklore and Folk Songs
Amy L. Cohn; Scholastic, 1993

> A large, illustrated collection of short folktales, poems, and traditional songs (with music) for kids of all ages.

John Henry: An American Legend
Ezra Jack Keats; Alfred A. Knopf, 1987

The story of the famous steel-driving man who became a legend working on the railroad.

Tall Tales Series

Steven Kellogg; William Morrow
Titles include *Johnny Appleseed* (1996), *Mike Fink* (1998), *Paul Bunyan* (1994), *Pecos Bill* (1992), and *Sally Ann Thunder Ann Whirlwind Crockett* (1995).

Yankee Doodle: A Revolutionary War Tale
Gary Chalk; Dorling Kindersley, 1993
The words and music to "Yankee Doodle," plus a rhyming account of the American Revolution as told by a patriotic mouse.

6. Know about the many different professions that enable a community to function. Kids show know about the workings of the fire and police stations, the post office, the bank, the newspaper office, the public transportation system, the telephone company, and so on. An excellent opportunity for local field trips.

AMERICAN HISTORY: CHRONOLOGICAL SURVEY

This topic will be reviewed and repeated in greater detail as kids pursue their educational careers. In first grade, the emphasis should be on great stories, fiction and nonfiction, folktales and legends, and topic-related activities. (Kids who love history, learn history.) For a more broad-based understanding, correlate material to timelines and maps.

A list of general topics to cover follows. There are many innovative books and resource materials for teaching American history to kids of all ages (See *The Complete Home Learning Source Book*; Rebecca Rupp; Three Rivers Press, 1998).

BLUESTOCKING PRESS
An excellent source for American history materials of all kinds for students in grades K–12. Resources are categorized by time period, from the pre-Columbian era to the present day. Bluestocking Press, Box 2030, Shingle Springs, CA 95682-2030; (800) 959-8586.

Also see *Social Studies Through Children's Literature*, page 37, and *Appleseeds*, page 163.

1. The arrival of the ancestors of the American Indians and the establishment of early civilizations. Kids should study the lifestyles, customs, and legends of representative American Indian tribes.

If You . . . Series

Scholastic
Relevant titles include *If You Lived in the Day of the Wild Mammoth Hunters* (Mary Elting and Franklin Folsom) and *If You Lived with the Sioux Indians* (Ann McGovern). Kid-friendly information delivered in a conversational question-and-answer format.

See *More Than Moccasins*, page 37.

Native American Legends Series

Terri Cohlene; Watermill Press, 1991
A series of charmingly illustrated picture books, each retelling an American Indian legend. In each, an appendix gives information about the relevant Indian tribe, illustrated with colorful maps and photographs. Titles include *Dancing Drum: A Cherokee Legend; Turquoise Boy: A Navajo Legend;* and *Little Firefly: An Algonquian Legend.*

Wild and Woolly Mammoths
Aliki; HarperCollins, 1998
A picture-book account of the woolly mammoths and the Stone Age tribes that hunted them.

2. The Maya, Aztec, and Inca civilizations of Central and South America.

New True Books: Ancient Civilizations

Patricia C. McKissack; Children's Press, 1985
Titles include *The Maya, The Aztec,* and *The Inca.* All are simple large-print overviews of ancient civilizations, illustrated with color pictures and photographs.

3. The arrival of Columbus in 1492; the Spanish conquistadors and early Spanish settlements.

Follow the Dream
Peter Sis; Dragonfly, 1996
> A simple history of Columbus's first and most famous voyage, for beginners.

Also see *The Discovery of the Americas* and *The Discovery of the Americas Activity Book*, page 166.

4. English colonization in the New World, including the stories of the "lost colony" of Roanoke, the settlement of Jamestown, the arrival of African slaves and the establishment of the first southern plantations, and the Pilgrims and Puritans in Massachusetts.

Colonial Kids: An Activity Guide to Life in the New World
Laurie Carlson; Chicago Review Press, 1997
> Historical background information, a timeline, and many creative activities and projects for kids aged 5–10.

If You . . . Series

Scholastic
> Relevant titles include *If You Lived in Colonial Times* (Ann McGovern) and *If You Grew Up with George Washington* (Ruth Belov Gross). Interesting information in a conversational question-and-answer format.

On the Mayflower: Voyage of the Ship's Apprentice and a Passenger Girl
Samuel Eaton's Day: A Day in the Life of a Pilgrim Boy
Sarah Morton's Day: A Day in the Life of a Pilgrim Girl
Tapenum's Day: A Day in the Life of a Wampanoag Boy
Kate Waters; Scholastic
> Picture-book accounts of life in the Pilgrim era illustrated with color photographs of reenactors from the living history museum at Plimouth Plantation.

5. The American Revolution.

Ben and Me
Robert Lawson; Little, Brown, 1988
> A wonderful, humorous, read-aloud subtitled "The Astonishing Life of Benjamin Franklin as written by his Good Mouse Amos." A mouse's view of Franklin's life and the American Revolution in fifteen delightful chapters.

The Fourth of July Story
Alice Dagliesh; Aladdin, 1995
> The picture-book story of the Declaration of Independence and the glorious Fourth of July.

Young John Quincy
Cheryl Harness; Simon & Schuster, 1994
> An overview of the early days of the Revolution through the eyes of eight-year-old John Quincy Adams.

6. The early exploration of the American West, including the stories of Daniel Boone and the Lewis and Clark Expedition.

Across America: The Story of Lewis and Clark
Jacqueline Morley; Franklin Watts, 1998
> An illustrated account of the famous Lewis and Clark Expedition, from choosing the supplies and planning the route to the safe return home. Also see *Lewis and Clark: Explorers of the Far West* (Steven Kroll; Holiday House, 1994).

If You Traveled West in a Covered Wagon
Ellen Levine; Scholastic, 1992
> Kid-friendly information in question-and-answer format. "How would you cross rivers when there were no bridges?" "What kind of clothes did people wear?" "What did you eat?"

WORLD HISTORY

A good choice for first-grade world history is an introductory foray into ancient history, correlating material to maps and time-lines. Kids should be encouraged to use a wide variety of resources, including fiction and nonfiction books, coloring and paper-crafts books, and video and audio materials. They should participate in hands-on projects and activities and, where possible, relevant field trips.

1. Compare and contrast everyday life in different cultures and times.
Through a combination of fiction and nonfiction books, folktales, myths, and legends, and hands-on activities, kids should learn about life in different times and places. Suggested resources

include multicultural picture books and folktale series, accounts of holidays and festivals around the world, and multicultural arts and crafts activities.

Encourage kids to trace changes in technology over time, making illustrated timelines. For example, they might chart changes in communication, from the origin of writing to the computer, or changes in transportation, from the wheel to the space shuttle.

CREATE-A-TIMELINE

Conveniently reusable blank panels for timeline makers with laminated surfaces that can be written upon (with dry markers) and erased. Pictures can be taped or glued in place and then peeled off. Crystal Productions, Box 2159, Glenview, IL 60025-2159; (800) 255-8629; www.crystalproductions.com.

Timeliner

A software program that allows kids to create, illustrate, and print their own timelines. Available as a Mac/Win CD-ROM. Tom Snyder Productions, 80 Coolidge Hill Rd., Watertown, MA 02472; (800) 342-0236; www.tomsnyder.com.

Visual Timeline of Transportation
Anthony Wilson; Dorling Kindersley, 1995

An illustrated history of transportation in drawings and color photographs, from 10,000 B.C. to the present.

2. **Study prehistory to the beginnings of civilization.** Topics to cover include early humans, Stone Age cultures, and the birth of civilization in the Tigris-Euphrates Valley. When our kids first studied Stone Age cultures, a popular activity was making their own decorated caves from big cardboard packing boxes.

Prehistoric People
Ovid K. Wong; Children's Press, 1988

A simple explanation of the history of early humans and the scientists who study them, illustrated with color photographs, maps, and paintings.

Prehistory to Egypt
Gloria Verges and Oriol Verges; Barrons Juveniles, 1988

An illustrated thirty-two-page history of the beginnings of civilization for beginning readers, told through a fictionalized story.

The Stone Age News
Fiona Macdonald; Candlewick Press, 1998

> A "newspaper" in book form all about early humans, with updates on the disappearing Neanderthals, reports on the new-fangled practice of farming and the best in cave art, and a double-page spread on how to make the most of your mammoth.

3. Survey ancient Egypt. Topics to cover include the Nile River, pyramids, pharaohs, mummies, gods and goddesses, the Sphinx, and hieroglyphic writing. Read ancient Egyptian legends; try your hand at hieroglyphic writing; visit an art museum and check out the ancient Egyptian artifacts.

Mummies Made in Egypt
Aliki; HarperTrophy, 1985

> A beautifully illustrated account of Egyptian religion, funeral rites, mummy-making, and pyramids.

Pyramids: 50 Hands-On Activities to Experience Ancient Egypt
Avery Hart and Paul Mantell; Williamson, 1997

> Games, arts and crafts projects, recipes, and more, all centering around the culture of ancient Egypt, for kids aged 4–9.

4. Survey ancient Greece. Topics to cover include the geography of Greece and its surroundings, the city-states of Athens and Sparta, the origin of democracy, Greek gods and goddesses, the Olympic Games, the Persian and Peloponnesian Wars, and such famous historical persons as Pericles, Socrates, Plato, Aristotle, and Alexander the Great. Read Greek myths and children's versions of Homer's *Iliad* and *Odyssey*.

Classical Kids: An Activity Guide to Life in Ancient Greece and Rome
Laurie Carlson; Chicago Review Press, 1998

> Background information and games, projects, recipes, and art activities for kids aged 5–10.

The Greeks
Sally Hewitt; Children's Press, 1995

> An introduction to ancient Greek history and culture for young readers, with related craft projects.

5. Survey ancient Rome. Topics to cover include the geography of the Roman Empire and the Mediterranean region, the legend of

Romulus and Remus, the Latin language, Roman numerals, Roman religion and mythology, and daily life in Roman times. An overview of Roman history should cover the Roman Republic, the Punic Wars (includng the famous tale of Hannibal and his elephants), the Roman Empire, and the decline and fall of Rome.

First Facts About the Ancient Romans
Fiona MacDonald; Peter Bedrick Books, 1996
> The life and times of ancient Rome, presented in a series of creatively illustrated double-page spreads, variously titled "Rich Romans Ate Flamingos and Peacocks" and "Many Roman Soldiers Couldn't Speak Latin."

Spend the Day in Ancient Rome: Projects and Activities That Bring the Past to Life
Linda Honan; John Wiley & Sons, 1998
> In the heyday of the Roman Empire, kids join a tpyical Roman family at a festival in honor of Jupiter. Activities include making a toga and a gladiator's shield, playing Roman games, and experimenting with Roman recipes.

6. Survey major world religions. Kids should be introduced to the principal tenets of Christianity, Judaism, and Islam through a variety of nonfiction books, story retellings, and other materials.

The Story of Religion
Betsy Maestro; Clarion, 1996
> A picture-book history of the world's religions for kids aged 7–12, covering the earliest religions, the beliefs of the ancient Egyptians and Greeks, and the tenets of Hinduism, Buddhism, Judaism, Christianity, and Islam.

Tales from the Old Testament
> Marvelous retellings by storyteller Jim Weiss. Seven tales, including the stories of Noah and the Ark, Queen Esther, and David and Goliath. Greathall Productions, Box 5061, Charlottesville, VA 22905-5061; (800) 477-6234; www.greathall.com.

Also see The Children's Picture World History Series, page 131.

Geography

1. Know the uses of maps and globes. Understand the meaning of a map's *key* and the use of map legends and symbols. First-graders should know which parts of maps and globes represent land and bodies of water and be able to identify rivers, lakes, and mountains.

Geography From A–Z
Jack Knowlton; HarperTrophy, 1997
> A brightly illustrated picture glossary of geography terms from archipelago to zone.

How We Learned the Earth Is Round
Patricia Lauber; HarperCollins, 1992
> First-graders should know that they live on a round globe; this simple picture book clearly explains why we know this is true.

2. Know the cardinal directions: north, east, south, and west. Let your kids experiment with compasses.

North, South, East, West
Allan Fowler; Children's Press, 1993
> A Rookie Read About Science Book that explains the four principal directions of the compass.

3. Be able to identify the world's major oceans and continents, the equator, the northern and southern hemispheres, and the North and South Poles. Kids should know the locations of the Atlantic, Pacific, Indian, and Arctic Oceans, and some basic information about each. First-graders should learn, for example, that three-quarters of the world is covered with water; that the oceans contain salt, rather than fresh, water; and that the Pacific is the world's largest ocean.

In studying the continents, kids should learn about the animal inhabitants of each and should be introduced to notably prominent continental features, such as Mount Everest, the Sahara Desert, the Amazon rain forest.

Count Your Way Series

Jim Haskins; Carolrhoda
> A series of short picture books in which kids discover interesting facts about the geography and culture of a featured country or

world region while learning to count to ten in the country's language. In *Count Your Way Through Japan,* for example, "one" is for one Mount Fuji.

NEW TRUE BOOKS: CONTINENTS

David Petersen; Children's Press
One book on each of the seven continents, each with a simple, large-print text and beautiful color photographs. Titles are *Africa, Antarctica, Asia, Australia, Europe, North America,* and *South America.*

Oceans
Seymour Simon; William Morrow, 1990
Short, simple, scientific explanations plus spectacular color photographs.

4. First-graders should know their town or city, state, and country, and be able to locate the United States, Canada, and Mexico on a world map.

SCIENCE

Most professional and commercial curricula list an admirable, but vague, selection of goals for early science programs. Kids, for example, should demonstrate curiosity, develop "critical response" skills, trust their senses, "be in awe and wonder" of their environment. The bottom line: Kids should know what it means to think like a scientist. That is, they should be able to look at what's happening, suggest explanations, and devise experiments for figuring out whether or not their proposed explanation is true. They should realize that science is not a static body of facts, but an ongoing process. Science is a worldview that shifts and changes with each new discovery; it is not a matter of belief, but a matter of evidence. The first time a kid says, "Show me," that's science.

There are two major approaches to science curricula. One favors a separation of scientific disciplines, such that biology, earth and space science, chemistry, and physics are taught in succeeding years; the other favors a simultaneous presentation of the major subdivi-

sions of science, emphasizing the connections and interrelationships among them. Inevitably the latter occurs: Astronomy overlaps
with physics ("What's the speed of light?") and chemistry ("What
are stars made of?"); earth science overlaps with biology ("What
kind of animal made this fossil?" "What does *extinct* mean?"); and
so on, as kids build and expand their frameworks of knowledge.
Again, science programs should be skewed toward the interests of
the students. Your kid is obsessed with telescopes; the curriculum
calls for amphibians. What to do? Whatever works best. You may
end up studying both at once (after all, it's the rare child who
doesn't like frogs). You may end up covering amphibians with one
quick picture book and a trip to the neighborhood pond. You may
ignore amphibians altogether—at least for the moment—in favor
of stargazing, building a telescope, assembling a solar system
mobile, and mapping the moon. This last—science being the
tightly woven web that it is—brings you back to frogs again. Some
cultures claim to see a frog (not a man) on the face of the full moon.

Any science program should concentrate on hands-on experiments and active investigations. Activities should be supplemented
with nonfiction and fiction books and with grade-appropriate
biographies of scientists.

Physical Science

1. Understand the basic premise of atomic theory: that is, all things are made of very small particles called atoms.

What's Smaller Than a Pygmy Shrew?
Robert W. Wells; Albert Whitman & Co., 1995
> A delightful and informative introduction to the very small, mov-
> ing downward from the pygmy shrew to the ladybug to the para-
> mecium, then to the molecule, atom, electron, and quark.

2. Know the three states of matter: solids, liquids, and gases.

Kids should know that matter has weight and takes up space. They
should be able to define and differentiate among solids (which
have a definite shape), liquids (which flow to fit the shape of their
container), and gases (which have no shape at all).

Air Is All Around You

Franklyn Branley; HarperCollins, 1986

A Let's-Read-and-Find-Out science book that explains the nature of air.

The Berenstain Bears' Science Fair

Stan and Jan Berenstain; Random House, 1984

A humorous introduction to physical science for beginners, including explanations of the three states of matter, the nature of simple machines, and the major sources of energy.

What Is the World Made Of? All About Solids, Liquids, and Gases

Kathleen Weidner Zoehfeld; HarperCollins, 1998

A clever reader-friendly explanation of the three states of matter, with memory-sticking examples from everyday life. ("Have you ever played with a lemonade doll or put on milk for socks?")

3. Investigate electricity and magnetism. Kids should experiment with static electricity, assemble simple electrical circuits, experiment with magnets, and differentiate among materials with magnetic properties.

CHARGE IT! STATIC ELECTRICITY

ELECTRICAL CONNECTIONS

MAGNET MAGIC

Delta Science Nutshell kits for elementary-level scientists, including a teacher's guide, student activity journal, and all necessary materials for many different experiments. Delta Education, Box 3000, Nashua, NH 03061-3000; (800) 442-5444; www.delta-ed.com.

Switch On, Switch Off

Melvin Berger; HarperTrophy, 1989

A simple picture-book introduction to electricity and electrical circuits for kids 4–8. Includes instructions for making an electromagnet.

What Magnets Can Do

Allan Fowler; Children's Press, 1995

A Rookie Read-About Science book for scientific beginners.

LIFE SCIENCE

1. Know that different animals have different habitats. Kids should know about forest, pond, desert, prairie, arctic, and ocean habitats and the different plants and animals that live there.

WHO'S AT HOME?

A board game of animal habitats around the world. Players move from polar regions to woodlands, urban centers, wetlands, deserts, grasslands, rain forests, and mountains, learning about animal adaptations and behaviors. Aristoplay, 8122 Main St., Dexter, MI 48103; (800) 634-7738; www.aristoplay.com.

2. Understand the food chain. Kids should also know that animals can be classified according to what they eat: *carnivores, herbivores, insectivores,* and (us) *omnivores.*

Everybody's Somebody's Lunch
Cherie Mason and Judy Kellogg Markowsky; Tilbury House, 1998
Multidisciplinary activities for elementary-aged children centering around predator-prey relationships in nature.

Who Eats What?
Patricia Lauber; HarperCollins, 1995
A straightforward explanation of food chains and food webs for young children.

3. Know that plants require soil, water, air, sunlight, and nutrients to grow. Kids should participate in a number of hands-on activities involving sprouting seeds and growing plants.

TOPS RADISHES

A creative botany unit for elementary students, using simple homemade materials and radish seeds, which grow very fast. TOPS Learning Systems, 10970 S. Mulino Rd., Canby, OR 97013; (888) 773-9755; www.topscience.org.

Also see *All About Seeds*, page 44, and *From Seed to Plant*, page 44.

4. Survey animal taxonomy. Introduce the basic principles of taxonomy (classification). Kids should know that animals can be grouped into *classes* and *families*—insects, fish, amphibians, reptiles, birds, mammals—and should learn basic characteristics of each. Pair with fiction and nonfiction books and poems about representative animals, as well as field trips and hands-on activities.

Benny's Animals and How He Put Them in Order
Millicent Selsam; HarperCollins, 1966
> A first introduction to taxonomy. Benny, who likes to sort and classify things, is struggling to put his enormous collection of animal pictures into some kind of order.

QUICK PIX: ANIMALS
> A colorfully illustrated card game in which kids match individual animal pictures to their proper group (marsupials, arachnids, birds, crustaceans, amphibians, whales/dolphins, hoofed mammals, dinosaurs, rodents, or primates). Plenty of visual cues to aid the confused. Aristoplay, 8122 Main St., Dexter, MI 48130; (800) 634-7738; www.aristoplay.com.

Also see Animal Classifications, page 175.

5. Define and discuss extinction and endangered species. Kids should learn about *extinction* as part of the long process of life on earth and should understand what an *endangered species* is today. First-graders love dinosaurs; try a multifaceted study of these "thunder lizards," encompassing fiction and nonfiction books, poems, projects, and field trips.

Dinosaur Hunters
John R. Jones and Kate H. McMullan; Random House, 1989
> An easy-to-read account of what paleontologists do.

Let's-Read-and-Find-Out Science Series: Paleontology
HarperTrophy
> Simple informational texts with appealing illustrations for kids aged 4–9. Relevant titles include *Dinosaur Bones* (Aliki, 1990), *Digging Up Dinosaurs* (Aliki, 1988), *Fossils Tell of Long Ago* (Aliki, 1990), and *What Happened to the Dinosaurs?* (Franklyn Branley, 1991).

V for Vanishing: An Alphabet of Endangered Animals
Patricia Mullins; HarperCollins, 1993

Paper collage illustrations depict twenty-six endangered animals around the world.

6. Understand the dangers of pollution and environmental destruction, and the benefits of conservation and recycling. Kids should understand the causes and effects of air and water pollution and learn how conservation and recycling help preserve the environment. An excellent opportunity for a unit study on rain forests.

A BEAUTIFUL PLACE
A cooperative board game in which kids make the earth a "beautiful place" by recycling, saving energy, feeding birds, and so on. For each good deed, they remove a puzzle piece of a polluted dead landscape in the center of the board to reveal a green landscape below. Animal Town Game Company, Box 757, Greenland, NH; (800) 445-8642; www.animaltown.com.

Oil Spill!
Melvin Berger; HarperCollins, 1994
A picture-book explanation of oils spills and their consequences.

Ozone Hole
Darlene R. Stille; Children's Press, 1991
A simple explanation of the causes and effects of ozone depletion, illustrated with color photographs.

Save the Rain Forests
Allan Fowler; Children's Press, 1996
An easy-to-read book about the endangered rain forest, illustrated with beautiful color photographs of rain forest plants and animals.

Where Does the Garbage Go?
Paul Showers; HarperCollins, 1994
"Each person in the U.S. creates about four pounds of trash a day." A short, simple explanation of recycling.

7. Know that the human body is made up of several different physiological systems; understand the germ theory of disease. Kids should know that their bodies are composed of skeletal, muscular, digestive, circulatory, and nervous systems and have a general idea of what each system does. They should also know that "germs"—bacteria and viruses—are reponsible for many diseases and should understand the reason for vaccinations.

Germs, Germs, Germs!
Bobbi Katz; Cartwheel Books, 1996
   A short rhyming text describes the evil habits of germs.

Germs Make Me Sick!
Melvin Berger; HarperCrest, 1995
   A simple explanation of bacteria, viruses, contagious diseases, and immunity, for beginners.

Let's-Read-and-Find-Out Science Series: The Human Body
HarperTrophy
   Relevant titles include *The Skelton Inside You* (Philip Balestrino, 1989), *You Can't Make a Move Without Your Muscles* (Paul Showers, 1982), *Hear Your Heart* (Paul Showers, 1987), and *What Happens to a Hamburger* (Paul Showers, 1987).

Also see SomeBody, page 138, and *Watch Me Grow!*, page 138.

EARTH/SPACE SCIENCE

1. Study basic features of sun, moon, and stars. Kids should know that the earth rotates on its axis (which causes day and night) and revolves around the sun (which takes one entire year). They should also know that the sun is a star that generates heat and light, and that the moon orbits the earth and goes through a series of changing shapes each month called *phases.* They should be aware that the stars of the night sky are said to be arranged in patterns called *constellations,* and be able to identify some of the more obvious constellations, such as the Big Dipper.

The Big Dipper and You
E. C. Krupp; William Morrow, 1989
   All about our best-known constellation, with intriguing illustrations and many interesting and unusual facts.

Let's Read-and-Find-Out Science Series: Astronomy
Franklyn M. Branley; HarperTrophy
   A series of simple informational picture books for early elementary students, with an interesting kid-friendly text. Titles include

The Sun: Our Nearest Star, The Moon Seems to Change, What Makes Day and Night, and The Planets in Our Solar System.

Stargazers
Gail Gibbons; Holiday House, 1992
A charmingly illustrated introduction to astonomy for kids aged 4–8, with explanations of what stars and constellations are and how telescopes work.

2. Know the names and characteristics of the planets. Kids should know the names of the planets in order and some of their major features. Which is the largest planet? Which planet is closest to the sun? Which planet is called "the Red Planet"?

Naturescope Astronomy Adventures
National Wildlife Federation; McGraw-Hill, 1997
Well-presented (and substantive) information, games, and activities categorized by grade level: primary (K–2), intermediate (3–5), and advanced (6–8). Includes an unforgettable song for learning the names of the planets in order, sung to the tune of "When Johnny Comes Marching Home."

Seymour Simon's Astronomy Series

Seymour Simon; William Morrow
A volume for each planet, illustrated with wonderful color photographs.

Also see *The Magic School Bus Lost in the Solar System,* page 178.

3. Understand the composition of the earth. Kids should be introduced to the inner layers of the earth and their compositions: crust, mantle, outer core, and inner core. They should understand what causes volcanoes, know that there are three major kinds of rocks (*igneous, sedimentary,* and *metamorphic*) and understand the major differences among them. A perfect time to start your own rock collection.

How to Dig a Hole to the Other Side of the Earth
Faith McNulty; HarperTrophy, 1990
A little boy, armed first with a shovel, then with a truly amazing drilling machine, manages to dig a hole all the way through the earth, describing his discoveries as he goes.

Let's-Read-and-Find-Out Science Series: Geology

HarperTrophy
> Short, informative, and cheerfully illustrated picture books on a range of geological topics for kids aged 4–9. Titles include *Let's Go Rock Collecting* (Roma Gans), *Volcanoes* (Franklyn Branley), and *How Mountains Are Made* (Kathleen Weidner Zoehfeld).

4. Observe and identify weather changes, both daily and seasonal. Try charting daily weather changes on a calendar. A useful resource here is a back-porch or kitchen-window thermometer: Take daily temperature readings. Weather observations should be linked to fiction and nonfiction books, poems, songs, and hands-on activities.

Let's-Read-and-Find-Out Science Series: Weather

Franklyn M. Branley; HarperTrophy
> Titles include *Sunshine Makes the Seasons; Flash, Crash, Rumble, and Roll;* and *Snow Is Falling.*

Rainy, Windy, Snowy, Sunny Days

Phyllis J. Perry; Teacher Ideas Press, 1996
> An annotated list of fiction and nonfiction books about the weather for elementary-level students, with discussion questions, project suggestions, and multidisciplinary activities for each. For example, to accompany James Stevenson's *Brrr!* (Greenwillow, 1991), Grandpa's hilarious (and very tall) tale about the frigid winter of 1908, suggestions include writing a winter tall tale, researching world snowfall records, and estimating (then determining) how long it takes an ice cube to melt. Teacher Ideas Press/Libraries Unlimited; (800) 237-6124; www.lu.com/tips.

Also see *Puddle Jumpers,* page 46.

FOREIGN LANGUAGE

See Kindergarten Foreign Language, pages 46–47.

ART

Kids at all levels should experience a varied approach to art, incorporating art history, art theory, art criticism and evaluation, and hands-on experimentation in a wide range of media. Where possible, kids should visit artists and craftspersons at work in varied fields, such as painting, printmaking, photography, sculpture, ceramics, textile arts, and architecture. They should also visit art galleries and museums. Go as a family group and take time to talk as you tour. Take sketchbooks.

Art should be incorporated in all subjects across the curriculum: During first-grade studies of ancient Egypt, for example, kids should be exposed to ancient Egyptian paintings, engravings, sculptures, and architecture.

1–8 ART CURRICULUM
Click on the appropriate grade level for creative art lessons on many topics, covering art techniques, multicultural art, and the works of famous artists. Under "Grade 1," for example, there are lesson plans on cartooning, soap carving, mask making, and the works of Andy Warhol, Vincent van Gogh, and Mary Cassatt. Web site: courier.esu11.k12.ne.us/per4/art/artcuric.html.

1. Know the primary colors and how these are mixed to produce secondary colors. Kids should know that the three primary colors are red, blue, and yellow, and should have hands-on experience with mixing these to discover that red plus blue makes purple; red plus yellow, orange; and blue plus yellow, green. They should observe and discuss the use of color in famous paintings.

Hailstones and Halibut Bones
Mary O'Neill; Doubleday, 1989
A collection of color poems; an excellent literature link to color experiments.

Mouse Paint
Ellen Stoll Walsh; Voyager, 1995
Three white mice fall into pots of primary-colored paints; then, as they splash about in painty puddles, they demonstrate the principles of color mixing.

2. Be familiar with the elements of line, shape, texture, space, light, and shadow. Discuss these elements using examples of artworks. Different kinds of lines, for example, include vertical and horizontal, curved and diagonal, thick and thin; textures include smooth, rough, bumpy, fuzzy, and so on.

What Makes a Shadow?
Clyde Robert Bulla; HarperCollins, 1994
   An explanation of shadows, with pictures of shadows in everyday life.

3. Be able to identify different kinds of pictures: portraits, still lifes, abstract art, and landscapes.

4. Study the works of a selection of well-known artists. Full-color postcard reproductions of artists' works are an excellent resource here: These are inexpensive, easy to handle, and attractive. Kids should have ample opportunity to examine and discuss features of each artwork. For greater understanding and interest, the works should be linked to simple biographies of artists, timelines, hands-on projects, and material covered in other academic disciplines. A study of Degas sculptures, for example, might be paired with a biography of Degas, fiction and nonfiction books on the ballet, and a hands-on clay modeling project.

Getting to Know the World's Greatest Artists Series
Mike Venezia; Children's Press
   A large and delightful series of thirty-two-page picture-book biographies of famous artists, with a simple text, humorous illustrations, and color reproductions of artworks. Many titles, among them *Diego Rivera* (1994), *Georgia O'Keeffe* (1993), *Henri Matisse* (1997), *Picasso* (1988), *Paul Gauguin* (1992), and *Van Gogh* (1988).

Move Over, Picasso! A Young Painter's Primer
Ruth Aukerman; Pat Depke Books and the National Gallery of Art, 1994
   Color reproductions of famous paintings paired with related art activities.

Also see *How to Use Child-Size Masterpieces for Art Appreciation*, page 48, and Discovering Great Artists, page 141.

5. Experiment with a range of art techniques. The sky's the limit. Examples include drawing, painting, collage, modeling media, printmaking, and weaving.

Drawing with Children
Mona Brookes; J. P. Tarcher, 1996
> A drawing program for kids aged 4 and up using the "Monart method," with which kids first reproduce a series of black-line patterns, then move on to more complex projects. Most six- to eight-year-olds are ready for the Level 2 series of lessons.

Mudworks: Creative Clay, Dough, and Modeling Experiences
MaryAnn Kohl; Bright Ring, 1989
> Over 100 creative modeling projects, using an interesting range of homemade doughs, pastes, clays, and more.

MUSIC

First-graders should participate in a multifaceted music program, combining music history, music theory, music appreciation, and musical performance.

1. Understand *rhythm* and *melody, pitch* (high/low), *dynamics* (loud/soft), *tempo* (fast/slow) and *timbre* (sound quality). Relate these concepts to sample musical selections. Kids should also experiment with simple rhythm instruments.

See *Kids Make Music: Clapping and Tapping to Bach and Rock,* page 49.

2. Memorize and sing simple songs. Learn an assortment of traditional folk songs, spirituals, pariotic songs, campfire tunes, and just plain silly songs.

Gonna Sing My Head Off! American Folk Songs for Children
Kathleen Krull; Alfred A. Knopf, 1994
> Words and music to sixty-two favorite American folk songs, with colorful illustrations and a brief paragraph of historical background for each.

Also see Wee Sing Series, page 49, and *From Sea to Shining Sea,* page 83.

3. Listen and respond to selections by famous composers. Suggestions for beginners include Tchaikovsky's *Nutcracker Suite,* Prokofiev's *Peter and the Wolf,* Saint-Saëns's *Carnival of the Animals,* Paul Dukas's *The Sorcerer's Apprentice,* and selections by Bach, Beethoven, Mozart, Scott Joplin, Duke Ellington, and George Gershwin. Sources include the Educational Record Center; (800) 438-1637; www.erc-inc.com; and Music for Little People; (800) 346-4445; www.mflp.com.

Pair listening sessions with biographies of composers, fiction and nonfiction books, and related activities.

Getting to Know the World's Greatest Composers Series

Mike Venezia; Children's Press
> Simple thirty-two-page biographies with humorous illustrations, photographs, and portraits. Many titles, including *Ludwig van Beethoven* (1996), *Wolfgang Amadeus Mozart* (1995), and *Duke Ellington* (1995).

4. Know the four families of instruments in the orchestra: strings, brass, woodwinds, and percussion. Kids should be able to identify instruments by look and sound and be able to group instruments into appropriate categories.

MUSIC MAESTRO PARADE
> A game of musical instruments in which kids match the sounds of the instruments on cassette tape to the pictured instruments on labeled cards. Aristoplay, 450 S. Wagner Rd., Ann Arbor, MI 48107; (800) 634-7738; www.aristoplay.com.

The Orchestra

Peter Ustinov
> A wonderful recording in which kids are introduced to the major instrumental families of the orchestra, using excerpts from well-known classical pieces as musical illustrations. On audiocassette or CD from Educational Record Center, 3233 Burnt Mill Dr., Suite 100, Wilmington, NC 28403-2698; (800) 438-1637; www.erc-inc.com.

Zin! Zin! Zin! A Violin
Lloyd Moss; Simon & Schuster, 1995

> A rhyming introduction to ten instruments of the orchestra, including examples of strings, reeds, and brasses. Kids are also introduced to the names of musical groups, starting with a trombone solo, through duo, trio, quartet, and chamber group.

HEALTH AND PHYSICAL EDUCATION

1. Kids should understand the importance of good nutrition, adequate sleep, cleanliness, tooth care, and regular exercise. In homeschool environments, parents generally take care of all this in the course of daily living. School-mandated curricula often require "abuse" education from the early grades on, in which children are cautioned about the evils of tobacco, alcohol, drugs, and sexual molestation. It's always a good idea to teach children techniques to ensure personal safety.

The Berenstain Bears and Too Much Junk Food
Stan and Jan Berenstain; Random House, 1985

> Brother and Sister Bear, stuffed on treats, are getting pudgy; they get a helpful lesson on diet and exercise.

The Berenstain Bears Learn About Strangers
Stan and Jan Berenstain; Random House, 1995

> Brother Bear is cautious; Sister Bear talks to everybody in sight. A lesson in how to deal with strangers for elementary-aged readers.

2. First-graders should be able to skip, run (without falling over), and throw and catch beanbags and balls. Play simple ball games; experiment with jump ropes; play running games.

3. Participate in athletic indoor and outdoor activities. Do calisthenics in the living room; hike; take walks; go to the playground.

Physical Education Plans for Grades 1–2
Bette J. Logsdon, et al. Human Kinetics, 1997

> Age-appropriate games, gymnastics lessons, and dance.

GAMES KIDS PLAY

Rules for all the classic playground games, including hide-and-seek, duck duck goose, tag (many), multicultural games, and more. The site also includes a selection of jump rope rhymes, just in case you've forgotten them. Web site: www.gameskidsplay.net.

GAME CENTRAL STATION

Search for games by name, grade, or featured skill (agility or strength, for example). The site includes a message board for questions and physical education–related lesson plan links. Web site: www.gamecentralstation.com.

Also see *Fit Kids!* and *Home School Family Fitness*, page 50.

GRADE TWO

The memory of being read to is a solace one carries through adulthood. It can wash over a multitude of parental sins.

KATHLEEN ROCKWELL LAWRENCE

LANGUAGE ARTS

READING

Basically, second-graders are expected to enhance and expand upon the skills acquired in grade one, honing their decoding (sounding out) abilities, and increasing vocabulary and reading fluency.

CYBERGUIDES

Teachers' guides and student lesson plans based on well-known books for students in grades K–12. Lesson plans include multidisciplinary activities, links, and teaching suggestions. After reading Russell Hoban's *Bread and Jam for Frances,* for example, kids visit an on-line wild animals photo site and make notes in a scientific journal, play food pyramid games, make their own jam and bread, and write Frances-style poems. Web site: www.sdcoe.k12.ca.us/score/cyberguide.html.

JUNIOR GREAT BOOKS PROGRAM

An excellent reading and discussion program for kids in grades 2–9. Reading selections are accompanied by thought-provoking questions which lead to in-depth discussions. Selections for second-graders include *The Tale of Squirrel Nutkin* by Beatrix Potter, "How the Camel Got His Hump" by Rudyard Kipling, and *The Red Balloon* by Albert Lamorisse. Great Books Foundation, 35 E. Wacker Dr., Suite 2300, Chicago, IL 60601-2298; (800) 222-5870; www.greatbooks.org.

LEARNING LANGUAGE ARTS THROUGH LITERATURE

The Red Book, for second-graders, teaches spelling, grammar, handwriting, and thinking skills through classic children's books. Titles include Else Holmelund Minarik's *Little Bear,* Donald Hall's *Ox-Cart Man,* Don Freeman's *Corduroy,* and Edgar and Ingri Parin D'Aulaire's *Abraham Lincoln.* Christian orientation, but generally can be adapted for those who aren't. Common Sense Press; (352) 475-5757; www.cspress.com.

Also see Five in a Row, page 53, Learning Links, page 60, and Novel Units, page 60.

Phonics, Decoding, and Word Recognition

1. Decode regular two-syllable words. The next step after *cat* and *mat* is the ability to decipher such doubleheaders as *rocket* and *butter.*

2. Understand basic rules of syllabication. Second-graders should know how to divide words into syllables. In words with a VCV (vowel-consonant-vowel) pattern, for example, syllables are divided V/CV, as in *di/ver* or *ri/der.* In words with a VCCV pattern, syllables are divided VC/CV, as in *din/ner* or *flip/per.*

3. Increase knowledge of sight words. See Dolch Word List, page 23. There are approximately fifty sight words recommended for memorization by second-graders, among them *always, because, does, these, those, which, why,* and *would.*

4. Know meanings of common abbreviations. Examples include personal titles (Mr., Ms., Dr.), months and days of the week (Dec., Mon.), and abbreviations commonly found in addresses (Rd., St.).

5. Read grade-appropriate materials aloud with proper expression and intonation. Representative titles for second-graders include *Stellaluna* by Janell Cannon; *Sylvester and the Magic Pebble* by William Steig; *Two Bad Ants* by Chris Van Allsburg; and *Where the Wild Things Are* by Maurice Sendak. For more recommendations, see Reading Comprehension below, and Book Lists, pages 400–402.

READING COMPREHENSION

1. Discuss previously read material, recalling and describing details of plot, characters, and setting. Kids should be able to compare books by different authors, contrasting plots, characters, or settings. They should also be able to compare different versions of the same story (as in "Cinderella" stories from several different cultures); and to propose alternative outcomes for stories. Inventing alternative endings or fractured fairy-tale variations on classic plots was always a favorite among our kids. If you need examples to get the imaginations off the ground, try Jon Scieszka's *The True Story of the 3 Little Pigs* (Puffin, 1996), a hilarious version of the tale told from the wolf's point of view; or Janet Perlman's *Cinderella Penguin* (Viking, 1993), in which all the characters, from prince to wicked stepsisters, are penguins, and Cinderella goes to the ball in a little glass flipper.

2. Obtain specific information from print materials. Second-graders should be able to use structural features of the text—table of contents, chapter headings, index—to locate specific factual information. They should also be able to interpret material presented in diagrams, charts, and graphs.

3. Follow two-step written instructions.

4. Identify rhyme, rhythm, alliteration, simile, and metaphor in poetry. Read and recognize limericks.

I'm Nobody! Who Are You?
Emily Dickinson; Stemmer House, 1991.
   An illustrated collection of Dickinson's poems selected for readers
   aged 6–10.

Lots of Limericks

Myra Cohn Livingston; Margaret McElderry, 1991

> An illustrated collection of over 200 limericks by many different poets on everything from "Peculiar People" to "Outer Space."

The Random House Book of Poetry for Children

Jack Prelutsky, ed.; Random House, 1983

> An illustrated anthology of over 500 poems, categorized by subject.

A Surfeit of Similes

Norton Juster; William Morrow, 1989

> A delightful rhyming introduction to similes (that is, comparisons using *like* or *as*).

5. **Experience a wide range of literary materials, including fiction and nonfiction books, myths, folktales, and fables, multicultural stories, and the like. Kids should read silently to themselves, aloud to others, and should listen to read-alouds.** Your public library will have collections of book reviews and lists of recommendations for kids of different ages. Some examples include the *Reading Rainbow Guide to Children's Books* by Twila C. Ligget and Cynthia Mayer Benfield (Citadel Press, 1996), reviews of books for kids aged 4–9 from the popular (and excellent) *Reading Rainbow* television program; *The Read-Aloud Handbook* by Jim Trelease (Penguin, 1995); and *Classics to Read Aloud to Your Children* by William F. Russell (Crown, 1992). Also see *A to Zoo: Subject Access to Children's Picture Books* by Carolyn W. Lima and John A. Lima (R. R. Bowker, 1998). This is a standard reference work for children's library rooms, a massive collection of over 18,000 children's picture books, categorized by title, author, and subject.

Also see *Spider* (page 59) and Book Lists (pages 400–402).

WRITING

99 Ways to Get Kids to Love Writing and 10 Easy Tips for Teaching Them Grammar

Mary Leonhardt; Three Rivers Press, 1998

> Games, activities, and creative suggestions for beginning writers, plus helpful hints for teaching grammar.

1. Practice manuscript handwriting skills, improving accuracy and legibility. Like first-graders, second-graders ordinarily use paper with a five-eighths-inch horizontal ruling, plus a broken midline for guidance in forming letters. Handwriting improves with practice; encourage kids to write daily.

See Handwriting Without Tears and Zaner-Bloser, page 26, Handwriting Worksheets, page 27, and *Draw Write Now*, page 61.

2. Experiment with a range of writing projects, including short stories, poems, nonfiction reports, journal keeping, and letter writing.

Write From the Edge
Ken Vinton; Free Spirit Publishing, 1997
   Innovative creative writing projects of all kinds for kids in grades K–6.

Also see *Creative Journal for Children* and *Rainbow Writing*, page 62, *Doing the Days: A Year's Worth of Creative Journaling, Drawing, Listening, Reading, Thinking, Arts & Crafts for Children Ages 8–12*, page 150, and *If You're Trying to Teach Kids How to Write, You Gotta Have This Book!*, page 150.

3. Know and use the correct format for a friendly letter, including date, salutation, body, closing, and signature. The best way to perfect one's letter-writing skills, of course, is by writing letters. Encourage your kids to correspond with friends and family. Track down pen pals.

Messages in the Mailbox: How to Write Letters
Loreen Leedy; Holiday House, 1994
   The little animals in Mrs. Gator's class learn the proper format for several kinds of letters, including friendly letters, thank-you letters, invitations, and fan letters.

KIDS' PEN PALS
   Pen pals for kids of all ages, at home and abroad; pen pal crafts; and letter writing tips; Web site: kidspenpals.about.com.

4. Recognize complete and incomplete sentences; be able to identify subject and predicate. The subject of a sentence is what the sentence is all about; the predicate is the sentence's main verb.

A simple sentence contains one subject and one predicate. Kids should be able to identify subject and predicate is such sentences as "The cat sat on the mat" and "The cow jumped over the moon."

5. Be able to identify nouns, verbs, and adjectives and use adjectives in a comparative sense by adding *er* or *est*.

THE GRAMMAR GORILLA
An on-line game about parts of speech. Beginners are challenged to identify nouns and verbs; advanced players, all parts of speech. Answer correctly and the gorilla gets a banana. Web site: www.funbrain.com/grammar.

For picture books about the parts of speech, see pages 62–63.

6. Identify synonyms, antonyms, and homonyms. Second-graders, given a sample word, should be able to come up with an appropriate synonym or antonym, and should recognize common homonyms.

Opposites
Richard Wilbur; Harcourt Brace, 1991
A humorous new view of antonyms, in rhyme. ("What's the opposite of riot?/*It's lots of people keeping quiet.*")

For more on synonyms, antonyms, and homonyms, see pages 64–65.

7. Change regular verbs to the past tense by adding *ed*; know the present and past tenses of common irregular verbs. The past tense of *jump* is *jumped*; the past tense of *walk* is *walked*. Kids should also know the irregular past tenses of such verbs as *to be, to have, to see, to do, to go, to come, to run, to give, to sing,* and *to ring*.

I Think I Thought and Other Tricky Verbs
Marvin Terban; Houghton Mifflin, 1984
An illustrated introduction to irregular verbs for early elementary students.

8. Change regular nouns to plural form by adding s; change nouns ending in s, ss, sh, ch, or x to plural form by adding es.

Your Foot's on My Feet! And Other Tricky Nouns
Marvin Terban; Houghton Mifflin, 1986
An illustrated collection of nouns with irregular plurals.

9. Spell phonetically regular words and second grade–level sight words from dictation.

For grade-appropriate spelling programs and sight-word lists, see page 64.

HANGMAN

The classic guess-and-spell game, complete with gallows, on-line. Web site: www.kidscom.com.

SPELLING ZONE

Spelling rules and quizzes. Topics covered include plural nouns, comparatives, superlatives, and word endings. Web site: members.home.net/englishzone/spelling/spelling.html.

SPICE UP YOUR SPELLING WORDS

Lots of ideas to enhance spelling lessons. Spell with pasta alphabet-soup letters, make clay words, spell in Morse code. Web site: www.teachnet.com/lesson/langarts/spellingwds040299.html.

10. Capitalize proper nouns, the first word of sentences, the pronoun *I*, the names of holidays, months, and days of the year, the names of countries, cities, and states, and the main words in book titles.

11. Know the correct use of periods, question marks, exclamation points, and quotation marks. Use commas correctly in dates and addresses.

LISTENING AND SPEAKING SKILLS

1. Be able to retell stories in proper sequence.
After hearing the tale of Jack and the magical beanstalk, for example, kids should be able to retell the story in their own words. Try recording kids' oral stories on audiocassettes and playing them back so that the kids can hear themselves talk.

BOOKWORM

A superb board game of "reading and remembering" for kids aged 6 and up. Players move around an alphabet-patterned board, listening to short selections from classic works of children's literature and answering questions about what they've just heard. The selections, printed on individual cards, are taken from 112 children's books, among them *Winnie-the-Pooh; The Lion, the Witch, and the Wardrobe;* and *The Jungle Book,* as well as much more challenging literary works, such as *The Red Badge of Courage* and *The Swiss Family Robinson.* Appropriate for a range of ages, with appropriate card choices. Published by Oxford Games, Ltd.; available from game stores.

2. Memorize and recite short poems and rhymes. Possibilities include Christina Rossetti's "Who Has Seen the Wind?," Carl Sandburg's "Fog," and Emily Dickinson's "I'm Nobody! Who Are You?"

3. Be able to give a short oral report based on facts drawn from a number of different sources. Challenge kids to give frequent short oral reports on topics of personal interest: crickets, penguins, submarines, dinosaurs, pianos, the moon.

STUDY SKILLS

Starting Early With Study Skills: A Week by Week Guide for Elementary Students
Judith L. Irvin and Elaine O. Rose; Allyn & Bacon, 1994
Activities and reproducible worksheets teach young children the basics of effective study skills.

1. Use a "first dictionary" to check word definitions and spellings. There are many illustrated beginner dictionaries for kids in this age group (see page 67).

MERRIAM-WEBSTER DICTIONARY FOR KIDS
An on-line student dictionary with many creative features, including a "Build-Your-Own-Dictionary," "Verse Composer," the "Daily Buzzword," and a list of teacher resources and dictionary-related lesson plans.

2. Be able to alphabetize to the second or third letter. Kids should be able to order such words as *bat, bean,* and *bog;* or *cart, castle,* and *candy.*

MATHEMATICS

A major advance for second-grade-level mathematicians is the introduction of multiplication as a fast and fancy way to add. Some programs and resources for second-grade math include:

EVERYDAY MATHEMATICS SERIES

A highly recommended activity-based program for grades K–6. Includes teacher's guide, student journals, and activity books, and a kit of manipulatives. Sample second-grade project titles are "Geoboard Fractions," "Polygons from Straws," "Chinese Calendar," and "Dates on Pennies." Everyday Learning Corporation, 2 Prudential Plaza, Ste. 2200, Chicago, IL 60601; (800) 382-7670; www.everydaylearning.com.

Math 2
Nancy Larson; Saxon Publishers, 1994

The home-study kit includes a teacher's manual of 132 very thorough lessons, plus student workbooks. Users will need to purchase a set of manipulatives. Saxon Publishers, Inc., 2450 John Saxon Blvd., Norman, OK 73071; (800) 284-7019; www.saxonpub.com.

MATH-IT

A collection of memorize-and-practice math games for kids aged 6–9. The kit includes boards and playing cards for "Addit," which teaches basic addition facts; "Dubblit," which teaches number doubling; and "Timzit," which teaches the multiplication tables from 1×1 to 9×9. The Sycamore Tree, 2179 Meyer Pl., Costa Mesa, CA 92627; (800) 779-6750; www.sycamoretree.com.

Miquon Math Series

Innovative workbooks covering the basics of second-grade math in a manner that stresses problem-solving and creative thinking. The Blue and Green books are recommended for grade 2. Key Curriculum Press, Box 2304, Berkeley, CA 94702-0304; (800) 995-MATH; www.keypress.com.

SRA Math: Explorations and Applications Series
Stephen S. Willoughby; SRA/McGraw-Hill
A creative and comprehensive math program for kids in grades K–6. Second-grade book and materials promote problem-solving skills through games and activities, calculator and computer use, math journaling, "thinking stories," and cross-curricular connections. SRA/Math; (888) SRA-4543; www.sra4kids.com.

Also see *Family Math for Young Children*, page 30, *A Collection of Math Lessons from Grades 1 through 3*, page 69, *Mathematics Their Way*, page 30, *Anno's Math Games*, page 68, and Math Stories, page 69.

Number Theory

1. Recognize and write numbers 0 to 1,000. Be able to read and write number words to 100.

How Much Is a Million?
David Schwartz; Mulberry Books, 1993
A delightful and hilarious picture-book introduction to increasingly big numbers, all the way up to a million, a billion, and a trillion. Second-graders, in theory, should only be interested in counting to 1,000, but *everybody* loves enormous numbers.

2. Order and compare numbers to 1,000 using "greater than" (>), "lesser than" (<), and "equals" (=) signs.

3. Be able to count to 100 by 2s, 3s, 5s, and 10s. Second-graders should also be able to count by 10s starting with any given number (e.g., 23, 33, 43, 53), and by 50s and 100s to 1,000. Useful resource: the hundred chart (see page 69).

The 512 Ants on Sullivan Street
Carol A. Losi; Scholastic, 1997
Counting by 2s all the way up to 512, as a horde of busy ants swipe food from a picnic basket.

4. Understand place values for 1s, 10s, 100s, and 1,000s.
Math By All Means: Place Value, Grades 1–2
Marilyn Burns; Marilyn Burns Education Association, 1994
See page 72.

The Case of the Missing Birthday Party
Joanne Rocklin; Cartwheel Books, 1997

Pauline's hamster has chewed up her birthday invitation, leaving nothing of the street address but the number 5. Finding the location of the party turns out to be an exercise in place value skills.

DINO MATH TRACKS

A terrific mathematical board game for kids aged 6 and up, with several playing permutations. Players advance their dinosaur (or woolly mammoth) pieces along a color-coded four-lane track that represents number places for 1s, 10s, 100s, and 1,000s. From toy and game stores.

5. Round numbers to the nearest 10. Before tackling this one, kids should be comfortable with the concept of place value. Rounding to the nearest 10, in a nutshell: Look at the number in the 1's place. If that number is 5 or greater than 5, the number in the 10's place is rounded *up*, or increased by 1. If the number in the 1's place is 4 or less, the number in the 10's place stays the same.

The number 347, rounded to the nearest 10, is 350. The number in the 1's place—7—is 5 or greater than 5; therefore the number in the 10's place (4), is increased by 1.

The number 71, rounded to the nearest 10, is 70. The number in the 1's place—1—is 4 or less than 4; therefore the number in the 10's place (7) stays the same.

6. Be able to write numbers in "expanded" form through the 100s. In "expanded" form, numbers are dissected into their component 1s, 10s, 100s, and so on, a process that reinforces the concept of place value and gives kids another slant on the structure of multidigit numbers. In expanded form, 729 = 700 + 20 + 9.

7. Understand the concept of *even* and *odd* numbers. Kids should also know the meanings of *dozen, half dozen,* and *pair.*

Among the Odds & Evens: A Tale of Adventure
Priscilla Turner; Farrar, Straus & Giroux, 1999

A delightful numerical tale in which X and Y, travelers from the distant Land of Letters, arrive in the peculiar Kingdom of Wontoo.

There they discover two kinds of resident Numbers: the Odds, all zanily outfitted eccentrics, and the Evens, all orderly, conservative, and predictable. Peculiarly enough, however, while two Even parents have only Even children, two Odd parents produce Even children too.

8. Use tallies for counting and score keeping.
See page 71.

9. Identify ordinal positions from first through twentieth.
See pages 32, 71.

10. Recognize and write fractions from ⅒ to ½.
Kids should be introduced to the terms *numerator* and *denominator*; and should know which fractions are equal to 1. (Three ⅓ pieces (³⁄₃), for example, equals 1 whole.)

Action Fractions!
A hands-on introduction to fractions for kids aged 7 and up, with accompanying set of pattern blocks and fraction dice. Kids play a variety of pattern-building and fraction-manipulating games, including "How Many Ways Can You Make a '1'?" Institute for Math Mania, Box 910, Montpelier, VT 05601-0910; (800) NUMERAL; members.aol.wm/mathmania/.

Fraction Fun
David A. Adler; Holiday House, 1996
A detailed and brightly illustrated explanation of fractions.

FRACTION CIRCLES/SUPER FRACTION CIRCLES
Color-coded plastic circles, variously divided into halves, thirds, fourths, fifths, sixths, eighths, tenths, and twelfths, for hands-on experimentation. ETA/Cuisenaire, 500 Greenwood Ct., Vernon Hills, IL 60061; (800) 445-5985; www.etauniverse.com or www.cuisenaire.com.

PATTERN BLOCKS
Pattern blocks on-line. Kids can experiment with fractions, tessellations, and pattern-making. Web site: www.best.com/~ejad/java/patterns/patterns_j.shtml.

Sources for real-live pattern (or "attribute") blocks include ETA/Cuisenaire and Creative Publications, 5623 W. 115th St., Alsip, IL 60803; (800) 624-0822; www.creativepublications.com.

11. Recognize and extend repeating patterns using symbols, pictures, or manipulatives.

12. Collect, organize, and record data using pictorial and bar graphs. Collect data in real-life situations. What is the most common eye color among the kids in your play group, art class, or soccer team? Draw a picture of each person showing the color of his or her eyes and paste it to your graph in the correct column. In which month do your friends have birthdays? When rolling a pair of dice, which sum is rolled the most often? In each case, what does the data look like? What does the graph show?

Lemonade for Sale
Stuart J. Murphy; HarperCollins, 1998
> Four kids (and a zany green parrot) discover bar graphs through their sidewalk lemonade business. Humorous illustrations, clear explanations, and activities.

Sorting: Groups and Graphs
Susan Jo Russell and Rebecca B. Corwin; Dale Seymour Publications
> One of the "Used Numbers: Real Data in the Classroom" series. Creative hands-on math lessons in which kids collect information, organize it systematically, and analyze it using simple graphs.

Also see Exploring Data (page 33).

OPERATIONS

1. Know basic addition and subtraction facts through 20.

QUICK PIX MATH

A simple, fast-paced card game in which kids match addition and subtraction problem cards to their proper answers. Aristoplay, 8122 Main St., Dexter, MI 48130; (800) 634-7738; www.aristoplay.com.

QUIA!

On-line educational games for all ages in a wide range of academic subjects. The mathematics section includes several addition and subtraction facts activities. Web site: www. quia.com.

Also see Pre-Math-It, page 74, Math-It, page 115, and Mathwork, page 70.

2. Understand the inverse relationship between addition and subtraction. Or, if you prefer, subtraction is the opposite of addition. $4 + 2 = 6$ and $6 - 2 = 4$.

3. Understand the relationships within the addition and subtraction fact "families." This is basically an expansion of the concept taught in number 2 (above). A fact family is a group of related math facts such as the following:

$3 + 5 = 8$

$5 + 3 = 8$

$8 - 3 = 5$

$8 - 5 = 3$

4. Review the commutative property of addition. Kids have already learned this concept in first grade. In simple language, it means that no matter what order numbers are added in, the answer comes out the same.

5. Be able to estimate sums and differences to 100. Estimation skills—a down-to-earth commonsense component of math—are of inestimable value to mathematicians of all ages. Estimation ability to 100 requires a good grasp of rounding to the nearest 10 (see Number Theory 5, page 117). Kids should be able to assess such problems as $38 + 37 + 11$ and know that the answer is somewhere around 90.

6. Be able to solve two- and three-digit addition and subtraction problems with and without regrouping. To cope with *regrouping*, kids will need a solid understanding of place value. *Regrouping* is a collective term for "carrying" or "borrowing," the process by which number quantities are passed back and forth from one decimal place to another in the course of solving a problem.

A good preparation for regrouping is playing base-10-block "trading games," in which kids roll dice to earn units, which can be traded in for 10s, and eventually for 100s—or the reverse, in which players start with a 100 square and roll dice to subtract units, racing to be the first to reach 0.

See place value, pages 71–72.

POLYHEDRAL DICE GAMES

Inexpensive games using assorted polyhedral dice; all reinforce basic arithmetic operations and place-value concepts. Institute for Math Mania, Box 910, Montpelier, VT 05601-0910; (800) NUMFRAL; members.aol.com/mathmania/.

7. Recognize the multiplication sign (×); know the definitions of *factor* **and** *product*. In the multiplication problem $5 \times 3 = 15$, 5 and 3 are the *factors*; 15 is the *product*.

Amanda Bean's Amazing Dream
Cindy Neuschwander; Scholastic, 1998
Why multiply? Because it's a lot easier and quicker than counting. Amanda Bean counts everything, from library books to popcorn kernels, one by one by one—until a mathematical nightmare about counting way too many sheep shows her the benefits of multiplication.

8. Know the commutative property of multiplication. This is a fancy way of saying that numbers can be multiplied in any order: 3×4, for example, generates the same result as 4×3.

9. Know multiplication facts through the "five times" table. Second-graders should also know how to multiply by 0, 1, and 10.

MATH SMART

A bright-colored game of math dominoes: one half of each card shows a math problem; the other half the answer to a math problem. The trick is to lay out the cards in interconnected patterns such that problems and answers match. Available in "Addition," "Subtraction," "Multiplication," and "Division" packs for young facts learners. Talicor, 8845 Steven Chase Ct., Las Vegas, NV 89129; (800) 433-4263; www.talicor.com.

10. Understand the use of variables and use these in number sentences. A first exposure to algebra. A variable is a numerical unknown, generally represented in mathematical equations by a letter, such as the ever-popular x. Kids should be able to interpret such simple equations (number sentences) as $4 + x = 7$.

11. Solve simple one-step addition, subtraction, and multiplication problems, including both horizontal and vertical numerical problems and word problems. Kids should be encouraged to apply a number of techniques to problem-solving, to model problems with symbols or manipulatives, and to describe problems and their solutions in everyday language. To model the subtraction problem $569 - 231$, for example, kids might try using base 10 blocks. Five 100 squares, six 10 bars, and 9 units are equivalent to the number 569. Then kids can physically remove 231—two 100 squares, three 10 bars, and 1 unit—to find the difference.

Describing math problems and their solution in everyday language is a technique with multiple benefits. It simultaneously clarifies thought processes, hones language skills, and enhances mathematical expertise. Such written descriptions are an integral part of Writing Across the Curriculum (WAC) programs, in which kids are encouraged to write in all academic disciplines. In several popular math programs, including the Everyday Mathematics Series (page 115) and SRA Math (page 116), kids keep math journals.

12. Apply mathematical knowledge to other areas of the academic curriculum and to everyday situations. Memory thrives on connections. This is why cross-curricular studies—in which kids cover many different aspects of a given topic from a range of perspectives—are so effective; the multifaceted approach provides an immense number of interlinked associations. The principle similarly applies to mathematics: The skills kids learn are reinforced by application in a variety of academic and daily-life situations.

See *Picturing Math*, page 30.

MONEY AND MEASUREMENT

1. Recognize and know the relative values of pennies, nickels, dimes, quarters, half dollars, and dollar bills.
See *Math By All Means*, page 75.

2. Be able to determine values of given combinations of bills and coins, and to write the amount using either the cent sign or the dollar sign and decimal point.

Bunny Money
Rosemary Wells; Dial Books for Young Readers, 1997

Max and his big sister Ruby (rabbits) go shopping for their grand-mother's birthday present with $15 in cash—which they spend every cent of over the course of the day, ending up with just enough money for bus fare home. (Grandma gets a great set of glow-in-the-dark vampire teeth.) A fun mathematical and mone-tary exercise for beginners.

3. Be able to add and subtract money and make change.

KIDS' MONEY PAGE

Games, activities, books, and general information about money. Participate in an allowance survey; Web site: www. kidsmoney.org.

PRESTO CHANGE-O

An attractive money-based board game for kids aged 6–9. Players hop their pieces around the board earning, spending, and sav-ing small amounts of money, supplied in fake paper bills and plastic coins. ("Lose a tooth: earn $1.50.") First kid to save $10 wins. From game stores or Educational Insights, 16941 Keegan Ave., Carson, CA 90764; (800) 933-3277; www. educationalinsights.com.

4. Compare and order objects by length, weight, and volume.

Kids should experiment with rulers, measuring tapes, arm and pan balances, and liquid measures. Second-graders should become familiar with both English and metric measures of length: inch (in.), foot (ft.), yard (yd.), and centimeter (cm.). They should also know that 1 foot contains 12 inches; that 1 yard contains 3 feet; and that 1 centimeter is about half the size of an inch. They should know that weight is measured in pounds (lbs.) and ounces (oz.); and volume (capacity) in cups (c.), pints (pt.), quarts (qt.), and gallons (gal.). They should also know that the metric measure, 1 liter, is approximately equal to 1 quart.

How Tall, How Short, How Faraway?
David A. Adler; Holiday House, 1999
> A picture-book explanation of the origins of measurement in ancient Greece and Rome, the development of standards, the beginning of the metric system, and ways of measuring length, height, and distance.

Measuring Penny
Loreen Leedy; Henry Holt, 1998
> Lisa and dog Penny tackle measurement in both standard and nonstandard units, variously determining heights, weights, volumes, times, and temperatures. Excellent.

5. Be able to read a thermometer, measure temperatures in degrees Fahrenheit, and recognize the degree (°) sign.

Hot and Cold
Allan Fowler; Children's Press, 1995
> A Rookie Read About Science book that explains the measurement of temperature.

6. Know the names of the months of the year in order. Kids should be able to use a calendar to determine day, date, week, and month.

For a source for a downloadable blank calendar, see page 76.

Calendar Bears
Kathleen Hague; Henry Holt, 1997
> A rhyming tour of the twelve months of the year with bright-colored illustrations of bears, variously shown making Valentines, splashing in spring puddles, watching Fourth of July fireworks.

The Story of Clocks and Calendars: Marking a Millenium
Betsy Maestro; Lothrop, Lee & Shepard, 1999
> A colorfully illustrated multicultural history of timekeeping, from prehistoric calendar sticks to the atomic clock.

7. Tell time to the quarter hour.

Exploring Time
Gillian Chapman; Millbrook Press, 1995
> A hands-on approach to time for kids aged 7 and up, covering many different aspects of time, from time in daily life to the broad

sweep of geological time. Projects include making timelines, sun-dials, sand timers, and time capsules.

Also see *One Hand at a Time*, page 76.

GEOMETRY

1. Identify the basic two-dimensional figures: circle, square, rec-tangle, and triangle. A good resource for enhancing geometrical thinking is a set of *Tangrams*, a collection of seven geometric pieces that can be used to solve a wide variety of puzzles. Sources for Tan-grams, geometric pattern blocks, and related activity books include ETA/Cuisenaire; (800) 445-5985; www.etauniverse.com or www.cuisenaire.com; and Creative Publications; (800) 624-0822; www.creativepublications.com.

Also see *Math By All Means: Geometry, Grades 1–2* (page 77) and *Shape Up!* (page 161).

2. Identify the basic three-dimensional figures: sphere, cube, cone, pyramid, and cylinder. Identify three-dimensional shapes around the house, yard, and neighborhood. Try making the geo-metric solids from clay or modeling compound.

Easy-to-Make 3-D Shapes in Full Color
A. G. Smith; Dover Publications, 1989
  A paper-crafts book from which young geometry students can cut, paste, and assemble an assortment of attractive, brightly colored polyhedrons, starting with the cube.

Three-Dimensional Shapes
David L. Stienecker; Benchmark Books, 1997
  A picture-book introduction to solid geometry, starting with the (Egyptian) pyramids.

3. Recognize and differentiate among horizontal, vertical, par-allel, and perpendicular lines.

Straight Lines, Parallel Lines, Perpendicular Lines
Mannis Charosh; Thomas Y. Crowell
  One of the Young Math Books series. Short, informative, interest-ing, and sadly out of print, but available from most libraries.

4. Be able to identify *congruent* figures. Congruent figures have both the same shape and the same size. Kids should be able to pick these out regardless of orientation or position.

5. Be able to identify and create symmetrical figures and designs. See *M Is for Mirror*, page 78.

6. Define and measure *perimeter* and *area*. Kids should know that perimeter is measured in units of length, while area is measured in square units, such as square inches, square feet, and square centimeters. Encourage kids to participate in hands-on activities: Measure and compare perimeters of objects around the house, using rulers or measuring tapes; cover outlined figures with small congruent shapes such as pattern-block squares (see geometry number 1, above). How many squares does it take to cover a picture book or a place mat?

Spaghetti and Meatballs for All
Marilyn Burns; Scholastic, 1997
> A family reunion, with an ever-expanding group of dinner guests, is an exercise in measuring perimeter and area, as tables and chairs are moved and moved again.

HISTORY AND GEOGRAPHY

Curricula, being arbitrary, disagree over both the content and the order in which certain academic subjects are presented to schoolchildren. More recently designed history standards often stress the importance of history as stories, urge a broad-based presentation of the multicultural aspects of history, and suggest that world and American history be introduced at early ages and repeated in greater depth as students reach the older grades. Homeschoolers, who have freedom to follow their own interests, may want to substitute alternative topics for those listed below or to pursue some of the listed topics for greater periods of time and in greater detail.

Remember: A curriculum isn't an assignment. It's a guideline, a suggestion list, a series of academic guesses. You know your kids best. Listen to them.

Reinforce history lessons with timelines, hands-on activities, videos, music, art projects, field trips, and reading material of all kinds, including fiction and nonfiction books, biographies of prominent people, legends and folktales, and poems.

AMERICAN HISTORY

Since a general overview of history through the Revolutionary War was presented to kids in first grade, second-grade history takes the story up where last left off: with the framing of the American Constitution.

See Bluestocking Press, page 84, *Social Studies Through Children's Literature,* page 37, and *Appleseeds,* page 163.

1. Know the basic purpose and content of the United States Constitution and understand the structure and function of the federal government. Topics to cover include the reason for laws; the rocky history of the writing of the Constitution, including the stories of the Virginia Plan, the New Jersey Plan, and the Connecticut Compromise; the Preamble to the Constitution, the Bill of Rights, and the definition of *amendment;* and the *executive* (President), *legislative* (Congress: the Senate and the House of Representatives), and *judicial* (Supreme Court) branches of government and their functions.

The Bill of Rights

The Constitution
Warren Colman; Children's Press, 1987
An explanation of each in a simple, large-print text illustrated with color photographs.

If You Were There When They Signed the Constitution
Elizabeth Levy; Scholastic, 1992
A detailed story of the Constitution in reader-friendly (and discussion-provoking) question-and-answer format.

We the People
Peter Spier; Doubleday, 1991
> An account of the Constitutional Convention, followed by the illustrated text of the Preamble.

2. The War of 1812. Topics to cover include the reasons for the war, James and Dolley Madison and the burning of the White House, "Old Ironsides," and the writing of "The Star-Spangled Banner."

An American Army of Two
Janet Greeson; Carolrhoda, 1992
> During the War of 1812, the two daughters of a Massachusetts lighthouse keeper fool the British into retreating by playing "Yankee Doodle" on the fife and drum.

By Dawn's Early Light: The Story of the Star-Spangled Banner
Steven Kroll; Scholastic, 1994
> A picture-book account of the War of 1812, including the dramatic story of Francis Scott Key, the attack on Fort McHenry, and the writing of our national anthem.

3. Westward expansion: wagon trains, steamboats, the transcontinental railroad, and the impact on the American Indians. Topics to cover include the building of the Erie Canal, the invention of the steamboat (and the steam-powered locomotive), the Pony Express, the building of the transcontinental railroad, the Oregon Trail and the wagon trains, and the Indian removal and the Cherokee "Trail of Tears."

Ahyoka and the Talking Leaves
Peter and Connie Roop; Beech Tree Books, 1994
> A fictionalized biography of Sequoyah, inventor of the Cherokee alphabet.

The Amazing Impossible Erie Canal
Cheryl Harness; Simon & Schuster, 1995
> A fascinating account of the building of the Canal for young readers, illustrated with diagrams (find out how a canal lock works) and maps.

They're Off! The Story of the Pony Express
Cheryl Harness; Simon & Schuster, 1996

> The short, exciting life of the Pony Express, with illustrations, maps, information about background events of the time, and particularly interesting facts in boxes.

Westward Ho! An Activity Guide to the Wild West
Laurie Carlson; Chicago Review Press, 1998

> Projects, games, arts and crafts, and recipes for kids aged 5–10 based on the nineteenth-century American West.

Also see *If You Traveled West in a Covered Wagon,* page 87.

4. An overview of the Civil War. Topics to cover include the conflict over slavery, the Abolitionists and the Underground Railroad, the opposing sides during the Civil War (Union and Confederacy; Yankees and Rebels), prominent Civil War–era Americans (such as Harriet Tubman, Abraham Lincoln, Ulysses S. Grant, and Robert E. Lee), key events of the war, and the importance of the Emancipation Proclamation and the Gettysburg Address.

Abe Lincoln Goes to Washington
Cheryl Harness; National Geographic Society, 1997

> A picture-book biography of Lincoln's later years, from his arrival in Springfield, Illinois, through his presidency, the war, and his tragic assassination.

The Civil War for Kids
Janis Herbert; Chicago Review Press, 1999

> Maps, period photographs, capsule biographies of famous people, anecdotes, and lots of truly terrific activities. Included are instructions for reenacting the Battle of Antietam.

If You Traveled on the Underground Railroad
Ellen Levine; Scholastic, 1988

> Lots of interesting and discussion-provoking information, in fun-to-read question-and-answer format.

5. Immigration. Topics to cover include the many different reasons immigrants came to the United States, their countries of origin, the symbolism of the Statue of Liberty, Ellis Island, the process of becoming an American citizen, and the many ethnic groups and cultural traditions found in the United States today.

If Your Name Was Changed at Ellis Island
Ellen Levine; Scholastic, 1994
> What it was like to be an immigrant, in question-and-answer format. ("Why did people leave their homelands?" "Where would you eat and sleep on the ship?")

Lily and Miss Liberty
Carla Stevens; Scholastic, 1992
> Kids learn about immigration and the Statue of Liberty through Lily, who is earning money for the statue's pedestal fund by making paper liberty crowns. (Pattern included.)

6. Civil rights: women's suffrage, integration, the rights of workers.
Topics to cover include suffrage and voting rights, prominent suffragists (including Susan B. Anthony and Elizabeth Cady Stanton), the struggle for workers' rights and the abolition of child labor, the civil rights movement, and the stories of prominent civil rights leaders (such as Rosa Parks and Martin Luther King Jr.).

The Ballot Box Battle
Emily Arnold McCully; Alfred A. Knopf, 1996
> Young Cordelia learns about women's rights from a formidable neighbor, Elizabeth Cady Stanton.

Fire at the Triangle Factory
Holly Littlefield; First Avenue Editions, 1996
> A fictionalized account of two young workers at the Triangle Shirtwaist Factory, where a terrible fire in 1911 spurred on the campaign for workers' rights.

A Picture Book of Martin Luther King, Jr.

A Picture Book of Rosa Parks
David A. Adler; Holiday House
> Simple picture-book biographies for young readers.

See Picture Book Biography Series, page 38.

World History

The Children's Picture World History Series
Anne Millard; EDC/Usborne Publishing

A multivolume history of the world in picture books, heavily illustrated with wonderful little pictures, colorful maps, and diagrams. Titles include *The First Civilizations, Warriors and Seafarers,* and *The Age of Revolutions.*

1. Survey the history of Asia, covering landmark events, culture and religion, and geography. Concentrate on the countries of China, Japan, and India. Under each, kids should locate the country and identify its major geographical features on the world map, discuss cultural and religious features, read associated fiction and nonfiction books, legends, folktales, and poems, and participate in hands-on projects and activities. While studying India, for example, they might read the story of the elephant-headed god Ganesh and make their own elephant-head masks; while studying China, they might read about the building of the Great Wall, learn to count to ten in Chinese, and try their hands at making paper; and while studying Japan, they might experiment with origami and try eating a Japanese meal with chopsticks.

ANCIENT CHINA TREASURE CHEST

A beautiful box stuffed with information on ancient China and materials for related activities. Includes charts and maps, a short text, brush, ink, and instructions for drawing Chinese characters, patterns and paper for making a fan, I Ching coins, and much more. From bookstores or Running Press; (800) 345-5359.

The Great Wall of China
Leonard Everett Fisher; Aladdin, 1995

A picture-book history of the famous Great Wall, with dramatic illustrations.

Made in China: Ideas and Inventions from Ancient China
Suzanne Williams; Pacific View Press, 1997

A chronological account of Chinese discoveries and inventions, including paper, silk, the compass, the crossbow, and porcelain. Illustrated with photographs, prints, and paintings.

MR. DONN'S ANCIENT HISTORY PAGE
An immense and superb collection of ancient history lesson plans
and activities for a range of grade levels, as well as maps and timelines. Many categories, among them China, India, and Japan. Web
site: members.aol.com/DonnandLee/.

A Samurai Castle
Fiona MacDonald; Peter Bedrick Books, 1995
An Inside Story book that shows the structure and function of an
ancient Japanese samurai castle and the everyday life of the
people who lived and worked in and around it. Detailed and colorful illustrations.

2. Survey the medieval to early Renaissance period (A.D.
400–1600). Topics to cover include the Dark Ages following the fall
of Rome, the rise of Christianity, feudal society and everyday life in
the medieval period, the Norman conquest of England, the Magna
Carta and its importance, the Black Death, the rise of Islam, and
the Crusades. Suggested literature links include children's versions
of *Beowulf* and Chaucer's *Canterbury Tales*, legends of King Arthur
and his knights, tales of Robin Hood, and the stories of Shakespearean plays.

Castle
David Macauley; Houghton Mifflin, 1982

Cathedral
David Macauley; Houghton Mifflin, 1973
Marvelously illustrated accounts of medieval building projects,
from the choosing of the site to the final completion of a Welsh
castle or French cathedral. Video versions of the books, each an
appealing combination of animation, narration, and live-action
footage, are available from Zenger Media; (800) 421-4246;
www.zengermedia.com.

**Knights and Castles: 50 Hands-On Activities to Experience the
Middle Ages**
Avery Hart and Paul Mantell; Williamson Publishing, 1998
Games (including chess), projects, activities, thought-provoking
questions, and historical background information on the medieval
period.

KNIGHTS AND CASTLES

A board game of chivalry, knighthood, and medieval life for kids aged 6–10. Aristoplay; (800) 634-7738; www.aristoplay.com.

KNIGHTS TREASURE CHEST

An activity kit containing a book of historical background information, a map of medieval Europe, and materials for many medieval projects and games, among them a working catapult model and "stained-glass" Gothic windows to color. From bookstores or Running Press; (800) 345-5359.

MR. DONN'S ANCIENT HISTORY PAGE

Detailed lesson plans on all aspects of ancient history, including the Middle Ages and Renaissance. Excellent. Web site: members. aol.com/DonnandLee/.

Also see *Gargoyles: Monsters in Stone*, page 141.

GEOGRAPHY

1. Name and locate the seven continents and four major oceans on a world map and globe.
See New True Books: Continents, page 92.

2. Name and locate Canada, the United States, and Mexico on maps and globes; continue to expand geographical knowledge based on studies in other academic disciplines. State and world geography should be reinforced across the curriculum. Use maps to locate states and countries mentioned in literature selections; link geography closely to history topics, as in studies of China, India, and Japan.

3. Make "story maps." This is an excellent way to reinforce geographical skills. Have kids listen to a story and then draw illustrative maps. After hearing the tale of "The Three Little Pigs," for example, kids should be able to invent a map showing the locations of the pigs' mother's house, the houses of straw, sticks, and bricks, the wolf's den, and so on.

The Once Upon a Time Map Book
B. G. Hennessy; Candlewick Press, 1999
> Wonderful maps of such magical places as Peter Pan's Neverland, Alice's Wonderland, and the gigantic kingdom Jack reached by climbing up the beanstalk.

Which Way to the Revolution?
Bob Barner; Holiday House, 1999
> Readers map Paul Revere's ride, with the help of a band of mice (and the hindrance of a bunch of evil rats). An appendix includes notes for other mapmaking projects.

4. Understand the use of a map key or legend; know the cardinal directions (north, east, south, and west).

5. Define and locate northern and southern hemispheres, the equator, and the North and South Poles. Introduce concepts of latitude and longitude. For reinforcing the concepts in 4 and 5, see:

Maps and Globes
Jack Knowlton; HarperTrophy, 1986
> An introduction to all the map basics, with attractive bright-colored illustrations.

Maps and Mapping
Barbara Taylor; Kingfisher Books, 1993
> An activity-based approach to maps and mapmaking for beginners. The book, illustrated with photographs and diagrams, covers different kinds of maps and essential elements of maps, including symbols and scale, and latitude and longitude.

Also see *Geography from A–Z*, page 91, and Count Your Way Series, page 91.

SCIENCE

Science is an active and investigative discipline; kids should participate in direct observations, exploration, and hands-on experimentation. The importance of the *scientific method* should be emphasized throughout: that is, the process of observation, hypothesis, testing through experimentation, and assessment of results that gradually leads researchers toward scientific truth.

Science should also be linked to other disciplines across the curriculum: to math, history, literature, and the arts. To accompany a study of ancient Greece, for example, kids might learn about ancient Greek science, read a biography of Archimedes, and perform experiments based on some of his discoveries.

From Butterflies to Thunderbolts: Discovering Science With Books Kids Love
Anthony D. Fredericks; Fulcrum Publishing, 1997
An annotated list of picture books categorized by science topic and paired with experiments and multidisciplinary activities. Topics include animals, plants, the environment, dinosaurs, the earth, the oceans, weather, and space. Sample book titles include Barbara Cooney's *Miss Rumphius,* Lynne Cherry's *The Great Kapok Tree,* and Verna Aardema's *Bringing the Rain to Kapiti Plain.*

Also see *Science Through Children's Literature,* page 42.

PHYSICAL SCIENCE

1. A very first introduction to Newtonian physics: Students should investigate objects in motion and learn that force is required to change an object's speed.

The Magic School Bus Plays Ball: A Book About Forces
Joanna Cole; Scholastic, 1998
The incredible bus plunges into a physics book where Ms. Frizzle's class learns all about motion and forces through a (frictionless) game of baseball.

Pushing and Pulling
Gary Gibson; Copper Beech Books, 1996
Simple experiments that demonstrate the science of pushing and pulling, gravity, friction, and more.

2. Sometimes forces are applied by simple machines. Know the basic simple machines (lever, wedge, inclined plane, wheel, screw) and how they work.

How Do You Lift a Lion?
Robert E. Wells; Albert Whitman, 1996

How do you lift a lion? With a lever. A delightfully illustrated introduction to simple machines.

EARLY SIMPLE MACHINES KIT

LEGO TECHNIC STARTER KIT

Creative and educational building kits using the ever-popular Lego blocks. Both include gears, pulleys, wheels, axles, and levers, plus "Activity Cards" with instructions for building an assortment of working machines. "Early Simple Machines" includes 71 Duplo-size pieces and is more suitable for younger children; "Lego Technic I," for more skilled Lego builders, includes 179 standard Lego-size pieces. Lego Dacta; (800) 362-4308; www.pitsco-legodacta-store.com.

Simple Machines
Deborah Hodge; Kids Can Press, 1998

Clear explanations and appealing hands-on experiments for early elementary students.

Also see Delta Science Nutshell Science Kits, page 43.

3. Define and explain friction.

4. Investigate magnetism.
Kids should continue the investigations begun in grade 1 (see page 94). Points to cover include lodestones and electromagnets, magnetic fields, the earth's magnetic poles and the workings of a compass, and the laws of magnetism (like poles repel; unlike poles attract).

What Makes a Magnet?
Franklyn M. Branley; HarperTrophy, 1996

A nice, clear, and delightfully illustrated explanation of magnets and magnetism, with instructions for making your own magnet and compass and playing a fishing-with-magnets game.

5. Understand that sound is caused by vibration.
Through demonstrations and hands-on experiments, kids should discover that sound is caused by vibration and that changes in the speed of the vibration changes the *pitch* of a note. Sound studies mesh readily

with music and studies of the biology of the senses. Kids should demonstrate, for example, that faster vibrations generate a higher pitch and slower vibrations, a lower pitch, and they should know that human speech results from vibration of the *vocal cords* or *larynx*.

The Science Book of Sound
Neil Ardley; Harcourt Brace, 1991
> Simple experiments that demonstrate the principles of sound, vibrations, and music.

Sounds All Around
Wendy Pfeffer; HarperCollins, 1999
> All about sound and hearing for kids aged 5–8. The book discusses vibration and sound waves and how hearing operates in people and animals; and gives instructions for sound-related activities.

LIFE SCIENCE

1. Understand and be able to describe the varied life cycles of plants and animals. A range of different species should be covered, including birds (from egg to adult), frogs, butterflies, trees, and flowers. Kids should be able to define and describe the process of *metamorphosis*.

Lifecycles Series
Gerald Legg; Franklin Watts
> Short picture books that trace the life cycles of flowers, frogs, butterflies. Titles include *From Seed to Sunflower* and *From Tadpole to Frog*.

Pumpkin Circle
George Levenson; Tricycle Press, 1999
> From seed to flower to fat orange jack-o'-lantern, illustrated with wonderful color photographs.

What Is a Life Cycle?
Bobbie Kalman; Crabtree, 1998
> Many examples of life cycles, including both plants and animals (insects, amphibians, reptiles, fish, birds, mammals, and human beings), illustrated with color photographs.

2. **Understand and be able to describe seasonal changes as they affect plants and animals.** Points to cover include the reasons for and features of seasons, migration, hibernation, camouflage, and dormancy.

How Do Birds Find Their Way?
Roma Gans; HarperTrophy, 1996
   The author explains several theories that account for the mystery of bird migration. Illustrated with maps and paintings.

3. **Understand cell theory.** Kids should know what a *cell* is and understand that the body is composed of different types of cells, which are organized into *tissues, organs,* and *systems.*

Cells Are Us
Fran Balkwill and Mic Rolph; First Avenue Editions, 1994
   A delightfully illustrated overview of cell biology for beginners. The book covers the structures and functions of the major types of body cells, as well as DNA, chromosomes, and cell division. Excellent.

For activities centered around human cells, see *Watch Me Grow,* below.

4. **Continue and expand upon the study of human body systems begun in grade 1 (see pages 97–98).** Review the digestive and excretory systems in greater detail. Kids should know the structure and function of salivary glands, esophagus, stomach, liver, small and large intestines, kidneys, bladder, urethra, and anus.

   SOMEBODY
   A game of human anatomy for kids aged 6–10. Players stick (reusable) vinyl pictures of body parts to the right place on the outlined bodies of cheerful, but transparent, kids in response to such anatomical questions as "Which body part has 4 chambers and pumps blood through your body?" Aristoplay, 8122 Main St., Dexter, MI 48130; (800) 634-7738; www.aristoplay.com.

Watch Me Grow: Fun Ways to Learn About Cells, Bones, Muscles, and Joints
Michelle O'Brien-Palmer; Chicago Review Press, 1999
   Experiments and activities about the parts of the human body for kids aged 5–9. For example, kids maintain a science journal,

make charts and graphs, play question-and-answer games, and make working models of body parts.

5. Be able to identify and describe the five senses and their respective systems. Topics to cover include all five senses—seeing, hearing, taste, touch, and smell—using a range of fiction and non-fiction books and hands-on projects and activities.

The Magic School Bus Explores the Senses
Joanna Cole; Scholastic, 1999
> Ms. Frizzle's class magically shrinks to tour the human senses. Humorous, appealing, and a lot of solid information. Kids learn about the interconnections of the nervous system, the rods and cones of the eye, the olfactory cells of the nose, and more.

You Can't Smell a Flower with Your Ear!
Joanna Cole; Price Stern Sloan, 1994
> All about the five senses, with everyday examples, fun cartoons, and simple diagrams of eye, ear, nose, and tongue.

EARTH SCIENCE

1. Understand and be able to describe the water cycle. Topics to cover include the processes of evaporation, cloud formation, condensation, and precipitation; water vapor in the air (*humidity*); and groundwater. Kids should know the major types of clouds (*stratus*, *cirrus*, and *cumulus*).

The Magic School Bus at the Waterworks
Joanna Cole; Scholastic, 1995
> Ms. Frizzle's science class shrinks, evaporates, falls to earth in raindrops, and tours the town's water system.

2. Continue and expand upon previous studies of weather. Encourage students to take measurements and record weather data. Possible projects include making weekly and monthly temperature graphs, assembling a scrapbook of cloud photographs, and making an anemometer and a rain gauge.

The Weather Sky
Bruce McMillan; Farrar, Straus & Giroux, 1996

All the basics of weather, with beautiful color photographs, corresponding weather maps, and charts showing cloud heights.

Weatherwatch
Valerie Wyatt; Addison-Wesley, 1990

Weather information, projects, puzzles, and activities for elementary students. Kids can make a cloud in a bottle, measure raindrops, and build a barometer.

Also see *Puddle Jumpers*, page 46, Let's-Read-and-Find-Out Science Series: Weather, page 100, and *Rainy, Windy, Snowy, Sunny Days*, page 100.

FOREIGN LANGUAGE

As kids progress in their foreign-language studies, programs should cover written as well as spoken language. Kids should read texts appropriate to their skill level, write sentences and short passages using correct grammar and vocabulary, and practice their chosen language in skits, recitations, and conversations.

See resources, page 46–47.

ART

Kids should experiment with a range of art media and techniques to create original artworks. They should also continue to develop their knowledge of historical and multicultural art. Art can be readily incorporated into all subjects across the curriculum. When studying pattern-block tessellations in geometry, for example, show kids the artwork of M. C. Escher; when studying life in the Middle Ages, view illuminated manuscripts and period paintings.

Also see 1–8 Art Curriculum, page 101, and *Art Through Children's Literature*, page 48.

1. Understand the function of the color wheel; know the rules of color mixing; experiment with tints and shades. Kids should know the primary and secondary colors and be familiar with the rules of color mixing. (See page 101.) They should try mixing white with various colors to create *tints* and black with various colors to make *shades* and should understand the concept of *warm* and *cool* colors.

2. Be familiar with the elements of line, shape, texture, space, light, and shadow. Identify these in a range of different types of artworks.

3. Identify different kinds of pictures: portraits, still lifes, abstract art, and landscapes. Experiment with matching or grouping paintings by style, by subject, and by artist.

A Child's Book of Art: Discover Great Paintings
Lucy Micklethwait; Dorling Kindersley, 1999
> Kids study thirteen paintings from seven centuries. Each double-page spread includes thought-provoking questions about the paintings and brief information about the artist and time period.

Discovering Great Artists
MaryAnn F. Kohl and Kim Solga; Bright Ring Publishing, 1996
> Project-centered art appreciation for kids aged 4–12. The book includes brief biographies of artists and creative activities based on their works. For example, kids make a leaf-print Rousseau jungle and a Jackson Pollock spatter painting.

Also see I Spy Series, page 48, *How to Use Child-Size Masterpieces for Art Appreciation*, page 48, and *Art Through Children's Literature*, page 48.

4. Continue to experience and discuss a variety of artworks by well-known artists throughout history and examples of arts and crafts from a range of countries and cultures. Know that architecture is the art of designing buildings. Students should become familiar with a range of styles of architecture and be able to define such architectural terms as *column*, *dome*, and *arch*.

Gargoyles: Monsters in Stone
Jennifer Dussling; Grosset & Dunlap, 1999
> All about gargoyles for elementary-aged students, with architectural details, intriguing history, and interesting facts.

***Round Buildings, Square Buildings, and Buildings That Wiggle
Like a Fish***
Philip M. Isaacson; Alfred A. Knopf, 1988

> A round-the-world tour of many different and interesting examples of architecture, illustrated with photographs.

What It Feels Like to Be a Building
Forrest Wilson; National Trust for Historic Preservation, 1988

> A very personal experience of architecture. Clever illustrations explain how the different parts of a building would feel if they were people.

5. Experiment with different art media and techniques to produce original artworks. Try watercolor and tempera painting, pastels, sidewalk chalk, and modeling compounds; make mobiles, murals, simple weavings, junk sculptures.

See *Kids Create!*, page 49, *Drawing With Children*, page 103, and *Mudworks*, page 103.

MUSIC

Kids should participate in a multifaceted music program, including music participation, appreciation, history, and theory.

1. Know the definitions of *scale, staff,* and *treble clef*; know the names of the lines and spaces of the treble clef. Names and positions of musical notes can be taught through the familiar acronyms FACE (the notes of the spaces of the treble clef) and EGBDF or Every Good Boy Does Fine (the names of the lines). Kids should be able to sing the C major scale (do, re, mi, fa, sol, la, ti, do).

2. Identify whole, half, and quarter notes and whole, half, and quarter rests.

Music Theory for Beginners
Emma Danes; EDC Publications, 1997

> A humorously illustrated introduction to the basics of music theory for elementary students.

Rabbit-Man Music Books Series

Julie Albright and Vincent Fago; Diversity Press
Very simple music theory workbooks for beginners, illustrated with cheerful rabbits. Diversity Press, Box 376, Bethel, VT 05032; (802) 234-9179.

3. Experiment with simple musical instruments. Often at this age kids begin to learn to play the soprano recorder—a nice choice for beginning musicians, since it is inexpensive, easy to play, and fun. Other popular choices for young beginners include the piano (or keyboard) and the violin (available in graded sizes).

ALFRED PUBLISHING COMPANY

Resources include Alfred's Basic Piano Course for beginning piano students aged 7 and up. Each of the seven levels of the course includes music, music theory, activities, and ear-training exercises. The company also publishes Music for Little Mozarts, a piano series for preschoolers; and Alfred's Piano Prep Course, for kids aged 5–7. Alfred Publishing Company, Box 10003, Van Nuys, CA 91410-0003; (818) 891-5999; www.alfredpub.com.

The First Book of the Recorder

Philip Hawthorne; Usborne, 1986.
A friendly introduction to the recorder, fingering, and music theory with a collection of bright-colored blobby little cartoon characters. Other Usborne books for beginners include *The First Book of the Piano* and *The First Book of the Keyboard*. EDC Publications; (800) 475-4522; www.edcpub.com.

RECORDERS

From Rhythm Band Instruments, Box 126, Fort Worth, TX 76101-0126; (800) 424-4724; www.rhythmband.com; or West Music, 1212 Fifth St., Box 5521, Coralille, IA 52241; (800) 397-9378; www.westmusic.com.

4. Listen and respond to varied selections by famous composers. Kids should also listen to multicultural musical selections. Listen to Chinese bamboo flute music, for example, while studying ancient China; to digeridoo music while studying Australia. Try an

assortment of Civil War ballads to accompany nineteenth-century American history. Accompany selections with biographies of composers and other related resource books. (For example, see Getting to Know the World's Greatest Composers Series, page 104.)
Also see Classical Kids, page 183.

5. Know the names of the instrument families of the orchestra and their individual members. Kids should recognize individual instruments and be able to group them in families (*strings, woodwinds, brass, percussion*). Drums, xylophones, cymbals, triangles, and tambourines, for example, are all percussion instruments; flutes, piccolos, clarinets, saxophones, oboes, and bassoons are woodwinds. Kids should also be familiar with keyboard instruments: upright and grand piano, harpsichord, and organ.

Music
Neil Ardley; Alfred A. Knopf, 1989
> One of the popular Eyewitness series. Each double-page spread covers a different music topic or instrumental family. Illustrated with wonderful color photographs.

Musical Instruments Coloring Book
Ellen J. McHenry; Dover Publications
> Black-line drawings of all the instruments of the orchestra, plus some extras. From bookstores or Dover Publications, Inc., 31 E. Second St., Mineola, NY 11501.

The Young Person's Guide to the Orchestra
Anita Ganeri; Harcourt Brace, 1996
> An overview of the instruments of the orchestra through a combination of book (illustrated with color photographs), narration, and Benjamin Britten's *Composition* on CD.

Also see Music Maestro, *The Orchestra,* and *Zin! Zin! Zin! A Violin,* page 105.

HEALTH AND PHYSICAL EDUCATION

1. Be familiar with the elements of good nutrition and the structure of the *food pyramid.*

The Edible Pyramid
Loreen Leedy; Holiday House, 1996
> A humorous introduction to nutrition from the headwaiter at the Edible Pyramid Restaurant.

Good Enough to Eat: A Kid's Guide to Food and Nutrition
Lizzy Rockwell; HarperCollins, 1998
> A bright and friendly explanation of the principal food groups, the elements of nutrition, serving size and number, and digestion. (Plus healthful recipes.)

2. As a general rule, second-graders should be able to skip (forward and backward), to stop, start, and abruptly change direction while running, to throw and catch a ball accurately from a distance of ten feet, to kick a moving ball, and to dribble and bounce a ball against a wall.

3. Participate in athletic indoor and outdoor activities. There are many ways in which homeschoolers can enjoy an active athletic program. Join a community children's soccer team, take swimming, gymnastics, or dancing lessons, skate, hike, or learn to ride a two-wheeled bicycle.

See *Fit Kids!* and *Home School Family Fitness*, page 50, and *Physical Education Plans for Grades 1–2* and other resources, page 105.

GRADE THREE

> It should be noted that children at play are not merely play-
> ing about; their games should be seen as their most serious-
> minded activity.
>
> MONTAIGNE

LANGUAGE ARTS

READING

Once kids have mastered the technical hurdles of learning to read,
reading "instruction" becomes largely a matter of practice. Kids
should simply be encouraged to read, moving from picture books
into short chapter books and then on to increasingly complex
works of literature.

BEYOND FIVE IN A ROW

A literature-based study unit curriculum for kids aged 8–12.
Featured titles include *The Boxcar Children* by Gertrude Chandler
Warner, *Homer Price* by Robert McCloskey, and *Sarah Plain
and Tall* by Patricia MacLachlan. Lessons cover language arts,
fine arts, science, history, and geography. Five in a Row, Box 707,

Grandview, MO 64030-0707; (816) 331-5769; www.fiveinarow.
com.

CYBERGUIDES

Excellent multidisciplinary lesson plans for a wide range of books for kids of all ages. Sample featured titles for third-graders include *Little House in the Big Woods* by Laura Ingalls Wilder, *Charlotte's Web* by E. B. White, *The Great Kapok Tree* by Lynne Cherry, and *Ben and Me* by Robert Lawson. (Also see CyberGuides, page 246). Web site: www.dscoe.k12.ca.us/score/cyberguide.html.

JUNIOR GREAT BOOKS PROGRAM

A superb reading and discussion program for kids in grades 2–9. Reading selections are accompanied by thought-provoking questions guaranteed to promote in-depth discussions. Third-grade selections include Hans Christian Andersen's *The Ugly Duckling,* Crockett Johnson's *Ellen's Lion,* excerpts from Kenneth Grahame's *The Wind in the Willows,* and many multicultural folktales. Great Books Foundation, 35 E. Wacker Dr., Suite 2300, Chicago, IL 60601-2298; (800) 222-5870; www.greatbooks.org.

Also see the Great Books Read-Aloud Program, page 59.

LEARNING LANGUAGE ARTS THROUGH LITERATURE

The Yellow Book, for third-graders, teaches spelling, grammar, and handwriting skills through a selection of classic children's books, including Elizabeth Shub's *The White Stallion,* Ludwig Bemelmans's *Madeline,* and Alice Dagliesh's *The Courage of Sarah Noble.* Christian orientation. Common Sense Press; (352) 475-5757; cspress.com.

Also see Learning Links, page 60, Novel Units, page 60, and Book Lists, pages 400–402.

1. Know common third grade–level sight words. The Dolch Word List (see page 23) lists about fifty common sight words for kids at this grade level, among them *about, laugh, only, together, eight, light, myself,* and *today.*

2. Decode phonetically regular multisyllabic words. That is, using their knowlege of phonics, kids should be able to decipher such long, but logical, words as *abracadabra.*

3. Identify antonyms, synonyms, homophones (homonyms), and homographs. Homophones are words that sound the same but are spelled differently and have different meanings, such as *there, their,* and *they're.* Homographs are words that are spelled alike but have different pronunciations and meanings, as in *lead* (the metal) and *lead* (the opposite of follow).

Eight Ate: A Book of Homonym Riddles
Martin Terban; Houghton Mifflin, 1982

The Dove Dove: Funny Homograph Riddles
Martin Terban; Clarion, 1988
    Illustrated word play for kids aged 8–11.

LEARNING WRAP-UPS: SYNONYMS, ANTONYMS, HOMONYMS
An unusual hands-on matching quiz. Each set (Synonyms, Antonyms, or Homonyms) contains ten "boards" and a packet of precut string; kids wind the string around the boards, connecting word matches. A total of 240 words per set. Learning Wrap-Ups, 1660 W. Gordon Ave. #4, Layton, UT 84041; (800) 992-4966; www.learningwrapups.com.

QUIA! A FEAST OF HOMONYMS
The site includes an immense collection of on-line games, categorized by academic subject. Under English, see "A Feast of Homonyms" for four on-line games. Web site: www.quia.com.

4. Use *index, glossary,* and *table of contents* to locate information in books.

5. Read grade-appropriate fiction and nonfiction material fluently, both silently and aloud. Sample recommended books for third-graders include *Bunnicula* by James Howe; *Dominic* by William Steig; *Little House in the Big Woods* by Laura Ingalls Wilder; *Mr. Popper's Penguins* by Richard and Florence Atwater; and *Ramona Quimby, Age 8* by Beverly Cleary.
See Book Lists, pages 400–402.

6. Show comprehension by answering questions about a finished text. This is often accomplished naturally in the course of ordinary conversation. Discuss books around the dinner table, in the car, while standing in line at the grocery store. "Why on earth did they think that Bunnicula was a vampire?" "In the Little House books, did Laura have any brothers?" "Were Pooh and Piglet really following a Heffalump?" And the kids will tell you.

Quizzes for 220 Great Children's Books
Polly Jeanne Wickstrom; Teacher Ideas Press, 1996
> Kids earn points for reading books and passing true/false and multiple-choice quizzes on the material they have read. Each listed book is rated on the basis of length and reading difficulty. For kids in grades 3–8.

BOOK ADVENTURE
> A free on-line reading incentive program for kids of all ages. Read the book, take a short multiple-choice quiz, and earn points for prizes. Includes reading recommendations by age and progress reports. Web site: www.bookadventure.com.

NAME THAT BOOK
> A quiz that tests kids' knowledge of juvenile literature, plus reading recommendations. Web site: members.home.net/ddays/book.html.

Also see Bookworm, page 113.

7. Experience a wide range of literature selections, including fiction and nonfiction books, multicultural folktales, myths and legends, and poetry. Be able to describe and define *simile, metaphor, alliteration,* and *onomatopoeia.*

Poems Go Clang! A Collection of Noisy Verse
Candlewick Books, 1997
> Noisy and onomatopoeic poems from a range of poets, including Dr. Seuss, Rudyard Kipling, William Jay Smith, and Robert Louis Stevenson.

Also see *A Surfeit of Similes,* page 110.

8. Differentiate between *fiction* and *nonfiction, biography* and *autobiography.*

9. Follow multistep written instructions. Examples: assembling a model or following the directions for playing a game.

Writing

Usually it is in third grade that kids make the transition from manuscript handwriting to cursive, a process from which numerous handwriting programs are commercially available. (See Handwriting Without Tears, page 26, and Zaner-Bloser, page 26.) Or you can invent your own, which is what we did: All you need is a paper tablet with ruled lines and a reasonable recollection of what your third-grade teacher's handwriting looked like.

In recognition of their developing motor skills, third-graders are generally given writing paper with narrower lines: a three-quarters-inch ruling, with marked broken midline (for guidance purposes).

1. Switch to cursive in all written work, with practice to perfect letter shape, size, slant, and spacing.

2. Write frequently, exploring a range of genres, including stories, personal narratives, poems, essays, and reports. Suggestions for young writers include journal keeping, maintaining a book diary, writing a family newsletter, and corresponding with a pen pal. Kids should be familiar with the process of proofreading, editing, and revising a written work.

Doing the Days: A Year's Worth of Creative Journaling, Drawing, Listening, Reading, Thinking, Arts & Crafts for Children Ages 8–12
Lorraine M. Dahlstrom; Free Spirit Publishing, 1994
> Writing projects and other fun activities for every day of the year, all related to holidays, famous birthdays, and unusual anniversaries.

If You're Trying to Teach Kids How to Write, You've Gotta Have This Book!
Marjorie Frank; Incentive Publications, 1995
> A terrific collection of innovative writing activities for kids aged 8 and up. Among the suggestions: Write instructions for "How to Pet a Lion"; put together a history book illustrated with Polaroid photos; make a word mobile; experiment with concrete poems.

INTERACTIVE WRITING: FIRST STEPS
A daily-use essay-writing program for kids in grades 3–5. Interact; (800) 359-0961; www.interact-simulations.com.

Also see *Write From the Edge* and Kids' Pen Pals, page 111.

3. Organize writing in coherent paragraphs. Kids should be able to research a topic using a number of different sources and present their findings in the form of an organized report, divided into paragraphs. Each paragraph should begin with an indented *topic sentence*, followed by supporting facts or additional details.

4. Know and use the correct format for a friendly letter— including heading, salutation, body, and closing—and the correct way to address an envelope.
For more on friendly letter format, see *Messages in the Mailbox,* page 111.

5. Distinguish between complete and incomplete sentences. Kids should be able to identify the subject and predicate of a sentence and identify the four major sentence types: *declarative, interrogative, imperative,* and *exclamatory.*

6. Use capital letters correctly.

7. Use periods, question marks, exclamation points, and quotation marks correctly. Use commas between the day and year when writing a date, between city and state when writing an address, and in series within sentences. An example of commas used to separate a series: The goat ate a tin can, two newspapers, a bicycle tire, and fifteen tomatoes.

8. Use apostrophes in contractions and in singular and plural possessive nouns.

9. Identify common prefixes and suffixes. Third-graders should be able to deal with such prefixes as *re, un,* and *dis*; and such suffixes as *less, ly, er,* and *or.*

10. Know common abbreviations. Kids should know, for example, the spellings and proper abbreviations of the months of the year, days of the week, titles (Mr., Ms., Dr., Capt.), and locations (Rd., St., Ave.).

11. Identify nouns, proper nouns, pronouns, verbs, and adjectives; and past, present, and future tenses of verbs.
For grammar concepts listed in numbers 5–11:

G.U.M. PROGRAM

G.U.M. stands for Grammar, Usage, and Mechanics. This is a grammar program for kids in grades 3–8. Each workbook is a collection of fifty short lessons. Zaner-Bloser; (800) 421-3018; www.zaner-bloser.com.

POP-UP GRAMMAR

Quizzes on parts of speech, verb tenses, and sentence fragments, and a "Find the Subject" quiz in which kids identify the subject word or words in simple sentences. Web site: www.brownlee.org/durk/grammar.

QUIA!

Games for all ages in all academic subjects. Includes games and quizzes on contractions, parts of speech, prefixes, word roots, homophones, and more. Web site: www.quia.com.

Also see The Grammar Gorilla, page 112.

12. Use conventional spelling for the bulk of written work. Third-graders are generally expected to have reached the transitional or correct stages of spelling (see page 63). They should be familiar with the rules of consonant doubling, know how to spell the plurals of words ending in *y* ("change the *y* to an *i* and add *es*"), and know the spellings of common homophones.

For grade-appropriate spelling programs, see page 64; also see resources, page 113.

Listening and Speaking Skills

1. Make short oral reports. Encourage kids to take turns giving "family reports" on a particular topic of interest, descriptions of a good book they've recently read, or accounts of a field trip, extracurricular class, or social event.

2. Tell stories to a group; present short dramatizations.

LIFESTORIES

A superb board game for families, suitable for players of all ages. As players move their pieces around the board, they draw cards that call for personal stories: "Tell a story about a pet or an animal." "Tell about a time when you slept outdoors." From game stores.

Out of the Bag: The Paperbag Players Book of Plays
Judith Martin; Disney Press, 1997
> A collection of short plays for kids aged 8–12, with easy-to-make props and costumes, many of them involving brown paper bags.

STORYTELLING, DRAMA, CREATIVE DRAMATICS, PUPPETRY, AND READER'S THEATER FOR CHILDREN AND YOUNG ADULTS

A very large list of resources for all forms of dramatic arts, including downloadable scripts of "The Three Billy Goats Gruff" and "The Little Red Hen." Web site: falcon.jmu.edu/~ramseyil/drama.htm.

Also see Reader's Theatre, page 66.

3. Memorize and recite short poems.

STUDY SKILLS

Often in third grade kids take their first standardized tests. In some states, standardized tests are required of all homeschooled students. Test preparation resources for kids in this age group include:

Dr. Gary Gruber's Essential Guide to Test-Taking for Kids: Grades 3, 4, and 5
Gary Gruber; William Morrow, 1986
> Test-taking strategies and practice exercises.

A Parent's Guide to Standardized Tests: How to Improve Your Child's Chances for Success
Peter Cookson, Joshua Halberstam, and Kristina Berger; Learning Express, 1998
> General information for parents on test components, test-taking skills and preparation, and interpretation of test scores.

Scoring High Series
SRA
> Practice tests and test-taking hints for students in grades 1–8. Books are available for several different tests, including the

California Achievement Test, the Iowa Test of Basic Skills, and the Stanford Achievement Test. From bookstores or the Sycamore Tree; (800) 779-6750; www.sycamoretree.com.

Spectrum Test Prep Series
McGraw-Hill
Test-preparation workbooks for kids in grades 3–8, with test-taking tips, practice exercises, and answer keys. From bookstores or McGraw-Hill; (800) 352-3566; www.mhkids.com.

1. **Be able to use the dictionary, encyclopedia, and thesaurus.**

2. **Be able to use the telephone directory.**

3. **Alphabetize material to the third or fourth letter.** Given a list of words on index cards, for example, kids at this level should be able to alphabetize *greeting, grumble,* and *grape* or *peanut, peacock,* and *pear.*

4. **Be familiar with the use of the library.** Best resource: Visit it frequently. Kids should know how to use the card catalog and be familiar with library organization and resources (fiction and non-fiction books, reference works, periodicals).

Books and Libraries
Jack Knowlton; HarperCollins, 1991
A short illustrated history of books and libraries from cave paintings to the Library of Congress. The book includes an explanation (with colorful diagram) of the Dewey Decimal System for cataloging books.

MATHEMATICS

Landmark events for kids at this grade level are the acquisition of the times tables and the introduction of the concept of division. Many of the listed topics are expansions of skills introduced in earlier grades; see relevant sections in grade 2.

A Collection of Math Lessons from Grades 3–6
Marilyn Burns; Marilyn Burns Education Association, 1986

Creative hands-on investigations for multiplication, fractions, statistics, pattern formation, and more for kids aged 8–12.

Everyday Mathematics Series

A highly recommended activity-based math series for grades K–6. The third-grade program includes teacher's guide, student books and journals, and a set of manipulatives. Games include "Factor Bingo" and "Angle Race;" sample projects include "Dodecahedron Calendar" and "How Far Can We Travel in a Million Steps?" Everyday Learning Corporation, 2 Prudential Plaza, Ste. 2200, Chicago, IL 60601; (800) 382-7670; www.everydaylearning.com.

Math 3
Nancy Larson; Saxon Publishers, 1994

The home-study kit includes a detailed teacher's manual (140 very thorough lessons) and student workbooks; a set of hands-on manipulatives must be purchased separately. Saxon Publishers, Inc., 2450 John Saxon Blvd., Norman, OK 73071; (800) 284-7019; www.saxonpub.com.

Miquon Math Series

Thought-provoking workbooks covering all the basics of third-grade math in a manner that promotes problem-solving skills and creative thinking. The Yellow and Purple books are recommended for third-graders. Key Curriculum Press, Box 2304, Berkeley, CA 94702-0304; (800) 995-MATH; www.keypress.com.

SRA Math: Explorations and Applications Series
Stephen S. Willoughby; SRA/McGraw-Hill

An excellent math program for kids in grades K–6. Third-grade book and materials promote creative thinking and problem-solving skills through games and hands-on activities, calculator and computer use, math journaling, cooperative learning projects, "thinking stories," and cross-curricular connections. SRA Math; (888) SRA-4543; www.sra4kids.com.

Also see *Family Math for Young Children,* page 30, *A Collection of Math Lessons from Grades 1 through 3,* page 69, and *Mathematics Their Way,* page 30.

Number Theory

1. Know numbers through the hundred thousands; be able to write these in both numerals and words.

Can You Count to a Googol?
Robert E. Wells; Albert Whitman & Co., 2000
A great visual introduction to huge numbers, as in 100,000 scoops of ice cream and 1,000,000 dollars. Also included is a short history of the enormous googol, named by a nine-year-old boy.

Also see *How Much Is a Million?,* page 116, *The Magic of a Million Activity Book,* page 192, and *On Beyond a Million,* page 193.

2. Order and compare numbers to 999,999 using greater than (>), lesser than (<), and equals (=) signs.

3. Be able to count by 2s, 3s, 5s, and 10s; and by 10's starting with any given number.

4. Understand place value through the hundred thousands.

5. Round numbers to the nearest 10 and 100.

6. Be able to write numbers in "expanded" form through the thousands. For example, $7863 = 7000 + 800 + 60 + 3$

7. Review the concept of odd and even numbers.
See *Among the Odds and Evens,* page 117.

8. Identify ordinal numbers through one hundredth.
For more on ordinal numbers, see pages 32 and 71.

9. Know the meaning of *square number.* Kids should use concrete models to establish the concept of "square" number. Using Cuisenaire rods or equivalent manipulatives, for example, kids can build the perfect squares, from 2×2 to 10×10, demonstrating that two 2-bars (a total of four) indeed forms a perfect square.

Know the perfect squares and square roots through 100; recognize the square root sign.

10. Know Roman numerals from I to XX (1 to 20).

Roman Numerals
David A. Adler; HarperCollins, 1987
  A simple picture-book introduction to Roman numerals and how we still use them today.

Roman Numerals I to MM
Arthur Geisert; Houghton Mifflin, 1996
  A wonderful picture book of Roman numerals illustrated with many, many (more than XX) pigs.

QUIA!

On-line games and quizzes for all ages in all academic subjects, including an elementary-level Roman numerals game. These test kids on their knowledge of the numerals I to XII using matching exercises, flash cards, and a concentration-type game. Web site: www.quia.com.

11. Understand the concept of *negative numbers.*

Kids should experiment with negative numbers in hands-on fashion, using a number line that lists number below zero. They should also be introduced to the use of negative numbers in daily life, as in below-zero temperatures.

50 Below Zero
Robert N. Munsch; Annick Press, 1989
  A picture book about Jason's sleepwalking father on a very cold night.

LINE JUMPER

The "Hard" and "Superbrain" levels of this on-line number line game use negative numbers. Web site: www.funbrain.com/linejump/.

12. Identify and compare fractions from $\frac{1}{2}$ to $\frac{1}{10}$.

Kids should know the meaning of *numerator* and *denominator.* They should be able to compare fractions with like denominators using greater than (>), lesser than (<), and equals (=) signs, and should be able to identify equivalent fractions.

See *Action Fractions!, Fraction Fun,* and Fraction Circles, page 118 and Mathwork, page 70.

13. Recognize and write mixed numbers. Mixed numbers are numbers that combine a whole number and a fraction, as in $3\frac{1}{2}$.

14. Read and write decimal numbers through the hundredths place. Kids should model decimals using base-10 blocks and grid paper. They should also know the decimal equivalents of ¼, ½, and ¾.

Hot Math Topics: Fractions and Decimals
Carole Greene; Prentice Hall, 1999
  Real-world math problems explain fractions and decimals for kids in grades 1–5.

Making Fractions
Andrew King; Copper Beech Books, 1998
  Projects, games, and hands-on activities demonstrating the many different aspects of fractions, including decimals, percents, and ratios.

15. Collect, organize, and analyze data using bar and line graphs. Discuss the results. What does this graph tell us? Does it make sense?

Measuring: From Paces to Feet
Rebecca B. Corwin and Susan Jo Russell; Dale Seymour Publications
  One of the Used Numbers: Real Data in the Classroom series, targeted at kids in grades 3–4. Kids use a variety of measurement techniques to collect data, then organize, display, and interpret the results using tables and graphs.

Also see Exploring Data, page 33.

16. Locate points on a coordinate grid. The idea of plotting points on a two-dimensional grid originated with French mathematician René Descartes, which is why this form of mathematical representation is called a *Cartesian graph*. In this first introduction to Cartesian graphing, kids should learn the names and positions of x and y *axes* and how to locate a point on a grid based on known values of x and y.

The Fly on the Ceiling: A Math Myth
Julie Glass; Random House, 1998
  The story of René Descartes and Cartesian coordinates.

Great Graphing
Martin Lee and Marcia Miller; Scholastic, 1993

Exercises in using tallies and tables, pictographs, bar graphs, and coordinate grids for kids in grades 1–4.

BATTLESHIP

An excellent (and just plain fun) resource to reinforce the concepts of Cartesian graphing is a game of "Battleship." This can be played with pencils on graph paper. On-line versions include:

ARMADA

Web site: scv.bv.edu/~aarondf/java/battleship.html

WEB BATTLESHIP

Web site: genesis.ne.mediaone.net/battle/

OPERATIONS

1. Review basic addition and subtraction facts.

2. Recognize addition and subtraction as inverse operations. Kids should know that addition can be used to check the answers to subtraction problems and vice versa.

3. Be able to add and subtract, with and without regrouping, with numbers up to five digits.

4. Know basic multiplication facts through 10 × 10.

There are many on-line sources of games to reinforce basic arithmetic facts and skills. See Quia! (www.quia.com), Funbrain (www.funbrain.com), A+ Math (www.aplusmath.com), and Cool Math (www.coolmath.com).

Also see Math-It, page 115, Quick Pix Math, page 119, and Math Smart, page 121.

5. Be able to multiply two- and three-digit numbers by single whole numbers.

6. Estimate answers to addition, subtraction, and multiplication problems.

7. Recognize multiplication and division as inverse operations; know the definitions of *dividend, divisor,* **and** *quotient.*

Math By All Means: Multiplication
Marilyn Burns; Marilyn Burns Educational Association, 1993

Math By All Means: Division
Susan Ohanian and Marilyn Burns; Marilyn Burns Association, 1997
Targeted at kids in grade 3, these are investigation-based mathematics programs in which kids learn the basics of multiplication and division through hands-on explorations and real-world challenges.

8. Be able to divide two- and three-digit numbers by single whole numbers. Kids should know that division problems can be checked by multiplying, and should be able to solve division problems involving *remainders.*

9. Understand the use of parentheses in mathematical sentences to indicate the order of operations. That is, whatever is in parentheses is done first.

In the number sentence $(3 \times 2) + (4 \times 6)$, for example, the multiplication steps are performed first, then the addition step.

10. Solve two-step word problems using all four basic arithmetic operations. See Math Stories at www.mathstories.com for a large selection of creative word problems for kids in grades 1–8.

11. Recognize and continue repeating patterns with numbers, symbols, or manipulatives.

12. Apply mathematical knowledge to other areas of the academic curriculum and to everyday situations.

Money and Measurement

1. Be able to write amounts of money using dollar or cent signs and decimal points.

2. Perform basic arithmetical operations with money. Kids should be able to add and subtract money and multiply and divide amounts of money by single-digit whole numbers.
See Presto Change-O, page 123.

3. Be able to select appropriate measuring instruments for determining length, surface area, volume (liquid and dry), and weight using standard and nonstandard units. Kids at this level should know English and metric measures for length, surface area, volume/capacity, and weight/mass. Known units of length should include millimeter, centimeter, meter, and kilometer; and inch, foot, yard, and mile. Units of surface area include the square equivalents of units of length. Units of volume/capacity should include milliliter and liter; and ounce, cup, pint, quart, and gallon. Units of weight/mass should include gram and kilogram; and ounce and pound.

Kids should know the accepted abbreviations for each unit and be able to identify approximate equivalencies between and within English and metric systems. That is, they should know that three feet equals one yard (within the system) and that one yard equals approximately one meter (between systems).

4. Be able to measure temperature in both degrees Fahrenheit and Centigrade (Celsius). Kids should know the freezing and boiling points of water in both systems.

5. Be able to tell time to the nearest minute. Kids should know the difference between A.M. and P.M.; be able to use a calendar to determine month, day, and date; and know the meaning of the terms *decade* and *century*.

GEOMETRY

1. Recognize and identify basic and more complex two-dimensional figures. Kids should be familiar with the triangle, square, rectangle, and circle, as well as such multisided *polygons* as the pentagon, hexagon, and octagon.

Shape Up! Fun with Triangles and Other Polygons
David A. Adler; Holiday House, 1998
> A brightly illustrated introduction to geometry. Kids learn how to tell an isosceles triangle from a right triangle, a pentagon from an octagon, a square from a rhombus, and more.

Also see Shapes in Math, Science, and Nature Series, page 196.

2. Recognize and identify common three-dimensional figures (geometric solids). Kids should be familiar with the sphere, cube, rectangular solid, pyramid, cone, and cylinder.

See *Easy-to-Make 3-D Shapes in Full Color* and *Three-Dimensional Shapes*, page 125.

3. Recognize and identify horizontal, vertical, parallel, and perpendicular lines. Kids should also know the definitions of *point*, *line segment*, and *ray*.

4. Be able to define *vertex* and *angle*. Kids at this level should know how angles are identified by letter names and be able to describe and recognize *right angles*.

5. Compare and contrast *similar* and *congruent* figures. Congruent figures have the same size and shape; similar figures have the same shape but are different in size. Kids should be able to identify these regardless of orientation or position. They should also be able to define what kind of positional change a geometric figure has undergone: a *slide* (simply moves one way or another, without changing orientation), a *rotation*, or a *flip*.

6. Calculate perimeter and area.

See *Spaghetti and Meatballs for All*, page 126.

7. Define and measure *circumference* and *diameter*. Initial investigations of circumference should involve hands-on measurements of circles of various sizes (use pieces of string or cloth measuring tapes).

Sir Cumference and the First Round Table
Cindy Neuschwander; Charlesbridge Publishing, 1997
> The mathematical tale of King Arthur's round table. Sir Cumference, his wife, Lady Di (who comes from Ameter), and their son, Radius, struggle with the design of the original rectangular table, sequentially converting it into a square, diamond, octagon, oval, and finally a perfect circle.

HISTORY AND GEOGRAPHY

The presentation of history varies near-astronomically from state to state and from packaged curriculum to packaged curriculum. In this guideline, kids will continue to expand upon past history lessons, covering in greater depth American history topics introduced in first and second grade and continuing ongoing world history narratives. In all cases, historical topics should be accompanied by maps and timelines, a range of reading material, including fiction and nonfiction books, age-appropriate biographies of famous persons, folktales, myths and legends, and poems. Studies should also be supplemented with hands-on projects and activities, field trips (where possible), and elements from other subjects across the academic curriculum. American and world history topics should be closely linked to geography. When studying the Spanish exploration of the American Southwest, for example, kids should trace routes on the map and learn the locations of relevant sites, such as Texas, New Mexico, Arizona, California, the Grand Canyon, and the Rio Grande River.

AMERICAN HISTORY

History is full of stories—true stories, the best ever.

JOY HAKIM

A History of US Series

Joy Hakim; Oxford University Press
A ten-book series covering American history from the first inhabitants to modern times. Each book is about 150 pages long, filled with wonderful stories, well-researched information, maps, photographs, period reproductions, quotations, and timelines. Excellent. For kids aged 8–13.

Appleseeds

An illustrated themed magazine for kids aged 7–9. Each issue centers around a topic in the fields of American history, world history, geography, or science. Sample issue titles include "Growing Up in Colonial Williamsburg," "Children of Ancient Egypt," and "Mapping the World." Each issue includes theme-related short articles, games, projects, recipes, math challenges, vocabulary facts, and a supplementary reading list. Cobblestone Publishing, 30 Grove St., Peterborough, NH 03458-1454; (800) 821-0115; www.cobblestonepub.com.

Also see Bluestocking Press, page 84, and *Social Studies Through Children's Literature*, page 37.

1. Early migrations into North America and the establishment of the first civilizations. Topics to cover include the Stone Age–era migration across the Bering land bridge; the Inuits, including geographical location, culture, and lifestyle; the Anasazi and the pueblo civilizations of the American Southwest; and the Mound Builders.

The Anasazi
Leonard Everett Fisher; Atheneum, 1997
A simple history of the Anasazi civilization of the Southwest.

Before You Came This Way
Byrd Baylor; E. P. Dutton, 1969
A picture-book story of life in the Southwest before the arrival of the European explorers.

Also see A History of US, Volume I, *The First Americans*, page 163.

2. Survey American Indian life and culture. Kids should compare and contrast the cultures and lifestyles of a variety of tribes from different regions of the country, such as the Iroquois and Abenaki of the Northeast; the Cherokees of the Southeast; the Lakota Sioux of the Great Plains; the Hopi and Navajo of the Southwest; and the Chinooks of the Pacific Northwest. Studies should be supplemented with fiction and nonfiction books, native legends, representative arts and crafts projects, and hands-on activities. For example, kids might make sand paintings, pottery, or model totem poles, experiment with native recipes, or plant an Indian-style garden.

Earthmaker's Lodge: Native American Folklore, Activities, and Food
E. Barrie Kavasch; Cobblestone, 1994
Indian stories, legends, and poems, with related activities and projects, categorized by region, from the Arctic to Mexico.

HONOR

A simulation of an American Indian coming of age before the arrival of the Europeans. Kids read native legends and then participate in a simulated adventure, tracing their movements on a map, making decisions based on "Fate Cards," and keeping a journal in invented picture language. All materials included. Interact; (800) 359-0961; www.interact-simulations.com.

A TIME FOR NATIVE AMERICANS

A two-sided card game for kids aged 8 and up. One side of each card has a portrait and brief biography of a famous American Indian; the other side is a piece of a puzzle map of North America, showing tribal regions. Instructions are included for four different games. Aristoplay, 8122 Main St., Dexter, MI 48130; (800) 634-7738; www.aristoplay.com.

True Books: American Indians Series

Children's Press
The series includes thirty-two short chapter books on individual American Indian tribes, targeted at kids in grades 2–4. Each book has a simple text and many colorful illustrations, including photographs, historical engravings, and maps.

Also see *More Than Moccasins*, page 37, and Native American Legends Series, page 85.

3. European exploration of North America: the Vikings. Topics
to cover include the geography of Scandinavia, the culture and lifestyle of the Vikings, Erik the Red and the discovery and settlement of Greenland, and Leif Eriksson and the discovery of Vinland.

Myths and Legends of the Vikings Coloring Book

Viking Ships to Cut Out and Put Together
Coloring and paper-crafts activities with Viking themes. Bellerophon Books; (800) 253-9943; www.bellerophonbooks.com.

Viking Adventure
Clyde Robert Bulla; Thomas Y. Crowell, 1963
A chapter book for kids aged 7–10. Sigurd, who loves his father's tales about Leif Eriksson, goes along on a journey to "Wineland" in distant North America.

Vikings

Peter Crisp; World Book, 1999

> An illustrated overview of Viking life, religion, culture, and customs through the eyes of an eight-year-old girl, Thora, who lives on the Orkney Islands. The book includes suggestions for related projects and activities.

The Vikings

Neil Grant; Oxford University Press, 1998

> An elaborately illustrated introduction to the Vikings, covering everyday life, religion, ships and navigation, arts and poetry, and conquests and empire building.

4. Explorers who followed Columbus. Kids should study the exploits of the Spaniards in the American South and Southwest, and of the French, Dutch, and British in Canada and the Northeast. They should know the names and accomplishments of prominent explorers and be able to locate their discoveries on the map. They should also be aware of the impact of the explorers on the American Indians.

A Coloring Book of Great Explorers

> Columbus, Balboa, Cortés, John and Sebastian Cabot, and many more, with a brief informative text. Bellerophon Books; (800) 253-9943; www.bellerophonbooks.com.

The Discovery of the Americas

Betsy and Giulio Maestro; Mulberry Books, 1991

The Discovery of the Americas Activity Book

Betsy and Giulio Maestro; Lothrop, Lee, & Shepard, 1992

> The book is a chronological account of the "discoveries" of the Americas, from the crossing of the Asia-to-Alaska land bridge by Stone Age hunters to Magellan's trip around the world. Terrific illustrations and colorful maps. The accompanying activity book describes games, projects, and activities of all kinds based on the text. For example, kids write newspapers, make board games, or put on puppet shows based on famous explorers and their journeys.

Exploration and Conquest: The Americas After Columbus 1500–1620

Betsy and Giulio Maestro; Lotherop, Lee & Shepard, 1994

A beautifully illustrated account of the many explorers who followed Columbus, including Cortés, Pizarro, De Soto, Champlain, and Hudson.

5. European exploration of North America: the Spaniards and the settlement of the Southwest.
Topics to cover include Ponce de León's search for the Fountain of Youth and the exploration of Florida, Hernando de Soto, the founding of St. Augustine, Coronado and the Seven Cities of Gold, and the establishment of the Spanish missions of Texas and California.

California Missions to Cut Out: Books I and II
Easy-to-assemble paper models. Bellerophon Books; (800) 253-9943; www.bellerophonbooks.com.

6. European exploration of North America: Canada and the search for the Northwest Passage.
Topics to cover include John Cabot and the exploration of Newfoundland, Samuel Champlain and the settlement of New France, and the voyages of Henry Hudson.

7. A survey of the thirteen colonies.
Kids should know the names and geographic locations of the original thirteen colonies, the names and locations of important colonial cities (Boston, Philadelphia, New York, Charleston, Williamsburg), and the climatic differences among colonies that led to variations in lifestyles and agricultural practices. (Or why the South had planations.)

Colonial Kids: An Activity Guide to Life in the New World
Laurie Carlson; Chicago Review Press, 1997
Historical background information, a timeline, and many creative hands-on projects. For example, kids churn butter, make trenchers, piece a quilt, and write an almanac.

If You Lived in Colonial Times
Ann McGovern; Scholastic, 1992
A delightful question-and-answer book about life in colonial New England. "What did colonial boys and girls wear?" "What happened to people who broke the laws?"

The New Americans: Colonial Times 1620–1689
Betsy Maestro; Lothrop, Lee & Shepard, 1998

A detailed picture-book history of the colonies, covering the arrival of the Pilgrims, the settlement of New Amsterdam and New Sweden, and the French voyageurs, illustrated with paintings and maps.

8. The Southern colonies: Virginia, Maryland, the Carolinas, and Georgia. Topics to cover include Sir Walter Raleigh and the "Lost Colony" of Roanoke, the settlement of Jamestown, the rise of tobacco as a cash crop, the beginning of the slave trade, the growth of the southern plantations, Lord Baltimore and the Maryland colony, and James Oglethorpe and the Georgia colony.

9. The New England colonies: Massachusetts, New Hampshire, Connecticut, and Rhode Island. Topics to cover include the Pilgrims and the establishment of the Plymouth colony; the Mayflower Compact; the Puritans and the establishment of the Massachusetts Bay Colony; Roger Williams, Anne Hutchinson, religious tolerance issues, and the establishment of Rhode Island.

10. The Middle Atlantic colonies: New York, New Jersey, Delaware, and Pennsylvania. Topics to cover include the Dutch and New Netherland; the English conquest and the establishment of New York; and William Penn, the Quakers, and the Pennsylvania colony.

Also see A History of US, Volume 2, *Making Thirteen Colonies,* page 163.

World History

Third-graders, taking up approximately where second grade left off, cover the Renaissance through the mid-nineteenth century. This period will be studied again in greater detail in seventh grade. Supplement studies with maps and timelines, historical fiction books and age-appropriate biographies, audiocassettes and videos, hands-on projects and activities, and relevant field trips. For example, listen to selections of sixteenth-century music, build models of Columbus's ships, visit a museum to view Renaissance paintings. See Social Studies School Service, page 197, Mr. Donn's Ancient History Page, page 132, and The Children's Picture World History Series (page 131).

1. The Renaissance. Topics to cover include the meaning of the word *Renaissance* (the "rebirth" of art and learning), the rise of the

Italian city-states as centers of trade, prominent Renaissance figures, such as Leonardo da Vinci, Michelangelo, and the Medicis, Renaissance ideals and values, including the concept of the "Renaissance man," and everyday life in the Renaissance period.

Italian Renaissance
John Clare; Gulliver Books, 1995
> One of the Living History series, in which background information is accompanied by color photographs of historical reenactors in period costumes.

Leonardo da Vinci for Kids
Janis Herbert; Chicago Review Press, 1998
> The life and times of Leonardo, with timelines, historical and biographical information, gorgeous color reproductions of Leonardo's work, photographs of Leonardo-related locations, and creative hands-on activities. For example, kids made a shoebox lute, plant Renaissance herbs, and experiment with Leonardo's mirror-writing.

LEONARDO DA VINCI SCIENCE KIT
> Creative activities based on Leonardo's inventions. For example, kids build replicas of Leonardo's crane, helicopter, and pyramid-shaped parachute. Wild Goose Science Company; (888) 621-1040; www.wildgoosescience.com.

Michelangelo and His Times
Veronique Milande; Henry Holt, 1996
> A graphically creative overview of the Renaissance centering around the life and works of Michelangelo. The book presents substantive history through maps, timelines, cartoons, drawings and fictionalized interviews.

Rats, Bulls, and Flying Machines
Deborah Mazzotta Prum; Core Knowledge Foundation, 1999
> A history of the Renaissance and Reformation through a terrific reader-friendly text, colorful maps and illustrations, and clever fact boxes. Core Knowledge Foundation; (800) 238-3233; www.coreknowledge.org.

Also see Mr. Donn's Ancient History Page, page 132.

2. The Reformation. Topics to cover include Gutenberg and the invention of the printing press, Martin Luther and the beginning of Protestantism, and the conflicts between science and church, as exemplified by Copernicus and Galileo.

See *Rats, Bulls, and Flying Machines* (page 169).

GALILEO HISTORY OF SCIENCE KIT

Background historical information plus materials to replicate several of Galileo's best-known experiments. For example, kids build and use a pendulum and a simple telescope. Scientific Explorer, Inc.; (800) 900-1182; www.scientificexplorer.com.

Gutenberg
Leonard Everett Fisher; Macmillan, 1993

An excellent illustrated biography of the fifteenth-century German who revolutionized the world with the invention of movable type.

3. England to the Age of Exploration. Topics to cover include Henry VIII and the establishment of the Church of England; Elizabeth I and the Elizabethan Age; the rise of the British sea power; the defeat of the Spanish Armada; early exploration and colonization; and everyday life in the fifteenth and sixteenth centuries.

Good Queen Bess: The Story of Queen Elizabeth I of England
Diane Stanley; Four Winds, 1990

A beautifully illustrated short biography of Elizabeth I, beginning with Henry VIII and his break from the Catholic Church.

William Shakespeare and the Globe
Aliki; HarperCollins, 1999

Charmingly illustrated account of William Shakespeare's life and times.

The World of Captain John Smith
Genevieve Foster; Beautiful Feet Books, 1998

What was happening in different parts of the world when John Smith was a small boy, a young soldier, an adventurer in the New World? World history that reads like a storybook. Beautiful Feet Books; (800) 889-1978; www.bfbooks.com.

4. The Age of Exploration. Topics to cover include the importance of the spice trade and its impact on exploration; the voyages of the Portuguese (including Prince Henry the Navigator, Bartolomeu Dias and the Cape of Good Hope; Vasco da Gama and the route to India; and Cabral and the annexation of Brazil); and the voyages of the Spanish (including Columbus and the discovery of the "New World"; the Treaty of Tordesillas; Magellan and the circumnavigation of the globe; and Balboa and the Pacific Ocean); the voyages of England and France (including the search for the Northwest Passage, the colonization of North America and the West Indies, and the establishment of trading posts in India); the voyages of the Dutch (including the annexation of Portuguese trading posts and colonies, the colonization of South Africa, and the establishment of New Netherland).

Around the World in a Hundred Years: From Henry the Navigator to Magellan
Jean Fritz; Putnam, 1994

> Told as only Jean Fritz can tell it, the tale of the Age of Exploration, covering the exploits of ten major explorers, including Bartholomeu Dias, Christopher Columbus, Juan Ponce de León, and Vasco Núñez de Balboa. In-depth information, human interest, and a sense of humor.

The History News: Explorers
Michael Johnstone; Candlewick Press, 1997

> A history of exploration in humorously illustrated newspaper format, with cartoons, maps, charts, interviews, up-to-the-minute reports, want ads, and advertisements.

The World of Columbus and Sons
Genevieve Foster; Beautiful Feet Books, 1998

> What was happening all over the world as Columbus was growing up and setting out on his voyages of discovery? An enthralling storylike approach to world history, covering such prominent figures as Prince Henry the Navigator, Czar Ivan III, Leonardo da Vinci, Mohammed II, Martin Luther, and Copernicus. Beautiful Feet Books; (800) 889-1978; www.bf.books.com.

5. The Age of Revolution. Topics to cover include French kings and queens from Louis XIV to Louis XVI and Marie Antoinette, the American Revolution, the French Revolution, the Reign of Terror, Napoléon Bonaparte and the French Empire, and the restoration of the Bourbons.

George Washington's World
Genevieve Foster; Beautiful Feet Books, 1998
> What was happening all over the world in the 1700s while George Washington was growing up in Virginia, commanding the Revolutionary army, serving as first president of the United States? Beautiful Feet Books; (800) 889-1978; www.bf.books.com.

The King's Day
Aliki; HarperCollins, 1989
> A marvelously illustrated picture-book history of life at the court of Louis XIV.

6. The Industrial Revolution. Topics to cover include major advances in transportation and industry, including James Watt and the steam engine, Eli Whitney and the cotton gin, and the rise of factories and mills.

GEOGRAPHY

As in other grades, geography studies should be closely linked to history and other academic subjects. For example, kids should trace the routes of famous fifteenth- and sixteenth-century explorers and discover just where Balboa stood for his first view of the Pacific Ocean.

Discovering Geography of North America With Books Kids Love
Carol J. Fuhler; Fulcrum Publishing, 1998

Discovering World Geography With Books Kids Love
Nancy A. Chicola and Eleanor B. English; Fulcrum Publishing, 1999
> Lesson plans and activities based on favorite books for kids in grades 3–6.

Also see geography resources, page 204.

1. Review and reinforce basic geographical concepts covered in previous studies. Kids should continue to expand their geographical vocabulary. For example, they should be able to recognize and define *peninsula, strait, gulf, bay, isthmus,* and *plateau.*

They should use and read a variety of different map types, be able to use map scales to measure distances between two locations, and be able to find locations on an *alphanumeric* (grid-style) map.

2. Define and describe the major kinds of climate and relate these to geographical locations. Kids should know the features and locations of the *tropical* (torrid), *temperate,* and *polar* (arctic) zones, and how these different climatic conditions affect living things—human, plant, and animal.

IMAGINE LIVING HERE SERIES

Vicki Cobb; Walker & Co.
What life is like for animals, plants, and people in different climatic regions of the world. Titles include *This Place Is Cold, This Place Is Dry, This Place Is High, This Place Is Wild,* and *This Place Is Lonely.*

3. Survey the major rivers of the world. Kids should know the definitions of *source, mouth, delta, tributary,* and *drainage basin.* They should also be able to name, describe, and locate the major rivers of each continent on the world map.

Great Rivers Series
Michael Pollard; Benchmark Books
A series of forty-five-page books illustrated with color photographs and maps, each featuring one of the world's great rivers. Titles include *The Amazon, The Ganges, The Mississippi,* and *The Yangtze.*

Rookie Read-About Geography Series
Allan Fowler; Children's Press
Titles include *The Nile River* and *The Mississippi River,* both thirty-two-page illustrated picture books.

SCIENCE

Science should be an interactive hands-on discipline, with plenty of opportunity to experiment, investigate, and explore.

See *Science Through Children's Literature,* page 42, and *From Butterflies to Thunderbolts,* page 135.

PHYSICAL SCIENCE

1. Explore and understand the properties of light. Topics to cover include light sources, the speed of light and its mode of travel (in straight lines), transparent and opaque objects, the behaviors of mirrors and lenses, and the prism and the spectrum of visible light.

Kids should know the differences between convex, concave, and plane mirrors and lenses; should be able to put a numerical value to the speed of light (186,000 miles/second); should understand the principles of *reflection* and *refraction*; and should know that white sunlight is composed of many different colors of light, which can be separated by a prism. They should know the colors of the spectrum in order and be familiar with the acronym ROY G BIV.

Kids might try making their own periscopes and kaleidoscopes.

The Optics Book
Shar Levine and Leslie Johnstone; Sterling Publications, 1998
    An excellent introduction to light, vision, and assorted optical instruments through clever experiments, helpful diagrams, and perfectly clear explanations.

Mirrors: Find Out About the Properties of Light
Bernie Zubrowski; Beech Tree Books, 1992
    The science of light with mirrors and flashlights. A Boston Children's Museum Activity Book.

2. Explore and understand the properties of heat. Kids should know that heat is a form of energy, and should be able to describe the various sources of heat, including geothermal, nuclear, and solar sources. Through direct observation and experiment, they should learn how heat moves by *conduction, convection,* and *radiation.* They should also investigate the relationships between light, color, and heat absorption.

Amazing Sun Fun Activities
Michael J. Daley; McGraw-Hill, 1997
    A hands-on introduction to solar energy with many creative activities, including instructions for making a solar water heater out of a soda can.

Heat FUNdamentals: Funtastic Science Experiments for Kids
Robert W. Wood; McGraw-Hill, 1996

Simple activities, background information, and catchy little facts that demonstrate such heat-related concepts as conduction, convection, expansion and contraction, evaporation, and energy conversion.

LIFE SCIENCE

1. Understand the concept of *balance of nature*, the elements of the food chain, and the definition of *ecosystem*. Kids should understand that living things exist in complex interdependent arrangements called *ecosystems*. They should know about the interactions of *producers, consumers,* and *decomposers* and be able to discuss the impact of human lifestyles on natural environments. They should also understand the dangers of air and water pollution.

2. Continue studies of animal classification introduced in grade 1. Kids should know the differences between cold- and warm-blooded animals; and between *vertebrates* and *invertebrates*; and be able to name examples of each. They should also know the distinguishing characteristics of the major classes of vertebrates: fish, amphibians, reptiles, birds, and mammals.

ALPHA ANIMALS

A board game of animl names and classification. Kids hop around an alphabet-patterned board, naming animals according to letter of the alphabet. Animal class (fish, amphibian, reptile, bird, insect, or mammal) is determined by a roll of dice. From game stores or www.areyougame.com.; (800) 471-0641.

Classroom Critters and the Scientific Method
Sally Stenhouse Kneidel; Fulcrum, 1999

Over thirty experiments using small animals such as mice, hamsters, and goldfish. Includes instructions and worksheets.

ANIMAL CLASSIFICATIONS

An explanation of animal classification with many links to Mammals, Amphibians, Reptiles, Birds, and Fish. For grades K–12; Web site: falcon.jmu.edu/~ramseyil/vertebrates.htm.

3. Continue studies of human anatomy and physiology. Kids at this level should build upon previous knowledge of the human body, studying the muscular, skeletal, and nervous systems. They should know the difference between *voluntary* and *involuntary* muscles; the basic components of the skeletal system; the means by which bones and muscles interact and interconnect; the basic components of the nervous system; and the means by which the nervous system communicates with other body systems.

Blood and Gore Like You've Never Seen
Vicki Cobb; Scholastic, 1998

No, not a slasher novel. This is a wonderful computer-enhanced collection of electron micrographs, with a brief kid-friendly text delivering interesting information about bone, muscle, nerves, skin, and blood.

The Body Book: Easy-to-Make Hands-On Models That Teach
Donald M. Silver and Patricia J. Wynne; Scholastic, 1995

Instructions and patterns for making paper models of the systems and individual organs of the human body, plus lesson plans.

The Brain
Seymour Simon; Mulberry Books, 1996

An excellent explanation of the human brain and nervous system, with colorful computer-enhanced electron micrographs, diagrams, and lots of information.

Gray's Anatomy Coloring Book
Freddy Stark; Running Press, 1991

Simplified to-be-colored diagrams of all body systems, an interesting kid-friendly text, plus intriguing fact boxes.

How the Body Works
Steve Parker; Reader's Digest, 1994

Over 100 creative activities on the structure and function of body systems, all illustrated with superb color photographs and diagrams, plus background information, capsule biographies of famous scientists, and interesting facts.

Earth/Space Science

Third-graders commonly enlarge upon and reinforce the studies of geology and astronomy introduced in grade 1 (see pages 98–100).

1. Define *fossil* and know how fossils are formed.

FOSSIL FORMATIONS
A Delta Nutshell kit (see page 43) that includes samples of real fossils, instructions and materials for making model fossils of your own, and a detailed activity guide with background information and supplementary project suggestions. For one to three kids aged 7–11. From Delta Education, Box 3000, Nashua, NH 03061-3000; (800) 442-5444; www.delta-ed.com.

Also see *Is There a Dinosaur in Your Backyard?* (below).

2. Know the difference between a *rock* and a *mineral*; and the characteristics of the three major groups of rocks: *sedimentary*, *igneous*, and *metamorphic*.

Is There a Dinosaur in Your Backyard?
Spencer Christian; John Wiley & Sons, 1998
A clever and information-packed introduction to fossils, rocks, and minerals in 128 pages, all with cartoons, diagrams, experiments and activities, and many unusual attention-catching facts. Try this: the emperor Nero wore sunglasses with emerald lenses.

A Look at Minerals: From Galena to Gold
Jo S. Kittinger; Franklin Watts, 1999

A Look at Rocks: From Coal to Kimberlite
Jo S. Kittinger; Franklin Watts, 1998
Basic overviews of minerals and rocks, with clear explanations and nice color photographs.

The Magic School Bus Inside the Earth
Joanna Cole; Scholastic, 1987
Ms. Frizzle's class sets out on a rock-collecting expedition and ends up burrowing toward the center of the earth. Lots of geological information, humorous illustrations, and a volcanic explosion.

4. Know the names and order of the planets in our solar system and be able to define *orbit*, *rotation*, and *revolution*. Supplementary

activities might include making solar system models, inventing a solar system game, and reading biographies of such famous astronomers as Galileo (discoverer of the rings of Saturn), William Herschel (discoverer of Uranus), and Clyde Tombaugh (discoverer of Pluto).

The Magic School Bus Lost in the Solar System
Joanna Cole; Scholastic, 1990

Ms. Frizzle's class, quietly en route to the planetarium, ends up on a journey into outer space, where they visit earth's moon and each of the planets, learning as they go.

THURSDAY'S CLASSROOM

An astronomy site for kids hosted by a NASA-affiliated science professor. Lesson plans and activity sheets, links, and astronomy-related stories in the news, available at grade 2–4 or grade 5–8 reading levels. Web site: www.thursdaysclassroom.com.

Also see Seymour Simon's Astronomy Series, page 99, and Naturescope Astronomy Adventures, page 99.

5. Understand the big bang theory and be aware of the size and composition of the universe.

The Beginning of the Earth
Franklyn M. Branley; HarperCollins, 1988

A simple explanation of big bang cosmology for readers aged 5–9.

Galaxies
Seymour Simon; Mulberry Books, 1991

All about the major types of galaxies, with spectacular photographs.

The Universe
Seymour Simon; William Morrow, 1998

An overview of the unimaginably enormous universe, from the solar system through galaxies, nebulae, and quasars, all impressively illustrated with photographs.

6. Be able to define *gravity* and describe its effects.

Gravity Is a Mystery
Franklyn M. Branley; HarperTrophy, 1986

A simple picture-book explanation of the difficult concept of gravity for kids aged 5–9. The book includes an account of what would happen if you fell into a hole reaching all the way through the center of the earth and a chart showing the weight of a sixty-pound kid on every planet in the solar system.

SIR ISAAC NEWTON HISTORY OF SCIENCE KIT
A collection of experiments demonstrating Newton's discoveries in the field of motion and gravity. For example, kids build a color-viewing box and launch a rocket. The kit includes an informational booklet with activity suggestions and a brief account of Newton's life and work. Scientific Explorer, Inc., 2802 E. Madison, Suite 114, Seattle, WA 98112; (800) 900-1182; www.scientificexplorer.com.

7. Define and describe lunar and solar eclipses. Demonstrate with model and diagrams. Best, of course, is to observe one.

UPCOMING ECLIPSES OF THE SUN AND MOON
Dates, descriptions, and locations. Web site: aa.usno.navy.mil/AA/data/docs/UpcomingEclipses.html.

8. Be familiar with the common constellations. The very best way to do this is to stargaze—for which kids and parents need little more than a star map and assorted curious pairs of eyes. Pair these with fiction and nonfiction books about the stars, including mythological and multicultural tales about the origins of the constellations.

The Stars: A New Way to See Them
H. A. Rey; Houghton Mifflin, 1980
Simplified diagrams and descriptions of all the major constellations, plus viewing hints and seasonal star charts.

The Ultimate Guide to the Sky: How to Find the Constellations and Read the Night Sky Like a Pro
John Mosley; Lowell House, 1997
A stargazer's guide with constellation descriptions and monthly star charts, targeted at beginners.

9. Survey the history of space exploration. Kids might make an illustrated timeline to accompany these studies. (For more on timelines, see page 88.)

The History News: In Space
Michael Johnstone; Candlewick, 1999

A big, colorful, newspaper-style overview of the history of space exploration, from the ancient Greeks to modern times—including a review of Ptolemy's brand-new astronomy book, an interview with the Russian cosmonaut Yuri Gagarin, and the latest in space fashions.

History of Space Exploration Coloring Book
Bruce LaFontaine; Dover Publications

From the launching of Robert Goddard's first liquid-fuel rocket in a Massachusetts cow pasture to the moon landing and the space shuttle, all in black-line pictures with a brief descriptive text. Dover Publications, 31 E 2nd St., Mineola, NY 11501.

Moonwalk: The First Trip to the Moon
Judy Donnelly; Random House, 1989

A Step into Reading book for kids in grades 2–4.

FOREIGN LANGUAGE

Kids should read foreign-language texts appropriate to their skill level, write sentences and short passages using correct grammar and vocabulary, and practice their chosen language in skits, recitations, and conversations.

See resources, page 47.

ART

Kids should continue to experiment with a wide range of art media and techniques to create original artworks. They should also continue to develop art appreciation skills and to expand upon their knowledge of historical and multicultural art.

See *Art Through Children's Literature,* page 48, Getting to Know the World's Greatest Artists Series, page 102, and *How to Use Child-Size Masterpieces for Art Appreciation,* page 48.

1. **Review the color wheel, know primary, secondary, and intermediate colors (red-orange, yellow-orange, yellow-green, blue-green, blue-violet, and red-violet).** Define *value* as the lightness or darkness of a color.

2. **Recognize *foreground, middle ground,* and *background* in works of art.** Recognize how the elements of an artwork (such as color, shape, line, and texture) are organized to create a focus or center of interest.

3. **Identify *balance* and *symmetry* in works of art. Recognize patterns and differentiate between *figure* and *ground*.**

SYMMETRY AND PATTERN: ORIENTAL CARPETS

Information about pattern and symmetry and a colorful gallery of patterned Oriental carpets. Web site: forum.swarthmore.edu/ gcomtry/rug3.

4. **Connect art to other academic disciplines across the curriculum.** At this grade level, for example, kids might study the art of the American Indians, colonial folk art, and the art of the Renaissance.

Artists' Workshop Series

Penny King and Clare Roundhill; Crabtree Publishing
Titles in the series include *Animals, Landscapes, Portraits,* and *Stories.* Kids do projects based on famous works of art. In *Stories,* for example, kids make a tapestry based on the Bayeux Tapestry and design a Chinese Willow-pattern plate.

A Child's Book of Art

Lucy Micklethwait; Dorling Kindersley, 1993
Over 100 full-color reproductions of paintings from a wide range of times and places, grouped by theme.

The Usborne Story of Painting: Cave Painting to Modern Art

Anthea Peppin; Usborne, 1980
A thirty-page history, crammed with colorful little drawings and reader-friendly information.

5. Experiment with a variety of art media and techniques, including drawing, painting, sculpture, printmaking, pottery, and textile or fiber arts.

Also see *Drawing with Children*, page 103, *Move Over, Picasso!*, page 102, and *Discovering Great Artists*, page 141.

MUSIC

Kids should participate in a multifaceted music program that combines active participation, music appreciation, music theory, and music history. The program should include listening to a range of pieces by famous composers and to selections of multicultural music; experimenting with musical instruments; singing; and using varied print materials including fiction and nonfiction books, legends and folktales related to music, songbooks, and age-appropriate biographies of composers and musicians.

1. Reinforce and expand upon the musical concepts taught in earlier grades. Kids should know the names of the notes and spaces of the treble clef and should recognize and understand symbols for *bar line, double bar, measure,* and *repeat.*

Making Music

Learn music by doing on Mac/Win CD. Kids can compose their own pieces, experimenting with melody, pitch, rhythm, tempo, and instrumentation. Learn Technologies Interactive; (888) 292-5584; www.voyager.learntech.com.

2. Recognize and understand symbols for whole, half, quarter, and eighth notes and whole, half, and quarter rests. See *Music Theory for Beginners*, page 142.

3. Recognize and understand 4/4, 2/4, and 3/4 meter signatures and the symbols *p, pp, f,* and *ff*. A meter signature defines the tempo of a musical piece. In 2/4 time, for example, there are 2 beats per measure and a quarter (1/4) note gets one beat.

The *p* and *f* symbols indicate how softly or loudly a piece should be sung or played: *p* (*piano*) means softly; *pp* (*pianissimo*), very softly; *f* (*forte*), loudly; and *ff* (*fortissimo*), very loudly.

4. Review the families of instruments in the orchestra and the individual instruments that make up each family.

Alligators and Music
Donald Elliott; Harvard Common Press, 1984
> A humorous and informative explanation of the families of orchestral instruments for kids aged 8–12.

Also see *Music, Musical Instruments Coloring Book,* and *The Young Person's Guide to the Orchestra,* page 144.

5. Listen to a range of pieces by well-known composers and to a variety of multicultural selections. For a broader musical experience, pair listening sessions with biographies of composers, fiction and nonfiction books about a featured culture, and hands-on activities.

CLASSICAL KIDS SERIES
> A superb series of stories based on the lives of famous composers, paired with many selections from their best-known works. Available materials include audiocassettes or CDs, videos, books, and "Teacher's Notes" with detailed lesson plans and many suggestions for supplementary activities. Many titles, including *Beethoven Lives Upstairs, Mr. Bach Comes to Call, Mozart's Magic Fantasy, Vivaldi's Ring of Mystery,* and *Hallelujah Handel!* Sources include West Music, 1212 5th St., Coralille, IA 52241; (800) 397-9378; www.westmusic.com.

Also see Getting to Know the World's Greatest Composers Series, page 104.

HEALTH AND PHYSICAL EDUCATION

1. By the end of third grade, kids should usually be able to run, dodge, and change direction while running; throw and catch both small- and large-size balls with reasonable accuracy; hit a volleyball; jump rope; dribble, pass, and shoot basketballs; and kick balls, as in soccer.

2. Know which physical activities are associated with cardiovascular strength, muscular strength and endurance, and flexibility.

3. Participate in age-appropriate indoor and outdoor athletic activities. In a homeschool situation, this may encompass any number of activities: calisthenics; hiking; biking; active outdoor play; dancing, swimming, or gymnastics lessons; participation on a school, community, or neighborhood sports team.

Physical Education Unit Plans for Grades 3–4
Bette J. Logsdon, Luann M. Alleman, Sue Ann Straits, David E. Belka, and Dawn Clark; Human Kinetics, 1997
   Grade-appropriate ball and field games, gymnastics, and dance activities.

Also see *Fit Kids!*, page 50, *Home School Family Fitness*, page 50, Game Central Station, page 106, and Games Kids Play, page 106.

4. Understand the negative aspects of alcohol, tobacco, and other drugs.

5. Be familiar with basic first-aid practices. Kids should know what to do in the case of bleeding wounds, choking, or poisoning.

Kids to the Rescue! First Aid Techniques for Kids
Maribeth Boelts and Darwin Boelts; Parenting Press, 1992
   Basic first-aid procedures explained in a simple illustrated text.

GRADE FOUR

An adventurous child, thanks to the gods.

HORACE

LANGUAGE ARTS

READING

By fourth grade, kids in public school classes are expected to be competent readers, using their expertise for a wide variety of literary and informational purposes. The truth of the matter, of course, is that—due to developmental, motivational, and just plain whimsical differences—kids attain literary fluency at different ages. Some are startlingly early readers; some are late readers. Homeschool, mercifully, adapts and adjusts to individual paces and interests in reading—as it does to everything else. For reading suggestions for advanced or lagging readers, see curriculum suggestions for higher or lower grades, or Book Lists (pages 400–402).

CYBERGUIDES

Detailed multidisciplinary lesson plans for many children's books, categorized by grade level. Fourth-grade selections include Elizabeth George Speare's *The Sign of the Beaver,* E. B. White's *Trumpet of the Swan,* and Robert C. O'Brien's *Mrs. Frisby and the Rats of NIMH.* Plans include hands-on projects and activities and related Internet links. Web site: www.sdcoe.k12.ca.us/score/ cyberguide.html.

JUNIOR GREAT BOOKS PROGRAM

An excellent "interpretive reading" program for kids in grades 2–9, in which participants read a selection, then join in an in-depth discussion. Discussion questions are enlightening and thought-provoking. Selections for fourth-graders include Rudyard Kipling's "The Elephant's Child," A. A. Milne's "Prince Rabbit," Eleanor Farjeon's "The Goldfish," and many other classic and multicultural tales. Superb for small home groups. Great Books Foundation, 35 E. Wacker Dr., Suite 2300, Chicago, IL 60601-2298; (800) 222-5870; www.greatbooks.org.

LEARNING LANGUAGE ARTS THROUGH LITERATURE

The fourth-grade *Orange Book* teaches reading, writing, spelling, and grammar skills through well-known children's books. Featured titles include Gertrude Chandler Warner's *The Boxcar Children,* Augusta Stevenson's *The Wright Brothers,* and Elizabeth George Speare's *The Sign of the Beaver.* Units cover research, journal writing, poetry, journalism, and making books. Christian orientation, but can usually be adapted for those with other philosophies. Common Sense Press; (352) 475-5757; cspress.com.

Also see Beyond Five in a Row, page 146, Learning Links, page 60, and Novel Units, page 60.

1. **Read a wide range of grade-appropriate fiction and nonfiction materials.** Kids should read a mix of classic and contemporary literature, nonfiction selections, poetry, magazine articles, and newspapers.

Recommended fiction titles for kids in grade 4 include *Chocolate Fever* by Robert Kimmel Smith; *Half Magic* by Edward Eager; *The Cricket in Times Square* by George Selden; *The Indian in the*

Cupboard by Lynne Reid Banks; and *The Chronicles of Narnia* by C. S. Lewis.

Cricket

An exceptional monthly literary magazine for kids aged 9–14. Selections include stories, legends, and folktales; science and nature nonfiction articles; poems; puzzles; and contests. Cricket Magazine Group, Box 7434, Red Oak, IA 51591-4434; (800) 827-0227; www.cricketmag.com.

See Book Lists, pages 400–402.

2. Be able to identify and analyze the main events of the plot, and discuss character traits and motivations.

3. Define elements of figurative language. Kids should be able to recognize and define *simile, metaphor, onomatopoeia, hyperbole,* and *personification.* Fourth-graders should also be exposed to a range of poetic forms, including limericks, haiku, tanka, narrative poems, sonnets, and couplets.

Poetry A to Z
Paul B. Janeczko; Simon & Schuster, 1994

A collection of poems of all kinds, arranged alphabetically by theme, with accompanying suggestions for poetry-writing projects.

Rose, Where Did You Get That Red?
Kenneth Koch; Vintage Books, 1990

A superb program for teaching great poetry to children. The works of many famous poets serve as jumping-off points for student projects.

POETRY AT ABOUT.COM

Poetry selections categorized by genre and historical era; games, contests, how-tos, and kids' poetry links; Web site: poetry.about. com.

POETRY PALS

All kinds of creative poetry activities and lesson plans for kids in grades K–12; Web site: www.geocities.com/EnchantedForest/ 5165/lessons2.html.

Also see *Poems Go Clang!*, page 149.

4. Use a variety of sources to obtain information. Kids should be able to obtain information on a given topic from a number of sources—including books, reference works, periodicals, and the Internet—and to compare and contrast the results. They should be able to differentiate between fact and opinion.

5. Understand and follow multiple-step written directions from a technical manual or instruction booklet. Kids should be able, for example, to follow the instructions for installing a computer software program, for programming a VCR, or for assembling a model rocket.

WRITING

Fourth-graders should have mastered cursive handwriting: The aim is that kids at this grade level write "fluidly and legibly." Often keyboarding skills (read "touch typing") are introduced in fourth grade: Our three children felt strongly that competent keyboarding in company with a word processor should excuse them from all further struggles with penmanship. Ordinarily this attitude is not shared by the public schools.

We taught our kids to type by showing them where to put their fingers on the keyboard; they taught themselves from there. They all peek when it comes to numbers and semicolons, so this may not have been as effective a method as some.

EASY TYPE

An on-line typing tutorial for kids at two different age levels. Web site: www.easytype.com.

Jumpstart Typing

A typing program for kids aged 7–10. It consists of thirty-three lessons, with animations, games, time tests. Knowledge Adventure, Inc.; (800) 545-7677; www.jumpstart.com or www.knowledgeadventure.com.

Mavis Beacon Teaches Typing!

A popular program for ages 7 and up, with sequential lessons, demonstrations, games, tests, and progress charts. Mattel Interac-

tive; (800) 395-0277; www.mattelinteractive.com or www.
MavisBeacon.com.

1. Write frequently, exploring a range of genres, including short stories, personal narratives, poems, essays, and research reports.

Encourage kids to maintain a daily journal; establish a family newsletter or literary magazine; write and make their own small books; correspond with a pen pal.

Word Wizardry

Margaret E. Kenda and William Kenda; Barrons Juveniles, 1999
Your kids don't like writing? Try this irresistible information-and-activity book. Kids can play name games, send secret messages, experiment with calligraphy, and much more, while learning fascinating facts about the history and structure of the English language.

Also see *Doing the Days, If You're Trying to Teach Kids How to Write, You've Gotta Have This Book,* and Interactive Writing: First Steps, page 150.

2. Create multiparagraph compositions. Include introductory, supporting, and concluding paragraphs, each with proper indentation and topic sentences.

3. Differentiate between complete and incomplete sentences; identify and correct run-on sentences. Kids should be able to identify the subject and predicate of a sentence and should recognize the four major sentence types: *declarative* ("I see a dog."), *interrogative* ("Do you see a dog?"), *imperative* ("Drop the bone."), and *exclamatory* ("He bit me!").

4. Use capital letters correctly. Kids should be familiar with previously covered usages of capitals; and should also know that capital letters are used for the names of magazines, newspapers, artworks, musical compositions, and organizations.

5. Use punctuation marks correctly. Fourth-graders should be familiar with the use of periods, question marks, exclamation points, commas, quotation marks, and apostrophes. They should know that book titles are underlined or italicized in written work and should understand the use of parentheses.

6. Recognize an expanding vocabulary of prefixes and suffixes.
Kids at this grade level should know the meanings of such prefixes as *im, in, non, mis, en,* and *pre* and such suffixes as *ily, y, ful, able/ible,* and *ment.*

7. Recognize and identify the common parts of speech, including nouns, verbs, adjectives (including articles), adverbs, conjunctions, and interjections.

8. Expand upon previous spelling skills.
See age-appropriate spelling programs (page 64).

Fourth-graders should have mastered the correct spelling and use of such homophones as *there/their/they're, you're/your, its/it's,* and *to/too/two.*

For age-appropriate grammar books, games, and programs, see pages 152, 219–220.

LISTENING AND SPEAKING SKILLS

1. Make both narrative and informational oral presentations.
Kids should be able to tell personal stories or deliver informational reports in an organized and coherent manner.

2. Give oral summaries of books, stories, or articles.

3. Memorize and recite poems. Kids might tackle more challenging poetry selections of two to three stanzas, or participate in brief dramatizations.

STUDY SKILLS

Help for fourth-graders faced with standardized tests:

How to Do Your Best on Tests
Sara D. Gilbert; Beech Tree Books, 1998
　　Everything from classroom quizzes to standardized tests, with helpful hints on how to study. The book even includes a test on taking tests.

True or False? Tests Stink!
Trevor Romain and Elizabeth Verdick; Free Spirit Publishing, 1999
　　How to tackle tests without succumbing to stress, for kids aged 8–13.

Also see test-taking resources, pages 153–154.

1. **Become familiar with the practice of** *outlining*. Kids should be able to identify main topics and subtopics in a given short passage and list them in proper outline form.

2. **Expand upon previous library skills.**

Find It! The Inside Story at Your Library
Claire McInerney; Lerner, 1989
> How to find and use the various references and resources available at the library, for kids aged 9–12.

DEWEY DECIMAL COLLECTION
> An explanation of the Dewey Decimal system with many interesting links from the kids' section of the Internet Public Library; Web site: www.ipl.org/youth/dewey/.

MATHEMATICS

Sample grade-appropriate programs and resources for fourth-grade math include:

Everyday Mathematics Series
> A highly recommended activity-based math program for grades K–6. The fourth-grade program includes a teacher's guide, student books and journals, and a kit of manipulatives. Kids cover math through exercises, games, and projects, including the "World Tour Project," a year-long mathematical trip around the globe. Everyday Learning Corporation, 2 Prudential Plaza, Suite 2200, Chicago, IL 60601; (800) 382-7670; www.everydaylearning.com.

HANDS-ON EQUATIONS
> A hands-on progam using simple manipulatives (pawns and number cubes) to teach algebraic concepts to kids in grades 3–8. Borenson and Associates, Box 3328, Allentown, PA 18106; (800) 993-6284; www.borenson.com.

How Math Works
Carol Vorderman; Reader's Digest, 1996
> A beautifully illustrated hands-on approach to math for kids aged 8–14. Information, capsule biographies of famous mathematicians, and terrific projects for many fields of mathematics. For example,

kids build a simple computer, measure heights of trees with a homemade astrolabe, and play negative-number hopscotch.

The I Hate Mathematics! Book
Marilyn Burns; Little Brown, 1974

Math for Smarty Pants
Marilyn Burns; Little Brown, 1982
Very creative, informative, and fascinating math activities and information for kids aged 9–12. Topics include statistics and probability, topology, geometry, logic, prime numbers, immense numbers, and much more. ETA/Cuisenaire; (800) 445-5985; www.etauniverse.com or www.cuisenaire.com.

Math 54
Stephen Hake and John Saxon; Saxon Publishers, 1995
A comprehensive fourth-grade math program, covering whole number concepts and computation, mental math, patterns and functions, measurement, geometry, fractions, decimals, and statistics and probability. Many practice problems and continual review of previously covered concepts. Saxon Publishers, Inc., 2450 John Saxon Blvd., Norman, OK 73071; (800) 284-7019; www.saxonpub.com.

SRA Math: Explorations and Applications Series
Stephen S. Willoughby; SRA/McGraw-Hill
A varied and excellent program, incorporating hands-on activities, calculator and computer use, math journaling, math "thinking stories," cooperative learning projects, cross-curricular connections, and much more. SRA/McGraw-Hill; (888) SRA-4543; www.sra4kids.com.

NUMBER THEORY

1. Know numbers through the millions; be able to write these in both numerals and words.

The Magic of a Million Activity Book
David M. Schwartz; Scholastic, 1998
Interesting activities and reproducible worksheets for the investigation of huge numbers.

On Beyond a Million: An Amazing Math Journey
David M. Schwartz; Bantam Doubleday Dell, 1999

Amazing facts about perfectly enormous numbers, funny and helpful illustrations, and a nice explanation of exponents.

Also see *Can You Count to a Googol?*, page 156, and *How Much Is a Million?*, page 116.

2. Order and compare numbers to 999,999,999 using greater than (>), lesser than (<), and equals (=) signs.

3. Understand place value to 100 million.

4. Be able to round numbers to the nearest 10, 100, and 1,000.

5. Know the perfect squares and square roots through 144; recognize the square root sign.

6. Know Roman numerals to 1,000 (M).

COMPUTER ROMANUS

A Roman numeral calculator and a lot of general information. Can also be used "to convert barbaric numbers to proper Roman numerals"; Web site: www.naturalmath.com.

Also see *Roman Numerals I to MM*, page 157.

7. Identify positive and negative numbers on a number line.

See Line Jumper, page 157.

Probability and Statistics

1. Collect, organize, and interpret data using bar and line graphs. *The I Hate Mathematics! Book* and *Math for Smarty Pants*, page 192, both contain creative data-collecting projects for kids in this age group.

Also see *Measuring: From Paces to Feet*, page 158, and Exploring Data, page 33.

2. Plot points on a coordinate grid.

See resources on Cartesian graphing, pages 158–159.

Fractions and Decimals

Key to Fractions Series

Key to Decimals Series

Self-guided workbook series for kids in grades 4 and up. *Key to Fractions* includes four workbooks, variously covering fraction concepts, mathematical operations with fractions, and mixed numbers. *Key to Decimals* includes four workbooks, covering decimal concepts, mathematical operations with decimals, and common uses of decimals. Key Curriculum Press; (800) 995-MATH; www.keypress.com.

Also see *Hot Math Topics: Fractions and Decimals* and *Making Fractions*, page 158.

1. Identify and compare fractions from $\frac{1}{2}$ to $\frac{1}{12}$. Kids should know the meaning of *numerator* and *denominator*, should be able to compare fractions with like denominators, and should recognize equivalent fractions, such as $\frac{1}{2}$ and $\frac{3}{6}$.

2. Add and subtract fractions with like denominators.

3. Identify mixed numbers and improper fractions. Be able to convert mixed numbers to improper fractions and vice versa.

4. Read and write decimal numbers through the thousandths place. Kids at this level should also be able to read and write decimals as fractions ($.02 = \frac{2}{100}$) and should know the decimal equivalents for halves, quarters, eighths, and tenths.

5. Compare decimals using greater than ($>$), lesser than ($<$), and equals ($=$) signs.

6. Round decimals to the nearest tenth and hundredth.

7. Add and subtract decimals to two places.

OPERATIONS

1. Know basic multiplication facts through 10×10 and equivalent basic division facts.
See on-line math games, page 157.

2. Multiply multidigit numbers by single whole numbers with regrouping.

3. Understand that multiplication and division are inverse operations. Be able to identify *dividend, divisor,* and *quotient*. Kids should know the three different ways of representing division problems. They should understand that numbers cannot be divided by 0, and should know that any number divided by 1 remains the same.

4. Divide multidigit numbers by single whole numbers, with and without remainders.

5. Estimate answers to multiplication and division problems. Kids should also be able to check multiplication problems by changing the order of the factors, and division problems by multiplying (and adding any remainder).

6. Solve two-step word problems and numerical problems involving more than one operation. Kids should understand the use of parentheses to indicate order of operations—that is, whatever is inside the parentheses is done first.

For an on-line source of word problems for kids in grades 1–8, see Math Stories at www.mathstories.com.

7. Identify repeating patterns formed by multiples, factors, and powers of 10.

Money and Measurement

1. Solve money problems involving multiplication and division with single whole numbers.

2. Make change in amounts up to $100.

3. Estimate and measure length, weight, and capacity/volume. Kids at this level should have an increasing knowledge of English and metric equivalencies. They should know, for example, that 1 foot = 12 inches; 1 yard = 3 feet = 36 inches; and 1 mile = 5,280 feet = 1,760 yards; and that 1 centimeter = 10 millimeters; 1 meter = 1,000 millimeters = 100 centimeters; and 1 kilometer = 1,000 meters.

Key to Measurement Series

Key to Metric Measurement Series

Self-guided workbook sets for students in grades 4 and up. *Key to Measurement* covers length, perimeter, area, volume, weight, capacity, temperature, and time using English units; *Key to Metric Measurement* is an equivalent series using metric units. Key Curriculum Press; (800) 995-MATH; www.keypress.com.

4. Understand the concept of time zones.

This Book Is About Time
Marilyn Burns; Little Brown, 1978

Activities, humor, and information on time for kids aged 9–12, including a history of clocks and timepieces, an explanation of time zones, and information on your own biological clock. ETA/Cuisenaire; (800) 445-5985; www.etauniverse.com or www. cuisenaire.com.

GEOMETRY

Key to Geometry Series

An eight-workbook set covering lines and segments, circles, constructions, perpendiculars, squares and rectangles, angles, chords and tangents, parallel lines, triangles, and similar polygons. Key Curriculum Press; (800) 995-MATH; www.keypress.com.

1. Recognize and identify common two-dimensional figures (polygons). Kids should know *triangle, quadrilateral, pentagon, hexagon, octagon, parallelogram, trapezoid, rectangle,* and *square.*

O! EUCLID!

A geometry game for kids aged 9 and up in which players assemble fourteen geometric shapes from an assortment of puzzle cards and match completed puzzles to correct geometric name. Shapes include equilateral, isosceles, and right triangles plus squares, rectangles, parallelograms, trapezoids, pentagons, hexagons, octagons, circles, ellipses, parabolas, and hyperbolas. Ampersand Press, 8040 NE Day Rd. W, Bainbridge Island, WA 98110; (206) 780-9015; www.ampersandpress.com.

Shapes in Math, Science, and Nature Series

Catherine Sheldrick Ross; Kids Can Press

A multidisciplinary and activity-oriented approach to geometry. In *Squares* (1996), kids learn about area and perimeter, square cities (including Rome), square buildings, and square numbers, and experiment with origami, prisms, cuboctahedrons, and polyominoes. In *Triangles* (1994), they learn about angles, Pascal's triangle, Platonic solids, and Alexander Graham Bell's tetrahedrons, and experiment with hexaglexagons, toothpick architecture, and Leonardo da Vinci's pyramidal parachute.

2. Identify and classify three-dimensional figures (solids/polyhedrons) by vertices, edges, and face shapes.

See *Easy-to-Make 3-D Shapes in Full Color* and *Three-Dimensional Shapes,* page 125.

3. Recognize and identify horizontal, vertical, perpendicular, parallel, and intersecting lines. Geometry students at this level should also be able to identify *points, line segments,* and *rays* and *right, obtuse,* and *acute* angles.

4. Compare and contrast congruent and similar figures. Be able to identify congruent and similar figures regardless of position and identify positional changes, such as flips, turns, and slides.

5. Calculate perimeters of polygons, and areas of rectangles and squares.

6. Recognize and define *circumference, radius,* and *diameter* of a circle.
See *Sir Cumference and the First Round Table,* page 162.

HISTORY AND GEOGRAPHY

History and geography studies continue to build and expand upon topics introduced in the earlier grades, using a wide variety of resources, including fiction and nonfiction books, folktales and legends, audiocassettes and videos, games, hands-on projects and activities, and field trips.

SOCIAL STUDIES SCHOOL SERVICE
A superb source of history materials of all kinds for elementary, middle, and high school students. Multiple catalogs cover world and American history, global studies, government, and geography. 10200 Jefferson Blvd., Box 802, Culver City, CA 90232-0802; (800) 421-4246; www.socialstudies.com.

American History

See A History of US Series, page 163.

Kids' America
Steven Caney; Workman, 1978
> An excellent resource for kids in this age group. Historical information, projects, recipes, arts and crafts, and games from all eras of American history.

USKids History Series

Howard Egger-Bovet and Marlene Smith-Baranzini; Little, Brown
> Titles in the series include *Book of the American Indians, Book of the American Colonies, Book of the American Revolution, Book of the New American Nation,* and *Book of the American Civil War.* The books include first-person narratives from primary sources, background information, maps, illustrations, and diagrams, and suggestions for crafts, projects, and supplementary reading.

Cobblestone
> A monthly American history magazine for kids in grades 4–9. Each issue is centered around a single American history topic and includes fiction and nonfiction articles, plays, poems, maps, timelines, games and puzzles, and instructions for hands-on projects. A superb resource. All back issues continuously available. Cobblestone Publishing, Inc., 30 Grove St., Peterborough, NH 03458-1454; (800) 821-0115; www.cobblestonepub.com.

Also see Bluestocking Press, page 84.

1. The French and Indian War. Topics to cover include causes of the war, major events of the war, including the story of Montcalm, Wolfe, and the Battle of Quebec, and the financial implications of the British victory.

Indian Captive: The Story of Mary Jemison
Lois Lenski; HarperTrophy, 1995
> The story of a young girl captured by the Seneca Indians during the French and Indian War.

The Matchlock Gun
Walter D. Edmonds; Troll Associates, 1990

While his father is off fighting in the French and Indian War, ten-year-old Edward must fend off an Indian attack with his Dutch great-grandfather's enormous matchlock gun.

Also see *From Colonies to Country,* Volume 3 in A History of US Series, which covers the period from the French and Indian War to the Constitutional Convention.

2. Causes of the American Revolution. Topics to cover include the Stamp Act, the Intolerable Acts, Thomas Paine and *Common Sense,* the concept of "taxation without representation," the Boston Tea Party, and the Boston Massacre.

And Then What Happened, Paul Revere?

Can't You Make Them Behave, King George?

Where Was Patrick Henry on the 29th of May?

Why Don't You Get a Horse, Sam Adams?

Will You Sign Here, John Hancock?
Jean Fritz; Paper Star
   Clever, entertaining, and very well researched short biographies covering major events of the Revolutionary War period.

3. The Declaration of Independence. Topics to cover include the meeting of the Continental Congress, Thomas Jefferson and the writing of the Declaration of Independence, major points of the Declaration, and the significance of July 4, 1776.

4. Main events of the American Revolution. Topics to cover include Paul Revere's ride, the Battles of Lexington and Concord and Bunker Hill, conflicts between Loyalists/Tories and Rebels, the Battle of Saratoga, Valley Forge, the Battle of Yorktown and the surrender of Lord Cornwallis, famous men of the Revolution (including George Washington, Thomas Jefferson, Lafayette, Thaddeus Kosciusko, Baron von Steuben, Benedict Arnold, Nathan Hale, and John Paul Jones), and famous women of the Revolution (including Betsy Ross, Molly Pitcher, Deborah Sampson, Sybil Ludington, and Phillis Wheatley).

If You Were There in 1776
Barbara Brenner; Simon & Schuster, 1994
   A global view of the world in 1776, including descriptions of the varied life of the colonists (in New England, on a southern

plantation, on the western frontier), the native Americans, and the slaves.

The Story of the American Revolution Coloring Book
Peter F. Copeland; Dover Publications
Includes scenes from the Boston Massacre and the Battle of Lexington and Concord to the surrender at Yorktown. Dover Publications, 31 E. Second St., Mineola, NY 11501.

Also see *George Washington's World* (page 172).

5. The Constitution.
Topics to cover include the Articles of Confederation, the Constitutional Convention, James Madison: "Father of the Constitution," the Preamble to the Constitution, features of the Constitution, including the three branches of the federal government and the concept of checks and balances, and the Bill of Rights.

If You Were There When They Signed the Constitution
Elizabeth Levy; Scholastic, 1992
The story of the Constitutional Convention in kid-friendly question-and-answer format.

A Kids' Guide to America's Bill of Rights
Kathleen Krull; Avon Books, 1999
A fascinating and reader-friendly explanation of the Bill of Rights, with many anecdotes, examples, case studies, and places to contact for additional information.

A More Perfect Union: The Story of Our Constitution
Betsy and Giulio Maestro; Mulberry Books, 1990
A simple straightforward text, colorful illustrations, and useful fact lists.

Shh! We're Writing the Constitution
Jean Fritz; Paper Star, 1998
A thoroughly fascinating account of the writing of the Constitution, including all the historical basics, plus a lot of human interest.

6. Early days of the new nation.
Topics to cover include George Washington and John Adams as first president and vice president of the United States, the formation of the cabinet, the establish-

ment of a national capital at Washington, D.C., political parties then and now, the philosophical differences of Thomas Jefferson and Alexander Hamilton, and Jefferson's presidency, including the Lewis and Clark expedition and the Louisiana Purchase.

See *The New Nation*, Volume 4 in A History of US Series (page 163), which covers the period from the election of George Washington to the 1830s.

7. The War of 1812 and beyond. Topics to cover include James Madison and the War of 1812, James Monroe and the Monroe Doctrine, and the presidencies of John Quincy Adams and Andrew Jackson.

Old Ironsides: Americans Build a Fighting Ship
David Weitzmann; Houghton Mifflin, 1997
> A blow-by-blow description of the building of the famous ship, illustrated with detailed drawings and diagrams. An epilogue describes the War of 1812 battle during which the ship earned its nickname.

The Star-Spangled Banner
Peter Spier; Yearling, 1992
> An illustrated history of the War of 1812 for kids aged 6–10, including a reproduction of Francis Scott Key's original manuscript of "The Star-Spangled Banner."

8. Reformers and humanitarians. Topics to cover include abolitionists, Jane Addams and social work, and women's suffrage.

You Want Women to Vote, Lizzie Stanton?
Jean Fritz; Putnam, 1995
> A short chapter biography of Elizabeth Cady Stanton, meshing historical background information with fascinating facts and anecdotes.

World History

History studies should be closely linked to geography and to themes from other academic disciplines. Kids should be encouraged to make interconnections among historical studies and to order events on timelines. They should also approach history through a range of resources, including fiction and nonfiction books, legends and folktales, biographies of famous people, audio and video materials, games, and arts and crafts activities.

Calliope

A monthly illustrated world history magazine for kids in grades 4–8. Each issue centers around a single topic or theme and includes fiction and nonfiction articles, folktales and myths, maps, timelines, hands-on projects, and a list of suggestions for supplementary reading. An excellent resource. Back issues continuously available. Cobblestone Publishing, Inc., 30 Grove St., Peterborough, NH 03458-1454; (800) 821-0115; www.cobblestonepub. com.

Kids pursuing a classical curriculum in history (see pages 79–80) have reached the modern era by grade 4, a course of study that will be repeated in grades 8 and 12. Other possibilities include surveys of African and Central and South American history.

1. Survey of early and medieval kingdoms of Africa. Topics to cover include the geography of Africa, the cultures of the early African kingdoms, the rise of Mali, Ghana, and Songhai, the establishment of Timbuktu as a center of trade and learning, and stories of prominent people, including Ibn Battutah, Sundiata, and Mansa Musa.

African Beginnings

Jim Haskins, Kathleen Benson, and Floyd Cooper; Lothrop, Lee & Shepard, 1998

A forty-eight-page history of eleven ancient African civilizations, illustrated with maps, timelines, and colorful paintings. Includes a supplementary reading list.

African History for Young Beginners

Susan David and Ron David; Writers and Readers Publishing, 2000

An illustrated survey of African history from the ancient kingdoms to the arrival of the European explorers, the slave trade, colonization, and conflict.

A Coloring Book of Ancient Africa

Illustrations taken from ancient African art with an explanatory text. Bellerophon Books; (800) 253-9943; www.bellerophonbooks.com.

2. Survey of ancient civilizations of Central and South America.

Topics to cover include the geography of Central and South America, the major social, political, and economic features of Maya, Aztec, and Inca civilizations, and the arrival of the Spanish explorers.

Aztec, Inca, and Maya

Elizabeth Baquedanco; Alfred A. Knopf, 1993

One of the Eyewitness series, illustrated with color photographs, drawings, and diagrams. Each double-page spread covers a different aspect of ancient American culture and history.

The Aztec News

Philip Steele, Penny Bateman, and Norman Rosso; Candlewick, 1997

The history and culture of the Aztecs in creative newspaper format, giving all the latest in politics, religion, fashion, and sports, recipes, classified ads, and the scoop on the newly arrived Europeans.

Mexico! 50 Activities to Experience Mexico Past and Present

Susan Milord; Williamson Publishing, 1999

Creative activities and projects based on the history and culture of Mexico.

Montezuma and the Aztecs

Mathilde Helly and Remy Courgeon; Henry Holt, 1997

A graphically creative approach to the history of Aztec civilization and the arrival of the Spanish conquistadors. The book includes maps, timelines, short biographies, and a lot of fascinating historical information, innovatively presented. An illustrated double-page spread, for example, compares "Things That Did Not Exist in Spain" (jaguars, turkeys, tomatoes, hummingbirds) to "Things That Did Not Exist in Mexico" (horses, pigs, wool, ships).

3. Central and South American colonization.

Topics to cover include colonization of Central and South America and the Caribbean, the establishment of the Caribbean sugar plantations, and the development of the "triangular" transatlantic slave trade.

Bound for America: The Forced Migration of Africans to the New World

Jim Haskins; Lothrop, Lee & Shepard, 1999

An illustrated history of the New World slave trade for readers aged 9–12.

4. Central and South American independence movements. Topics to cover include Toussaint-L'ouverture and the Haitian Revolution, the Mexican Revolution, the South American liberators (including Simon Bolívar, José de San Martín, and Bernardo O'Higgins), and Brazilian independence.

The Story of Mexico
A coloring book of Mexican history from Montezuma to modern times, with accompanying text. Bellerophon Books; (800) 253-9943; www.bellerophonbooks.com.

GEOGRAPHY

Kids should sketch and model a variety of maps, and should use maps and globes frequently in the course of daily life. Relate geography to other academic subjects. While learning about Meso-American civilizations, for example, kids should study the geography of Central and South America.

NATIONAL GEOGRAPHIC
Information, activities and lesson plans, virtual tours, games, many maps, and a geobee. The site includes subscription information for *National Geographic World* for readers aged 6–12; Web site: www.nationalgeographic.com.

Geography Wizardry for Kids
Margaret Kenda and Phyllis S. Williams; Barrons Juveniles, 1997
Over 200 creative multidisciplinary geography activities and projects for kids aged 9–12.

Where in the U.S.A. Is Carmen Sandiego?

Where in the World Is Carmen Sandiego?
Creative geography on CD-ROM (Mac or Windows) for kids aged 8–14. Kids travel the United States or the world tracking down a gang of innovative and humorous criminals. Interesting information, clever facts, illustrations, video clips, color photographs, audio clips of music and foreign language phrases, and much more. Mattel Interactive; (800) 395-0277; www.mattelinteractive.com.

Also see *Discovering Geography of North America With Books Kids Love* and *Discovering World Geography With Books Kids Love,* page 172.

1. Review and reinforce concepts covered in previous geographical studies. Kids should be familiar with a range of different kinds of maps, including political, physical, population density, relief, and thematic maps. They should be able to use map scales to measure distances between locations, should know that latitude and longitude are measured in *degrees,* and should be able to find a location on the map, given latitudinal and longitudinal coordinates. They should be able to define and locate the *prime meridian* and the *international date line.*

2. Survey the major mountain ranges of the world. Kids should know the definitions of *ridge* and *valley* and be familiar with the rain-shadow effect. They should be able to name, locate, and describe the major mountain ranges and peaks of the world, including the Andes, Rockies, Appalachians, Himalayas, Urals, Atlas, and Alps.

3. Relate studies in other disciplines to geographical concepts, features, and locations. Studies of Africa, for example, should include location and description of the bordering Mediterranean Sea, Red Sea, Atlantic Ocean, and Indian Ocean; the Cape of Good Hope; the Atlas Mountains and Mount Kilimanjaro; the Nile, Niger, and Congo Rivers; the Sahara and Kalahari Deserts; and the Sudan.

4. Learn the names of the states and their capitals. By time-honored tradition, fourth grade is the year when kids often memorize the names of the states and their capitals. In theory this is useful; in practice, all you need to know is how to look them up.

STATELY KNOWLEDGE

Click on a state name for information and interesting links; Web site: www.ipl.org/youth/stateknow.

STATES AND CAPITALS

Click on a state for a long list of useful information: state capital, bird, flag, famous people, and fascinating facts; Web site: www.50states.com.

Kids Learn America
Patricia Gordon and Reed C. Snow; Williamson, 1992

> Information about all fifty states, with maps, projects, puzzles, quotations, fascinating facts, information about famous state people, and silly little mnemonics that help kids remember the state capitals.

> For an on-line game to teach state capitals, see Geography at www.quia.com.

SCIENCE

The basis of science is answering questions by means of experimentation and investigation. As in the previous grades, kids should be encouraged to approach science in an exploratory hands-on fashion. Studies should be supplemented with a range of print materials, including fiction and nonfiction books, biographies of famous scientists, and activity books.

PHYSICAL SCIENCE

1. Explore and understand the properties of electricity and magnetism. Topics to cover include current and static electricity; electrical circuits, electromagnets, conductors and insulators; the conversion of electrical energy to heat, light, and motion; electrical safety precautions and electrical hazards; and the uses of electricity in daily life.

Kids should understand that an electrical current is caused by the flow of electrons. Try designing and building series and parallel circuits using simple electrical components. They should also know that an electric current generates a magnetic field. They'll never forget this if they make and experiment with an electromagnet.

Electricity and Magnetism FUNdamentals
Robert W. Wood; McGraw Hill, 1996

> Experiments, explanations, and colorful illustrations. Kids build an electromagnet, a motor, a compass, a galvanometer, and map the magnetic field of the earth.

ELECTRICITY

MAGNETISM

Creative investigative science units that use very simple (but highly effective) homemade materials and instruments. Kids use paper clips, rubber bands, clothespins, masking tape, and foil to perform an impressive array of experiments, including bursting a balloon with electricity and mapping a magnetic field. For grades 3–8. TOPS Learning Systems, 10970 S. Mulino Rd., Canby, OR 97013; (888) 773-9755; www.topscience.org.

The Magic School Bus and the Electric Field Trip
Joanna Cole; Scholastic, 1997

Ms. Frizzle, science teacher extraordinaire, takes her class on an amazing electrical field trip. Lots of humorously presented information, plus instructions for making an electromagnet.

Shocking Science
Shar Levine and Leslie Johnstone; Sterling Publications, 1999

Great experiments and clear explanations for kids aged 9–12. (Make a battery with lemons.)

2. Explore and understand the basic concepts of chemistry. Topics to cover include the structure of the atom, the physical and chemical properties of matter, concepts of mass and density, features of elements and compounds, and features of diluted, concentrated, and saturated solutions.

Kids should be introduced to the planetary and Bohr models of the atom, and should know the definitions of *proton, neutron,* and *electron.* They should know that an object's *mass* is a measure of its actual amount of matter, while *weight* varies with gravity, and they should be able to calculate and compare *densities.* They should know that elements—the basic units of matter—consist of only one kind of atom and that there are over 110 known elements; they should also be able to name and describe assorted basic elements. They should be able to define *solvent* and *solute,* and should experiment with a range of dilute, concentrated, and saturated solutions (as in the making of rock candy).

GEMS CHEMISTRY HANDBOOKS
Study units for kids of all ages. Sample titles include "Discovering Density," "Chemical Reactions," and "Involving Dissolving." Lawrence Hall of Science; (510) 642-1016; www.lhs.berkeley.edu.

Also see chemistry resources, pages 235–237.

LIFE SCIENCE

1. Reinforce and expand upon earlier studies of ecosystems. Kids should recognize and identify structural and behavioral *adaptations* that allow plants and animals to survive in specific environments. They should understand the relationship between available natural resources and population densities and be able to define and cite examples of *carnivores, herbivores, omnivores,* and *decomposers.*

2. Continue studies of human anatomy and physiology. Kids should build upon existing knowledge of the human body and its systems, studying the circulatory and respiratory systems.

Topics covered should include the structure and function of the heart, the major components of blood, types of blood vessels (*arteries, veins,* and *capillaries*), the blood clotting process, causes and treatments of heart attacks, blood types and blood transfusions, the components of the respiratory system and the process of respiration, the structure and function of the lungs, and the relationship between smoking and lung cancer.

How the Body Works
Steve Parker; Reader's Digest, 1994
A superb collection of projects and experiments for kids (and parents) about the workings of the human body, with background information, capsule biographies of scientists, fascinating facts, diagrams, and hundreds of terrific color photographs.

The Heart
Seymour Simon; Mulberry Books, 1996
A clear and kid-friendly explanation of the heart and circulatory system, illustrated with colorful computer-enhanced electron micrographs and diagrams.

Also see anatomy and physiology resources, page 176.

Earth Science

1. Continue and expand upon the studies of geology introduced in previous grades. Topics to cover include the inner structure of the earth, the theory of plate tectonics, earthquakes and volcanoes, Pangaea and the theory of continental drift, the process of mountain formation, the contrast between rapid and slow geologic processes (for example, volcanism and earthquakes versus weathering and erosion), and the rock cycle and soil formation.

Geology: The Active Earth
National Wildlife Federation; McGraw-Hill, 1997
A volume in the Naturescope Series filled with detailed scientific information, photographs and diagrams, many multidisciplinary activities and projects, and more. An excellent resource, usable by kids from grades K–8. Activities are categorized by grade level.

Geology Rocks! 50 Hands-On Activities to Explore the Earth
Cindy Blobaum; Williamson Publishing, 1999
A creative activity book filled with information, fun facts, projects, language links, capsule biographies of famous geologists, and more. Kids make a miniglacier, an earth model, a Pangaea puzzle, and a mancala game (they collect the pebble playing pieces).

How the Earth Works
John Farndon; Reader's Digest, 1992
An excellent and comprehensive hands-on approach to earth science, covering the structure of the earth and ocean, rocks and soils, and the atmosphere. Activities include making a continental jigsaw and a clay model demonstrating the process of mountain formation. For kids ages 8–14.

2. Continue and expand upon studies of meteorology introduced in previous grades. Topics to cover include the layers of the atmosphere, the causes of wind, air pressure, cold and warm fronts, clouds and cloud types, storms, and weather instruments and forecasting.

For example, kids should be able to define *troposphere, stratosphere, mesosphere,* and *ionosphere* and identify *stratus, cumulus,* and *cirrus* clouds. They should know that air pressure is measured with a barometer and understand the implications of barometric pressure changes for weather prediction. They should also understand the causes of thunder and lightning, and know the difference between *weather* and *climate*.

How the Weather Works
Michael Allaby; Reader's Digest, 1999
> A collection of excellent meteorological experiments and activities for kids aged 8–14, plus information, capsule biographies of scientists, detailed diagrams, and hundreds of wonderful color photographs.

Wild About Weather
National Wildlife Federation; McGraw-Hill, 1997
> An activity book in the Naturescope Series filled with interesting scientific information, illustrations, charts, and diagrams, creative multidisciplinary activities, experiments, projects, and more. Kids experiment with air pressure, make a cloud book and a weather wheel, launch a hot-air balloon, and put on a weather radio play. Can be used with kids from grades K–8.

FOREIGN LANGUAGE

Kids should read foreign language texts appropriate to their skill level, write sentences and short passages using correct grammar and vocabulary, and practice their chosen language in skits, recitations, and conversations.

See resources, page 47.

ART

Art, as in the previous grades, should consist of a multifaceted program, incorporating hands-on art experiences, art appreciation, and art history. Kids should: experiment with a wide range of art techniques and media, including drawing, painting, printmaking, sculpture, pottery, and fiber arts; approach art through fiction and nonfiction books, folktales and legends, poems, and biographies of famous artists; and take field trips to artists' studios, art galleries, exhibits, and museums.

Lives of the Artists : Masterpieces, Messes (and What the Neighbors Thought)
Kathleen Krull; Harcourt Brace, 1995

An illustrated collection of short, engaging biographies of sixteen famous artists from Leonardo da Vinci to Andy Warhol.

The Louvre: Museums of the World for Kids

With Open Eyes

Tours of the Louvre and the Art Institute of Chicago on Win/Mac CD-ROM. Programs include images and close-ups of each artwork or artifact, a virtual gallery with audio narration, games and puzzles, and interactive maps and timelines that allow kids to put artworks in historical and geographical context. Learn Technologies Interactive; (800) 292-5584; voyager.learntech.com.

Also see 1–8 Art Curriculum, page 101, *How to Use Child-Size Masterpieces for Art Appreciation*, page 48, and Getting to Know the World's Greatest Artists Series, page 102.

1. Use knowledge of the basic elements of art and principles of design to discuss works by famous artists and to create original artworks. For example, kids should be familiar with the color wheel and should be able to identify *primary, secondary, complementary,* and *neutral* colors as well as define *hue, intensity,* and *value.*
See *Move Over, Picasso!*, page 102, *Discovering Great Artists,* page 141, and Artists' Workshop Series, page 181.

2. Experiment with a variety of art media and techniques, including drawing, painting, sculpture, printmaking, pottery, and fiber arts. Kids might also explore the use of technology in art, experimenting with computers, cameras, and video recorders.
See *Drawing With Children,* page 103.

3. Study art in conjunction with other academic disciplines across the curriculum. History and geography studies, for example, should include overviews of the art of the featured historical period or world region.

WORLD CRAFT SERIES

Franklin Watts

Craft projects from around the world. There are many titles in the series, among them *Textiles, Puppets, Masks, Musical Instruments,* and *Papercrafts.* Each illustrated book includes background information and detailed instructions. *Textiles,* for example, features Chinese silk painting, Indian tie-dye, and African kente cloth. (And more.)

MUSIC

As in art, kids should pursue a multifaceted music program, including instrumental and vocal activities, music appreciation, music theory, and music history. This should include listening to a range of pieces by famous composers and to selections of multicultural music as well as using a range of print materials, including fiction and nonfiction books, legends and folktales, songbooks, and biographies of famous composers and musicians.

In the public schools, fourth grade is often the year in which kids begin to play a band or orchestral instrument.

Lives of the Musicians: Good Times, Bad Times (and What the Neighbors Thought)
Kathleen Krull; Harcourt Brace, 1993

An illustrated collection of nineteen short biographies of nineteen famous musicians in chronological order from Vivaldi to Gershwin. Historical information, fun facts, and human interest.

Also see Getting to Know the World's Greatest Composers Series, page 104.

1. Reinforce and expand upon the musical concepts covered in earlier grades. Kids should know the notes of the treble clef; recognize whole, half, quarter, and eighth notes, and whole, half, and quarter rests; and recognize and know the meaning of *tied* and *dotted* notes and *sharps* and *flats*.

Music Ace

Music theory for beginners on Mac/Win CD-ROM. A series of twenty-four lessons covers note reading, sharps and flats, key signatures, keyboard basics, major scales, octaves, the grand staff, and more through colorful animations and games. A Music Doodle Pad feature lets kids compose their own music. Harmonic Vision; (800) 474-0903; www.harmonicvision.com.

Also see *Music Theory for Beginners*, page 142, and *Making Music*, page 182.

2. Be able to recognize the orchestral families and their individual members by sight and sound. Kids should also know the difference between an *orchestra* and a *band*.

The Young Person's Guide to the Orchestra
Benjamin Britten
An excellent introduction to the varied instruments of the orchestra through a piece by composer Henry Purcell, with narration. From music stores on audiocassette or CD.

Also see *Alligators and Music*, page 183, and resources, page 143.

3. Recognize and identify vocal ranges. Kids should know the sounds of *soprano, mezzo soprano, alto, tenor, baritone,* and *bass.* See opera resources, page 313.

4. Listen and respond to a range of pieces by well-known composers and to folk and ethnic musical selections. Kids should be able to identify repeating and contrasting phrases and simple formal structures in music. They should also be able to associate certain selections with the appropriate composer.
See Classical Kids, page 183.

5. Participate in instrumental and vocal performances, group and solo. Kids should experiment with musical instruments or participate in a program of formal musical instrument instruction; and they should continue to refine their singing skills, singing melody and harmony.

They should also be encouraged to write and perform their own musical compositions.

HEALTH AND PHYSICAL EDUCATION

1. Identify a range of activities associated with the major components of physical fitness: cardiovascular health, muscular strength and endurance, and flexibility.

2. **Participate in a range of age-appropriate indoor and outdoor athletic activities.** Suggestions for homeschoolers include individual, small group, and team activities, such as gymnastics, dance, swimming, skating, hiking, skiing, and soccer.

See *Physical Education Unit Plans for Grades 3–4*, page 184, *Fit Kids!*, page 50, and *Home School Family Fitness*, page 50.

3. **Participate in a program of drug education.** Kids should understand the negative aspects of alcohol, tobacco, and illegal drug use, and they should be aware of safe practices for the use of prescription and nonprescription drugs.

4. **Understand the elements of good nutrition, and the relationship between diet, health, and energy.**

The Healthy Body Cookbook: Over 50 Fun Activities and Delicious Recipes for Kids
Joan D'Amico and Karen Eich Drummond; John Wiley & Sons, 1999
Health and science for kids aged 9–12. The book emphasizes the crucial role diet plays in the development of healthy hearts, bones, muscles, teeth, and nervous systems, and it reinforces concepts through hands-on investigations and fun-to-make recipes.

Janice Van Cleave's Food and Nutrition for Every Kid
Janice Van Cleave; John Wiley & Sons, 1999
Food facts and experiments for kids aged 8–12. Kids learn about the basic food groups, the importance of vitamins and minerals, the relationship between food and energy, and much more, with simple activities and exercises.

5. **Know basic first-aid practices.**
See *Kids to the Rescue!*, page 184.

GRADE FIVE

> All men who have turned out worth anything have had the chief hand in their own education.
>
> SIR WALTER SCOTT

LANGUAGE ARTS

LITERATURE

By fifth grade, kids should generally be competent and independent readers, pursuing their own interests through a wide variety of books and periodicals. A buzz phrase for such independent readers is "sustained silent reading," which in practice means kids should curl up on a bed, chair, couch, or living room rug and read to themselves. Formal curricula often recommend at least thirty minutes of this daily.

JUNIOR GREAT BOOKS PROGRAM

Selections for kids in grade 5 include "Thank You, M'am" by Langston Hughes, "The Happy Prince" by Oscar Wilde, "The Fifty-First Dragon," by Heywood Broun, "Alberic the Wise" by

Norton Juster, and "The Bat-Poet" by Randall Jarrell. Each selection is followed by a series of thought-provoking questions for in-depth discussion. Great Books Foundations, 35 E. Wacker Dr., Suite 2300, Chicago, IL 60601-2298; (800) 222-5870; www.greatbooks.org.

LANGUAGE LEARNING THROUGH LITERATURE

The Purple Book for fifth-graders teaches creative writing and composition, grammar and spelling, speech, and study skills through well-known books. Featured titles include *Farmer Boy* by Laura Ingalls Wilder, *Trumpet of the Swan* by E. B. White, and *Caddie Woodlawn* by Carol Ryrie Brink. Christian orientation, but generally adaptable for a secular audience. Common Sense Press; (352) 475-5757; cspress.com.

CYBERGUIDES

Multidisciplinary lesson plans for many books, categorized by grade level. Fifth-grade selections include E. L. Konigsberg's *From the Mixed-Up Files of Mrs. Basil E. Frankweiler,* Scott O'Dell's *Island of the Blue Dolphins,* Carol Ryrie Brink's *Caddie Woodlawn,* and many more. Plans include hands-on activities, projects, and related Internet links. Web site: www.sdcoe.k12.ca.us/score/cyberguide.html.

Also see Learning Links, page 60, and Novel Units, page 60.

1. Read a wide range of grade-appropriate fiction and non-fiction materials. Kids should be encouraged to read a mix of classic and contemporary literature, nonfiction works, myths and legends, fables and folktales, poetry, magazines, and newspapers.

Fiction suggestions for fifth-graders include:

The Adventures of Tom Sawyer (Mark Twain; Puffin, 1995)

The Adventures of Sherlock Holmes (Sir Arthur Conan Doyle; Penguin, 1993)

Alice in Wonderland (Lewis Carroll; Scholastic, 1988)

Anne of Green Gables (L. M. Montgomery; Bantam Books, 1984)

The BFG (Roald Dahl; Puffin, 1998)

Caddie Woodlawn (Carol Ryrie Brink; Aladdin, 1997)

The Hobbit (J. R. R. Tolkien; Houghton Mifflin, 1997)

Mrs. Frisby and the Rats of NIMH (Robert C. O'Brien; Aladdin, 1986)

Sarah, Plain and Tall (Patricia MacLachlan; HarperTrophy, 1987)

The Sign of the Beaver (Elizabeth George Speare; Yearling Books, 1994)

The Secret Garden (Frances Hodgson Burnett; Signet Classics, 1994)

Stuart Little (E. B. White; HarperCollins, 1999)

Tuck Everlasting (Natalie Babbitt; Farrar, Straus & Giroux, 1988)

Also see Book Lists, pages 400–402, and *Cricket,* page 187.

2. Evaluate works of literature through discussion, debate, and written critique. Kids should be familiar with such literary features as story development, author's purpose, narrative point of view, conflict and resolution, character motivation, and theme. They should be able to discuss main ideas presented in a written work, draw conclusions based on the text, and support these conclusions with evidence drawn from the text.

See Junior Great Books Program, pages 215–216.

3. A first introduction to full-text Shakespeare: Read and discuss *A Midsummer Night's Dream*. Literature programs vary as to when Shakespeare is best introduced to young readers. Many parents may prefer to begin earlier with versions of Shakespearean plays tailored to early elementary–aged students, of which there are many available.

Reinforce studies of Shakespeare with supplementary reading materials, hands-on projects, and cross-curricular connections.

Bard of Avon
Diane Stanley and Peter Vennema; Morrow Junior Books, 1992

A beautifully illustrated account of Shakespeare's life, times, and plays for readers in grades 4–8.

SHAKESPEARE CATALOG

Books, activity books, games, videos, computer software, and other materials for Shakespeare students of all ages. The Writing Company, 10200 Jefferson Blvd., Rm. K711, Box 802, Culver City, CA 90232-0802; (800) 421-4246; www.writingco.com.

Shakespeare for Kids: His Life and Times
Colleen Aagesen and Margie Blumberg; Chicago Review Press, 1999

History, biographical information, selected accounts of poems and plays, and many creative projects and hands-on activities for kids aged 9–13. For example, kids make and write with a quill pen, play Elizabethan games, make a sword and choreograph a sword fight, write a sonnet, and enact a short scene from *Julius Caesar*.

4. Read a varied range of poetic forms. Kids should be able to identify and define *simile, metaphor, onomatopoeia, hyperbole, personification,* and *alliteration*.

See poetry resources, page 187.

5. Understand and follow multiple-step written directions. Common examples include the instructions found in technical manuals.

WRITING

THE WRITING COMPANY

A large and creative assortment of writing resources, programs, activity books, and skills manuals for kids in grade 4 and up. The Writing Company, Box 802, Culver City, CA 90232-0802; (800) 421-4246; www.writingco.com.

1. Write frequently, producing a variety of works, including reports, essays, short stories, poems, narratives, journal entries, and letters. Fifth-graders should be able to use a multistep writing process, involving prewriting, writing a first draft, revising, editing, and writing a final version of a work.

Kids should be able to obtain information from a variety of sources and reference works, and incorporate their findings into well-organized nonfiction reports. At this level, reports should include a coherent multiparagraph structure with a well-defined main idea, an introduction and conclusion, key points illustrated with relevant examples, and a simple bibliography.

2. Identify and correct incomplete and run-on sentences. Kids at this level should also be able to identify and use *prepositional phrases, appositives,* and *independent* and *dependent clauses*.

3. Use punctuation marks correctly. Reinforce and expand upon knowledge acquired in earlier grades. Kids should also be familiar with the use of the *colon* (before a list).

4. Continue to expand knowledge of prefixes and suffixes and the way in which these affect word meaning. Fifth-graders should be familiar with the use and meaning of such prefixes as *anti, co, fore, inter, mid, post,* and *semi,* and such suffixes as *ist, ish, ness,* and *tion/sion.*

5. Recognize and identify the common parts of speech, including nouns, pronouns, verbs, adjectives (and articles), adverbs, conjunctions, and interjections. Kids should know the proper use of such problematic verbs as lie/lay, sit/set, and rise/raise, and the correct use of *nominative, objective,* and *possessive* pronouns.

6. Expand upon previous spelling and vocabulary skills. For age-appropriate spelling programs, see page 64.

GRAMMAR RESOURCES AND SUPPLEMENTS FOR NUMBERS 2–6 INCLUDE:

Nitty-Gritty Grammar
Edith H. Fine and Judith P. Josephson; Ten Speed Press, 1998
All the parts of speech, the grammar of sentences (including subject and predicate, clauses and phrases, misplaced modifiers, and diagramming), and complete guides to punctuation and spelling, all with many examples. Illustrated with hilarious panel cartoons.

SCRABBLE
What better resource for spelling? The classic board game is available at game and toy stores. The Official Scrabble Homepage online includes Scrabble in four languages, an Anagram Builder, a dictionary; Web site: www.scrabble.com.

SUE PALMER'S LANGUAGE LIVE!
Spelling, punctuation, and grammar through a series of witty and humorous games. Try the S.P.E.L.L. Fantasy Theme Park, the Home for Abused Apostrophes, or Words at Work, Home of Norman Noun, Angelica Adjective, Vera Verb, and Ashley Adverb. Web site: www.nuff.ox.ac.uk/users/martin/languagelive. htm.

WILD WORLD OF WORDS

Spelling, word decoding, and vocabulary games and puzzles (involving idioms, rhymes, and homophones), all available at Beginning, Medium, and Advanced levels. Web site: www.ash. udel.adv/ash/challenge/.

Also see *Princeton Review Grammar Smart Junior,* page 250.

LISTENING AND SPEAKING SKILLS

1. Listen to and make narrative and informational oral presentations. Kids should be able to make oral presentations of their own in an organized and well-delivered fashion; conversely, they should be able to understand, draw conclusions, and ask appropriate questions based on oral presentations made by others. They should be able to analyze and critique oral presentations and media messages for bias, persuasion, fallacies, opinion cited as fact, and unsupported generalities. (Does your family watch the evening news? Talk about it.)

2. Follow multiple-step oral directions.

3. Give oral summaries of books, stories, articles, or spoken presentations.

4. Memorize and recite poems. Kids might also participate in creative dramatic activities such as plays, puppet shows, choral speaking presentations, and storytelling.

See Storytelling, Drama, Creative Dramatics, Puppetry and Reader's Theater for Children and Young Adults, page 153.

STUDY SKILLS

1. Know how to use dictionaries, thesauri, atlases, almanacs, periodicals, and encyclopedias as sources of information.

The Kid's Guide to Research
Deborah Heiligman; Scholastic, 1999

A kid-friendly explanation of research techniques with the help of the experts at the New York Public Library. The book covers library reference tools, library catalogs, the Internet, interviews, surveys, and site visits, and tips on evaluating sources for accuracy and bias.

2. Use electronic media as research tools. Kids should be familiar with the Internet and the use of search engines for tracking information.

INTERNET TUTORIALS

A range of Internet tutorials for preschoolers, kids, teens, and adults; Web site: www.mckinley.lib.oh.us/internettutorial/tutorial.htm.

INTERNET TUTORIALS

Information, activities, and tutorials for persons at all levels; Web site: Familyinternet.about.com.

3. Develop a simple outline from a short written selection.

4. Practice effective study techniques. Kids should be encouraged to pursue their studies in an organized fashion. Examples of tried-and-true techniques include PQRST (an ordered process of "Preview, Question, Read, Study, Test"), SQ3R ("Survey, Question, Read, Recite, Review"), and 4R ("Research, Read, Review, Report").

STUDY GUIDES AND STRATEGIES

A comprehensive page covering study techniques, writing and reading skills, test preparation, note taking, scheduling, and much more. Web site: www.iss.stthomas.edu/studyguides/

Also see test prep resources, pages 153–154, and the Writing Company, page 218, for study guides, research manuals, and test preparation materials for all ages.

MATHEMATICS

SAMPLE GRADE-APPROPRIATE PROGRAMS AND RESOURCES INCLUDE:

Everyday Mathematics Series

A highly recommended activity-based series for grades K–6. The fifth-grade program includes a teacher's guide, student books and journals, and a kit of manipulatives. Kids cover math through exercises, games, and projects, including the year-long "American Tour Project," a mathematical survey of American history and geography.

Everyday Learning Corporation, 2 Prudential Plaza, Suite 2200, Chicago, IL 60601; (800) 382-7670; www.everydaylearning.com.

Fractals, Googols and Other Mathematical Tales
Theoni Pappas; Wide World Publishing/Tetra, 1993

A fascinating exploration of mathematical concepts for kids in the company of Penrose, the mathematical cat. Activities, puzzles, fact boxes, and illustrations teach kids about decimal points, number lines, Fibonacci sequences, prime numbers, topology, pi, zero, and impossible geometry.

FUNBRAIN

On-line educational games for kids of all ages. Math games for kids in this age group challenge them to calculate areas and perimeters, make change, identify equivalent fractions, and more. www.funbrain.com.

G Is for Googol
David Schwartz; Tricycle Press, 1998

An illustrated math alphabet book filled with all things math, from Abacus and Binary to Zillion. The book combines historical background information with creative explanations and colorful diagrams. *E* is for Exponent, which concept is explained through multiplying jellybeans; *Y* for Y-axis, under which kids learn about bar and line graphs.

Math 65
Stephen Hake and John Saxon; Saxon Publishers, 1995

A basic fifth-grade text, covering whole number concepts and computation, patterns and functions, measurement, fractions, mixed numbers, decimals, geometry, percents, negative numbers, and probability and statistics. Saxon Publishers, Inc., 2450 John Saxon Blvd., Norman, OK 73071; (800) 284-7019; www.saxonpub.com.

SRA Math: Explorations and Applications Series
Stephen S. Willoughby; SRA/McGraw-Hill

A creative and comprehensive math program for kids in grades K–6, approaching math skills through practice problems, games, calculator and computer use, math journaling, cooperative learning projects, "thinking stories," cross-curricular connections and more. SRA/McGraw-Hill; (888) SRA-4543; www.sra4kids.com.

THE MATH FORUM

A superb Web site for mathematicians of all ages. Includes "Ask Dr. Math," a math library, math Web units and lessons, and math resources listed by subject and grade, including Internet resources and projects, lesson plans, software, and discussion groups. Topics covered include arithmetic, discrete math, precalculus, algebra, geometry, calculus, and probability and statistics. Web site: forum.swarthmore.edu.

Also see *Mathematics: A Human Endeavor*, page 253.

NUMBER THEORY

1. Know numbers through the billions; be able to write these in both numerals and words.
See *The Magic of a Million Activity Book* and *On Beyond a Million*, page 187.

2. Order and compare numbers to 999,999,999 using greater than (>), lesser than (<), and equals (=) signs.

3. Write numbers in expanded form. That is, $896,432 = 800,000 + 90,000 + 6,000 + 400 + 30 + 2$.

4. Reinforce concepts of place value.

5. Round numbers to the nearest 10, 100, 1,000, or 10,000.

6. Compare and order negative numbers on a number line. Kids should be able to define *integer*; and should know that the sum of any integer and its opposite is 0.
See *Line Jumper*, page 157.

7. Study the concept of exponents. Kids should know the perfect squares and square roots through 144, understand the terms *squared, cubed,* and *to the nth power,* and understand the relationship between exponents and repeated multiplication. They should be able to identify powers of 10 through 10^6 (= $10 \times 10 \times 10 \times 10 \times 10 \times 10$ or 1,000,000).

Powers of Ten
Philip Morrison and Phylis Morrison; W. H. Freeman, 1994
A spectacular journey from the subatomic particle to the edge of the universe in twenty-five exponential jumps.

8. Identify, create, and experiment with numerical patterns such as triangular numbers, square numbers, and arithmetic and geometric sequences. Kids should approach such patterns in varied ways, using manipulatives, paper and pencil, and calculators. Given a starting number and a basic rule, kids should be able to generate number sequences of their own.

Sites for creative math puzzles include K–8 Math at www.csun.edu/~vceed009/math.html and Interactive Math Puzzles at www.cut-the-knot.com.

9. Define *prime* and *composite* numbers. Be able to identify prime and composite numbers to 100.

PROBABILITY AND STATISTICS

1. Collect, organize and interpret data using line, bar, and circle ("pie") graphs, tables, and stem-and-leaf and scatter plots.
Statistics: The Shape of the Data
Susan Jo Russell and Rebecca B. Corwin; Dale Seymour Publications
 One of the Used Numbers Series, see pages 119 and 258. Data analysis through investigation for kids in grades 4–6. Students experiment with a number of ways of organizing and describing data and learn about such statistical basics as average, median, and stem-and-leaf plot. ETA/Cuisenaire; (800) 445-5985; www.etauniverse.com or www.cuisenaire.com.

Also see Exploring Data, page 33.

2. Solve problems involving the interpretation of graphs and tables. Good sources for real-life data include news magazines and the daily newspaper.

3. Find the average (mean) of a set of numbers.

4. Perform simple probability experiments. Use a variety of methods for generating random outcomes: flipped coins, dice, and spinners, for example.

5. Plot points on a coordinate grid.
See Cartesian graphing, pages 158–159.

FRACTIONS AND DECIMALS

See Key to Fractions Series and Key to Decimals Series, pages 193–194, and *Hot Math: Fractions and Decimals* and *Making Fractions*, page 158.

1. Express relationships as simple ratios. Introduction to ratio should be approached in hands-on fashion. For example, kids should make simple scale drawings using ratios.

2. Recognize equivalent fractions. For an on-line exercise in equivalent fractions, see Fresh-Baked Fractions at www.funbrain.com.

3. Determine the least common denominator of fractions with unlike denominators. Kids at this grade level should also be able to reduce fractions to their lowest terms.

4. Compare fractions with like and unlike denominators using greater than (>), lesser than (<), and equals (=) signs.

5. Add, subtract, and multiply fractions with like and unlike denominators.

6. Identify mixed numbers and improper fractions; change mixed numbers to improper fractions and vice versa. Kids should be able to add, subtract, and multiply mixed numbers and improper fractions.

7. Round fractions to the nearest whole number.

8. Read, write, and order decimals to the ten-thousandths place.

9. Round decimals to the nearest tenth, hundredth, and thousandth.

10. Add and subtract decimals to four places.

11. Multiply and divide decimals by 10, 100, and 1,000; multiply decimals by whole numbers and by other decimal numbers.

12. Write fractions as decimals and vice versa.

OPERATIONS

1. Know the basic multiplication facts through 12×12; and the equivalent basic division facts.

2. **Define and understand the *commutative* and *associative* properties of addition and the commutative, associative, and *distributive* properties of multiplication.** These rules are used to determine whether or not two mathematical expressions are equivalent.

The *commutative* property of addition shows that it doesn't matter in what order two numbers are added; the answer will always come out the same. Or, in mathematical terms, for any two numbers a and b: $a + b = b + a$.

The *associative* property of addition shows that the same holds true for more than two numbers. In mathematical terms, for any three numbers, a, b, and c: $(a + b) + c = a + (b + c)$.

The *commutative* property of multiplication similarly shows that it doesn't matter in what order two given numbers are multiplied. In other words, for any two numbers a and b: $a \times b = b \times a$.

The *associative* property of multiplication carries this principle a step further, to more than two numbers. For example, for any three numbers, a, b, and c: $(a \times b) \times c = a \times (b \times c)$

The *distributive* property of multiplication shows how multiplication is related to addition and subtraction. For any two numbers a and b: $a (b + c) = ab + ac$ and $a (b - c) = ab - ac$.

3. **Add, subtract, multiply, and divide numbers to four digits with and without regrouping.** For example, kids should be able to multiply two factors of up to four digits each; and should be able to divide dividends of up to four digits by one- to three-digit divisors. Kids should be familiar with the use of calculators for arithmetic operations.

4. **Estimate answers to arithmetical problems. Check answers using appropriate strategies.**

5. **Solve multistep word problems and numerical problems involving more than one operation.**
See Math Stories at www.mathstories.com for a wide range of word problems categorized by grade level (K–8).

MONEY AND MEASUREMENT

1. **Solve money problems using all arithmetical operations.**

2. Be familiar with English and metric measurements of length, volume, capacity, and weight/mass; measures of time; and measures of temperature in degrees Fahrenheit and Centigrade (Celsius). Kids should know measurement equivalencies (such as 1 foot = 12 inches, 1 kilometer = 1,000 meters) and should be able to convert to common units of measurement in problems involving different units. In a problem in which measurements are given in both yards and feet, for example, kids should know that one must be converted to the other before a solution can be found.

See Key to Measurement Series and Key to Metric Measurement Series (page 195).

3. Solve problems on elapsed time with and without regrouping. In multiplication and division problems involving time, for example, kids should be able to regroup, converting minutes to hours as necessary.

GEOMETRY

See Key to Geometry Series (page 196).

1. Recognize and identify common polygons and polyhedrons. Kids should know that *regular polygons* have sides of equal length and angles of equal measure.

> **A-MAZE-ING SHAPES**
> A multidisciplinary study unit on plane geometry and maze construction for kids in grades 4–8. Students identify geometric shapes, calculate areas and perimeters, design a maze, maintain a geometry journal, and read related literature. Interact; (800) 359-0961; www.interact-simulations.com.

See *Easy-to-Make 3-D Shapes in Full Color,* page 125, *Shape Up!,* page 161, Shapes in Math, Science, and Nature Series and O! Euclid!, page 196.

2. Identify similar and congruent figures and symmetrical and asymmetrical figures. Encourage kids to experiment with transformational motions of plane figures, including translations (slides), rotations (turns), and reflections (flips).

3. Recognize right, acute, and obtuse angles. Kids should be able to use a *protractor* to draw and measure angles. They should know that a right angle equals 90 degrees; that an acute angle is less than 90 degrees; an obtuse angle, more than 90 degrees; and a straight angle, 180 degrees.

4. Calculate the perimeters of polygons and the areas of rectangles, squares, and right triangles. Kids should know that the area of a rectangle can be determined using the formula A = lw (Area = length × width) and the area of a right triangle using the formula A = $\frac{1}{2}$ bh (Area = $\frac{1}{2}$ × base × height). They should also know that area is measured in square units.

See A-Maze-ing Shapes, page 227.

5. Identify the various parts of a circle. Kids at this level should be able to identify *circumference, diameter, radius, arc,* and *chord.* They should draw circles of given radii or diameters, using a *compass,* and should calculate the circumference of a circle using the formula C = πd.

See *Sir Cumference and the First Round Table* (page 162).

HISTORY AND GEOGRAPHY

History and geography studies continue to build and expand upon previously covered topics. Both history and geography should be approached using a wide range of resources, including fiction and nonfiction books, biographies, multicultural folktales and legends, timelines, audiocassettes and videos, games, hands-on projects and activities, and field trips. The two disciplines should be closely correlated: When studying the history of early Japan or the nineteenth-century American West, for example, kids should study the corresponding geography.

Kids should be encouraged to see history as an ongoing pursuit of truth, continually subject to analysis and reinterpretation. They should analyze and interpret primary historical sources, such as letters, journal excerpts, and newspaper articles, and should approach historical events from a range of perspectives—viewing the Civil War, for example, from the varying points of view of southern plantation owners, southern small farmers, northern factory workers, "Yankee" and "Rebel" soldiers, and slaves.

See A History of US Series, page 163. Volumes that cover the American history topics listed below are *Liberty for All?*, *War, Terrible War*, and *Reconstruction and Reform*.

U.S. History Through Children's Literature
Wanda J. Miller; Teacher Ideas Press, 1997
An annotated list of fiction and nonfiction books for kids aged 8–14, categorized by American historical periods. Each book listing is accompanied by discussion questions and suggestions for projects and activities.

Also see USKids History Series, page 198, *Kids' America*, page 198, Social Studies School Service, page 197, Bluestocking Press, page 84, and *Cobblestone*, page 198.

1. Westward expansion. Topics to cover include Daniel Boone and the Wilderness Trail, the Lewis and Clark Expedition, the mountain men and the fur trade, Zebulon Pike and Pike's Peak, the building of the Erie Canal, traveling west with the pioneers, the Santa Fe and Oregon Trails, the Mormon settlement of Utah, the California gold rush of 1849, and nineteenth-century conflicts with the Indians.

The West: An Illustrated History for Children
Dayton Duncan; Little, Brown, 1996
The book covers the history of the American West from the days of the pre-Columbian native peoples to the early twentieth century. An interesting text and fascinating human interest stories, heavily illustrated with period photographs and prints.

2. The Mexican War. Topics to cover include the concept of Manifest Destiny, the American settlement of Texas, the Battle of the Alamo, Henry David Thoreau and civil disobedience, and the results of the Mexican War.

3. Prologue to the Civil War. Topics to cover include John C. Calhoun and states' rights, slave life and slave rebellions, the abolitionist movement, the drawing of the Mason-Dixon Line, the Missouri Compromise of 1820, the impact of the Dred Scott Decision, Harriet Beecher Stowe and *Uncle Tom's Cabin*, John Brown and Harper's Ferry, the Lincoln-Douglas debates, and southern secession.

4. The Civil War. Topics to cover include Fort Sumter, the establishment of the Confederacy, "Yankees" and "Rebels," the First Battle of Bull Run, the ironclad ships (the *Monitor* and the *Merrimack*), the Battle of Antietam, the Emancipation Proclamation, the Battle of Gettysburg and the Gettysburg Address, Sherman's march to the sea. Lee's surrender at Appomatox Courthouse, and Lincoln's assassination by John Wilkes Booth.

> THE CIVIL WAR
>
> A simulation of Civil War history for kids aged 10 and up. Participants move through the five years of the war, fighting all the battles (with maps and "Combat Cards") and keeping journals about their experiences. They also play Civil War games, listen to period music, compete in a Gettysburg Address contest, and reenact the surrender at Appomatox Courthouse. Interact; (800) 359-0961; www.interact-simulations.com.

Also see *The Civil War for Kids,* page 129.

5. Reconstruction. Topics to cover include the postwar devastation of the South, the Radical Republicans and the impeachment of Andrew Johnson, carpetbaggers and scalawags, the Thirteenth, Fourteenth, and Fifteenth Amendments, the Black Codes and the Ku Klux Klan, and the end of Reconstruction and the Compromise of 1877.

6. Continued westward expansion, Indian resistance, and the Indian Wars. Students might begin by reviewing previous studies of Indian life and culture in different regions of North America (see pages 164–165).

Topics to cover include Tecumseh, William Henry Harrison, and the Battle of Tippecanoe; Osceola and the Seminoles; the Homestead Act of 1862; the building of the transcontinental railroad; the extermination of the buffalo; the cowboy era and cattle drives; Wild West legends (Buffalo Bill, Annie Oakley, Billy the Kid); "Buffalo soldiers"; government policies toward Indians and the establishment of the Bureau of Indian Affairs; forced removal to reservations; the Battle of Little Bighorn; the Ghost Dance movement; the purchase of Alaska from Russia; and the significance of the closing frontier.

See *The West: An Illustrated History for Children,* page 229.

WORLD HISTORY

One good choice for fifth-grade world history is to explore in greater depth the period from prehistory to the fall of Rome, first introduced in the first grade (see pages 88–90).

Literature Connections to World History: K–6

Literature Connections to World History: 7–12
Lynda G. Adamson; Libraries Unlimited, 1998
> Two fat annotated collections categorized by historical period, world region, grade level, and author. Listings include historical fiction, nonfiction, biographies and collective biographies, CD-ROMs, and videos.

The Story of Mankind
Hendrik Willem Van Loon; Liveright, 1994
> This edition is an update of the original Newbery Award winner. The book covers the history of mankind from prehistory to modern times, in thorough but friendly fashion. An excellent resource.

Also see Social Studies School Service, page 197, Mr. Donn's Ancient History Page, page 132, *Calliope*, page 202, and *Cartoon History of the Universe*, page 331.

1. Prehistory to the beginning of civilization. Topics to cover include early hominids and the first human beings, Stone Age hunter-gatherer culture, the evolution of tools and weapons, prehistoric art, language, and religion, the domestication of animals, the agricultural revolution, and the establishment of settled communities. Kids should know the difference between an *anthropologist* and an *archaeologist*.

> BONES AND STONES
> A simulation of Stone Age life for kids in grades 4–8. Sample topics include "Survival," "Language," "Cave Art," and "Megaliths." The unit includes readings, activities, and discussion. Interact; (800) 359-0961; www.interact-simulations.com.

Early Humans
Nick Merriman; Alfred A. Knopf, 1989
> An Eyewitness book on human prehistory, illustrated with excellent color drawings and photographs.

2. The rise of cities and the first civilizations. Topics to cover include the geography and cultures of ancient Mesopotamia, notably the Sumerians, Babylonians, and Assyrians, the developing use of metals, the invention of *cuneiform* writing, and the significance of the Code of Hammurabi. Try reading a version of the world's oldest epic poem, the Mesopotamian "Epic of Gilgamesh."

Ancient Egyptians and Their Neighbors: An Activity Guide
Marian Broida; Chicago Review Press, 1999
  Historical background information, intriguing facts, maps, a detailed timeline, and many innovative projects centering around the ancient civilizations of the Mesopotamians, Nubians, Hittites, and Egyptians. For example, kids made a cylinder seal, and a model ziggurat and mud-brick house.

3. Ancient Egypt. Topics to cover include the geography and culture of ancient Egypt, an overview of ancient Egyptian history (from the beginning of civilization through the Old, Middle, and New Kingdoms), hieroglyphic writing, art and architecture, religion, science, and everyday life. Other possible topics include Egyptologists of the nineteenth and twentieth centuries and their discoveries, including the stories of Howard Carter and Tutankhamen's tomb and Champollion and the Rosetta stone.

Pharaohs of Ancient Egypt
Elizabeth Payne; Random House, 1998
  An interesting and well-written history of ancient Egypt in chapterbook form for young readers.

Pyramid
David Macauley; Houghton Mifflin, 1975
  A step-by-step description of the construction of a pyramid, from choosing the ground to the final closing of the tomb. Illustrated with wonderful detailed pen-and-ink drawings.

Pyramids of Ancient Egypt
John D. Clare; Harcourt Brace, 1992
  One of the Living History series in which a short historical text is illustrated with color photographs of reenactors. What things might have looked like if someone had visited the pharaoh's court with a camera.

The World in the Time of Tutankhamen
Fiona Macdonald; Dillon Press, 1997

What was happening all over the world when Tutankhamen was the ruler of Egypt?

4. Ancient Greece. Topics to cover include the rise of the Greek city-states and the origin of democratic government, the Persian Wars, Pericles and the Golden Age of Athens, the Peloponnesian Wars, Greek art and architecture, Greek science, everyday life in ancient Greece, the Olympic Games, the philosophy, life, and trial of Socrates, the philosophies of Plato and Aristotle, and the accomplishments of Alexander the Great.

Ancient Greek and Roman Resource Series

Golden Owl Publishing

Resource books for kids in grades 4–12 on the civilizations of ancient Greece and Rome. There are ten books in the series, each with lesson plans, worksheets, detailed background information, activity suggestions, and a bibliography. Included is the *Critical Bibliography for Teaching the Ancient World,* an annotated list of books, videos, CD-ROMs, and Internet sites, categorized by grade level. Jackdaw Publications, Box 503, Amawalk, NY 10501; (800) 789-0022; www.jackdaw.com.

GREEKS

A multidisciplinary simulation of life in ancient Greece in which kids debate fifth-century political and social issues, build model temples, write Greek-style plays, and more. Other simulations for this age group include *Romans* and *Egypt.* Interact; (800) 359-0961; www.interact-simulations.com.

5. Ancient Rome. Topics to cover include the Etruscans, the founding of Rome, the features of the Roman Republic, the structure of Roman society, the causes and events of the Punic Wars, the establishment of the Roman Empire, the Roman emperors, early Christianity in the Roman Empire, and the decline and fall of Rome. Kids should know the names and stories of famous Roman emperors and other well-known Romans, and be familiar with Roman myths and legends, art and architecture, and language and literature. They should also study the geography of the Roman Empire.

See Ancient Greek and Roman Resource Series and *Greeks*, page 233.

Ancient Rome: How It Affects You Today
Richard J. Maybury; Bluestocking Press, 1995
Roman political philosophy and the Roman model of government have had profound effects on the world ever since. A thought-provoking approach for kids aged 10 and up.

Augustus Caesar's World
Genevieve Foster; Beautiful Feet Books, 1998
A survey of world history at the time of Augustus Caesar. The book discusses both happenings in Rome and in other parts of the world in interesting story-style text. A good read-aloud. Beautiful Feet Books; (800) 889-1978; www.bfbooks.com.

6. Byzantium. Topics to cover include the establishment of the "eastern Roman empire;" centered in Constantinople; Constantine, the first Christian emperor; and Justinian's landmark Code of Law. Kids should also be familiar with the geography of the Byzantine Empire and with Byzantine art, architecture, and culture.

THE BYZANTINE EMPIRE
A portfolio of historical background essays and reproductions of primary-source materials, including a photograph of the Hagia Sophia, stories of famous persons of Byzantium, illustrations of mosaics and icons, and accounts of Byzantine civil law, home life, science, technology, and medicine. Jackdaw Publications; (800) 789-0022; www.jackdaw.com.

GEOGRAPHY

See geography resources, pages 204–206, and *Discovering Geography of North America With Books Kids Love* and *Discovering World Geography With Books Kids Love*, page 172.

1. Review and reinforce concepts covered in previous geographical studies. Fifth-graders should be familiar with a range of different kinds of maps and should be able to read maps and globes using coordinates of latitude and longitude. They should be able to locate and describe the major climatic zones (arctic, tropic, and temperate), should understand the concept of time zones, and should be able to locate the prime meridian in Greenwich, England (0 degrees longitude), and the international date line (180 degrees longitude).

2. Survey the great lakes of the world. Kids should be able to locate, for example, Asia's Caspian and Aral Seas, Africa's Lake Victoria, the Great Lakes of North America, and South America's Lake Maracaibo and Lake Titicaca.

3. Geography studies should be closely linked to history topics. In conjunction with American history studies, kids should cover corresponding American geography, for example, tracing the course of the Erie Canal, the path of the transcontinental railroad, and the Santa Fe and Oregon Trails; locating the Mason-Dixon Line; and identifying the site of major Civil War battles and events.

Kids should also know the characteristics of the major regions of the United States: New England, Mid-Atlantic, South, Midwest, Great Plains, Southwest, far West, and Pacific Northwest. They should know what the Gulf Stream is and be able to describe its effects on climate. They should also, according to most curricula, know the names and capitals of all fifty states (see pages 205–206). Similarly, geography should be linked to world history studies.

SCIENCE

Kids should approach science investigations by way of the *scientific method*—the ordered process of hypothesis, experiment, and analytical reassessment by which scientists answer questions and solve problems. Studies should be enhanced and supplemented with a range of varied resources, including fiction and nonfiction books, biographies of famous scientists, activity books, and field trips.

PHYSICAL SCIENCE

1. Review and expand upon studies of atomic structure. Topics to cover include the structure of the atom, types of subatomic particles, the concept of electron shells and energy levels, and molecules and compounds.

Kids should be able to describe current theories of atomic structure and name the three basic subatomic particles. They should know that *protons* are positively charged; *electrons*, negatively charged; and *neutrons*, neutral. They should understand the concept of electron orbital shells or energy levels, and should understand how individual atoms bond to form molecules and compounds.

Kids should also know the composition of some common compounds, such as water, table salt, and sugar.

Chemically Active!
Vicki Cobb; J. B. Lippincott,1985
An excellent introduction to chemistry for kids aged 10–13, covering solutions, distillation, crystallization, chemical reactions, electrolysis, oxidation, electrolytes, atomic structure and the periodic table, and analytical chemistry. Clear explanations and many better-than-average experiments. That said, the book, infuriatingly, is out of print. Look for it at the library.

Also see GEMS Chemistry Handbooks, page 208. Quia! at www.quia.com includes a number of on-line quizzes, exercises, and activities for chemistry students.

2. Survey the elements of the periodic table. Topics to cover include the definition of *element*, the organization and use of the periodic table of elements, the definitions of *atomic symbol, number,* and *weight,* and the characteristics of metals and nonmetals.

Kids should know that elements consist of only a single kind of atom and that the atoms of a given element are identified by their characteristic number of protons (the atomic number). They should review the organization of the periodic table of elements and learn the atomic symbols for representative common elements, such as oxygen (O), iron (Fe), gold (Au), copper (Cu), and so on. They should know that about two-thirds of the known elements are *metals,* which are characterized by electrical and thermal conductivity, malleability, ductility, and a shiny appearance. They should also know that some metals, such as bronze and brass, are *alloys:* combinations of two or more elemental metals.

CHEM4KIDS

The fundamentals of matter, atoms, elements, and chemical reactions with a kid-friendly text and colorful graphics. The site also includes biographies of famous chemists, games, and quizzes. www.chem4kids.com.

CHEMICOOL PERIODIC TABLE

Click on the image of an element on a big, colorful periodic table to access detailed information about each. wild-turkey.mit.edu/Chemicool.

PROTON DON

A game of chemical symbol identification played on the periodic table. Several levels of difficulty. www.funbrain.com.

3. Chemical and physical properties of matter. Topics to cover include the definitions and examples of physical and chemical changes, the ways in which chemists use chemical and physical properties to explore the composition of matter, and an overview of new compounds generated by chemical research (plastics, Teflon, Kevlar).

Kids should understand that physical changes alter only the physical properties or appearance of a substance. Examples include cutting a substance into smaller pieces or changing its state or phase, as in the freezing of water. Chemical changes, on the other hand, produce completely new substances. Examples include the rusting of iron and the burning of wood.

4. Review and reinforce studies of force and motion (see page 135). Topics to cover include potential and kinetic energy, Newton's laws of motion, and concepts of distance, rate, speed, acceleration, and gravity.

Kids should experiment with force and motion using simple apparatus such as balls and small toy cars, and should be able to define *potential energy, kinetic energy, force, velocity,* and *inertia.* They should be familiar with distance/rate/time interrelationships, and should be able, for example, to calculate the time it would take to travel a given distance at a given speed. They should be able to define *acceleration* and should understand the concept of acceleration of falling objects due to the force of gravity. To enhance these studies, kids should experiment with a variety of falling objects of varying masses, demonstrating, for example, the effect of air resistance on rate of fall. A historical accompaniment to the study of acceleration might be a biography of Galileo, including an account of his landmark experiments with falling bodies.

How Things Work: 100 Ways Parents and Kids Can Share the Secrets of Technology
Neil Ardley; Reader's Digest, 1995
> An excellent collection of projects, activities, experiments, and interesting information for kids aged 8–14, illustrated with diagrams, drawings, and color photographs.

MOTION MACHINES
> Creative hands-on study units in which kids learn substantive science using clever homemade equipment. The Motion module includes thirty-six detailed lessons; the Machines module, sixteen. TOPS Learning Systems; (888) 773-9755; www.topscience.org.

Also see the Galileo History of Science Kit, page 170.

LIFE SCIENCE

1. Enlarge and expand upon earlier studies of plant and animal classification. Topics to cover include the definition of *taxonomy*, an overview of the five kingdoms of living things (plants, animals, fungi, protists, and monerans), taxonomical subdivisions (kingdom, phylum, class, order, family, genus, and species), scientific names, and a review of the major classes of vertebrates and their characteristics: fish, amphibians, reptiles, birds, and mammals.

A supplement to this topic might be a biography of Carolus Linnaeus, the eighteenth-century scientist known as the "Father of Taxonomy."

Amazing Mammals

Birds, Birds, Birds

Incredible Insects

Let's Hear It for Herps!
National Wildlife Federation; McGraw-Hill, 1997

The Naturescope Series includes several books on various classes of vertebrates, each featuring detailed scientific information, illustrations, charts, and diagrams, and many experiments and multidisciplinary activities. For kids in grades K–8.

Also see Animal Classifications, page 175.

2. Enlarge and expand upon earlier introduction to cell biology. Topics to cover include cell theory; comparison of plant, animal, and bacterial cells; major cellular organelles and their functions; and the organization of cells into tissues, organs, and systems. See *Cells Are Us*, page 138, and Microexplorers Series, page 292.

3. Enlarge and expand upon studies of botany. Topics to cover include comparisons of vascular and nonvascular plants; the process of photosynthesis; vegetative and sexual reproduction; the anatomy of flowers; and seed and fruit production.

Kids should be able to describe the characteristics of nonvascular plants (such as algae) and vascular plants, which use *xylem* and *phloem* to transport water and nutrients. They should know the principles of the process of photosynthesis, including the functions of *chloroplasts* and *chlorophyll*. They should be able to describe and cite examples of vegetative reproduction in plants and should experiment with a range of examples: for example, sprouting potato eyes, ivy leaves, or carrot tops.

They should be able to compare and contrast reproduction in spore-bearing plants (such as ferns), nonflowering vascular plants (conifers), and flowering vascular plants. They should understand the functions of *sepals, petals, stamens, anthers, pistils, ovaries* and the various modes of *pollination*. Kids might collect and classify evergreen cones, dissect flowers, examine samples of pollen under a microscope or magnifying glass, and germinate and cultivate seeds.

Trees Are Terrific
National Wildlife Federation; McGraw-Hill, 1997

A volume in the Naturescope Series containing interesting information on all aspects of trees, illustrations and diagrams, and many multidisciplinary activities and projects for kids in grades K–8. Excellent.

A wealth of informational resources, including—under "Education"—instructions for hands-on experiments, lesson plans, games, and activities for kids of all ages; Web site: botany.about. com.

4. Reproduction in plants and animals. Topics to cover include asexual reproduction (including bacterial fission, sporulation, budding, and cloning) and sexual reproduction in plants (see above) and animals.

Kids should be able to define *gamete, testis,* and *ovary,* and should understand the process of fertilization and the developmental sequence from zygote to embryo to fetus to newborn.

5. Continue studies of human anatomy and physiology. Human anatomy and physiology studies can be used as a springboard to prepare kids in this age group for the onset of adolescence. Parents/teachers might want to use this opportunity to discuss bodily changes accompanying puberty: growth spurts, hair growth, voice changes, breast development, menstruation. (Or then again, depending on the needs and responses of their kids, they might not.)

Topics to cover include duct and ductless glands; the definition of *hormone* and examples; the pituitary, adrenal, and thyroid glands and their functions; the pancreas; and the male and female reproductive systems.

It's So Amazing: A Book about Eggs, Sperm, Birth, Babies, and Families
Robie H. Harris; Candlewick, 1999
Male and female anatomy inside and out, eggs and sperm, sex, gestation and childbirth, chromosomes and genes, warnings about sexual abuse, and information on HIV and AIDS. Clear, comfortable explanations (with the help of a large green bird and a big bee in sneakers) and helpful color illustrations.

Also see *How the Body Works,* page 176.

EARTH/SPACE SCIENCE

1. Review and reinforce geological studies covered in previous grades. Topics to cover might include the definition of *mineral* and the basic characteristics of minerals, the six crystal systems, the characteristics and sources of metamorphic, sedimentary, and igneous rock and common examples of each, the varied processes of erosion, volcanoes and earthquakes, and rocks from space (asteroids, meteorites, and impact craters). Take geological field trips. Collect rocks.

Discover Nature in the Rocks
Rebecca Lawton, Diana Lawton, and Susan Panttaja; Stackpole Books, 1997

Illustrated chapters cover minerals and rocks, volcanoes, sedimentation, fossils, erosion, continental drift and tectonic plate theory, earthquakes, and planetary geology, with many excellent projects and activities. The book includes patterns for making cardboard models of the six crystal systems.

Also see *Geology: The Active Earth, Geology Rocks!,* and *How the Earth Works,* page 209.

2. Study oceanography. Topics to cover include the topography of the ocean floor; currents, waves, and tides; properties of salt- and freshwater; marine ecosystems; the influence of the ocean on weather; and water pollution and other threats to life in the oceans.

Kids should understand the terms *continental shelf, slope,* and *rise; abyssal plain;* and *mid-ocean ridge* and *trench.* They should understand the causes (and effects) of the Gulf Stream; the reasons for daily high and low tides; the causes and characteristics of waves; and the definition of *tsunami.* They should also be familiar with oceanic life zones and their inhabitants, including the *pelagic* and *benthic* zones, and should understand the essential role plankton plays in marine ecosystems.

Diving into Oceans
National Wildlife Federation; McGraw-Hill, 1997

A Naturescope activity book on the ocean and marine life, including detailed scientific information, illustrations, charts, and diagrams, and many experiments and multidisciplinary projects for kids in grades K–8. Explore everything from the chemistry of saltwater to the biology of the giant squid.

Whales in the Classroom Series: Volume I, Oceanography
Larry Wade; Singing Rock Press

An illustrated information-and-activity book on ocean science, covering marine ecosystems and ecology, currents and tides, methods of conducting oceanographic studies, and interviews with marine biologists and oceanographers. Singing Rock Press, Box 1274, Minnetonka, MN 55345; (612) 935-4910; www. whalebooks.com.

Oceans
Diane M. Tyler and James C. Tyler; Running Press, 1990
A fact-filled informational coloring book for kids aged 9–12. A kid-friendly text, interesting fact boxes, and to-be-colored black-line drawings cover all aspects of oceanography.

Good supplements to this topic might include biographies of Rachel Carson and Jacques Cousteau.

FOREIGN LANGUAGE

Kids should display skills appropriate to their grade level in speaking, comprehension of spoken and written material, and grammar and vocabulary concepts.

See resources, page 47.

ART

A good art program should incorporate many aspects of art: hands-on activities and explorations, art theory, art appreciation, and art history. Kids should experiment with a wide range of art techniques and media. They should learn about art through varied print sources, including fiction and nonfiction books and biographies of well-known artists, and, if possible, should participate in field trips to artists' studios, galleries, exhibits, and museums.

See 1–8 Art Curriculum, page 101, *Lives of the Artists*, The Louvre, and With Open Eyes, page 211, *The Annotated Mona Lisa* and *Great Painters*, page 269, and *How to Use Child-Size Masterpieces for Art Appreciation*, page 48.

1. Use previously acquired knowledge of art elements and principles of design to analyze the artwork of others and to produce a

wide range of creative artworks. For example, kids should experiment with drawing, painting, printmaking, pottery and ceramics, sculpture, fiber arts, and electronic media.

See *Drawing With Children* (page 103).

2. Study art in conjunction with other academic subjects across the curriculum. History and geography studies, for example, should include overviews of the art of the featured historical period or geographical region.

In conjunction with ancient history studies, for example, kids might learn about Egyptian painting and sculpture, Greek and Roman art and architecture, and Roman mosaics.

MUSIC

A music program should encompass vocal and instrumental experimentation and performance, music theory, music appreciation, and music history. Kids should listen to a range of pieces by famous composers and to multicultural music selections. They should study music through varied print materials, including fiction and nonfiction books, songbooks, and biographies of famous musicians and composers, and should, if possible, attend varied musical performances.

Multimedia History of Music

Multimedia Musical Instruments

Interactive musical experiences on CD-ROM (Windows). In *History of Music,* kids can explore a musical timeline, read about the lives, works, and times of famous composers, and listen to music from each historical era. In *Musical Instruments,* kids can discover the history of the instruments of the orchestra, survey instruments from a range of other cultures, learn the parts of each instrument, hear musical selections, and view video clips of playing techniques. Voyetra Turtle Beach; (800) 233-9377; www.voyetra.com.

1. Reinforce and expand upon the musical concepts covered in earlier grades. Kids should be familiar with the terms *accelerando, ritardando, crescendo, decrescendo, legato,* and *staccato.* They should understand basic musical notation, including the notes of the treble clef, the significance of sharps and flats, and the meaning of meter signature (2/4, 3/4, 4/4, and 6/8).

See Music Ace, page 213, Music Ace 2, page 270, and Making Music, page 182.

2. Describe musical compositions in terms of melody, harmony, dynamics, rhythm, timbre, and texture. Kids should also be able to identify major and minor tonalities and identify themes, variations, and repeating structures.

3. Identify the major orchestral families and their individual instruments by sight and sound. Kids should continue to expand upon their knowledge of musical instruments to encompass ethnic, folk, acoustic, electronic, and historical instruments.

4. Listen and respond to a range of pieces by well-known composers and to folk and ethnic musical selections. Kids should be able to associate musical selections with the appropriate composer and associate musical compositions with their appropriate historical period or ethnic group/world region.

See Classical Kids, page 183.

5. Participate in instrumental and vocal performances, group and solo. Kids should be able to sing or play simple melodies while reading a musical score.

HEALTH AND PHYSICAL EDUCATION

1. Participate in a range of age-appropriate indoor and outdoor athletic activities designed to provide a well-rounded program of physical fitness. Kids should understand the health benefits of regular exercise; and know how various forms of exercise correlate to cardiovascular health, muscular strength and endurance, and flexibility.

See Fit Kids! and Home School Family Fitness, page 50.

2. Participate in a program of drug education.

3. Understand the distinction between communicable and noncommunicable diseases. Kids at this grade level should have a basic understanding of how the immune system works and know basic methods for preventing the spread of communicable (contagious) diseases.

Cell Wars
Fran Balkwill and Mic Rolph; First Avenue Editions, 1994
> An excellent explanation of the immune system and its components, the process of vaccination, and blood clotting, with clever illustrations and a kid-friendly text.

Also see *Your Body's Heroes and Villains* in the Microexplorers Series, page 292.

4. Be familiar with the elements of good nutrition and personal hygiene. Kids should be able to design a good dietary program based on the food pyramid and USDA dietary guidelines. They should know the functions and sources of the six major nutrients (carbohydrates, proteins, fats, vitamins, minerals, and water), and should understand the health problems associated with dietary deficiencies.
See *The Healthy Body Cookbook* and *Janice Van Cleave's Food and Nutrition for Every Kid,* page 214.

5. Know basic first-aid procedures for common injuries. Kids should be familiar with proper procedures for choking, bleeding, shock, poisoning, and minor burns.
See *Kids to the Rescue!,* page 184.

GRADE SIX

It is no matter what you teach them first, any more than
what leg you shall put into your breeches first.

SAMUEL JOHNSON

LANGUAGE ARTS

LITERATURE

CYBERGUIDES
Excellent multidisciplinary lesson plans for many well-known
books, categorized by grade level. Lesson plans appropriate for
sixth grade cover Elizabeth Janet Gray's *Adam of the Road,* Karen
Cushman's *Catherine, Called Birdy* Natalie Babbitt's *Tuck Everlasting,* and Gary Paulsen's *Hatchet.* Web site: www.sdcoe.k12.ca.
us/score/cyberguide.html.

JUNIOR GREAT BOOKS PROGRAM
Selections for kids in grade 6 include Paula Fox's "A Likely Place,"
Isaac Bashevis Singer's "The Mysteries of the Cabala," Jean
Stafford's "Bad Characters," Ray Bradbury's "The Veldt," and

William Saroyan's "The Parsley Garden." Each selection is accompanied by a list of discussion questions and writing suggestions, designed to promote critical thinking and analytical discussion. Great Books Foundation, 35 E. Wacker Dr., Suite 2300, Chicago, IL 60601-2298; (800) 222-5870; www.greatbooks.org.

LEARNING LANGUAGE ARTS THROUGH LITERATURE

The Tan Book, for sixth-graders, teaches grammar, spelling, thinking, and study skills through well-known books, among them Jean Latham's *Carry On, Mr. Bowditch,* Elizabeth George Speare's *The Bronze Bow,* and C. S. Lewis's *The Horse and His Boy.* Christian orientation, but generally adaptable for a secular audience. Common Sense Press; (352) 475-5757; cspress.com.

Also see Learning Links, page 60, Novel Units, page 60, the Shakespeare Catalog, page 217, and The Writing Company, page 218.

1. Read a wide range of age-appropriate fiction and nonfiction materials. Kids should read a mix of classic and contemporary literature, novels and short stories, myths and legends, fables and folktales, poems, plays, essays, magazine articles, and newspapers. Literary experiences should be enhanced with a range of supplementary resources, including biographies of writers, audio and video performances, and hands-on and cross-curricular activities.

Read All About It!: Great Read-Aloud Stories, Poems, and Newspaper Pieces for Preteens and Teens
Jim Trelease; Penguin, 1993
> Just because the kids are getting older doesn't mean you have to stop reading aloud to them. Suggestions from the author of the acclaimed *Read-Aloud Handbook* include selections by Harper Lee, Langston Hughes, Ellery Queen, Rudyard Kipling, Howard Pyle, Frederick Douglass, Mike Royko, Maya Angelou, Ray Bradbury, and many more.

READING SUGGESTIONS FOR SIXTH-GRADERS INCLUDE:

The Borrowers (Mary Norton; Harcourt Brace, 1998)
The Children of Green Knowe (L. M. Boston; Harcourt Brace, 1989)
The Chronicles of Prydain Series (Lloyd Alexander; Bantam Books, 1999)
The Dark Is Rising Series (Susan Cooper; Aladdin, 1999)

The Giver (Lois Lowry; Laurel Leaf, 1994)

Harry Potter and the Sorceror's Stone (J. K. Rowling; Arthur A. Levine, 1999)

Hitty: Her First Hundred Years (Rachel Field; Bantam Books, 1998)

Holes (Louis Sachar; Farrar, Straus & Giroux, 1998)

Matilda (Roald Dahl; Puffin, 1998)

The Prince and the Pauper (Mark Twain; Puffin, 1998)

The Westing Game (Ellen Raskin; Puffin, 1997)

The White Mountains (John Christopher; Aladdin, 1998)

The Witch of Blackbird Pond (Elizabeth George Speare; Laurel Leaf, 1978)

See Book Lists, pages 400–402.

2. Evaluate works of literature through discussion, debate, and written critique. Kids should be familiar with such literary elements and techniques as *plot, setting, theme, characters, conflict, figurative language,* and *point of view.*

3. Expand upon knowledge of the classics. Suggestions for kids at this grade level include Shakespeare's *Julius Caesar* and Homer's *The Iliad* and *The Odyssey.*

Black Ships Before Troy
Rosemary Sutcliff; Delacorte Press, 1993
The story of the Trojan War in exciting prose, for middle school–aged readers.

The Odyssey
A superb four-hour retelling on audiocassettes or CDs to an accompaniment of harp and twelve-string guitar. Narrated by storyteller Odds Bodkin, but it might be Homer himself. Rivertree Productions, Box 410, Bradford, NH 03221; (800) 554-1333; www.oddsbodkin.com.

Shakespeare Stories
Leon Garfield; Houghton Mifflin, 1991
An excellent introduction to Shakespeare for beginners aged 9–12. The book is a collection of prose retellings of twelve Shakespearean plays with dramatic description and enough of the original dialogue to give readers a feel for Shakespearean language.

Also see the Shakespeare Catalog, resources, page 217.

4. Read a varied range of poetic forms. Kids should be familiar with *imagery, simile, metaphor, onomatopoeia,* and *personification.* They should be able to analyze rhyme and rhythm schemes, define *meter* and *iamb,* and understand the meaning of *free verse.*

It Figures! Fun Figures of Speech
Marvin Terban; Clarion Books, 1993
A clever illustrated explanation of six common figures of speech: simile, metaphor, onomatopoeia, alliteration, hyperbole, and personification. The book includes definitions and great (and lousy) examples of each, plus writing exercises.

5. Understand and follow written multiple-step directions.

WRITING

1. Write frequently, producing a variety of works, including reports, essays, short stories, poems, narratives, journal entries, and letters. Kids should be familiar with a multistep writing process, involving prewriting, drafting, revising, editing, proofreading, and publishing a finished piece.

At this grade level, kids should learn the techniques of writing an effective multiparagraph essay: defining a main purpose or thesis, supporting the thesis with evidence and examples, distinguishing unsubstantiated opinion from proven fact, using relevant quotes from attributed sources, and providing a bibliography.

They should be able to tailor their writings to a chosen audience or purpose: personal, academic, or business, for example.

Princeton Review Writing Smart Junior
C. L. Brantley and Cynthia Johnson; Random House, 1995
The art and craft of writing for kids in grades 6–8. The book includes general information, many helpful hints, and writing exercises.

Also see The Writing Company, page 218.

2. Recognize and use correct sentence structure. Kids should know the four major types of sentences (declarative, interrogative, imperative, and exclamatory), should recognize and identify *simple, compound, complex,* and *compound-complex* sentences, and should be able to use all effectively in written work.

They should be able to identify and correct incomplete and run-on sentences, and should recognize and identify the principal parts of sentences: *subject, predicate, object,* and *modifiers.*

3. Use punctuation marks correctly. Reinforce and expand upon knowledge acquired in earlier grades. At this grade level, kids should be familiar with the uses of the *colon* and *semicolon.*

4. Recognize and identify common parts of speech, including nouns, pronouns, verbs, adjectives (and articles), adverbs, conjunctions, and interjections. Kids should be able to distinguish between verbs in the *active* and *passive* voice. They should understand *subject-verb agreement, pronoun-antecedent agreement* ("Give it to me" versus "Give it to I"), and the correct use of adjectives and adverbs.

For numbers 2–4, see:

Princeton Review Grammar Smart Junior
Liz Buffa; Random House, 1995
   "Good Grammar Made Easy" for kids in grades 6–8. Comprehensive information, examples, and exercises.

Also see grammar resources, pages 219–220.

5. Expand upon previous spelling and vocabulary skills. By this grade level, most kids should be reasonably competent spellers. Spelling exercises should concentrate on reinforcing common spelling rules and on correcting commonly misspelled words.

Kids should be aware of the proper usage of such common bugbears as *good* and *well, between* and *among, bring* and *take, accept* and *except, affect* and *effect, who* and *whom, capital* and *capitol, principle* and *principal,* and *like* and *as.*

WORDOPOLY
A fun and challenging vocabulary-building board game in which players compete to define words; complete clichés, aphorisms, and quotations; and identify abbreviations and foreign words. Included are over 700 words, selected from educational word lists and standardized tests. Word Wizard Corporation, Box 4000, Santa Cruz, CA 95063; www.wordopoly.com.

SPELLING AND VOCABULARY PLANS
A long list of spelling and vocabulary games and activities for kids in grades 5–6; Web site: www.knownet.net/users/Ackley/spell_plans.html.

Also see Spelling Programs, page 64, and Bethump'd with Words, page 324.

6. Know the meanings of foreign words commonly used in English and the meaning of Greek and Latin words that form common English word roots. Examples of the former include *fiesta* and *nom de plume;* examples of the latter include *bios* (life) as in *biology; phone* (sound) as in *telephone; post* (after) as in *posthumous;* and *pre* (before) as in *prepare* and *predict.*

7. Write business letters in correct format.

Listening and Speaking Skills

1. Listen to and make narrative and informational oral presentations. Kids should be able to make oral presentations in an organized and well-delivered fashion, tailored to suit the audience and situation. They should be able to understand, summarize, and ask pertinent questions based on oral presentations by others. By this grade level, kids should also be able to take notes from orally presented information.

They should also be able to analyze and critique oral presentations, speeches, and media messages for bias, persuasion, propaganda, fallacies, opinion presented as fact, and unsupported generalities.

2. Follow multiple-step oral directions.

3. Memorize and recite poems. Our oldest son by this age had amassed an impressive repertoire of memorized poems, among them Edgar Allan Poe's "The Raven," Lewis Carroll's "Jabberwocky," and big chunks of Samuel Taylor Coleridge's "The Rime of the Ancient Mariner." Our third son, at this age, learned Alfred Noyes's "The Highwayman," because he liked *Anne of Green Gables* and Anne, at some point in L. M. Montgomery's series, memorized "The Highwayman." Our second son by this age had given up poetry in favor of computer manuals. Conventional dogma holds that memorization of poetry enhances one's facility with language; it also broadens the mind, touches the heart, and provides near-endless amusement for those times when one is trapped in traffic jams. But then lots of other things do too. See how it goes.

Study Skills

1. Know how to obtain information from common print and electronic reference sources. Kids should be able to use dictionaries, thesauri, atlases, almanacs, periodicals, encyclopedias, and electronic multimedia technologies (databases and search engines).

Casting Your Net: A Student's Guide to Research on the Internet
H. Eric Branscomb; Allyn & Bacon, 1997
> All about the Internet and the World Wide Web and how best to use them, as well as explanations of Boolean logic, a survey of search engines, and more.

Also see Study Guides and Strategies and *The Kids' Guide to Research*, pages 220–221.

2. Be able to take effective notes and develop outlines from written selections.

3. Practice effective study techniques.

Test Smart!
Gary W. Abbamont and Antoinette Brescher; Prentice Hall, 1997
> Exercises, worksheets, and lessons on test-taking techniques for kids in grades 5–12.

See Study Guides and Strategies, page 221, and test preparation resources, pages 153–154, 190.

MATHEMATICS

<small>Sample grade-appropriate resources include:</small>

Connected Mathematics Project Series
> An investigative approach to mathematics. The curriculum is divided into several units each year, covering number theory and operations,

algebra, geometry and measurement, and probability and statistics. Sixth-grade units include "Data About Us," in which kids statistically document an "average" sixth-grader, and "Ruins of Montarek," in which they learn to create 2-D representations of 3-D objects. Prentice-Hall, Inc.; (800) 848-9500; www.phschool.com.

Everyday Mathematics Series

A highly recommended activity-based series for grades K–6. The sixth-grade program includes a teacher's guide, student books and journals, and a kit of manipulatives. Kids cover math through exercises, games, and projects, including the "Solar System Project" (a multilesson study of scientific notation), the "Paper Airplane Project," and "Perspective Drawing." Everyday Learning Corporation, 2 Prudential Plaza, Suite 2200, Chicago, IL 60601; (800) 382-7670; www.everydaylearning.com.

Exploring Math With Books Kids Love
Kathryn Kaczmarski; Fulcrum Publishing, 1998

Kids explore number theory, algebra, statistics, geometry, and measurement through favorite books, among them *The Phantom Tollbooth, The Westing Game, Tuck Everlasting,* and *Around the World in Eighty Days.* Challenging math projects, clear explanations, and supplementary reading lists.

Math 76
Stephen Hake and John Saxon; Saxon Publishers, 1992

A comprehensive text for sixth-graders. New concepts include exponents, square roots, geometric formulas, and mathematical operations with signed numbers. Saxon Publishers, Inc., 2450 John Saxon Blvd., Norman, OK 73071; (800) 284 7019; www.saxonpub.com.

Mathematics: A Human Endeavor
Harold R. Jacobs; W. H. Freeman & Company, 1994

A creative and mind-stretching approach to mathematics for kids aged 12 and up. The book is a wholly fascinating exploration of the real world of mathematics. Through intriguing examples and illustrations, Jacobs covers everything from number sequences to functions, logarithms, mathematical curves, statistics, and topology. A good bet for kids bored by rote exercise.

The Number Devil
Hans Magnus Enzenberger; Metropolitan Books, 1997

A delightful mathematical novel in which twelve-year-old Robert meets the Number Devil, a little bright-red man the size of a grasshopper. The Devil, in slightly muddled language, introduces Robert to infinity, prime numbers, repeating fractions, square roots, triangular numbers, Fibonacci numbers, factorials, topology, and much more. Includes a very useful index.

SRA Math: Explorations and Applications Series

Stephen S. Willoughby; SRA/McGraw-Hill
A creative and multifaceted math program for kids in grades K–6. The sixth-grade book and materials emphasize problem-solving and mathematical thinking. The program includes all the basics, plus hands-on activities and games, cooperative learning projects, math journaling, "thinking stories," and cross-curricular connections. SRA/McGraw-Hill; (888) SRA-4543; www.sra4kids.com.

SUPPLEMENTS

GRAPHING CALCULATOR GUIDE
On-line lessons and activities with graphing calculators for grades 7–12. Web site: cesme.utm.edu/math/grcalc/toc.html.

TI-73/TI-82
Calculators with accompanying Graph Explorer Software and computer link capabilities, recommended for middle school students. There are also many informational activity books available to support calculator activities. Texas Instruments, Box 650311, MS 3962, Dallas, TX 75265; (800) TI-CARES; www.ti.com.

Also see The Math Forum, page 223, *Family Math: The Middle School Years*, page 279, and Mathematics at about.com, page 328.

NUMBER THEORY

1. Read and write numbers through the trillions in both numerals and words.

2. Reinforce concepts of place value; recognize place value through the billions.

3. Round numbers to the nearest ten, hundred, thousand, ten thousand, hundred thousand, and million.

4. Reinforce concept of exponents introduced in previous grade. Kids should know the perfect squares and square roots through 144; understand the terms *squared, cubed,* and *to the nth power;* and be familiar with powers of 10.

See *Powers of Ten,* page 223.

5. Determine whether a given number is prime or composite.

6. Determine the greatest common factor (GCF) and least common multiple (LCM) of given numbers.

7. Explore a variety of alternative number systems, including ancient systems and alternate bases.

Can You Count in Greek?

Judy Leimbach and Kathy Leimbach; Dandy Lion Publications

> A workbook introduction to ancient number systems, including those of the Egyptians, Romans, Greeks, Babylonians, Hindus, and Maya, as well as quinary and binary systems. Dandy Lion Publications; (800) 776-8032; www.dandylionbooks.com.

How to Count Like a Martian

Glory St. John; Henry Z. Walck, Inc., 1975

> A history of counting systems from ancient times to the present, including the numerical systems of the ancient Egyptians, Babylonians, and Maya, and an explanation of how a computer counts in base 2 or binary.

Also see *Fractals, Googols and Other Mathematical Tales,* page 222, which includes an account of counting in base 12 with the 12-fingered inhabitants of planet Dodeka.

RATIO AND PERCENT

Key to Percent Series

> The three-workbook series covers percent concepts, percents and fractions, and percents and decimals. Key Curriculum Press; (800) 995-MATH; www.keypress.com.

1. Determine and express simple ratios. Kids should be able to use ratios and proportions to interpret map scales and scale drawings and to create accurate scale drawings of their own.

2. Solve problems involving ratios. For example, kids should be able to use ratios to determine the lengths of the sides of similar triangles.

3. Define and model percents. Kids should recognize the percent sign (%) and know that percent means "per hundred." Use grids or manipulatives to demonstrate percents.

4. Translate among fractions, decimals, and percents. Kids should be able to determine, for example, that $\frac{1}{10} = 0.1 = 10\%$, and should know that $\frac{1}{4} = 25\%$; $\frac{1}{2} = 50\%$; and $\frac{3}{4} = 75\%$.

5. Solve problems using percents. For example, kids should be able to determine percents of a given number, as in "What is 5% of 60?"

Fractions and Decimals

See Key to Fractions Series and Key to Decimals Series, pages 193–194.

1. Identify the reciprocal of a given fraction. Kids should also know that the product of a fraction and its reciprocal is 1.

2. Add, subtract, multiply, and divide fractions and mixed numbers with like and unlike denominators.

3. Compare and order fractions and decimals on a number line.

4. Add, subtract, multiply, and divide decimals. Kids should be able to add and subtract multidigit decimals and to multiply and divide decimals by 10, 100, and 1,000; by whole numbers; and by other decimals. They should know how to move the decimal point when multiplying or dividing by 10s.

Operations

1. Define and understand the commutative and associative properties of addition and the commutative, associative, and distributive properties of multiplication.

2. Add, subtract, multiply, and divide multidigit numbers with and without a calculator. Know methods for checking answers; be able to estimate answers.

3. Solve word problems with multiple steps and mathematical problems with more than one operation according to order of operations. For word problems for kids in grades K–8, see Math Stories at www.mathstories.com.

Measurement

See Key to Measurement Series and Key to Metric Measurement Series, page 195.

1. Compare and convert units of measurement within the English and metric measurement systems. Within systems, kids should be able to compare and convert measures of length, area, volume, capacity, and weight/mass. They should, for example, be able to convert square feet to square inches, liters to milliliters, and ounces to pounds.

2. Define *precision* and *accuracy* in measurement. *Accuracy* indicates how close a measurement is to its true value; *precision* refers to the reproducibility of the measured value (that is, if you take the measurement three times, how closely will the results agree?).

Probability and Statistics

1. Collect, organize, and interpret data using graphs, charts, plots, and tables. Kids should create their own graphic representations of data and should solve problems that require the interpretation of graphs and tables. They should experiment with the use of computer spreadsheets or calculators with graphing capabilities to display and categorize data.

See Exploring Data, page 33, and TI-73, TI-83, and Graphing Calculator Guide, page 254.

2. Determine range and measures of central tendency of a given set of numbers. Kids should be able to calculate *mean, median,* and *mode* and should know the appropriate use of each.

Statistics: Middles, Means, and In-Betweens
S. N. Friel, J. R. Mokros, and S. J. Russell; Dale Seymour Publications
This volume of the Used Numbers series, for kids in grades 5–6, covers mean, median, and mode through independent hands-on projects in data analysis. ETA/Cuisenaire; (800) 445-5985; www.etauniverse.com or www.cuisenaire.com.

3. Understand statistical sampling. Kids should understand the use of samples for making predictions and mathematical inferences.

Statistics: Prediction and Sampling
Rebecca B. Corwin and Susan N. Friel; Dale Seymour Publications
A volume of the Used Numbers series, covering sampling and its uses through hands-on projects and explorations. ETA/Cuisenaire; (800) 445-5985; www.etauniverse.com or www.cuisenaire.com.

4. Plot points on a coordinate grid using ordered pairs of positive and negative whole numbers. Kids should be familiar with the four quadrants of a coordinate grid and be able to locate the *origin*, *x-axis*, and *y-axis*.

5. Conduct simple probability experiments and express the results in decimals and percents.

GEOMETRY

See Key to Geometry Series, page 196.

1. Recognize, measure, and construct angles. Kids should be able to measure angles using a protractor; classify angles as acute, obtuse, or right; and construct angles of a given degree. They should also be able to classify angles as *interior, exterior, complementary,* or *supplementary.*

2. Calculate the perimeters and areas of plane figures. Kids should know the formulas for calculating the areas of rectangles, squares, triangles, and parallelograms. They should also be able to determine the areas of irregular polygons by dividing them into regular figures.

3. Calculate the circumferences and areas of circles. Kids should be able to construct circles of a given radius or diameter, using a compass, and should be able to calculate perimeter and area using the appropriate formulas.

4. Know the triangle sum theorem. Kids should know that the sum of the three angles of a triangle always equals 180 degrees and should be able to solve problems to find missing angles.

5. Identify and construct different kinds of triangles. Kids should be able to identify *right, isosceles, equilateral,* and *scalene* triangles and construct examples of each using protractors and rulers.

See Shapes in Math, Science, and Nature Series, *Triangles,* page 196.

6. Identify similar, congruent, and symmetrical figures. Kids should be familiar with the results of transformational geometry: translations, reflections, and rotations.

PREALGEBRA

1. Recognize variables and solve simple equations containing variables. Kids should be able to solve equations such as $x + 5 = 11$ and should be able to determine the value of an expression when given the replacement value of the variable: That is, they should be able to figure out the value of $8 - x$, given that $x = 2.5$.

2. Write and solve simple equations for word problems.

HISTORY AND GEOGRAPHY

History and geography studies, as in the earlier grades, should employ a wide range of resources, including fiction and nonfiction books, biographies, multicultural folktales and legends, timelines, audiocassettes and videos, games, hands-on projects and activities, and relevant field trips.

Kids should be encouraged to take an active approach to history, viewing historical events from a range of different viewpoints.

AMERICAN HISTORY

See A History of US Series, page 163. Volume 7, *Reconstruction and Reform,* and Volume 8, *An Age of Extremes,* cover the American history topics listed below. Also see Bluestocking Press, page 84, Social Studies School Service, page 197, and *Cobblestone* and USKids History Series, page 198.

1. Nineteenth-century immigration. Topics to cover include the many different groups of immigrants and their countries of origin, Ellis Island, famous immigrants and immigrant contributions to American society, the concept of the "melting pot," changing population demographics with immigration, and national resistance to immigration (for example, the Chinese Exclusion Act).

Immigrant Kids
Russell Freedman; Puffin, 1995
> The life of immigrant children around the turn of the century, illustrated with superb photographs.

I Was Dreaming to Come to America: Memories from the Ellis Island Oral History Project
Veronica Lawlor, ed.; Viking Children's Books, 1995
> A beautifully illustrated picture book based on first-hand accounts of immigrant experiences.

2. The United States as a world power. Topics to cover include the annexation of Hawaii, the Spanish-American War, the building of the Panama Canal, and Theodore Roosevelt's "Big Stick" policy.

Bully for You, Teddy Roosevelt!
Jean Fritz; Paper Star, 1997
> An excellent chapter biography for this age group.

The Panama Canal
Elizabeth Mann; Mikaya Press, 1998
> An interesting illustrated history from the struggles of the French under Ferdinand de Lesseps through the completion of the canal. A four-page foldout shows the enormous scope of the canal and the structure of locks. For younger readers, see *Locks, Crocs, and Skeeters: The Story of the Panama Canal* (Nancy Winslow Parker; Greenwillow, 1996).

3. The rise of industrialization. Topics to cover include post–Civil War industrialization and urbanization, political corruption and the rise of "machine politics" in major cities, labor conditions and the formation of the unions, big business and the "robber barons" (including Andrew Carnegie, J. P. Morgan, Cornelius Vanderbilt, and John D. Rockefeller), Theodore Roosevelt and "trust-busting," and increasing government regulation of business.

Fire!: The Beginnings of the Labor Movement
Barbara Diamond Goldin; Puffin, 1997

A fictionalized account of the 1911 Triangle Shirtwaist factory fire and its aftermath, as seen through the eyes of eleven-year-old Rosie, whose older sister Freyda is a garment worker.

4. Reform. Topics to cover include populism, the "muckrakers" (including Ida Tarbell and Upton Sinclair), Jane Addams and the establishment of settlement houses, Jacob Riis and city ghettos, fighters for the rights for black Americans (including Ida B. Wells, Booker T. Washington, and W. E. B. Dubois), women's suffrage and prominent women, and socialism.

WORLD HISTORY

Sixth-graders might repeat in greater depth the studies of the Middle Ages and Renaissance introduced in second grade (see pages 132–133). Supplement studies with historical fiction and nonfiction books, myths and legends, hands-on activities, and field trips. Visit a museum, for example, and view medieval armor.

Fictional accompaniments to studies of the Middle Ages might include Janet Gray's *Adam of the Road*, Karen Cushman's *Catherine, Called Birdy*, Marguerite de Angeli's *The Door in the Wall*, and Frances Temple's *The Ramsay Scallop*.

Picture the Middle Ages

An activity-based resource book on the medieval period for upper elementary and middle school students. The book covers daily life in the town, castle, monastery, and manor farm, music and dance, art, and literature. Many activities, a map, a timeline, and a reading list. Jackdaw Publications; (800) 789-0022; www.jackdaw.com.

The World in the Time of Marco Polo
Fiona Macdonald; Dillon Press, 1997

What was happening in seven different regions of the world while Marco Polo was traveling to Cathay? The books gives readers a historical perspective on the Hundred Years War, the Anasazi of the

American Southwest, the Byzantine Empire, the African kingdom of Mali, and the Mongol invasion of China. Also see Macdonald's *The World in the Time of Charlemagne* (Dillon Press, 1998).

Also see Social Studies School Service, page 197, *The Story of Mankind* and *Literature Connections to World History*, page 231, and *Calliope*, page 202.

1. The Dark Ages. The first three centuries after the fall of Rome (about A.D. 500 to A.D. 800) are generally referred to as the "Dark Ages." Topics to cover include the sack of Rome by the invading barbarians, Attila and the Huns, and other Germanic tribes, including the Vandals, Franks, Angles, and Saxons.

2. The rise of Christianity. Topics to cover include the rise of the Roman Catholic Church and the increasing power of the pope, the split between the Roman and Greek Orthodox churches, the rise of the monasteries, and Emperor Charlemagne and the Holy Roman Empire.

3. Feudal society. Topics to cover include castles and manors; everyday life in the medieval period; medieval social structure, including the relationships between lord and vassals; chivalry and knighthood; the rise of towns as centers of trade and commerce; and the development of guilds.

Medieval World
Jane Bingham; Usborne Publications, 1999
  Detailed descriptions of medieval life with many colorful illustrations and diagrams.

4. England in the Middle Ages. Topics to cover include the Norman Conquest, Henry II and Eleanor of Aquitaine, the Magna Carta and its importance, Parliament and the beginning of representative government, the Hundred Years War, and the Black Death.

KINGS AND QUEENS
Illustrated cards picturing all the kings and queens of England from 1066 to the present. A brief biography appears on the back of each. Excellent for ordering on timelines and inventing historical games. Aristoplay; (734) 424-0123; www.aristoplay.com.

5. The rise of Islam. Topics to cover include Muhammad and the basic tenets of Islam, the conquest of North Africa and Spain by Islamic Turks, and Arab contributions to civilization in the fields of science, medicine, mathematics, and the arts.

6. The Crusades. Topics to cover include the causes and major events of the Crusades, Richard the Lion-hearted and Saladin, and the far-reaching effects of the cultural exchange between Europe and the East.

GEOGRAPHY

See geography resources, pages 204–206, *Discovering Geography of North America with Books Kids Love* and *Discovering World Geography with Books Kids Love,* page 172.

1. Review and reinforce concepts covered in previous geographical studies. Kids should be familiar with the use and content of maps and globes, including names and locations of continents, major oceans, states and countries, climate and time zones, the prime meridian and the international date line, the Tropics of Cancer and Capricorn, and the Arctic and Antarctic Circles.

2. Survey deserts of the world. Kids should be able to explain the characteristics of deserts and be able to locate and discuss such major deserts as the Sahara, Kalahari, Gobi, Mojave, Sonoran, Patagonian, and the great central desert of Australia.

Discovering Deserts
National Wildlife Federation; McGraw-Hill, 1997
  Desert geography, science, and multidisciplinary activities for kids in grades K–8. Students make dioramas comparing the Sonoran and Sahara deserts, make a desert rain wheel, and research the dinosaurs of the Gobi.

3. Geography studies should be closely linked to history topics. In conjunction with sixth-grade world history studies, for example, kids should survey the geography of Western Europe and the Middle East and trace the paths of medieval explorers.

SCIENCE

Science, as in the previous grades, should involve hands-on experiments and investigations, as well as informational books, biographies of noted scientists, video and on-line resources, and relevant field trips.

PHYSICAL SCIENCE

Teaching Physics With Toys
Beverley A. P. Taylor, James Roth, and Dwight J. Portman; Tab Books, 1995

Basic physics principles are taught through common toys. Activities are categorized by grade (K–3, 4–6, and 7–9).

The Visual Dictionary of Physics
Jack Challoner; Dorling Kindersley, 1995

An overview of physics illustrated with terrific color photographs and diagrams. Topics include energy, electricity, magnetism, nuclear physics, and mechanics.

Also see Fizzics Fizzle!, page 384.

1. Investigate the properties of heat energy. Kids should be able to correlate heat to atomic/molecular activity. They should understand the three ways that heat energy can be transferred (via *conduction, convection,* or *radiation*), and should understand that heat transfer always proceeds from hotter to colder until equilibrium is reached.

HEAT

KINETIC MODEL

Investigative study units using inexpensive, simple equipment. Heat (twenty lessons) teaches kids about conduction, convection, and radiation, the greenhouse effect, and the relationship of mass and temperature to calories; Kinetic Model shows kids how to apply atomic and molecular theory to the behaviors of solids, liquids, and gases. TOPS Learning Systems; (888) 773-9755; www.topscience.org.

See *Heat FUNdamentals,* page 175.

2. Survey states of matter in terms of energy transfer. Kids should be able to describe the three states of matter (solid, liquid, gas) in terms of their relative atomic/molecular activities. They should understand that phase changes occur when energy is added or subtracted from a system, and should be able to explain the molecular basis for expansion or contraction in response to changes in temperature.

The Cool Hot Rod and Other Electrifying Experiments in Energy and Matter
Paul Doherty and Don Rathjen; John Wiley & Sons, 1996
> Information, education, and creative hands-on experiments in the fields of energy transfer, temperature, electricity and magnetism, and molecular behavior from the San Francisco Exploratorium.

3. Understand and explore the principle of distillation. Kids should know that each substance has a characteristic boiling and freezing point, and be able to state the boiling and freezing points of water in both degrees Fahrenheit and Centigrade (Celsius). They should be able to define and explain the process of *distillation* (separation of liquid mixtures based on differences in boiling point).

4. Investigate the properties of light energy. Kids should be able to define *reflection, refraction,* and *absorption.* They should understand how a prism works (play with one) and should be able to discuss and cite examples of how light energy can be transformed into heat, chemical, electrical, or mechanical energies.

> LIGHT
>
> A study unit about the properties of light using very inexpensive (but effective) homemade equipment. Kids learn about reflection and refraction, color, and the way lenses work. TOPS Learning Systems; (888) 773-9755; www.topscience.org.

Light Action!
Vicki Cobb; HarperCollins, 1993
> An excellent explanation of the principles of optics, with many demonstrations and activities. Topics include shadows, refraction and reflection, prisms and the visible spectrum, waves, polarized light, and photosynthesis.

Virtual Labs: Light

An optics lab on Win/Mac CD-ROM for grades 6–12. Kids can experiment with mirrors, lenses, and prisms while learning about the properties of light, incident and reflected rays, convergence, divergence, and focal points, and colors. Included is a manual of student worksheets and instructions. Edmark; (800) 362-2890; www.edmark.com.

5. Understand the law of the conservation of energy. Energy can neither be created nor destroyed, but it can be changed from one form to another.

LIFE SCIENCE

1. Explore concepts of energy transfer within ecosystems. Kids should be able to trace the transfer of energy through ecosystems, from light energy (sunlight) to chemical energy (photosynthesis) to stored energy (plant sugars), and then from one organism to another through terrestrial and aquatic food webs.

2. Describe and discuss interactions of organisms and their environment within ecosystems. Kids should be able to compare and contrast *coexistence, cooperation,* and *competition.* They should be able to define and cite examples of *symbiosis,* and should understand the impact of *limiting factors* on ecosystems and the results of external disruption of food webs.

3. Continue studies of human anatomy and physiology. Kids should briefly review body systems covered in previous grades and should engage in a detailed study of the body's immune system.

Topics to cover include the major components of the circulatory and lymphatic systems, antigens and antibodies, the structure and function of bacteria and viruses, bacterial diseases (including tetanus, typhoid, diphtheria, and tuberculosis), the discovery and mechanism of action of antibiotics, viral diseases (including the common cold, rabies, polio, and AIDS), epidemics, and the biological basis for vaccination.

Good supplements to this topic might include biographies of Edward Jenner, Louis Pasteur, and Alexander Fleming.

Cell Wars
Fran Balkwill and Mic Rolph; First Avenue Editions, 1994
> A detailed explanation of the workings of the immune system for
> kids aged 7–13, with humorous illustrations.

Also see *How the Body Works,* page 176, and the Microexplorers Series, page
292.

EARTH/SPACE SCIENCE

1. Investigate and explore the concept of plate tectonics. Topics
to cover include Alfred Wegener and the theory of plate tectonics,
the causes and effects of earthquakes, the Richter scale, geologic
"hot spots" and the formation of volcanoes and island chains, and
a survey of supportive evidence for plate tectonic theory.
See *How the Earth Works,* page 209, and *Discover Nature in the Rocks,* page 241.

2. Reinforce and expand upon studies of astronomy. Topics to
cover include Newton's universal law of gravitation; kinds and
classification of stars; the life history of stars, novas and super-
novas, galaxies, pulsars and quasars; and astronomical instruments
and the measurement of astronomical distances.

EARTH, MOON, AND SUN

THE PLANETS AND STARS
Comprehensive study units using simple homemade equipment.
Kids model the moon's phases with Ping-Pong balls and black
tape and make a 3-D map of the Big Dipper with pinheads. Each
unit contains twenty lessons. TOPS Learning Systems; (888) 773-
9755; www.topscience.org.

How the Universe Works
Heather Couper and Nigel Henbest; Reader's Digest, 1994
> Substantive activities and information on all aspects of astronomy
> for kids aged 9–14. The book includes capsule biographies of
> famous astronomers, fact boxes, and hundreds of color pho-
> tographs, diagrams, and charts.

Also see *Naturescope Astronomy Adventures,* page 99, and Thursday's Classroom, page 178.

FOREIGN LANGUAGE

Sixth-graders should show appropriate skills in speaking, comprehension of spoken and written material, and grammar and vocabulary. This will vary depending on the design of your curriculum or home-study program. Some kids do not start studying a foreign language until sixth grade or later. There are many resources for language students of all ages, including texts, audiocassettes, videos, and computer software programs.

LANGUAGE NOW! SERIES
An immersion approach to language learning on CD-ROM for students aged 12 and up. Covers speaking, reading, and grammar and vocabulary skills through interactive texts, games, quizzes, and puzzles. Available in many languages. Transparent Language; (800) 752-1767; www.transparent.com.

FOREIGN LANGUAGE LESSON PLANS AND RESOURCES
A long list of lesson plans, activities, resources, and information for many different languages and grade levels; Web site: www. csun.edu/~hced013/eslsp.html.

See foreign language resources, page 47.

ART

A sixth-grade art program should include hands-on activities, art theory, art appreciation, and art history. Kids should experiment with a wide range of art techniques and media. They should observe and interact with artworks from different historical periods and geographic regions and should learn about art through varied sources, including fiction and nonfiction books, biographies of famous artists, and videos. If possible, take field trips to artists' studios, art galleries, exhibits, and museums.

See 1–8 Art Curriculum, page 101, The Louvre and With Open Eyes, page 211, and *History of Art for Young People,* page 294.

1. Use knowledge of art elements and principles of design to produce a wide range of creative artworks. Kids should experiment with drawing, painting, printmaking, pottery and ceramics, sculpture, fiber arts, photography, and electronic media.

2. Use knowledge of art elements and principles of design to analyze and critique a variety of works by well-known artists and others. Kids should discuss and evaluate art in the context of its historical period. They should be able to compare and contrast the different purposes of art and the ways in which various artists communicate their message.

3. Study art in conjunction with other academic subjects across the curriculum.

4. Survey art history from the classical period to the nineteenth century. One possible approach to art studies is a structured concentration on art history. Topics to cover include features and concepts of classical, Gothic, Renaissance, baroque, rococo, neoclassical, romantic, and realistic art.

Kids should view, classify, and compare representative artworks from each period. They might also create art timelines and supplement art studies with a range of print materials, including fiction and nonfiction books and biographies of key artists.

The Annotated Mona Lisa
Carol Strickland and John Boswell; Andrews & McMeel, 1992
A creatively designed history of art from the cave painters to the twentieth century, with an informational text, fact boxes, sidebars, and many, many illustrations.

Great Painters
Piero Ventura; Putnam, 1984
A charmingly illustrated history of art, from the thirteenth-century fresco painters to the twentieth-century cubists.

MUSIC

As in the visual arts, a sixth-grade music program should be multifaceted and varied, including vocal and instrumental performance, music theory, music appreciation, and music history. Kids should listen to pieces by famous composers and to multicultural music selections. They should study music through fiction and nonfiction books, songbooks, and biographies of famous musicians and composers, and should attend varied musical performances.

See Multimedia History of Music and Multimedia Musical Instruments, page 243.

1. Reinforce and expand upon musical concepts introduced in earlier grades. Kids should know the meaning of such frequently used musical terms as *grave, largo, adagio, andante, moderato, allegro,* and *presto.* They should be familiar with major and minor scales and with keys up to three sharps or flats.

At this grade level, kids should be introduced to the notes of the *bass clef* and to the basics of *chords.*

Music Ace 2

A continuation of Music Ace (see page 213) on Mac/Win CD-ROM. In twenty-four lessons, the program covers standard notation, rhythm, half, quarter, eighth, and sixteenth notes, rests and measures, key signatures, major and minor scales, melody, harmony, syncopation, and much more. Animations, games, and progress tracking. Harmonic Vision; (800) 474-0903; www.harmonicvision.com.

2. Recognize and identify the major orchestral families and their individual instruments, historical instruments, and ethnic instruments by sight and sound. Kids should also be familiar with the major keyboard instruments.

3. Recognize and identify the major vocal ranges. Kids should know *soprano, alto, tenor, baritone,* and *bass* voices.

4. Survey music history from the baroque to the romantic period. Topics to cover include the music and prominent composers of the baroque period (including Johann Sebastian Bach and George Frideric Handel), the classical period (including Wolfgang Amadeus Mozart, Franz Joseph Haydn, and Ludwig van Beethoven), and the romantic period (including Franz Schubert and Frédéric Chopin). Kids should be able to identify and define *counterpoint, fugue, oratorio, symphony, concerto,* and *chamber music.*

Kids should listen to representative musical pieces from the surveyed historical periods, read biographies of famous composers, order musical pieces and composers on timelines, and associate musical developments with other historical trends and events.

See *Lives of the Musicians: Good Times, Bad Times (and What the Neighbors Thought)*, page 212.

5. Listen and respond to a range of musical pieces by well-known composers and to multicultural musical selections.

See Classical Kids, page 183.

6. Participate in instrumental and vocal performances, group and solo.

7. Create and play original musical compositions. Kids should also experiment with making and playing their own musical instruments.

Make Mine Music!
Tom Walther; Little, Brown, 1981

A delightful hands-on approach to music, covering the science of sound and the history and structure of the classes of musical instruments. Includes instructions for making an aeolian harp, a glockenspiel, a thumb piano, a sliding trumpet, and many more.

Rubber-Band Banjos and Java-Jive Bass: Projects and Activities on the Science of Music and Sound
Alex Sabbeth; John Wiley & Sons, 1997

Information and creative activities centering around the science of sound and music. Kids make their own saxophones, banjos, and drums using simple materials.

Making More Music

Music composition for kids on Mac/Win CD-ROM. Users can experiment with musical notation in "Chamber Music," develop rhythms with nine different percussion instruments in "Rhythm Band," and invent new variations on classical pieces. A sequel to *Making Music* (page 182). Learn Technologies Interactive; (888) 292-5584; www.voyager.learntech.com.

8. Study music in conjunction with other academic subjects across the curriculum.

HEALTH AND PHYSICAL EDUCATION

1. **Participate in a range of age-apropriate indoor and outdoor athletic activities designed to provide a well-rounded program of physical fitness.** Kids should participate in physical activity that sustains a target heart rate for a minimum of twenty minutes daily. See *Fit Kids!* and *Home School Family Fitness*, page 50.

2. **Participate in a program of drug education.**

3. **Understand the nature of sexually transmitted diseases and methods of prevention.** A standard for public school health curricula. Kids should be able to define HIV/AIDS and should know its causes and means of prevention.

It's Perfectly Normal: Changing Bodies, Growing Up, Sex and Sexual Health
Robie Harris; Candlewick, 1994
   All the basics for both boys and girls, from the onset of puberty to the nature of sexually transmitted diseases. Comfortably explained, with tasteful illustrations.

Also see *It's So Amazing*, page 240.

   ADOLESCENCE
   All about, including the social, biological, and cognitive transitions inherent in adolescence, typical problems, peer group influence, and effects on school, work, and family relationships. Web site: www.personal.pcu.edu/faculty/n/x/nxdlo/adolescence.htm.

4. **Be familiar with the elements of good nutrition and personal hygiene.**

5. **Know basic first-aid procedures for common injuries.** Kids should also know the symptoms, causes, and treatments for such "temperature emergencies" as hypothermia, heat exhaustion, and heat stroke.
See *Kids to the Rescue!*, page 184.

GRADE SEVEN

We teachers can only help the work going on, as servants wait upon a master.

MARIA MONTESSORI

LANGUAGE ARTS

LITERATURE

CYBERGUIDES

Multidisciplinary lesson plans for many well-known books, categorized by grade. Featured books for seventh-graders include *Bull Run* by Paul Fleischman, *The Egypt Game* by Zilpha Keatley Snyder, *The Giver* by Lois Lowry, and *The Old Man and the Sea* by Ernest Hemingway. Web site: www.sdcoe.k12.ca.us/score/cyberguide.html.

JUNIOR GREAT BOOKS PROGRAM

Selections for seventh-graders (Series 7) include Kurt Vonnegut's "Harrison Bergeron," Alice Munro's "Day of the Butterfly," and

Charles Dickens's *A Christmas Carol.* Each selection is followed by a list of discussion questions and writing-project suggestions, designed to promote critical thinking and analytical discussion. Great Books Foundation, 35 E. Wacker Dr., Suite 2300, Chicago, IL 60601-2298; (800) 222-5870; www.greatbooks.org.

LEARNING LANGUAGE ARTS THROUGH LITERATURE

While the LLATL program has a Christian orientation, most of the materials can be adapted by persons of all philosophies. Many of the reading choices for *The Green Book* for seventh-graders, however, center around creationism and will not suit nonfundamentalists. The book also features a study of Shakespeare's *Much Ado About Nothing.* Grammar, spelling, writing, and study skills taught through literature. Common Sense Press; (352) 475-5757; cspress.com.

Also see Learning Links, page 60, Novel Units, page 60, The Writing Company, page 218, and the Shakespeare Catalog, page 217.

1. Read a wide range of age-appropriate fiction and nonfiction materials. Seventh-graders should read a mix of classic and contemporary literature, novels and short stories, myths and legends, fables and folktales, biographies and autobiographies, poems, plays, essays, magazine articles, and newspapers.

READING SUGGESTIONS FOR SEVENTH-GRADERS INCLUDE:

Anne Frank: The Diary of a Young Girl (Anne Frank; Bantam Books, 1993)

The Bridge to Terabithia (Katherine Paterson; HarperTrophy, 1987)

The Call of the Wild (Jack London; Tor Books, 1990)

The Incredible Journey (Sheila Burnford; Laurel Leaf, 1996)

Johnny Tremain (Esther Forbes; Houghton Mifflin, 1992)

My Side of the Mountain (Jean Craighead George; Viking Press, 1991)

The Outlaws of Sherwood (Robin McKinley; Ace Books, 1989)

Redwall (Brian Jacques; Ace Books, 1998)

Treasure Island (Robert Louis Stevenson; Bantam Books, 1982)

A Wrinkle in Time (Madeleine L'Engle; Yearling Books, 1973)

See Book Lists (pages 400–402).

2. Evaluate works of literature through discussion, debate, and written critique. Seventh-graders should be able to discuss such literary elements as plot and subplot, setting, major and minor characters, theme, conflict, suspense, climax, and point of view. Kids should be able, for example, to identify events that advance the plot and determine how each either explains past actions or *foreshadows* future events. They should be able to: analyze characterization through an individual character's thoughts, words, or actions, or through outside descriptions and opinions; identify recurring themes within and among texts; and determine whether the narrative point of view is *omniscient* or *limited, subjective* or *objective,* or presented in the *first* or *third person.*

3. Expand upon knowledge of the classics. Suggestions for kids at this grade level include Edmond Rostand's *Cyrano de Bergerac* and Charles Dickens's *A Tale of Two Cities.*

4. Read and respond to a varied range of poetic forms. For example, kids should be familiar with ballads, sonnets, narrative and lyric poems, limericks, and haiku, and should be able to define *meter, iamb,* and *rhyme scheme.*

Rose, Where Did You Get That Red?
Kenneth Koch; Vintage Books, 1990
> A guide for "Teaching Great Poetry to Children." Kids read and discuss the work of famous poets and use these works as starting points for poetry-writing projects of their own. Many examples.

Talking to the Sun
Kenneth Koch and Kate Farrell, eds.; Henry Holt, 1985
> An anthology of poetry from many times and places, beautifully illustrated with artworks from the Metropolitan Museum of Art.

See poetry resources, pages 187, 323.

5. Understand and follow written multistep directions.

WRITING

1. Write frequently, producing a variety of works, including reports, essays, short stories, poems, narratives, journal entries,

and letters. At this grade level, kids should be able to write a well-organized research essay. Necessary skills include gathering data, taking notes, defining a thesis (main idea), organizing an outline, integrating appropriate quotations, acknowledging sources, and appending a bibliography.

Getting There: Seventh Grade Writing on Life, School, and the Universe

Kathryn Kulpa, and R. James Stahl, eds.; Merlyn's Pen, Inc., 1995
What do seventh-graders write? This is a book of excellent real-life examples: stories, narratives, and essays by talented seventh-graders, collected by the staff of the creative writing magazine *Merlyn's Pen*.

Merlyn's Pen: Middle School Edition

A high-quality collection of student writing by kids in grades 6–9. The magazine publishes short stories, poems, essays, reviews, and artwork. Merlyn's Pen, Inc., Box 910, E. Greenwich, RI 02818; (800) 247-2027; www.merlynspen.com.

RESEARCHPAPER.COM

A comprehensive site for research paper writers, including thousands of topic suggestions, on-line search help, a "Writing Center" of tips and techniques, and much more. For kids in grade 6 and up. Web site: www.researchpaper.com.

2. Identify and analyze the parts of a sentence. By this grade level, students should have a good grasp of English grammar. For example, kids should be able to classify sentences as *simple, compound, complex,* or *compound-complex,* and should be able to identify *subject, predicate, prepositional phrases, direct* and *indirect objects, independent* and *dependent clauses* (adjective, adverb, and noun), *gerunds* and *gerund phrases,* and *infinitives* and *infinitive phrases.*

3. Use punctuation marks correctly. Kids should be familiar with the rules of punctuation covered in previous grades and should understand the use of *hyphens, dashes, brackets,* and *semicolons.*

4. Identify common parts of speech, including nouns, pronouns, verbs, adjectives and articles, adverbs, conjunctions, and interjections. Kids should know rules for correct subject/verb agreement in sentences with compound subjects, compound subjects joined by *or*, and indefinite pronouns as subjects.

For numbers 2–4, see *Nitty-Gritty Grammar*, page 219, *Princeton Review Grammar Smart Junior*, page 250, and grammar resources, pages 299–300.

5. Expand upon previous spelling and vocabulary skills. Spelling, at this grade level, should emphasize commonly misspelled words. Kids should also know how to spell word derivatives formed by adding prefixes and suffixes.

They should be able to define and use *idioms* and *analogies* and distinguish between *literal* and *figurative* modes of speech.

In a Pickle: And Other Funny Idioms
Marvin Terban; Houghton Mifflin, 1983

Punching the Clock: Funny Action Idioms
Marvin Terban; Clarion Books, 1990
Humorously illustrated introductions to idioms and their origins, including "straight from the horse's mouth," "white elephant," "chip off the old block," and "raise the roof."

See Bethump'd With Words, page 324, Wordopoly, page 250, and spelling resources, pages 219–220.

6. Be familiar with the use of word processing and publishing software programs.

LISTENING AND SPEAKING SKILLS

1. Listen to and make narrative and informational oral presentations. Kids might participate in storytelling sessions, debates, group discussions, dramatic presentations, or give short oral reports on a nonfiction topic or summaries of books or articles.

2. Follow multiple-step oral directions.

3. Memorize and recite poems.

STUDY SKILLS

1. Know how to obtain information from print and electronic reference sources.
See *The Kid's Guide to Research*, page 220, and *Casting Your Net*, page 252.

2. Be able to take effective notes and develop outlines from written selections.

See Study Guides and Strategies, page 221.

3. Practice effective study techniques.

See test prep resources, pages 153–154, 190, 252.

MATHEMATICS

As kids move through math in the middle school grades, much of the emphasis is on expanding and reinforcing basic number sense—that is, the grasp of arithmetical concepts and number relationships that form the bedrock of all mathematical studies—and on preparing for a formal course in algebra, which usually takes place in either the eighth or the ninth grade. Often the course offered as seventh-grade math is titled "prealgebra."

SAMPLE GRADE-APPROPRIATE RESOURCES INCLUDE:

Basic College Mathematics
Charles D. Miller, Stanley A. Salzman, and Diana L. Hestwood; Harper-Collins College Publishers, 1995

Despite the title, this is quite manageable by most kids in grade 7 and up. A thorough coverage of basic math, from whole number operations through geometry, basic algebra, and statistics, with clear explanations and many practice exercises. A good alternative to the Saxon math texts. From bookstores or Bluestocking Press, Box 2030, Shingle Springs, CA 95682-2030; (800) 959-8586.

Connected Mathematics Project Series

A project-based approach to mathematics in an integrated program covering number theory and operations, algebra, geometry and measurement, and probability and statistics. Highly recommended. Seventh-grade units include "Stretching and Shrinking," an interactive approach to the concept of similarity, and "What Do You Expect?," a study of probability based on computer and carnival games. Prentice-Hall, Inc.; (800) 848-9500; www.phschool.com.

Family Math: The Middle School Years
Virginia Thompson and Karen Mayfield-Ingram; Lawrence Hall of Science, 1998

An excellent investigative approach to numbers and algebraic reasoning for kids in grades 6–9 using games, projects, and activities, as well as mathematical examples and helpful background information. Family Math, Lawrence Hall of Science no. 5200, University of California, Berkeley, CA 94720-5200; (800) 897-5036; equals.lhs.berkeley.edu.

Manipulative Activities to Build Algebraic Thinking Series
Bob Willcutt; Critical Thinking & Software Press

A series of three workbooks designed to help kids "build a hands-on bridge" to abstract algebraic thinking. The books use assorted manipulatives (you supply or make your own) with which kids make pattern sequences and translate these into algebraic expressions. Critical Thinking Books & Software, Box 448, Pacific Grove, CA 93950-0448; (800) 458-4849; www.criticalthinking.com.

Math 87
Stephen Hake and John Saxon; Saxon Publishers, 1991

In theory, if you've been a Saxon math student since elementary school, this is a seventh-grade text. It's also an appropriate eighth-grade text for kids whose interest/pace in mathematics is somewhat slower. It covers fractions, decimals, percents and ratios, basic geometry, exponents and scientific notation, and signed numbers, with much repetition and review. Saxon Publishers, Inc., 2450 John Saxon Blvd., Norman, OK 73071; (800) 284-7019; www.saxonpub.com.

Middle School Math: Course 2
Scott Foresman/Addison-Wesley

The text covers algebraic language, decimals and fractions, geometry and measurement, ratios and proportions, scale and similarity, exponents, squares and square roots, percents, integers, and equations and graphs. Reviewers describe it as a "pre-prealgebra text." The book includes reviews, practice problems, and technology exercises.

See pre-algebra texts, pages 302–303, *Mathematics: A Human Endeavor,* page 302, The Math Forum, page 223, graphing calculators and Graphing Calculator Guide, page 254, and Mathematics at About.com, page 328.

NUMBER THEORY

1. Identify factors, multiples, primes, and composite numbers. Kids should be able to identify the greatest common factor (GCF) and least common multiple (LCM) of given numbers.

2. Understand the properties of real numbers. Kids should know the definitions of *natural* numbers, *real* numbers, *rational* and *irrational* numbers, and *integers*. They should be able to describe any given number in terms of these number sets.

They should also be familiar with the associative, commutative, and distributive properties of the real number system; inverse relationships; and the properties of 0 and 1.

3. Understand the concept of *absolute value*. Kids should know the symbol for absolute value, should be able to find the absolute value of any real number, and should be able to use value properties to solve problems and evaluate mathematical expressions.

RATIO AND PERCENT/FRACTIONS AND DECIMALS

See Key to Percent Series, page 255, Key to Fractions Series, page 193, and Key to Decimals Series, page 194.

1. Use ratios and proportions to solve mathematical and real-world problems. Kids should be able to read, write, and compute ratios and proportions. They should also be able to determine missing terms in proportions and make accurate scale drawings based on proportions.

They should be able to use their knowledge of ratio and proportion to solve rate problems, using the formula d = rt (distance = rate × time).

2. Compare and order fractions, decimals, integers, and percents. Kids should be able to use fractions, decimals, and percents interchangeably and should recognize equivalent representations.

3. Solve mathematical and real-world problems involving percents. For example, kids should be able to use their knowledge of percents to solve problems involving sales tax and discounts.

OPERATIONS

1. Be able to add, subtract, multiply, and divide with both positive and negative numbers.

2. Round numbers to the appropriate significant digit.

3. Continue studies of exponents. Kids should understand positive and negative exponents and should know that any non-0 number to the 0 power is 1. They should understand why a negative number raised to an even power is positive, while a negative number raised to an odd power is negative, and they should be able to multiply exponential numbers.

They should also be able to convert numbers to and from *scientific notation.*

See *Powers of Ten,* page 223.

4. Experiment with a range of problem-solving strategies and tools, selecting the most appropriate for a given problem. For example, kids should tackle problems by drawing diagrams, making charts and tables, evaluating patterns, breaking a complex problem down into simpler components, and so on. They should be encouraged to experiment with a range of mathematical tools, from pencil and paper to concrete manipulatives, calculators, and computers.

5. Use estimation skills in all branches of mathematics.

MEASUREMENTS

See Key to Measurement Series and Key to Metric Measurement Series, page 195.

1. Select and use appropriate measures of length, area, volume, capacity, weight/mass, time, and temperature.

2. Compare and convert units of measure both within and between the English and metric systems. For example, kids at this grade level should be able to convert kilometers to miles, pounds to kilograms, and centimeters to inches, and vice versa.

3. Use measures expressed as rates or products to solve problems. Measures expressed as rates include speed (miles per hr; km per sec) and density (grams per cubic centimeter); measures expressed as products include kilowatt-hours and foot-pounds.

PROBABILITY AND STATISTICS

The Visual Display of Quantitative Information
Edward R. Tufte; Graphics Press, 1983
  A dramatically illustrated explanation of the theory and practice of graphs, with many intriguing examples.

Also see *How Math Works*, page 191, which includes an informative and interactive chapter on statistics, *Statistics: Middles, Means, and In-Betweens*, page 258, *Statistics: Prediction and Sampling*, page 258, and Exploring Data, page 33.

1. Collect, organize, and interpret data using a range of methods including bar graphs, line graphs, circle graphs, tables and charts, and *frequency distributions*. Kids should experiment with graphing calculators and computer software, see page 254.

2. Determine the theoretical probability of an event and compare with experimental results.

3. Find the number of combinations possible in a given situation using a variety of computational methods.

4. Show the relationship between two variables using a *scatter plot*. Kids should be able to distinguish between *independent* and *dependent* events.

5. Graph measures of variability. Kids should be able to identify and display *range, distribution,* and *outliers*, and describe the central tendencies of a data set using *mean, median,* and *mode*.

GEOMETRY

See Key to Geometry Series, page 196.

1. **Identify, classify, and construct regular and irregular polygons.** Kids should be able to determine perimeter, area, and sum of interior angles of each.

2. **Describe and construct common solids: right prisms, cylinders, cones, and spheres.** Kids should be able to calculate the surface areas and volumes of these solids using appropriate formulas.

3. **Know the properties of parallel lines, perpendicular lines, bisectors, transversals, and angles.** Kids should be able to construct parallel lines, perpendicular lines, transversals, bisectors, and angles using a protractor, compass, and/or straight edge. They should know the properties of angles formed by the transversal of parallel lines and should recognize and define various types and features of angles, including *congruent, vertical, complementary, supplementary, adjacent, corresponding,* and *alternate interior* and *exterior.*

4. **Know and understand the Pythagorean theorem and use it to solve geometrical problems.** In a right triangle, the square of the hypotenuse is equal to the sum of the squares of the other two sides.

5. **Analyze effects of basic transformations on geometric shapes.** Kids should be able to identify translations, reflections, and rotations. They should also be able to determine how changes of scale affect measures of perimeter, area, and volume.

Prealgebra

1. **Evaluate and solve algebraic equations and inequalities in one variable using addition, subtraction, multiplication, and division.**

Try this: $2(4x - 5) + x = 6(x + 3)$

Kids should be able to apply such concepts as the distributive property of multiplication and order of operations to algebraic equations. (See page 226.)

2. **Write and solve equations for word problems.**

3. Graph simple functions on a coordinate plane and solve related problems. Kids should be able to translate patterns and proportions into equations and graphs. For example, given a mathematical rule such as $y = 2x$, they should be able to create a table of values and represent the results as ordered pairs plotted on a coordinate grid. They should also be able to translate linear graphs into equations.

At this grade level, kids should understand the concepts of *function* and *slope*. They should be familiar with equations in the form $y = ax$, where a is the slope of the graphed line; and $y = ax + b$, where a is the slope of the line, and b the y-intercept.

4. Understand equality properties for equations. Kids should know that equations are equivalent when the same quantity is added or subtracted from each side of the equation; or when each side of the equation is multiplied or divided by a quantity other than zero.

HISTORY

AMERICAN HISTORY

Seventh-graders, building upon past history studies, might concentrate on the events of the 20th century to the end of World War II. Topics should be enhanced with historical fiction and nonfiction books, videos and audiocassettes, activities and projects, and relevant field trips.

AMERICAN HISTORY RE-CREATIONS
Interactive mini-units centering around crucial events in American history from the colonial period to modern times. Kids participate in research and discussion, and role-play in debates. Interact; (800) 359-0961; www.interact-simulations.com.

JACKDAW PUBLICATIONS
Portfolios of background essays, timelines, maps, photographs, and primary-source documents on a wide range of American and world history topics. Many titles are relevant to this time period, among them *World War I, The Russian Revolution, The New*

Deal, The Depression, and *The Holocaust.* Jackdaw Publications; (800) 789-0022; www.jackdaw.com.

See A History of US Series, page 163. Volume 8, *An Age of Extremes,* and Volume 9, *War, Peace, and All That Jazz,* cover twentieth-century American history. Also see *Literature Connections to World History,* page 231, *Literature Connections to American History,* page 365, and *Cobblestone,* page 198.

1. World War I. Topics to cover include causes and background of World War I, European imperialism in Africa, the major events of the war, the entry of the United States into the war, the Treaty of Versailles, the influenza epidemic of 1918, Woodrow Wilson's Fourteen Points, and the League of Nations.

First World War
John D. Clare; Gulliver Books, 1995
   A short history of World War I in the Living History Series, dramatically illustrated with color photographs of reenactors.

2. America between the wars. Topics to cover include the Roaring Twenties and Prohibition, the Scopes "Monkey Trial," women's suffrage and the passage of the Nineteenth Amendment, the Harlem Renaissance and the Jazz Age, and landmark technological advances of the early twentieth century.

3. The Great Depression and the New Deal. Topics to cover include the Wall Street crash of 1929, the presidency of Herbert Hoover, the Oklahoma dust bowl, Franklin Delano Roosevelt and the New Deal, the increasing power of unions, and the new social welfare programs.

4. World War II. Topics to cover include causes and historical background of the war, Mussolini's rise to power in Italy, Hitler and Nazi totalitarianism, the Soviet Union under Joseph Stalin, the Spanish Civil War, major events of World War II in Europe and the Pacific, the American home front, the Manhattan Project and the atomic bomb, the Nuremberg war trials, and the creation of the United Nations.

5. A survey of American government. Topics to cover include the structure, function, and powers of national, state, and local governments, the concept of balance of power, the election process, and the political party system.

WORLD HISTORY

In seventh grade, kids following a classical curriculum (see page 80) might review and repeat in greater detail studies of the period from the Renaissance to the nineteenth century first introduced in Grade 3 (see pages 168–172).

See *The Story of Mankind,* page 231, *Literature Connections to World History,* page 231, and *Calliope,* page 202.

1. The Renaissance. Topics to cover include the "rebirth" of Greek and Roman classicism and the humanist movement; the rise of the Italian city-states as centers of trade; prominent Renaissance figures, including Petrarch, Dante, Brunelleschi, and the Medicis; Renaissance ideals and values, including the concept of the "Renaissance man," everyday life in the Renaissance, arts and literature, major historical events of the period, and Machiavelli and his influential political treatise, *The Prince.* Kids should also study the "northern Renaissance" of the Low Countries.

Picture the Renaissance
An activity-based resource book for upper elementary and middle school students covering all aspects of Renaissance life and culture. Chapters include "The Passion for the Classical Past," "The Passion for Exploration," "Humanism and the Early Italian Renaissance," "Art of the Renaissance," "Science and Inventions," and "The Reformation." The book includes maps, a timeline, and suggestions for games, music, dance, costumes, and many other activities. Jackdaw Publications; (800) 789-0022; www.jackdaw.com.

RENAISSANCE
A simulation of life in Renaissance Italy in which kids choose a Renaissance identity, play a board game of Renaissance daily life, and complete a wide range of interdisciplinary activities in the fields of geography, math, science, art, and literature. Interact; (800) 359-0961; www.interact-simulations.com.

Also see *Michelangelo and His Times,* page 169, *Rats, Bulls, and Flying Machines,* page 169, and Mr. Donn's Ancient History Page, page 133.

2. The Reformation. Topics to cover include the ideas of Erasmus, Martin Luther and the rise of Protestantism, the course of the Reformation in Germany, Switzerland, and England, the Counter-Reformation, and the ensuing wars over religion.

MARTIN LUTHER

A portfolio of illustrated historical background essays and primary-source documents covering the life and times of Luther and the Protestant Reformation. Jackdaw Publications; (800) 789-0022; www.jackdaw.com.

3. European history to the Glorious Revolution. Topics to cover include Henry VIII and his heirs, the life and times of Elizabeth I, conflicts with Spain and the defeat of the Spanish Armada, the Thirty Years' War, Oliver Cromwell and the Puritan Revolution, the Restoration, and the Glorious Revolution. Kids should be able to define *divine right of kings*, and should understand the seventeenth century conflicts over the limitation of the monarchy.

4. The Age of Exploration. Topics to cover include the spice trade (and the geography of the Spice Islands), Prince Henry the Navigator and the development of the Portuguese maritime empire, Columbus and his voyages to the New World, the Treaty of Tordesillas and its implications, the Spanish conquistadors and their impact on the Americas, the circumnavigation of the globe, the voyages of the English, French, and Dutch, and early colonization. Kids should know the names and accomplishments of major explorers of the period and should understand that a corollary to the establishment of New World colonies was the growth of the African slave trade to provide labor for the Caribbean sugar plantations.

GALLEON

A simulation of sixteenth-century exploration on board a Spanish galleon or English privateer. Kids learn about such prominent explorers as Balboa, Vespucci, Ponce de León, Magellan, Cortés, and De Soto, while mapping their ship's course, maintaining a ship's log, and dealing with scurvy, storms, and enemies. Interact; (800) 359-0961; www.interact-simulations.com.

See *Around the World in a Hundred Years*, *The History News: Explorers*, and *The World of Columbus and Sons*, page 171. Jackdaw portfolios, page 284, relevant to this period include *Columbus and the Age of Explorers* and *Drake and the Golden Hinde*.

5. The Scientific Revolution and the Enlightenment. Topics to cover include the rise of faith in science and reason. Kids should be familiar with the scientific accomplishments of Copernicus, Kepler, Galileo, Galen, and Isaac Newton, and with the political philosophies of René Descartes, Thomas Hobbes, and John Locke. They should also understand the impact of these discoveries and philosophies on eighteenth-century thought, notably their influence on the rising revolutionary movements in the American colonies and France. In company with history studies, kids should survey the art, music, and literature of the period.

6. The Age of Revolution. Topics to cover include the rise of Prussia as a European power, the War of the Austrian Secession and the Seven Years' War, absolutism in France from Louis XIV to Louis XVI, the French Revolution, Napoléon Bonaparte and the French Empire, the Napoleonic Wars, and the restoration of the French monarchy. Kids should be familiar with the philosophy of Jean-Jacques Rousseau and the Romantic movement.

7. Russian history to the reign of Catherine the Great. Topics to cover include a survey of the history and culture of early Russia, the Eastern Orthodox Church, and the lives and times of Ivan III (the Great), Ivan IV (the Terrible), Peter the Great, and Catherine the Great.

Russia Under the Czars
James I. Clark; Raintree/Steck Vaughn, 1990
An illustrated overview of Russia under the czars from mid-800 to the Russian Revolution.

8. Russian revolution. Topics to cover include an overview of Russian history; the causes and events of the Russo-Japanese War; the Revolution of 1905; the last Romanovs; Nicholas and Alexandria; the Revolution of 1917; Lenin and revolutionary Marxism; Bolsheviks and White Russians; and the formation of the Soviet Union.

9. The Industrial Revolution. Topics to cover include landmark inventions, the rise of factories and their impact on society, the concept of capitalism, Adam Smith and the laissez-faire economy, socialism, and communism. They should be familiar with Karl Marx and understand the importance of *The Communist Manifesto*.

GEOGRAPHY

GEOGRAPHY AT ABOUT.COM

An excellent and enormous source of geographical resources for all ages on the Internet. Among the many topics covered are climate and weather, countries and nations, earthquakes, flags, geography education, geography for kids, time zones, physical geography, and all possible kinds of maps. Included is a list of sources for on-line and blank maps. Web site. www. geography.about.com.

Also see geography resources, pages 204–206, 306–307.

1. Survey the geography of Europe. In conjunction with history studies of the World Wars, kids should study the geography of Europe, covering countries, major cities, rivers, lakes, and mountain ranges, and historical and economic high points. Kids should also be aware of how the map of the world changed following the World Wars.

2. Survey the geography of Russia. In conjunction with studies of the Russian Revolution, kids should study the political, physical, and economic geography of Russia, covering climate, resources, mountains, lakes and rivers, boundaries, and major cities.

3. Survey the geography of the United States, expanding upon previous studies. Topics to cover include a survey of the major geographical regions of the United States (including political, social, and economic features), mountain ranges and notable mountain peaks, lakes and rivers, boundaries, the fifty states and their capitals (see page 206), major cities, territories, population demographics, natural resources, and landmark geographic features such as Niagara Falls, the Grand Canyon, and Death Valley.

SCIENCE

As science studies become more complex and specialized in the older grades, the question of sequence and organization becomes increasingly difficult. While there are any number of science curricula proposals for middle- and secondary-level students, most fall into one of three basic categories. Most common is a traditional curriculum in which "discipline-based courses"—earth/space science, biology, chemistry, and physics—are taught in sequence, one science per year through the end of twelfth grade. An alternative is a curriculum in which the discipline-based courses are taught in shorter series—that is, kids get a little of each every year, perhaps eight weeks of earth science, followed by eight weeks of biology, then eight weeks of chemistry, and finally eight weeks of physics. This approach, some science teachers feel, gives kids a more integrated view of science and a firmer grasp of its many interconnections. In some cases, the discipline-based courses might even be taught in parallel—that is, all four, all at once, with the entire course content stretched out over four years.

A more radical departure from the traditional curriculum completely reshuffles the sciences, centering science courses around a single overreaching "great idea." One candidate for such an organizing principle is *evolution*—which leads kids into a multifaceted study of plant and animal classification, adaptation and selective pressures, the fossil record and the age of the earth, the theory of continental drift, and even, on a galactic scale, the evolution of the universe. Other possibilities include *energy,* or *science and society.*

In some curricula, science specialization begins in seventh grade: Seventh-graders concentrate on the life sciences; eighth-graders on the physical sciences. In others, a "series" curriculum continues through the end of eighth grade: Kids study in sequence, over the course of a single year, topics in the physical, life, and earth/space sciences.

Homeschool families may want to emphasize one or another of these, depending on their children's interests and abilities.

Physical Science

1. Survey atomic theory. Topics to cover include the nature of atoms, molecules, and compounds, the history of chemistry from the ancient Greeks to Mendeleyev, models of atomic structure, and kinds of subatomic particles.

The World of Atoms and Quarks
Albert Stwertka; Twenty-first Century Books, 1995
   A short, illustrated history of particle physics from *Scientific American,* tracing the atom from the theories of the ancient Greeks through the modern-day "particle explosion."

2. Understand major types of chemical bonds and reactions. Topics to cover include the atomic basis of chemical bonds, ionic and covalent bonds, salts, oxidation and reduction reactions, acids and bases, and chemical equations.

3. Understand and use the periodic table of elements. Kids should be familiar with the organization of the periodic table, should understand *atomic number* and *atomic weight,* and should know the definition of *isotope.*

   A good supplement to studies of the periodic table might be a biography of Dmitry Mendeleyev.

   ELEMENT-O
   A Monopoly-style board game based on the periodic table of elements. Lewis Educational Games, Box 727, Goddard, KS 67052; (800) 557-8777.

See Quia! at www.quia.com for on-line games for chemistry students; also see chemistry resources, pages 237, 368–370.

Life Science

1. Compare and contrast structure and function of typical plant and animal cells. Kids should be able to identify and describe major cell organelles, including *nucleus, nuclear membrane, cytoplasm, cell membrane, vacuoles, Golgi bodies, lysosomes, endoplasmic reticulum* (rough and smooth), and *mitochondria.*

2. **Understand the processes of cell division.** Kids should be able to define, compare, and contrast *meiosis* and *mitosis* and should know what a *mutation* is.

3. **Survey the science of genetics.** Topics to cover include Gregor Mendel's experiments; definitions of *dominant* and *recessive* traits, *alleles, genotype,* and *phenotype*; chromosomes and genes; DNA structure and function; common genetic disorders; and genetic engineering.

For example, kids should understand the molecular basis for genetic change. They should also know how DNA is replicated and transcribed, and should understand the one gene–one protein hypothesis. Good supplements to these studies might be biographies of scientists James Watson, Francis Crick, Rosalind Franklin, and Barbara McClintock.

Microexplorers Series
Patrick Baeverle and Norbert Landa; Barron's Juveniles
A series of colorfully illustrated books about cell biology and genetics. Titles include *The Cell Works, Your Body's Heroes and Villains, How Y Makes the Guy,* and *Ingenious Genes.*

4. **Survey the science of evolution.** Topics to cover include the definition of evolution; concepts of *mutation, adaptation, natural selection, extinction,* and *speciation;* Charles Darwin and *The Origin of Species;* and an overview of the evidence for evolution from the fields of geology, paleontology, comparative anatomy, and molecular biology.

The Evolution Book
Sara Stein; Workman, 1986
Information, illustrations, and terrific hands-on activities trace four billion years of earth history.

Earth/Space Science

1. **Be familiar with the geological history of the earth.** Topics to cover include concepts of *uniformitarianism* and *catastrophism,* the rock cycle, stratigraphy, fossil formation, radioactive dating,

the age of the earth and the progression of life on earth, the means in which crustal plate movements have affected distribution of living things, and the Cretaceous extinction.

Kids should know that evidence from the geologic record and radioactive dating studies indicate that the earth is 4.6 billion years old and that life first appeared about 3 billion years ago. Good supplements to this study might include making geologic timelines, visiting a road cut or other geologic site to view rock layers, and reading biographies of Charles Lyell, Alfred Wegener, and Luis Alvarez.

2. Know the four major eras of geologic time and the characteristics of each. The four major geologic eras are the Precambrian, Paleozoic, Mesozoic, and Cenozoic.

FOREIGN LANGUAGE

Kids should show appropriate progress in speaking, comprehension of spoken and written material, and grammar and vocabulary. See resources, pages 47, 268.

ART

An art program should include both hands-on activities and studies of art theory, art appreciation, and art history. Field trips might include visits to artists' studios, art galleries, and museums.

1. Use knowledge of art elements and principles of design to produce a wide range of creative artworks. For example, kids might experiment with drawing, painting, printmaking, pottery and ceramics, sculpture, fiber arts, photography, and electronic media.

Drawing With Older Children and Teens
Mona Brookes; J. P. Tarcher, 1991
  A creative step-by-step drawing course for students aged 12 and up.

2. Use knowledge of art elements and principles of design to analyze and critique a variety of artworks by well-known artists

and works from a variety of multicultural sources. Kids should be able to discuss and evaluate art in the context of its historical period and world region. Try making timelines to trace developments in the field of art in various regions of the world.

3. Study art in conjunction with other academic subjects across the curriculum.

4. Survey major schools and periods in art history, from the impressionists to the twentieth century. For each school or period, kids should study representative artists and their artworks. They should know the major features of each genre of art and should be able to recognize and classify artworks by period and school. They should read biographies of famous artists, order artworks and artists on timelines, and associate artistic developments and innovations with other historical trends and events.

Topics to cover include *impressionism* (including the work of Degas, Renoir, Monet, and Cassatt), *postimpressionism* (including the work of Cézanne, Seurat, van Gogh, and Gauguin), *expressionism* (including the work of Matisse, Chagall, Munch, and Picasso), *abstract art* (including the work of Kandinsky, Klee, and Mondrian), *surrealism* (including the work of Dalí), and modern American painting (including the work of Hopper, Wyeth, O'Keeffe, Wood, Rockwell, and Rivera).

History of Art for Young People
H. W. Janson and Anthony F. Janson; Harry N. Abrams, 1997
An encyclopedic and superbly illustrated history of art for kids aged 12 and up. The book spans art from prehistoric times to the present day, covering painting, sculpture, architecture, and photography. All the names, dates, and definitions you'll ever need.

Also see 1–8 Art Curriculum, page 101, The Louvre and With Open Eyes, page 211, and *The Annotated Mona Lisa* and *Great Painters*, page 269.

MUSIC

As in the visual arts, a music program should include active participation in the form of vocal and instrumental performance, as well as music theory, music appreciation, and music history.

See Multimedia History of Music and Multimedia Musical Instruments, page 243.

1. Reinforce and expand upon musical concepts introduced in previous grades. Kids should know musical notation (both bass and treble clefs) and terms. They should recognize I, IV, and V7 chords and should be able to construct major and minor scales and chords in keys up to three sharps or flats. They should also be able to define *octave*.

See Music Acc 2, page 270.

2. Recognize and identify the major orchestral families and their individual instruments, keyboard instruments, historical instruments, and ethnic instruments by sight and sound.

3. Recognize and identify common musical forms. For example, kids should be able to identify *theme and variation, rondo, suite, opera, string quartet, sonata,* and *fugue.*

4. Survey music history from the romantic period to the twentieth century. Topics to cover include the romantic composers (including Brahms, Berlioz, Liszt, Wagner), the nationalist composers (including Dvořák, Grieg, and Tchaikovsky), and the American musical tradition (including blues and jazz).

Kids should listen to musical examples of each, read biographies of famous musicians and composers, order musical compositions and composers on timelines, and associate musical developments with other historical trends and events.

5. Listen and respond to a range of musical pieces by well-known composers and to multicultural musical selections.

6. Participate in instrumental and vocal performances, group and solo. Kids should also be able to conduct musical performances, using correct beat patterns.

7. Create and play original musical compositions. Kids should also experiment with making and playing original instruments (see page 271).

8. Study music in conjunction with other academic subjects. When studying World War II, for example, kids might listen to representative music of the period.

HEALTH AND PHYSICAL EDUCATION

1. Participate in a range of age-appropriate indoor and outdoor athletic activities designed to provide a well-rounded program of physical fitness. Kids should understand the value of practice and training.

See *Fit Kids!* and *Home School Family Fitness,* page 50.

2. Participate in a program of drug education.

3. Understand the nature of sexually transmitted diseases and methods of prevention. Kids should know how HIV/AIDS is transmitted and be able to explain its effects on the immune system.

See *It's Perfectly Normal* and Adolescence (page 272).

4. Be familiar with the elements of good nutrition and personal hygiene.

5. Know basic first-aid procedures for common injuries.

GRADE EIGHT

LANGUAGE ARTS

Literature

While reading is the crux of any literary program, a well-rounded program may also include audio and video presentations of literary material and field trips to theaters, plays, or poetry readings.

CYBERGUIDES
Excellent multidisciplinary lesson plans for a wide range of well-known books, categorized by grade level. Selections for eighth-graders include an overview of Civil War literature, Mildred Taylor's *Roll of Thunder, Hear My Cry,* Katherine Paterson's *Sign of the Chrysanthemum,* and Jules Verne's *20,000 Leagues Under the Sea.* Web site: www.sdcoe.k12.ca.us/score/cyberguide.html.

JUNIOR GREAT BOOKS PROGRAM
Selections for eighth-graders (Series 8) include William Saroyan's "The Summer of the Beautiful White Horse," Ivan Turgenev's "The

Watch," Frank R. Stockton's "The Griffin and the Minor Canon," and excerpts from Gary Paulsen's *The Winter Room* and Maya Angelou's *I Know Why the Caged Bird Sings*. Each selection is followed by a list of thought-provoking discussion questions and writing project suggestions. Great Books Foundation, 35 E. Wacker Dr., Suite 2300, Chicago, IL 60601-2298; (800) 222-5870; www.greatbooks.org.

LEARNING LANGUAGE ARTS THROUGH LITERATURE
Grammar, spelling, writing, and study skills taught through book selections. Featured readings for *The Gray Book* for eighth-graders include *Across Five Aprils* by Irene Hunt, *A Lantern in Her Hand* by Bess Streeter Aldrich, and assorted selections specifically targeted at Christian families. Common Sense Press; (352) 475-5757; cspress.com.

Also see Learning Links, page 60, Novel Units, page 60, The Writing Company, page 218, and the Shakespeare Catalog, page 217.

1. Read a wide range of age-appropriate fiction and nonfiction materials. Kids should read a mix of classic and contemporary literature, novels and short stories, myths and legends, fables and folktales, biographies and autobiographies, poems, plays, essays, magazine articles, and newspapers.

Reading suggestions for eighth-graders include:

Carry On, Mr. Bowditch (Jean Lee Latham; Houghton Mifflin, 1973)
Good Night, Mr. Tom (Michelle Magorian; HarperTrophy, 1986)
Hatchet (Gary Paulsen; Houghton Mifflin, 1995)
The Haunting (Margaret Mahy; Atheneum, 1982)
The House of Dies Drear (Virginia Hamilton; Aladdin, 1984)
Jacob I Have Loved (Katherine Paterson; HarperTrophy, 1990)
Julie of the Wolves (Jean Craighead George; HarperTrophy, 1974)
Roll of Thunder, Hear My Cry (Mildred D. Tayler; Puffin, 1997)
The Slave Dancer (Paula Fox; Laurel Leaf, 1989)
A String in the Harp (Nancy Bond; Aladdin, 1996)
Watership Down (Richard Adams; Avon Books, 1998)
Z for Zachariah (Robert C. O'Brien; Aladdin, 1987)

See Book Lists, pages 400–402. Also see On-line Book Lists for Teenagers, page 322, and *Cicada*, page 322.

2. Evaluate works of literature through discussion, debate, and written critique. Kids should be familiar with such literary elements as plot and subplot, setting, characters and characterization, theme, conflict, suspense and climax, and point of view. They should also be able to define and identify *protagonists* and *antagonists*.

Kids should be encouraged to build upon their literary experiences through projects and activities: for example, dramatizing excerpts from a reading selection, making original illustrations, writing critical essays, or researching a scientific, geographical, or historical aspect of the book.

3. Expand upon knowledge of the classics. Suggestions for kids at this grade level include George Orwell's *Animal Farm,* Pearl Buck's *The Good Earth,* and William Shakespeare's *Twelfth Night.*

Eighth-graders should be able to compare and contrast *tragedy* and *comedy* and should be familiar with such dramatic elements as *farce, satire, soliloquies,* and *asides.*

4. Read and respond to a varied range of poetic forms.

5. Understand and follow written multistep directions.

WRITING

1. Write frequently, producing a variety of works, including reports, essays, short stories, poems, narratives, journal entries, and letters. Kids should be able to write well-organized essays, including research essays. See Researchpaper.com.

2. Identify and analyze the parts of a sentence. Eighth-graders should be able to recognize and use *simple, compound, complex,* and *compound-complex* sentences and should be able to punctuate each correctly. They should be able to identify *subjects, predicates, complements* (including predicate adjectives, predicate nominatives, direct and indirect objects), *modifiers* (including phrases and clauses), and *appositives.*

LINGUA CENTER GRAMMAR SAFARI
Challenging activities for exploring grammar in the real world, with many examples of such parts of speech as phrases, gerunds,

infinitives, dangling prepositions, and more. Web site: deil.lang.
uiuc.edu/web.pages/grammarsafari.html.

For numbers 2–4, also see *Princeton Review Grammar Smart Junior,* page 250,
Nitty-Gritty Grammar, page 219, and grammar resources, pages 219–220.

3. Use punctuation marks correctly. Kids should be able to punctuate the four kinds of sentences (see above) and should be familiar with the punctuation of quotations, the use of parentheses, and
the use of hyphens, dashes, colons, semicolons, and italics.

**4. Identify common parts of speech, including nouns, pro-
nouns, verbs, adjectives and articles, adverbs, conjunctions, and
interjections.**

JABBERWOCKY
An on-line exercise in grammar: Kids read and identify parts of
speech in Lewis Carroll's poem. (Is *brillig* an adjective?) Web site:
www.col-ed.org/cur/lang/lang04.txt.

5. Expand upon previous spelling and vocabulary skills.
See Wordopoly, page 250, and Bethump'd With Words, page 324.

Eighth grade is the last year kids are eligible to enter the Scripps
Howard National Spelling Bee. Potential champions should contact Scripps Howard National Spelling Bee, Box 371541, Pitts-
burgh, PA 15251-7541; www.spellingbee.com.

Listening and Speaking Skills

1. Listen and respond to various forms of spoken literature.
Examples include plays, skits, and poetry and prose readings.

**2. Listen to and make narrative and informational oral presen-
tations.** Kids might participate in storytelling sessions, debates,
group discussions, or dramatic presentations; or give short oral
reports on a nonfiction topic. They should be able to listen critically, analyzing oral presentations and media messages for bias,
persuasion, propaganda, fallacies, opinion expressed as fact, and
unsubstantiated generalities.

They should also be able to give coherent oral summaries of books or articles.

ALLYN & BACON PUBLIC SPEAKING WEBSITE
Everything you need to know for making a speech, plus interactive activities, a "Speech Doctor," and related links. Web site: www. abacon.com/pubspeak/.

3. Follow multiple-step oral directions.

4. Memorize and recite poems.
See *A Poem A Day,* page 360.

STUDY SKILLS

1. Know how to obtain information from print and electronic reference sources. For example, kids should be able to use card catalogs, periodical indices, microfilm collections, and electronic databases and search engines.

2. Be able to collect and organize information for research projects. For a given research project, kids should be able to select appropriate sources, take notes, and organize and summarize the results. They should also know how to gather information from interviews.

3. Be able to take effective notes and develop outlines from written selections.

4. Practice effective study techniques.
See Study Guides and Strategies, page 221, and test preparation resources, pages 153–154, 190–191, and *Test Smart!,* page 252.

MATHEMATICS

Depending on interest, skills, and/or mathematical program design, eighth-graders may devote this year to a course in prealgebra, with accompanying reinforcement and expansion of previously studied arithmetical and geometrical concepts. Or they may take a beginning course in algebra (see pages 326–329).

Texts and Programs

Algebra 1/2
John H. Saxon, Jr.; Saxon Publishers, 1990

This text covers the topics ordinarily taught in prealgebra. It is intended as a precursor to a formal beginning algebra course, to be used by seventh-graders who plan to take algebra in eighth grade, or by eighth-graders who plan to take algebra in ninth. Either system works. *Algebra 1/2* reviews and reinforces basic mathematics, fractions and decimals, ratio and percent, statistics, geometry, exponents, scientific notation, algebraic equations, and graphing. The book is available as a "Home Study Kit" with accompanying teacher's manual, test booklet, and answer key. Saxon Publishers, Inc., 2450 John Saxon Blvd., Norman, OK 73071; (800) 284-7019; www.saxonpub.com.

Connected Mathematics Project Series

A highly recommended project-based mathematics program that combines number theory and operations, algebra, geometry and measurement, and probability and statistics. Grade 8 units include "Looking for Pythagoras," "Frogs, Fleas, and Painted Cubes," (quadratic relationships), and "Say It With Symbols" (algebraic reasoning). Prentice-Hall, Inc.; (800) 848-9500; www.phschool.com.

Mathematics: A Human Endeavor
Harold R. Jacobs; W. H. Freeman and Company, 1994

A highly creative alternative to run-of-the-mill textbooks. Jacobs teaches substantive math—including mathematical sequences, functions and their graphs, logarithms, symmetry, mathematical curves, probability and statistics, and topology—through a wealth of innovative real-world examples. A fascinating education in mathematical thinking.

Prealgebra
Margaret L. Lial, E. John Hornsby, Charles D. Miller, and Diana Hestwood; Longman Publishing Group, 1998

A comprehensive coverage of prealgebra, with many examples, review exercises, and tests. Topics include signed numbers, exponents, order of operations, variables and simple equations, rational numbers, ratio and proportion, percents, decimals, measurement, statistics, and graphs.

Pre-Algebra: An Integrated Transition to Algebra and Geometry
Glencoe/McGraw-Hill

Usable as a seventh- or eighth-grade text. The book contains excellent coverage of prealgebra concepts, including integers; one-step equations and inequalities; factors and fractions; mathematical patterns; functions and graphing; ratio, proportion, and percent; statistics and probability; geometry and algebra; and polynomials.

Also see *Basic College Mathematics*, page 278, *Family Math: The Middle School Years*, page 279, The Math Forum, page 223, and Mathematics at About.com, page 328.

Some basic requirements for a typical course in prealgebra:

1. Understand the use of real numbers, including fractions, decimals, percents, ratios, and exponents. Kids should be able to write numbers in scientific notation; identify *prime* and *composite* numbers; find the *greatest common factor* (GCF) and *least common multiple* (LCM) of two or more numbers; estimate square roots; and estimate sums, differences, products, and quotients of real numbers. They should also be able to interconvert among fractions, decimals, percents, and ratios and use fractions, decimals, percents, and ratios in real-world situations.

See Key to Fractions Series, page 193, Key to Decimals Series, page 194, and Key to Percent Series, page 255.

2. Know the basic properties of geometry. Students should be familiar with the classification and measurement of angles and lines. They should be able to identify similar, congruent, and similar figures and calculate perimeter and area of regular and irregular plane figures and surface area and volume of solid figures, including rectangular solids, pyramids, prisms, cones, and cylinders. They should know the Pythagorean theorem and be able to use it to solve problems, and they should be able to apply geometric principles to real-world situations.

See Key to Geometry Series, page 196.

3. Understand basic probability and statistics. Kids should be able to compare and contrast varying graphic representations of the same data. They should be able to use measurements of central tendency, including mean, mode, and median, and apply these appropriately to problem-solving situations. They should be able to find the mathematical and experimental probability of simple and compound events, using hands-on experiments, random number generation, computer simulation, and other methods, and they should be able to display and interpret data using scatter plots.

See resources.

4. Understand the introductory principles of algebra. Eighth-graders should be able to simplify numerical expressions using order of operations, and to describe and identify commutative and associative properties of addition and subtraction and distributive properties of multiplication. They should be able to translate word problems into algebraic expressions and to evaluate and solve simple equations. They should be able to solve simple inequalities and graph the solutions, to use graphs and tables to represent relations and functions, and extend and create geometric and numerical patterns.

Given a rule or function that describes a linear equation, they should be able to make a table and create a graph; given an algebraic formula, they should be able to make substitutions and solve for one unknown.

HISTORY

Many public school curricula concentrate on state history and geography during eighth grade. Homeschoolers designing their own history/geography programs may prefer to integrate state history into a more comprehensive ongoing program.

AMERICAN HISTORY

Eighth-graders, building upon past American history studies, might spend this year surveying modern times. Topics should be supplemented with historical fiction and nonfiction books, activities and projects, and relevant field trips.

The Century for Young People
Peter Jennings and Todd Brewster; Doubleday, 1999
>A decade-by-decade tour of the past century, filled with information, first-person stories, and many superb photographs.

Children's History of the 20th Century
Dorling Kindersley, 1999
>A survey of the people, events, and discoveries of the twentieth century through timelines and thousands of photographs.

Also see A History of US Series, page 163. Volume 10, *All the People,* covers the American history topics listed below (from Truman's presidency to the end of the cold war). Also see American History Re-Creations and Jackdaw Publications, page 284.

1. The cold war. Topics to cover include the world post–World War II, the Marshall Plan and the Truman Doctrine, the origins of the cold war, the "Iron Curtain" and Eastern European resistance, the Korean War, McCarthyism, Eisenhower and the military-industrial complex, the presidency of John F. Kennedy, the space program and the Apollo moon landing, and American culture in the 1950s and 1960s.

2. The civil rights movement. Topics to cover include early moves toward desegregation, Rosa Parks and the Mongomery bus boycott, Martin Luther King Jr., Lyndon Johnson and the Great Society, the Civil Rights Act of 1964, and the rise of African-American militancy movements.

3. The Vietnam War. Topics to cover include the historical background of the conflict, the "domino" theory, major events of the war, the antiwar protest movement, and Watergate and Richard Nixon's resignation.

4. Modern activism and reform. Topics to cover include feminism and the women's liberation movement, Cesar Chavez and the United Farm Workers, American Indian activism, and environmentalism.

WORLD HISTORY

See *The Story of Mankind,* page 231, *Literature Connections to World History,* page 231, and *Calliope,* page 202.

1. **Decline of European colonialism: the British Empire.** Topics to cover include the formation of the British Commonwealth, Irish nationalism (including the Easter Rebellion and the Irish Free State), and Indian nationalism (from the Sepoy Rebellion to Mahatma Gandhi).

2. **Decline of European colonialism: China.** Topics to cover include China under the Europeans, the Opium War and Boxer Rebellion, the policies of Sun Yat-sen, communism, Mao Zedong and the Long March, the defeat of nationalists under Chiang Kai-shek, and the establishment of the People's Republic of China.

3. **The Middle East.** Topics to cover include territorial mandates in the Middle East, the creation of Israel, the Suez crisis, the Palestine Liberation Organization, the Arab-Israeli Wars, the Camp David Peace Treaty, the Persian Gulf War, and the politics of oil.

4. **End of the cold war.** Topics to cover include the diplomatic reinstatement of China, Strategic Arms Limitation talks, the breakup of the U.S.S.R., the reunification of Germany, China under communism, the Cultural Revolution, European unity, the Common Market, conflict in the Balkans, and South Africa and the end of apartheid.

GEOGRAPHY

Eighth-graders should have a good grasp of the basic principles of geography. They should be familiar with the use of maps and globes; should be able to find specific locations on a map, given coordinates of latitude and longitude; and should have a well-developed geographic vocabulary.

Everything You Need to Know About Geography Homework
Anne Zeman and Kate Kelly; Scholastic, 1997
   An overview of geography for kids in grades 5–9, including all the basics, with colorful illustrations, charts, and diagrams.

Gumshoe Geography

Richard S. Jones; Zephyr Press, 1996

A fat collection of detective projects for young geographers. Kids use their map-reading skills to gather information on interesting and unusual sites around the globe.

Also see Geography at About.com, page 289.

1. Survey the geography of India. In conjunction with history studies (see above), kids should study the geography of India and southern Asia, covering major countries (India, Pakistan, Bangladesh, and Sri Lanka) and cities, mountain ranges, rivers, boundaries, climate, man-made monuments and structures (the Taj Mahal), and social and economic features.

2. Survey the geography of China. In conjunction with history studies (see above), kids should study the geography of China, covering major cities, mountain ranges, deserts (the Gobi Desert), rivers, boundaries, climate, man-made monuments and structures (the Great Wall), and social and economic features. Kids should know, for example, that China is the most heavily populated country in the world and the third-largest in terms of territory, and that Chinese culture is 4,000 years old.

3. Survey the geography of the Middle East. In conjunction with history studies (see above), kids should cover the major countries of the Middle East (Egypt, Israel, Lebanon, Jordan, Syria, Iraq, Iran, Kuwait, Saudi Arabia, Turkey), major cities, lakes and seas, rivers, mountain ranges, boundaries, climate, man-made monuments and structures, and social and economic features.

SCIENCE

While individual science curricula vary—sometimes widely (see page 290), eighth grade science often concentrates on physical science, a discipline that is repeated in more detail in twelfth grade.

PHYSICAL SCIENCE

Hands-On Physics Activities With Real-Life Applications
James Cunningham and Norman Herr; Center for Applied Research in Education, 1994
> Nearly 200 minilabs, investigations, demonstrations, and lesson plans for kids in grades 8 and up. Includes detailed background information and answer keys.

PHYSICS AT ABOUT.COM
> A wealth of physics resources on the Internet, categorized by topic. Among these are electricity and magnetism, classical mechanics, Newton's laws, particle physics, and optics. The site also includes links to books, educational resources, on-line texts and tutorials, and reference data. Web site: physics.about.com.

The Physical Universe
Konrad B. Krauskopf and Arthur Beiser; McGraw-Hill, 1996
> A beautifully illustrated introductory text on the physical sciences, covering basic physics, chemistry, earth science, and astronomy. Comes with a study guide that includes chapter summaries, lists of key equations and formulas, quizzes, and practice problems.

Using the Learning Cycle to Teach Physical Science: A Hands-On Approach for the Middle Grades
Paul C. Beisenherz and Marylous Dantonio; Heinemann, 1996
> The "learning cycle strategy" in an inquiry-based approach to science, in which kids first experience hands-on activities related to a featured scientific concept, then are introduced to the concept in formal terms, and finally learn about real-world applications of the concept. The book includes activity instructions and materials lists, teaching procedures, questions lists, and detailed background information.

Also see *Teaching Physics With Toys* and *Visual Dictionary of Physics*, page 264, and physics resources, pages 383–384.

1. Understand concepts of force and motion. Kids should know the definitions of *velocity* and *speed*, be familiar with the formula $s = d/t$, and be able to interpret graphs plotting position versus time and speed versus time. They should understand concepts of *force*, including *gravity*, *elasticity*, and *friction*; the effects of balanced and unbalanced forces on objects; and the relationship between force and mass.

Mechanics FUNdamentals
Robert W. Wood; McGraw-Hill, 1996

Explanations and interesting experiments demonstrating concepts of energy transfer, heat expansion, friction, balance, gravity, inertia and momentum, force, and more. The book also includes brief biographies of famous scientists and many fascinating facts.

MOTION

An investigative study unit using creative homemade equipment. Kids analyze and graph many forms of motion while studying concepts of mass, inertia, balanced and unbalanced forces, acceleration, action and reaction, and more. The unit contains thirty-six lessons for grades 7–12. TOPS Learning Systems; (888) 773-9755; www.topscience.org.

The Spinning Blackboard and Other Dynamic Experiments on Force and Motion
Paul Doherty and Don Rathjen; John Wiley & Sons, 1996

Hands-on activities and experiments demonstrating basic principles of force and motion from the San Franciso Exploratorium.

2. Understand concepts of density and buoyancy. For example, kids should be able to calculate *density* (given mass and volume); should understand the concept of *buoyancy* and know how to predict whether a given object will float or sink; and should understand *Archimedes's principle*.

FLOATING AND SINKING

A hands-on study unit on density and buoyancy for kids in grades 7–12. Uses simple homemade equipment to investigate complex concepts. TOPS Learning Systems; (888) 773-9755; www.topscience.org.

3. Understand concepts of work and power. For example, kids should be able to define *work* and *power*, to solve problems using the formulas w = fd (work = force x distance) and p = w/t (power =

work/time), and know common units of measure of work and power in both English and metric systems.

MACHINES
An investigative study unit in which kids build an array of machines from simple materials and use these to study work, power, and efficiency. Includes sixteen lessons for kids in grades 7–12. TOPS Learning Systems; (888) 773-9755; www.topscience.org.

4. Reinforce and expand upon previous studies of energy. For example, kids should know the definitions of *kinetic* and *potential* energy and be able to give examples of each. They should also understand the law of conservation of energy.

5. Reinforce and expand upon earlier studies of electricity and magnetism. For example, kids should be able to compare *current* and *static electricity*. They should know the characteristics and functions of *conductors*, *insulators*, and *capacitors*, should be able to define *amperes*, *watts*, and *ohms*, and should be able to solve problems using *Ohm's law* (watts = amperes × volts). They should also understand the relationship between electricity and magnetism and be able to cite practical applications of this phenomenon.

ELECTRICITY

MAGNETISM
Detailed investigative study units for kids in grades 8–12 using creative homemade materials. In Electricity, for example, kids study like and unlike charges, experiment with parallel and series circuits, make predictions based on Ohm's law, and build galvanometers, fuses, electroscopes, ammeters, and more. TOPS Learning Systems; (888) 773-9755; www.topscience.org.

Virtual Lab: Electricity
An interactive physical science curriculum on Win/Mac CD-ROM for kids in grades 6–12. The lab includes a versatile collection of tools with which kids can devise electrical experiments and conduct investigations, along with an accompanying book of instructions, background information, lab sheets, and suggestions for off-the-computer activities. Edmark; (800) 362-2890; www.edmark.com.

6. Understand concepts of sound and light and properties of wave propagation. Kids should understand the basic properties of waves, including *transverse versus longitudinal waves, wavelength, frequency,* and *amplitude.* They should know the properties of light and sound waves, be familiar with the composition of the *electromagnetic spectrum,* and understand the concepts of *wave interference, resonance,* and the *Doppler effect.*

See Virtual Labs: Light and other light resources, page 266.

FOREIGN LANGUAGE

Kids should show appropriate skills in speaking, comprehension of spoken and written material, and grammar and vocabulary.

See resources, pages 47, 268.

ART

As in the earlier grades, a comprehensive art program should include hands-on activities, art theory, art appreciation, and art history. If possible, kids should visit artists' studios, art galleries, and museums.

1. Use knowledge of art elements and principles of design to produce a wide range of creative artworks. Kids should experiment with many media and techniques, including drawing, painting, printmaking, pottery and ceramics, sculpture, fiber arts, photography, and electronic media.

See *Drawing With Older Children and Teens,* page 293.

2. Use knowledge of art elements and principles of design to analyze and critique a variety of artworks by well-known artists and works from a variety of multicultural sources. Kids should be able to discuss the influence of political and social developments on the art of a given historical period and should trace developments in art on timelines.

3. Study art in conjunction with other academic subjects across the curriculum. During a survey of the Middle East, for example, kids might study Arabic miniature painting. Studies of the Vietnam War might include the story of sculptor Maya Lin and the creation of the memorial wall.

4. Survey twentieth-century art and architecture. Kids should study representative artists and their artworks, should know characteristic features of each school or genre, and should be able to recognize and classify artworks accordingly.

Topics to cover include modern painters (including the work of Pollock, Rothko, Warhol, Lichtenstein, and Lawrence), photography (including the work of Steichen, Steiglitz, Bourke-White, and Adams), sculpture (including the work of Rodin, Brancusi, Picasso, Moore, Calder, Nevelson, and Oldenburg), and architecture (including the work of Wright, Gropius, Le Corbusier, and Mies van der Rohe).

See *History of Art for Young People*, page 294.

Discover America's Favorite Architects
Patricia Brown Glenn; John Wiley & Sons, 1996
Short biographies of famous American architects with illustrations of their most significant works. Among those featured are Thomas Jefferson, Frank Lloyd Wright, Julia Morgan, and I. M. Pei.

MUSIC

A music program should include active participation in the form of vocal or instrumental performance, music theory, music appreciation, and music history. If possible, kids should attend varied musical performances.

See Multimedia History of Music and Multimedia Musical Instruments, page 243.

1. Review and reinforce musical concepts introduced in the earlier grades. Kids should know musical notation (both bass and treble clefs) and musical terms. They should be familiar with major and minor chords, chord changes, and intervals, and should be able to construct major and minor scales in keys up to three sharps and flats.

See Music Ace 2, page 270.

2. Recognize and identify the major orchestral families and their individual instruments, keyboard instruments, historical instruments, and ethnic instruments by both sight and sound.

3. Recognize and identify common musical forms.

4. Continue survey of music history. Kids should listen to selections of famous works, read biographies of musicians and composers, order musical pieces and composers on timelines, and associate musical styles and developments with historical periods. For example, they should be able to recognize baroque, classical, and twentieth-century music and to describe its historical and cultural context.

Bach, Beethoven, and the Boys
David W. Barber; Sound and Vision, 1996

If It Ain't Baroque . . .
David W. Barber; Sound and Vision, 1992
"Music History as It Ought to be Taught," with an irreverent sense of humor. *Bach, Beethoven, and the Boys* covers music history through the biographies of famous composers; *If It Ain't Baroque . . .* is a chronological survey of musical genres, from "Really Early Music" through the Gregorian chant, the passion, the oratorio, the madrigal, the concerto, and the symphony. All musical terms are clearly defined.

Studies of music history at this grade level might also include an introduction to opera.

Music! Words ! Opera!
A multilevel curriculum for opera students in grades K–12. The program includes teacher's manual, audiocassette, and student workbooks. West Music; (800) 397-9378; www.westmusic.com.

When the Fat Lady Sings: Opera History as It Ought to be Taught
David W. Barber; Sound and Vision, 1990
A lighthearted and informative history of opera and famous operatic composers, from Monteverdi to the twentieth century.

Also see Multimedia History of Music and Multimedia Musical Instruments, page 243.

5. Listen and respond to a range of musical pieces by well-known composers and to multicultural musical selections.

6. **Participate in instrumental and vocal performances, group and solo.** Kids should also be able to conduct musical performances using a range of simple and compound meters.

7. Create and play original musical compositions.

8. **Study music in conjunction with other academic subjects across the curriculum.**

HEALTH AND PHYSICAL EDUCATION

1. **Participate in a range of age-appropriate indoor and outdoor athletic activities designed to provide a well-rounded program of physical fitness.** Kids should be able to design personal fitness programs, applying basic training principles to ensure cardiovascular health, strength, and flexibility.
See *Fit Kids!* and *Home School Family Fitness,* page 50.

2. Participate in a program of drug education.

3. **Understand the nature of sexually transmitted diseases and methods of prevention.** Kids should be familiar with the causes, symptoms, and means of prevention of HIV/AIDS.
See *It's Perfectly Normal* and Adolescence, page 272.

4. **Be familiar with the elements of good nutrition and personal hygiene.**

5. Know basic first-aid for common injuries.

HIGH SCHOOL: AN OVERVIEW

Commonly curricula become somewhat more amenable to individual interests in the high school years. Kids in secondary school generally have the option to select one or more elective classes each semester and often begin to concentrate their efforts in specific academic areas. States do have minimum requirements, however, for high school graduation; so do many colleges for enrollment eligibility.

MOST SECONDARY SCHOOL PROGRAMS REQUIRE A MINIMUM OF:

English/Language Arts: 4 years
Mathematics: 2 years
Science: 2 or 3 years
History/Geography: 2 or 3 years
Health and Physical Education: 4 years

In addition to these core basics, high school students must complete assorted electives—for example, additional mathematics or science, foreign language classes, civics, economics, psychology, art, music, and/or driver's education—thus earning a total number of required course credits. These are computed somewhat differently from school system to school system; as a rule of thumb, however, most secondary students take six to eight courses each school year. Community service or volunteer activities and part-time job, internship, or apprenticeship hours can often be used to fulfill high school credit requirements. Many homeschoolers take correspondence courses, on-line classes, or community college or university classes in their high school years (see Distance Learning, pages 403–408); often these can be used for high school (or future college) credit purposes.

A SAMPLE FOUR-YEAR PROGRAM MIGHT INCLUDE:

Grade Nine
    Language Arts
    Algebra I
    World History I
    Earth Science
    Foreign Language
    Art/Music
    Health and Physical Education

Grade Ten
    Language Arts
    Geometry
    World History II
    Biology
    Foreign Language
    Art/Music
    Health and Physical Education

Grade Eleven
    Language Arts
    Algebra II
    American History
    Chemistry
    Foreign Language

Art/Music
Health and Physical Education
Grade Twelve
Language Arts
Calculus
American Government
Physics
Foreign Language
Art/Music
Health and Physical Education

College-bound students generally take standardized college admissions tests during their high school years. Foremost among these are the SAT I (Scholastic Aptitude Test) and the ACT (American College Test), generally taken in the spring of junior year or the fall of senior year. In addition, high school students may also take the PSAT (Preliminary Scholastic Aptitude Test) in the fall of their sophomore or junior years; this serves as a dry run for the SAT and allows students to qualify for National Merit Scholarships. Students also have an option to take a battery of SAT II Subject Tests, which are achievement tests in a range of specific academic areas, including English literature, American history, biology, chemistry, and mathematics. Some colleges and universities require SAT II tests; often these are recommended to home-schoolers who lack conventional transcripts.

The SAT I is a three-hour exam that purports to measure verbal and mathematical reasoning skills. This is an *aptitude,* rather than an *achievement,* test, intended to assess a student's potential for succeeding in college. A perfect score on each section of the test is 800 points; thus absolute tops on the SAT is a score of 1600. The PSAT, in similar format, also is divided into verbal and mathematics sections, each with a possible perfect score of 800. The ACT measures achievement in math, English, reading comprehension, and science; get every single question right and you get a score of 36.

Many manuals and computer software programs are available to help students prepare for these tests.

For registration and information about the PSAT, SAT I, SAT II, or ACT exams, call your local high school or contact:

College Board SAT, Princeton, NJ 08541; (609) 771-7600; www.collegeboard.org; or ACT Registration Box 414, Iowa City, IA 52243-0414; (319) 337-1270; www.act.org.

Homeschooled kids have a wide range of options for fulfillment of high school education requirements. They may pursue a personal home-designed curriculum; take high school classes by correspondence or through on-line sources; attend community college or university classes; acquire mentors or enroll in apprenticeship programs; or gain practical skills through community service, volunteer work, or part-time jobs.

A note on texts: traditionally, school subjects are taught from textbooks. Such publications, even the best of their kind, almost invariably sacrifice quality for quanity—the unavoidable result of attempting to cram an immense amount of information into one (or two) portable volumes. High school texts thus tend to skim the surface of a discipline (hence the recurring terms "survey" and "overview"). While textbooks are useful as informational guidelines, often a much more compelling coverage of specific topics is found in the popular literature. Your teenager is interested in ancient China, medieval Europe, environmentalism, robotics? Let them concentrate. Supplement. Take them to the library.

RESOURCES FOR HOMESCHOOLED HIGH SCHOOL STUDENTS:

The Day I Became an Autodidact
Kendall Hailey; Delacorte Press, 1989
> Kendall Hailey left high school at sixteen to become an autodidact—a self-taught person. The book is her personal journal: a wonderful account of an innovative education, a self-designed literary life, and intellectual growth.

Homeschooling: The Teen Years
Cafi Cohen; Prima Publishing, 2000
> Anecdotes, advice, and suggestions for homeschooling teenagers. See the author's Web site (Homeschool/Teens/College), page 319.

The Teenage Liberation Handbook
Grace Llewellyn; Element, 1997
> A life instruction manual for teenagers, with many creative suggestions and resources for acquiring an education on their own.

The Teenager's Guide to the Real World
Marshall Brain; Byg Publishing, 1997

A proactive guide to life for teenagers. The book begins with an introduction to the "Hard Facts" (chapter titles include "Money Really Matters," "Teenagers Lack Experience," and "Adults Rule the World"), and continues through straightforward discussions of jobs and careers ("You Must Have a Job to Live Life"), love and marriage ("Marriage Is Forever"), attitudes and values ("Certain Mistakes Will Ruin Your Life"), success, financial security, and more.

THE HIGH SCHOOL HOME PAGE

A wealth of information for homeschooled secondary students. Web site: www.cis.upenn.edu/~brada/homeschooling.html.

HIGH SCHOOL HUB

On-line academic resources for high school students, including exam preparation help, a daily SAT question, learning games and study strategies, research and reference aids, college information, and a driver's quiz; Web site: highschoolhub.org.

HOMESCHOOL TEENAGERS

How to start homeschooling your teenager, curricula and approaches, and discussion groups for kids and parents. Web site: www.angelfire.com/la/homeschool.

HOMESCHOOL/TEENS/COLLEGE

Information on homeschooling teenagers and preparation for college, hosted by Cafi Cohen, author of *And What About College?* (Holt Associates, 1998). Web site: www.homeschoolteenscollege.net.

LEARN IN FREEDOM

Information for homeschooled teens plus a long list of colleges and universities that have accepted homeschoolers. Web site: www.learninfreedom.org.

GRADE NINE

It is very difficult to live among people you love and hold back from offering them advice.

Anne Tyler

LANGUAGE ARTS

As kids move through secondary school, language arts courses become more specialized. For example, literature students may have the option to concentrate on American literature, British literature, women's literature, world literature, mythology, or poetry; writers may study creative writing, journalism, or nonfiction writing. Those designing individualized homeschool curricula should base choices on their children's interests and skill levels.

Literature

CYBERGUIDES
On-line literature lesson plans and study units categorized by grade level. Guides for grades 9–12 cover *The Adventures of*

Huckleberry Finn, Hamlet, The Odyssey, To Kill a Mockingbird, Lord of the Flies, and many more. Web site: www.sdcoe.k12. ca.us/score/cyberguides.html.

JUNIOR GREAT BOOKS PROGRAM.
Selections for ninth-graders (Series 9) include Truman Capote's "Miriam," Robert Louis Stevenson's *The Strange Case of Dr. Jekyll and Mr. Hyde,* and H. G. Wells's *The Time Machine.* Each selection is followed by discussion questions and writing-project suggestions, all designed to promote critical thinking and excite debate. Great Books Foundation, 35 E. Wacker Dr., Suite 2300, Chicago, IL 60601-2298; (800) 222-5870; www.greatbooks.org.

Also see Learning Links, page 60, Novel Units, page 60, the Writing Company, page 218, and the Shakespeare Catalog, page 217.

1. Read a wide range of age-appropriate fiction and nonfiction materials. Students should use both print and nonprint resources to further their studies of literature. Curricular supplements might include biographies of well-known writers, audio and video performances, on-line resources, and field trips to theaters, lectures, or readings.

READING SUGGESTIONS FOR NINTH-GRADERS INCLUDE:

Across Five Aprils (Irene Hunt; Berkeley Publishing Group, 1991)

The Chocolate War (Robert Cormier; Laurel Leaf, 1991)

The Crystal Cave (Mary Stewart; Ballantine Books, 1996)

Dandelion Wine (Ray Bradbury; Bantam Books, 1985)

The Devil's Arithmetic (Jane Yolen; Puffin, 1990)

Dicey's Song (Cynthia Voigt; Fawcett Books, 1995)

Fahrenheit 451 (Ray Bradbury; Ballantine Books, 1995)

Island of the Blue Dolphins (Scott O'Dell; Yearling Books, 1987)

The Little Prince (Antoine de Saint-Exupéry; Harcourt Brace, 1982)

The Lord of the Rings Trilogy (J. R. R. Tolkien; Houghton Mifflin, 1999)

A Member of the Wedding (Carson McCullers; Bantam Books, 1985)

The Old Man and the Sea (Ernest Hemingway; Scribner, 1999)

One-Eyed Cat (Paula Fox; Yearling Books, 1985)

The Ramsay Scallop (Frances Temple; HarperTrophy, 1995)

Sounder (William H. Armstrong; HarperCollins, 1989)

A Tree Grows in Brooklyn (Betty Smith; HarperPerennial, 1998)

The True Confessions of Charlotte Doyle (Avi; Orchard Books, 1990)

ON-LINE BOOK LISTS FOR TEENAGERS:

BOSTON PUBLIC LIBRARY: TEEN LOUNGE
Several school reading lists for grades 9–12. Web site: www.bpl.org/WWW/KIDS/TeenLounge.html.

CARNEGIE LIBRARY OF PITTSBURGH'S YOUNG ADULT BOOK-LISTS
Good teen books, categorized by topic. Web site: alphaclp.clpgh.org/teens/.

OUTSTANDING BOOKS FOR THE COLLEGE BOUND
Annotated lists in five categories: fiction, nonfiction, biography, drama, and poetry. Web site: www.ala.org/yalsa/booklists/obcb/.

TEEN BOOK LISTS
Many categorized lists. Web site: www.mcpl.lib.mo.us/readers/lists/teen.

Also see Book Lists, pages 400–402.

Cicada
A high-quality literary magazine for teenagers. Includes fiction, nonfiction, poetry, and book reviews. The Cricket Magazine Group; (800) 827-0227; www.cricketmag.com.

2. Evaluate works of literature through discussion, debate, and written critique. Kids should read, discuss, and analyze works of fiction and nonfiction, including book-length works, short stories, essays, plays, and poems.

3. Expand upon knowledge of the classics. Suggestions for students at this grade level include William Shakespeare's *Romeo and Juliet* and/or *Antony and Cleopatra*, Dylan Thomas's *Under Milkwood*, Anton Chekhov's *The Sea Gull*, and selections from Greek, Roman, and Norse mythology.

4. Read and respond to a varied range of poetic forms.

INTERNATIONAL LIBRARY OF POETRY
Search by poet or title, biographies of poets, a list of the world's
one hundred greatest poems, and many useful links; Web site:
www.poetry.com.

How Does a Poem Mean?
John Ciardi; Houghton Mifflin, 1959
An analytic look at a wide range of poetry selections, from classical
to modern, with discussion questions to accompany each selection.

Also see poetry resources, pages 187, 275, 360.

WRITING

By this grade level, students should have mastered the elements of
English grammar, sentence structure, syntax, and spelling. Writing
studics should concentrate on refining skills, perfecting style, and
developing a distinctive personal voice.

**1. Write frequently and for many purposes, producing a range
of works including reports, essays, short stories, pocms, narratives, journal entries, and business and personal letters.** Kids
should be able to use an ordered writing process, involving
prewriting, drafting, revising, editing, proofreading, and publishing. They should be able to produce a well-organized research
report, gathering information from a variety of sources and
including a stylistically correct bibliography.

Merlyn's Pen: Senior Edition
A student-written literary magazine for kids in grades 9–12. Publishes stories, poems, essays, reviews, and artwork. Merlyn's Pen,
Inc., Box 910, E. Greenwich, RI 02818; (800) 247-2027; www.
merlynspen.com.

2. Be familiar with use of standard writers' reference works.
Kids should be able to use dictionaries, thesauri, quotations collections, style manuals, and usage handbooks.

The Elements of Style
William Strunk Jr., and E. B. White; Allyn & Bacon, 1999
Short, elegant, informative, timeless, and one of the few style
manuals that can be read with enjoyment from cover to cover.

3. **Use word processing and publishing software.**

4. **Survey the history of the English language.** One option for kids at this grade level is a survey of how the English language has evolved over time. Kids might study samples of literature from various periods in the history of English; review how English has been shaped by social, cultural, and geographical differences; learn about important influences, ancient and modern, on the shaping of English; and study the effects of such innovations as the printing press and the dictionary.

BETHUMP'D WITH WORDS

A creative board game based on the history of the English language. Players answer questions about word histories and origins, acronyms, eponyms, British and Australian English, slang, abbreviations, foreign words in English, and much more. Mamopalire, Box 24, Warren, VT 05674; (888) 496-4094; www.bethumpd.com.

The Story of English
Robert McCrum, William Cran, and Robert MacNeil; Viking, 1986
A fascinating and comprehensive history of the English language. Also available as a nine-video set. Zenger Media, 10200 Jefferson Blvd., Box 802, Culver City, CA 90232-0802; (800) 421-4246; www.zengermedia.com.

LISTENING AND SPEAKING SKILLS

1. **Listen and respond to various forms of oral presentations.** This should include plays, skits, and poetry and prose readings; and speeches, storytelling sessions, and lectures. Kids should be able to analyze material presented and ask substantive and appropriate questions. They should also be able to listen critically, evaluating oral presentations and media messages for bias, persuasion, propaganda, fallacies, opinion expressed as fact, and unsubstantiated generalities.

2. **Make well-organized oral presentations to a group.** Kids should be able to give an effective talk, appropriate to the audience and purpose.
See public speaking resources, page 301.

3. Analyze historically significant speeches. Examples might include Abraham Lincoln's "Gettysburg Address," Martin Luther King Jr.'s "I Have A Dream," and Sojourner Truth's "Ain't I a Woman?"

See *World's Greatest Speeches,* page 344.

4. Follow multiple-step oral directions.

STUDY SKILLS

1. Obtain information from a wide range of reference sources, including print and electronic sources, interviews, and site visits.

2. Practice effective study techniques.

Developing Study Skills, Taking Notes and Tests, Using Dictionaries and Libraries
Marcia J. Coman and Kathy L. Heavers; NTC Publishing Group, 1997
All you need to know in one handy informational volume.

Study Is Hard Work
William H. Armstrong; David R. Godine, 1998
A classic on the art of study, covering individual academic subjects, note taking and outlining, test taking, the effective use of libraries—and the all-important fact that all rewarding disciplines take effort.

For a large assortment of books and resources on enhancing study, writing, and research skills, and preparing for tests, see the Writing Company, page 218.

MATHEMATICS

Mathematics in the high school years may be taught in ordered traditional sequence—algebra (grade 9), geometry (grade 10), advanced algebra and trigonometry (grade 11), calculus (grade 12)—or may be taught in an integrated fashion, such that algebra, geometry, and trigonometry concepts are covered simultaneously over a two- to three-year period. Trigonometry, mathematical analysis, and linear algebra may also be combined in a precalculus course, taught in the eleventh or twelfth grade.

The popular Saxon math sequence, for example, includes courses in algebra 1 (grade 9), algebra 2 (grade 10), advanced mathematics (grade 11), and calculus (grade 12). In this series, algebra 1 and 2 incorporate geometry while advanced mathematics includes a mix of algebra, geometry, trigonometry, and mathematical analysis equivalent to a precalculus course. Selection of an appropriate course of study depends upon the interests, abilities, and goals of the individual student; parents and kids will have to decide among a range of options. Science- and technology-oriented students should take at least three—preferably four—years of mathematics.

SAMPLE GRADE-APPROPRIATE RESOURCES INCLUDE:

Algebra I
John H. Saxon, Jr.; Saxon Publishers, 1990

A beginning course in algebra and geometry, recommended for either eighth or ninth grade. The text covers signed numbers, exponents, equations in one variable, simultaneous equations, polynomials, functions and graphs, the Pythagorean theorem, solutions of quadratic equations, and direct and inverse variations. A thorough no-nonsense approach. Saxon Publishers, Inc., 2450 John Saxon Blvd., Norman, OK 73071; (800) 284-7019; www.saxonpub.com.

Algebra 1: Expressions, Equations, and Applications
Paul A. Foerster; Addison-Wesley, 1994

An excellent coverage of basic algebra in fourteen chapters, including linear equations and inequalities in one variable, linear functions, factoring and applications, laws of exponents, and radicals and radical expressions. Many student exercises, with an emphasis on application word problems.

Core-Plus Mathematics Project

An innovative mathematics series in which each year includes four interwoven strands of mathematical disciplines: algebra and functions, statistics and probability, geometry and trigonometry, and discrete mathematics. The program emphasizes mathematical modeling and the use of graphing calculators. Core-Plus Mathematics Project, Dept. of Mathematics and Statistics, Western Michigan University, Kalamazoo, MI 49008; (616) 387-4562; www.wmich.edu/cpmp.

Elementary Algebra
Harold R. Jacobs; W. H. Freeman and Company, 1979

A highly creative and thought-provoking approach to introductory algebra, appropriate for either eighth or ninth grade. The text covers fundamental operations, equations in one and two variables, simultaneous equations, functions and graphs, exponents, polynomials, factoring, quadratic equations, fractional equations, inequalities, and number sequences, all with clever illustrations and interesting real-world examples.

Interactive Mathematics Program

A nontraditional approach to mathematics. This is a multifaceted and problem-centered four-year program that combines a range of mathematical disciplines. In *IMP Year 1*, for example, kids cover five units: "Patterns," "The Game of Pig," "The Overland Trail," "The Pit and the Pendulum," and "Shadows." Concepts studies include functions, integers, polygons, probability, linear relationships, statistics, and trigonometry. Key Curriculum Press; (800) 995-MATH; www.keypress.com.

Introductory Algebra
Margaret Lial, John Hornsby, and Charles Miller;
Addison-Wesley, 1997

A complete first-year course in algebra. The emphasis is on problem-solving and mathematical thinking rather than rote exercises aimed at getting "the right answer." The book includes clear examples of all operations and many, many practice problems.

Key to Algebra Series

A first-year algebra course presented in a series of ten consumable workbooks, particularly recommended for kids who are struggling and intimidated by the very sound of the word *algebra*. The books are gently paced and include many demonstrations, illustrations, examples, and practice problems and activities. Titles are *Operations on Integers; Variables, Terms, and Expressions; Equations; Polynomials; Rational Numbers; Multiplying and Dividing Rational Expressions; Adding and Subtracting Rational Expressions;*

Graphs; Systems of Equations; and *Square Roots and Quadratic Equations.* Key Curriculum Press, Box 2304, Berkeley, CA 94702-0304; (800) 995-MATH; www.keypress.com.

Supplements:

Algebra Unplugged
Kenn Amdahl and Jim Loats; Clearwater Publishing, 1996
Short, humorous, and cheerfully nontechnical explanations of all the basics of algebra.

Algebra Word Problems Series

Anita Harnadek; Critical Thinking Press & Software
A series of twelve workbooks ranging from prealgebra to algebra 2, all emphasizing the process of translating word problems into algebraic expressions. Titles include *How to Solve Algebra Word Problems; Warm-Up; Ages and Coins; Mixtures;* and *Formulas, Rectangles, D = rt.* Critical Thinking Books & Software, Box 488, Pacific Grove, CA 93950-0448; (800) 458-4849; www. criticalthinking.com.

Hands-On Algebra
Frances M. Thompson; Prentice-Hall, 1998
Over 350 pages of creative games and activities for kids in grades 7 and up.

MATHEMATICS AT ABOUT.COM
A superb and comprehensive collection of math resources on the Internet, categorized by topic. Among these are *algebra, calculus, geometry, math history, math education, number theory,* and *statistics.* The site also includes links to math texts, tutorials, activities, and discussion groups. Web site: www.math.about.com.

TI-82 OR TI-83
Popular calculators for secondary-level mathematics, with advanced graphing capabilities. Many supplementary activity books and manuals relate calculator use to algebra, geometry, and calculus. Texas Instruments; (800) TI-CARES; www.ti.com.

Also see *Basic College Mathematics,* page 278, *Mathematics: A Human Endeavor,* page 253, and The Math Forum, page 223.

Some basic requirements for introductory algebra:

1. Understand the use of algebraic language. Students should be able to translate word problems and phrases into algebraic expressions and vice versa, and should be able to evaluate algebraic expressions and use algebraic formulas to solve problems.

2. Perform operations with real numbers. Kids should be able to simplify numeral expressions using order of operations; determine the additive or multiplicative inverse of a number; and distinguish between rational and irrational numbers. They should also be able to determine the absolute value of expressions, to estimate square roots, to simplify radical expressions, and to perform numerical operations with square roots.

3. Solve equations and inequalities with one variable. Kids should be able to solve simple equations both numerically and graphically. They should be able to solve simple equations involving fractions, absolute values, radicals, and exponents, and should be able to use equations and inequalities to solve problems.

4. Understand relations and functions. Kids should be able to define and distinguish *relation* and *function*. They should be able to graph ordered pairs of numbers on a coordinate plane, to graph a relation given an equation and a domain, and explore the graphs of functions using a graphing calculator or computer. They should be able to graph a linear equation, computing the x- and y- intercepts and determine the slope of a nonvertical line given either the graph or the equation of the line. They should know the slope-intercept form of an equation of a line. They should be able to graph a linear inequality in two variables, and should be able to apply their knowledge of relations and functions to real-world problems and situations.

5. Perform operations with polynomials. First-year algebra students should be able to define and identify *monomials, binomials,* and *polynomials.* They should be able to add and subtract polynomials, multiply and divide monomials, binomials, and polynomials, factor the difference of two squares, and factor a simple quadratic trinomial.

6. Reinforce and review knowledge of proportions, ratios, and percents. Kids should be able to simplify ratios involving algebraic expressions and use proportions, ratios, and percents in solving numerical and real-world problems.

7. Investigate, graph, and interpret non-linear equations. Kids should be able to graph quadratic equations, to solve quadratic equations using the quadratic formula, and to use quadratic equations to solve problems. They should be able to recognize an exponential function and use graphing calculators or computers to investigate problems involving nonlinear equations.

HISTORY AND GEOGRAPHY

Most public school curricula require kids to study two to three years of history/geography in order to obtain a high school diploma. Generally this includes courses in American history (one year), world history (one year), and civics or American government (one year), with options for more specialized electives such as ancient history, modern history, African-American history, women's history, world geography, comparative religion, anthropology, sociology, and economics. There are many ways of organizing history, geography, and related studies; a common approach is to study world history as a two-year sequence in ninth and tenth grades. World history 1 (grade 9) thus spans prehistory to about A.D. 1000; world history 2 (grade 10) covers the years from A.D. 1000 to modern times. Some programs split world history 1 and 2 at a somewhat later date, dividing the courses around A.D. 1500. Another alternative is to condense world history to a less detailed one-year course, covering prehistory to A.D. 1000 (or A.D. 1500) in the first semester, and A.D. 1000 (or A.D. 1500) to modern times in the second. In both cases, studies reinforce and expand upon topics introduced in the earlier grades.

Ninth-grade history studies should involve a range of resources and approaches, including fiction and nonfiction books, multicultural myths and legends, biographies of key historical figures, magazines and historical journals, maps, software programs and on-line resources, videos, hands-on investigations and activities, and field trips.

See Social Studies School Service, page 197, Jackdaw Publications, page 284.

See Social Studies School Service, page 197, Jackdaw Publications, page 284.

SUGGESTED GRADE-APPROPRIATE RESOURCES INCLUDE:

The Cambridge Introduction to World History Series

Trevor Cairns; Cambridge University Press
Illustrated texts plus supplementary "Topic Books" cover world history from the beginning of civilization to the mid-seventeenth century for kids in grades 7–12.

World History

World History: To 1800

World History: Since 1500

William J. Duiker and Jackson J. Spielvogel; Wadsworth Publishing, 1997
World History is a single-volume comprehensive introduction to the study of world civilizations from ancient to modern times. *World History: To 1800* and *World History: Since 1500* cover the same material in more detail, in two volumes.

World History: Patterns of Change and Continuity

Peter N. Stearns; Addison-Wesley, 1995
A thorough, illustrated textbook of world history from prehistory to modern times, including the rise of the first civilizations; China, India, Greece, and Rome; the rise of Islam; Byzantium and Russia; the Middle Ages; the civilizations in the Americas; the Mongols; the age of discovery and colonization, the Ottoman and Mughal Empires; the Industrial Revolution; western imperialism in Asia and Africa; and the world in the 20th century.

SUPPLEMENTS

The Cartoon History of the Universe I

Larry Gonick; Doubleday, 1990

The Cartoon History of the Universe II

Larry Gonick; Doubleday, 1994
Humorous but highly informational cartoon-illustrated histories of the universe, from the big bang to the fall of Rome. Fun for all; particularly good for the history-resistant.

World History Volume 1: From the Stone Age to 1500
Charles A. Frazee, ed.; Greenhaven, 1999

A collection of primary and secondary source documents, including timelines, maps, and discussion questions, to accompany world history studies. This volume contains, for example, the Mesopotamian creation myth, the Code of Hammurabi, Socrates's trial defense, Marco Polo's account of his meeting with Kublai Khan, and more.

(See volume 2, page 350.)

BASIC TOPICS TO COVER IN WORLD HISTORY 1 INCLUDE:

1. The development of the earliest human communities and the beginnings of agriculture. Topics include the paleontological evidence for human ancestry, the distinctions between *anthropology* and *archaeology*, techniques of anthropological and archaeological research, hunter-gatherer societies, toolmaking and the discovery of fire, and the rise of agrarian societies.

2. The first great civilizations. Topics include the civilizations of Mesopotamia, Egypt, and the Indus River valley; the social, political, religious, and economic features of each; and the landmark development of writing.

3. The history of ancient Greece: 2000 B.C.–300 B.C. Topics include the social, political, and economic features of ancient Greek civilization, Greek mythology and religion; the birth of democracy; the Persian and Peloponnesian Wars; the "Golden Age" of Athens; Greek science, literature, art, architecture, and philosophy; and Alexander the Great and the spread of Hellenism.

4. The history of ancient Rome: 700 B.C.–A.D. 500. Topics include social, political, and economic features of ancient Roman civilization; Roman mythology and religion; the Roman Republic; the Roman Empire; the origin, beliefs, and spread of Christianity; Roman science, literature, art, architecture, philosophy, and law; and the decline and fall of the Roman Empire.

5. The rise of Islam. Topics include the origin, beliefs, and spread of Islam; the social, political, and economic features of the Islamic nations; the multiple causes of the historic conflict between Muslims and Christians; and the impact of Arab culture on western civilization.

6. The Byzantine Empire. Topics include the establishment of Constantinople; the social, political, and economic features of the Byzantine Empire; the codification of Roman law under Emperor Justinian; the split between Roman Catholic and Greek Orthodox branches of the Christian church; Byzantine art and architecture; and the impact of the Byzantine Empire on Russia and Eastern Europe.

7. The great civilizations of Africa, Asia, and the Americas. Topics include the social, political, economic, and religious features of major eastern and western African kingdoms, including Kush and Ghana; the social, political, economic, and religious features of ancient India; Indian Hinduism; introduction of Islam to India with the conquest by the Muslim Turks; the social, political, economic, and religious features of ancient China and Japan; the features of Buddhism, Confucianism, Taoism, and Shintoism; and the social, political, economic, and religious features of the Maya, Aztec, and Inca civilizations.

8. Identify global trends from 4000 B.C. to A.D. 1000. As well as details, facts, and individual personalities, kids should study history in a broad sense, tracing population movements, the spread of religion, the multifaceted effects of technological and social developments, and the like. For these studies, they should use maps and timelines, along with other references and resources.

In all cases, geography should be incorporated into history studies. Kids should understand and be able to give examples of the major influences of geography upon civilization.

See Geography at About.com.

SCIENCE

Most public school curricula require two or three years of science studies in order to obtain a high school diploma. Depending on the scope of the local high school, students may fulfill this requirement from a battery of science choices, including geology, astronomy, biology, chemistry, physics, botany, and environmental science. In the traditional science sequence, kids usually study earth/space science in ninth grade (see below), biology in tenth (see page 352), chemistry in eleventh (see page 368), and physics in twelfth (see page 383). Homeschoolers, depending on the interests of their children, should adjust their science curricula accordingly.

Earth/space science should be approached through a range of resources and methods, including hands-on explorations and experiments, fiction and nonfiction books, magazines and professional journals, biographies of prominent scientists, videos, computer software programs and Internet resources, and field trips. Kids should also use maps (bathymetric, geologic, topologic, and weather), charts (including star charts), and globes.

EARTH/SPACE SCIENCE

RESOURCES: EARTH SCIENCE

The Blue Planet: An Introduction to Earth System Science
Brian J. Skinner, Stephen C. Porter, and Daniel B. Botkin; John Wiley & Sons, 1999
> A beautifully illustrated text that covers the earth in space, earth structure and geology, the oceans, the atmosphere, and the interrelationships of environment and life. Optional accompaniments include a teacher's manual, test bank, laboratory manual, student study guide, and CD-ROM.

Earth: The Making of a Planet
Roy A. Gallant and Christopher J. Schuberth; Marshall Cavendish, 1998
> The illustrated text covers earth's history from the big bang to the distant future, including the formation of continents, oceans, and the moon; the makeup of the earth's interior; meteorology; geology; and oceanography.

Earth Story: The Shaping of Our World
Simon Lamb and David Sington; Princeton University Press, 1998
> An enthralling account of the earth sciences, covering the plate-tectonics revolution, earthquakes and volcanoes, the earth's interior, mountain formation, oceanography, climatology, and more.

Exploring Earth

Jon P. Davidson, Walter E. Reed, and Paul M. Davis; Prentice Hall, 1996

An introduction to physical geology for beginners. The comprehensive text relates basic geologic premises to such topics as the eruption of Mount St. Helens, the formation of the Antarctic ozone hole, and acid rain.

RESOURCES: SPACE SCIENCE

Astronomy

Eric Chaisson and Steve McMillan; Prentice-Hall, 1997

A spectacularly illustrated, comprehensive, and thoroughly understandable introductory college-level text, appropriate for motivated high school students. Includes a CD-ROM.

The Friendly Guide to the Universe

Nancy Hathaway; Viking, 1994

A fascinating and fat compendium of astronomical information, including timelines, biographies of famous astronomers, anecdotes and quotations, and reader-friendly explanations of all basic astronomical concepts. An excellent supplement to a high school–level astronomy program.

COSMOS

A thirteen-part PBS video series narrated by astronomer Carl Sagan, dramatically covering all aspects of astronomy. PBS; (800) 645-4247; www.pbs.org.

ISAAC ASIMOV'S LIBRARY OF THE UNIVERSE

A multimedia tour of the universe on six CD-ROMs. The equivalent of a survey course in basic astronomy for high school or college students. Includes tests. Andromeda Software, Box 605-N, Amherst, NY 14226–0605; www.andromedasoftware.com.

BASIC TOPICS TO COVER IN EARTH/SPACE SCIENCE INCLUDE:

1. The formation of the sun, solar system, earth, and moon. Topics include big bang cosmology and its supporting evidence; the compositions of sun, terrestrial planets, and gas planets; theories for the origin of the moon; the effects of asteroid impacts on earth, moon, and planets; planetary orbits and retrograde motion; Kepler's laws; the relationship between earth's tilt and orbital position and the seasons; moon phases; and lunar and solar eclipses.

2. The earth in the universe. Topics to cover include composition of stars and galaxies, classification of stars, life histories of stars, origin of heavy elements in stars, Hertzsprung-Russell diagrams, astronomical instruments (including reflecting, refracting, radio, and X-ray telescopes), and the measurement of astronomical distances.

3. The structure of the earth. Topics include the shape of the earth (including polar flattening and equatorial bulge), the circumference of the earth (including measurements from the experiments of Eratosthenes to modern times), the structure of the earth's internal layers, the earth's magnetic field and its measurement, and gravity and its measurement.

4. Plate tectonics. Topics include the history and evidence for the theory of plate tectonics, characteristic tectonic processes (including subduction, rifting, sea floor spreading, and continental collision), the relationship between volcanoes and earthquakes and plate boundaries, the structure of the ocean floor, mountain formation, earthquakes and their measurement, and classification and features of volcanoes.

5. Rocks and minerals. Topics include a survey of the most common elements and most abundant minerals in the earth's crust; common rock types: igneous (intrusive and extrusive), sedimentary (clastic and chemical), and metamorphic (foliated and unfoliated); economically valuable minerals; identification of rocks and minerals; key properties; basic crystal systems; the rock cycle; the fossil record and the geologic time scale; and fossil fuels.

6. The hydrologic (water) cycle. Topics include clouds, precipitation, sources of freshwater on and under the earth, water capacity of soils and groundwater zones, the relationship between slope and run-off velocity, and the causes and effects of erosion; streams and rivers; flooding; and the source of minerals and salts in seawater.

7. Oceans. Topics include a survey of oceans as complex interactive systems, topographic features of the ocean floor, the layered structure of ocean waters, waves and currents, the Coriolis effect, the effects of ocean currents on climate, and the causes and effects of sea level and polar ice cap variations.

8. The atmosphere. Topics include the structure of the atmospheric layers, measurements and studies of atmospheric changes over geologic time, the origin of atmospheric oxygen, the causes and effects of variations in carbon dioxide concentration, atmospheric regulation mechanisms, the ozone layer and its disruption, and the atmospheres of other planets.

9. Energy transfer patterns: dynamics of earth systems. Topics to cover include the internal energy of the earth; solar energy and its effects and uses; causes and consequences of the greenhouse effect; differential heating and circulatory patterns of atmosphere and oceans (winds and currents); the effect of the earth's rotation on wind and ocean currents; causes and effects of temperature inversions; climatic zones; effects of geologic and geographic features on climate; interaction of wind, ocean currents, and mountain ranges in formation of global weather patterns; the distinctions between *weather* and *climate*; weather prediction; and climatic changes over time.

10. Biogeochemical cycles. Topics include the *carbon cycle* (photosynthesis and respiration); the global carbon cycle (including the transfer of carbon in the atmosphere, oceans, biomass, and fossil fuels); and the *nitrogen cycle*.

11. Correlate the earth sciences to state geographical features. Students should relate the principles learned in earth science studies to familar geographical features of their home states, explaining the causes and effects of mountain ranges, ocean currents, faults and seismic activity, and the like.

FOREIGN LANGUAGE

Students should show appropriate skills in speaking, comprehension of spoken and written material, and grammar and vocabulary.
See resources, pages 47, 268.

ART

As in the earlier grades, a comprehensive art program should include creative hands-on activities and explorations, art theory, art appreciation, and art history. If possible, students should participate in field trips to artists' studios, art galleries, and museums.

1. Apply knowledge of art elements and principles of design to produce a wide range of creative artworks.
See *Drawing With Older Children and Teens*, page 293.

2. Analyze and critique artworks by well-known artists and works from a variety of multicultural sources.
See *History of Art for Young People*, page 294.

SISTER WENDY'S STORY OF PAINTING
A history of art (and a stunning world tour) in a five-video series from PBS. PBS Home Video, 1320 Braddock Pl., Alexandria, VA 22314-1698; (800) 645-4727; www.pbs.org.

The Story of Painting: The Essential Guide to the History of Western Art
Sister Wendy Beckett; Dorling Kindersley, 1994
A gloriously illustrated history from cave paintings to modern art, with information on the lives and times of the painters, technical aspects of art, fact boxes, and timelines.

3. Study art in conjunction with other academic subjects across the curriculum. See World History 1 (pages 332–333). Art studies might be correlated with the chronological progression through world history, using a range of sources, including fiction and nonfiction books, magazines and journals, videos, computer software and Internet sources, and field trips.

Topics to cover include prehistoric art: cave paintings and early sculptures; the first architecture (including dolmens, menhirs, and cromlechs); Mesopotamia: ziggurats and bas-reliefs; the art and architecture of Ancient Egypt; the art and architecture of Ancient Greece; the art and architecture of Ancient Rome; pre-Columbian art and architecture in the Americas; early African art: masks and sculptures; and Byzantine art and architecture.

MUSIC

As in the earlier grades, a comprehensive music program should include active participation in the form of vocal or instrumental performance, music theory, music appreciation, and music history. The program should utilize a varied range of resources, including fiction and nonfiction books, biographies of famous musicians and composers, audio and video resources, computer software and Internet sources, and field trips to attend musical performances.

1. Use and understand musical concepts studied in the earlier grades. For example, kids should know musical notation (bass and treble clefs) and musical terms and should be familiar with scale patterns, intervals, chord progressions, and musical forms.

See Music Ace 2, page 270.

2. Recognize and identify the major orchestral families and their individual instruments, keyboard instruments, historical instruments, and ethnic instruments by both sight and sound.

See Multimedia Music Conservatory, page 340.

3. Listen and respond to a range of musical pieces by well-known composers and to multicultural selections. Kids should be able to identify musical genres from various selections, use their knowledge of musical concepts to analyze and critique assorted selections, and pair selected compositions with the appropriate composer.

4. Identify and classify musical selections according to historical and cultural context. Kids should arrange musical pieces and their composers on timelines; associate musical selections with particular historical periods and with cultural and social developments; and read biographies of representative composers.

Music Conservatory

An exploration of music history and theory on CD-ROM. Includes audio and video demonstrations of seventy-five orchestral instruments, a detailed musical glossary, biographies of famous composers with excerpts of their works, and a musical timeline. Voyetra Technologies, 5 Odell Plaza, Yonkers, NY 10701-1406; (914) 966-0600; www.voyetra.com.

See Multimedia History of Music, page 243, *Bach, Beethoven, and the Boys* and *If It Ain't Baroque . . .* , page 313.

5. Participate in instrumental and vocal performances, group and solo.

6. Create and play original musical compositions.

7. Study music in conjunction with other academic subjects across the curriculum.

HEALTH AND PHYSICAL EDUCATION

1. Participate in a range of age-appropriate indoor and outdoor athletic activities designed to provide a well-rounded program of physical fitness. Homeschooled kids might participate in a variety of individual, small group, or team sports, including gymnastics, dance, tennis, racquetball, skating, jogging, hiking, bicycling, swimming, volleyball, soccer, field hockey, football, baseball, and basketball.

See *Fit Kids!* and *Home School Family Fitness,* page 50.

2. Participate in a program of drug education. Kids should understand the dangers of tobacco, alcohol, and other drug use.

3. Understand the nature of sexually transmitted diseases and the methods of prevention. HIV/AIDS falls into this category in public school programs.

4. Know the elements of good nutrition and personal hygiene.

5. Know common first-aid and safety procedures.

GRADE TEN

Knowledge is of two kinds. We know a subject ourselves, or we know where we can find information upon it.

SAMUEL JOHNSON

LANGUAGE ARTS

For an overview of high school options in language arts, see page 320.

LITERATURE

INTRODUCTION TO THE GREAT BOOKS PROGRAM

This is a reading and discussion program for kids in grades 10–12. Selections include classical and contemporary literature, both fiction and nonfiction; all are chosen for their thought-provoking discussion potential. The "First Series," recommended for tenth-graders, includes "Why War?" by Sigmund Freud, "The Melian Dialogue" by Thucydides, "The Social Me" by William James, and "Rothschild's Fiddle" by Anton Chekhov. A superb and mind-expanding exercise in critical thinking. Great Books Foundation, 35 E. Wacker Dr., Suite 2300, Chicago, IL 60601-2298; (800) 222-5870; www.greatbooks.org.

Also see CyberGuides, pages 320–321, Learning Links, page 60, Novel Units, page 60, the Writing Company, page 218, and The Shakespeare Catalog, page 217.

1. Read a wide range of age-appropriate fiction and nonfiction materials.
Students should supplement their literature studies with a varied range of resources, including biographies of well-known writers, audio and video performances, Internet resources, and field trips to theaters, lectures, and prose or poetry readings.

Reading suggestions for tenth-graders include:

Babbitt (Sinclair Lewis; Signet Classics, 1998)
Catcher in the Rye (J. D. Salinger; Little, Brown, 1991)
Cold Sassy Tree (Olive Ann Burns; Delta, 1986)
Flowers for Algernon (Daniel Keyes; Bantam, 1984)
Go Tell It on the Mountain (James A. Baldwin; Laurel Leaf, 1985)
Gone With the Wind (Margaret Mitchell; Warner Books, 1994)
The Grapes of Wrath (John Steinbeck; Penguin, 1992)
The Heart Is a Lonely Hunter (Carson McCullers; Bantam Books, 1983)
I Never Promised You a Rose Garden (Joanne Greenburg; New American Library, 1984)
The Left Hand of Darkness (Ursula LeGuin; Ace Books, 1991)
Manchild in the Promised Land (Claude Brown; Simon & Schuster, 1999)
The Once and Future King (T. H. White; Ace Books, 1996)
One Flew Over the Cuckoo's Nest (Ken Kesey; Penguin, 1977)
Slaughterhouse Five (Kurt Vonnegut Jr.; Delta, 1999)
Walden (Henry David Thoreau; Beacon Press, 1998)

See Book Lists, pages 400–402, On-line Book Lists for Teenagers and *Cicada*, page 322.

2. Evaluate works of literature through discussion, debate, and written critique.
Students should read, discuss, and analyze works

of fiction and nonfiction, including book-length works, short stories, essays, plays, and poems.

3. Expand upon knowledge of drama, classic and contemporary. Recommendations for tenth-graders include William Shakespeare's *Henry V* and *The Taming of the Shrew,* Sophocles' *Antigone,* Lillian Hellman's *Watch on the Rhine,* Arthur Miller's *All My Sons,* and Eugene O'Neill's *Mourning Becomes Electra.*

4. Read and respond to a varied range of poetic forms. See poetry resources, pages 187, 275, 360.

WRITING

Writing at the high school level can encompass specialized courses such as creative writing, nonfiction writing, and journalism; or writing may be integrated with literature courses, as in "American Literature and Composition," "Multicultural Literature and Composition," "Contemporary Literature and Composition," and the like. Homeschoolers should select or design programs based on their children's individual interests and skill levels.

1. Write frequently and for many purposes, producing a range of works including reports, essays, short stories, poems, narratives, journal entries, and business and personal letters. Tenth-graders should use an ordered writing process, involving prewriting, drafting, revising, editing, proofreading, and publishing. They should be able to produce well-organized research reports, based on information gathered and synthesized from a wide range of sources and including a stylistically correct bibliography.

10,000 Ideas for Term Papers, Projects, Reports, and Speeches
Kathryn Lamm; IDG Books Worldwide, 1998
At a loss for ideas? This fat manual contains ten thousand suggestions in 130 subject areas for high school and college-level students.

Models for Writers
Alfred Rosa and Paul Eschholz, eds.; St. Martin's Press, 1992
A collection of short essays, each illustrating a basic principle, purpose, or technique of nonfiction writing, with accompanying writing projects for high school and beginning-college-level writers.

Also see Researchpaper.com, page 276, and *Merlyn's Pen,* page 323.

2. Be familiar with use of standard writers' reference works.
Students should use dictionaries, thesauri, quotation collections,
style manuals, and usage handbooks.

Writers Inc.: A Student Handbook for Writing and Learning
Patrick Sebranek, Verne Meyer, and Dave Kemper; Write Source, 1995
   A comprehensive reference handbook, including everything from
   the proper use of the semicolon and the important distinctions
   between *who* and *whom* to the proper formats for résumés,
   reports, and essays.

3. Use word processing and publishing software.

4. Expand upon knowledge of the history of the English language.
See *The Story of English* and Bethump'd With Words, page 324.

Listening and Speaking Skills

1. Listen and respond to various forms of oral presentations.
Such presentations should involve plays, skits, and poetry and
prose readings, speeches, storytelling sessions, and lectures. Kids
should be able to analyze presented material, evaluating the
speaker's purpose and identifying both verbal and nonverbal components of communication and should ask substantive and appropriate questions. They should also be able to listen critically,
evaluating oral presentations and media messages for bias, propaganda, fallacies, and the like.

2. Participate in group discussions both as a speaker and a listener.

3. Make well-organized oral presentations to a group. For example, kids should be able to present an argument in a persuasive and
orderly fashion.
See public speaking resources, pages 300–301.

4. Analyze historically significant speeches.

World's Greatest Speeches
   Over 400 great speeches on CD-ROM, with text, audio, and video
   clips, plus illustrated biographies of the speakers. Zenger Media,

10200 Jefferson Blvd., Box 802, Culver City, CA 90232-0802; (800) 421-4246; www.zengermedia.com.

5. Follow multiple-step oral directions.

STUDY SKILLS

1. Obtain information from a wide range of reference sources, including print and electronic sources, interviews, and site visits.

2. Practice effective study techniques. Students have an option to take the PSAT (Preliminary Scholastic Aptitude Test) in the fall semester of tenth grade. (See pages 317–318.)

Also see Study Guides and Strategies, page 221.

How to Improve Your Study Skills
Marcia J. Coman and Kathy L. Heavers; NTC Publishing, 1997
> Study skills for high school and college students. The books covers how to discover your personal learning style, basic study skills, note taking, tests, improving understanding and increasing speed, skimming and scanning, using basic references, library skills, and Internet research.

For books and resources on enhancing study, writing, and research skills, and on test preparation, see the Writing Company, page 218.

MATHEMATICS

For an overview of high school options in Mathematics, see pages 325–326.

Common recommendations for tenth-graders include algebra 2, geometry, and business mathematics. Parents should select programs based on their children's interests, goals, and skill levels. Also see Mathematics resources, grade 9 (pages 326–328).

TEXTS AND PROGRAMS

Algebra 2
John Saxon; Saxon Publishing, 1991
> This text includes both concepts ordinarily covered in a second-year algebra course and the equivalent of one semester of geometry. Topics include graphic solutions to simultaneous equations,

quadratic equations, exponential equations, polynomials, vectors, polar and coordinate systems, logarithms and antilogarithms, basic trigonometric functions, set theory, and probability and statistics. Saxon Publishers, Inc., 2450 John Saxon Blvd., Norman, OK 73071; (800) 284-7019; www.saxonpub.com.

Beginning and Intermediate Algebra

Margaret L. Lial, E. John Hornsby, and Charles D. Miller; Addison-Wesley, 1996

A comprehensive combined text covering both algebra 1 and 2, with chapter summaries, many review exercises, and tests. Topics covered include the real number system, linear equations and their applications, linear inequalities and absolute value, polynomials and exponents, factoring, rational expressions, the straight line, linear systems, roots and radicals, quadratic equations, quadratic functions and conic sections, inverse, exponential, and logarithmic functions, and sequences and series.

Business Mathematics

Charles D. Miller, Stanley A. Salzman, and Gary Clenenden; Addison-Wesley, 1999

The text reviews basic mathematics, including decimals, fractions, and percents, and covers introductory business mathematics, including bank services, payrolls, invoices and trade discounts, simple and compound interest, loans, taxes and insurance, depreciation, and more. A prerequisite for this course is *Basic College Mathematics* (see page 278).

Core-Plus Mathematics Project

See pages 326–327.

Essentials of Geometry

Margaret Lial, Arnold R. Steffensen, and L. Murphy Johnson; Addison-Wesley, 1990

Recommended for high school and beginning college students. The text covers all the essentials, with many illustrative examples and practice problems.

Geometry

Harold R. Jacobs; W. H. Freeman and Company, 1987

A substantive and highly creative approach to geometry, emphasizing real-world relationships and mathematical thinking. The book covers deductive reasoning, points, lines, and planes, rays and angles, congruent triangles, inequalities, parallel lines, quadrilaterals, transformations, area, similarities, right triangles, circles, concurrence theorems, regular polygons, geometric solids, and coordinate geometry.

Interactive Mathematics Program

In *IMP Year 2*, kids cover five interactive mathematical units variously involving statistics and probability, geometry and trigonometry, equations and graphs, and exponents. Unit titles are "Solve It!" "Is There Really a Difference?" "Do Bees Build It Best?" "Cookies," and "All About Alice." Comprehensive and creative. Key Curriculum Press; (800) 995-MATH; www.keypress.com.

Key to Geometry Series

A beginning geometry course presented in a series of eight consumable workbooks. Titles are *Lines and Segments; Circles; Constructions; Perpendiculars; Squares and Rectangles; Angles; Perpendiculars and Parallels, Chords and Tangents, Circles;* and *Triangles, Parallel Lines, Similar Polygons*. Gently paced, with many illustrations and practice problems. Key Curriculum Press; (800) 995-MATH; www.keypress.com.

Mathematics for Everyday Life Series

Roland E. Larson and Robert P. Hostetler; Meridian Creative Group
A series of worktexts for high school students centered around mathematics encountered in real-world situations. There are nine titles in the series, among them *The Mathematics of Saving, The Mathematics of Borrowing, The Mathematics of Investment,* and *The Mathematics of Taxes*. Meridian Creative Group, 5178 Station Rd., Erie, PA 16510; (800) 695-9417; www.home.meridiancg.com.

SUPPLEMENTS

The Joy of Pi

David Blatner; Walker & Co., 1997
Many fascinating facets of this all-important number; a mind-broadening supplement for young geometry students.

LIFE BY THE NUMBERS

A superb seven-part video series on the vast and multidimensional role mathematics plays in our lives. PBS Home Video; (800) 645-4727; www.pbs.org/shop.

Also see *Basic College Mathematics*, page 278, *Mathematics: A Human Endeavor*, page 253, Mathematics at About.com, page 328, and The Math Forum, page 223.

Basic topics covered in introductory geometry include:

1. Concepts of points, lines, and planes in one, two, and three dimensions. Students should be able to identify *points, lines, rays, segments,* and *planes,* to find the coordinates of a point in a plane or in space, identify the midpoint of a given segment on a line, and solve problems using lengths.

2. Composing valid proofs using a variety of reasoning strategies. Students should understand the process of *deductive reasoning* and be able to state the *converse, inverse,* and *contrapositive* of a conditional statement. They should be able to construct mathematical proofs using flow diagrams, two-column formats, and paragraph formats, and should be able to solve problems and write proofs using definitons of *adjacent, vertical, linear pair, complementary* and *supplementary angles,* the *angle addition postulate,* and the definitions of *angle bisectors, parallel lines, perpendicular lines,* and *perpendicular bisectors.* They should understand the relationships that exist between the pairs of angles formed by parallel lines and a transversal, and they should be able to use slopes to determine whether or not a given pair of lines is parallel or perpendicular.

3. Properties of polygons and polyhedrons. Students should be able to model and describe *convex* and *regular polygons* and use measures of interior and exterior angles and proportions to solve problems. They should understand the properties of *similar* and *congruent* polygons and should explore *polygonal transformations,* including *tessellations, slides, rotations,* and *flips,* in a coordinate plane. They should be able to model and describe *regular* and *irregular polyhedrons;* and identify *similar* and *congruent polyhedrons.*

4. Properties of quadrilaterals. Students should know the properties of *parallelograms, rectangles, rhombuses, squares,* and *trapezoids* and should use these to solve problems and write proofs.

5. Properties of triangles. Students should be able to classify triangles according to lengths of sides and angles, solve problems involving the interior and exterior angles of triangles, and use postulates and theorems to prove that two triangles are congruent. They should be able to apply theorems pertaining to isosceles triangles, altitudes, perpendicular bisectors, medians, segments joining midpoints of two sides of a triangle, and segments divided proportionally.

Students should also be familiar with the properties of right triangles, including the use of the Pythagorean theorem, and should know the definitions of *sine, cosine,* and *tangent* and use these to solve problems.

6. Properties of circles and spheres. Students should know the mathematical definition of a circle. They should understand the relationship between tangents and circles and the properties and theorems relating to *arcs, angles of circles, chords, tangents, secants,* and *radii.* They should know the relationship between the *equation of a circle* and its center and radius length; the relationships of *congruent, similar,* and *concentric circles*; and the properties of *spheres.*

7. Concepts of perimeter, area, and volume. Students should be able to determine the perimeters of geometric figures; the areas of triangles, parallelograms, trapezoids, and rectangles; and the circumferences and areas of circles. They should also be able to determine arc lengths and sector areas of circles and calculate the surface areas and volumes of *right prisms, pyramids, cylinders, cones,* and *spheres.*

HISTORY AND GEOGRAPHY

For high school–level history and geography options, see page 330.

A common choice for tenth-graders is World History 2 (A.D. 1000 to modern times), which builds upon the previous year's world history studies. Homeschoolers should select their course of study based upon their children's individual interests and goals.

World History: Since 1500
William J. Duiker and Jackson J. Spielvogel; Wadsworth Publishing, 1997

A history of world civilization from the Renaissance to modern times, with illustrations, maps, timelines, and primary source documents.

World History Volume 2: From A.D. 1500 to the Present
Charles A. Frazee, ed.; Greenhaven, 1999

An anthology of primary and secondary source documents to supplement world history studies, with background information, discussion questions, timelines, and maps.

World history should be approached through a range of resources and methods, including hands-on activities, fiction and nonfiction books, biographies of prominent persons, magazines and journals, computer software and Internet sources, and field trips. Students should make frequent use of maps, globes, and timelines, and should integrate world history with other academic subjects across the curriculum, including science, art, and music. See Social Studies School Service, page 197, Jackdaw Publications, page 284, and Annual Editions, page 365.

TOPICS TO COVER IN WORLD HISTORY 2 INCLUDE:

1. The world in A.D. 1000. Topics include the social, political, and economic aspects of feudalism; trade, commerce, and the rise of towns; the major countries and leaders of pre-A.D. 1000 western Europe; the major countries and leaders of Byzantium and the Middle East; the cultures and kingdoms of India, China, and Japan; the cultures and kingdoms of the Americas and Africa; the role of the Catholic Church in western and eastern Europe; and the conflict between Christians and Muslims.

2. The late Medieval Period. Topics include major political and social developments in Spain, France, England, and Russia; the Crusades; the Mongol invasions and conquests; the rise of the Ottoman Turks; and the causes and consequences of the Black Death.

3. The Renaissance. Topics include the rise of the Italian city-states; the blossoming of Renaissance art, architecture, literature, and science; Machiavelli and *The Prince*; and features of the northern Renaissance.

4. The Reformation. Topics include background history and causes of the Reformation; key Reformation figures including Martin Luther and John Calvin; Henry VIII and the establishment of the Anglican Church; and the impact of the Reformation on Europe.

5. Comparative religion worldwide. Topics include monotheism and polytheism; a survey of the major leaders, sacred writings, traditions and beliefs, and histories of Judaism, Christianity, Islam, Buddhism, and Hinduism; a survey of the geographic distributions of the world's great religions; political, social, and economic influences of the world's great religions; and major religious conflicts, past and present.

6. Exploration and colonization. Topics include the explorations and settlements by Europeans in the Americas (Spanish, French, English, and Portuguese), early settlement patterns, the impact of cultural and social exchange, the effects of colonization on native peoples, the slave trade, and the rise of mercantilism.

7. The Ages of Absolutism, Enlightenment, and Reason: Sixteenth to Eighteenth centuries. Topics include absolute monarchism in Europe, the impact of the Glorious Revolution, the science and philosophy of the Enlightenment and its impact, and the American and French Revolutions.

8. Western Europe in the nineteenth century. Topics include the Napoleonic Wars, the Congress of Vienna, the growth of democracy, the Revolution of 1848 and the British Reform Laws, the unification of Germany under Bismarck, and the unification of Italy under Garibaldi.

9. The Industrial Revolution. Topics include the rise of industrial economies; western imperialism in Africa and Asia; the social, political, and cultural impact of science and technology; the rise of capitalism and free enterprise economies; the impact of capitalism; and the rise of socialism and communism.

10. The twentieth century. Topics include the causes, events, and effects of World War I; the Russian Revolution; the rise of totalitarianism in Germany, Italy, Japan, and the Soviet Union; the worldwide economic depression of the 1930s; the causes, events, and effects of World War II; the Holocaust; political and social revolutions in Asia; independence of Asian and African colonies; the Korean and Vietnam Wars; the cold war; and the breakup of the Soviet Union.

SCIENCE

For high school science options, see page 333. A common choice for tenth-grade science is a survey course in general biology.

BIOLOGY

TEXTS:

Biology Fundamentals
Gil Brum, Larry McKane, and Gerry Karp; John Wiley & Sons, 1995
An introductory text covering everything from the cellular and molecular basis of biology to ecology and animal behavior. Chapters include discussions of famous scientists and their landmark discoveries, discussion questions, and quizzes.

Biology: The Science of Life
Robert A. Wallace, Gerald P. Sanders, and Robert J. Ferl; Addison-Wesley, 1996
An excellent and enormous introductory biology text, covering all the basics: cell biology, heredity, evolution, diversity, plant and animal structure and function, and ecology.

Biology: The Unity and Diversity of Life
Cecie Starr and Ralph Taggart; Wadsworth Publishing Company, 1997
A beautifully illustrated comprehensive text in biology, with helpful chapter summaries, review quizzes, and an accompanying CD-ROM. Topics are divided among seven major categories: cell biology, the principles of inheritance, evolution, evolution and diversity, plant structure and function, animal structure and function, and ecology.

Life: The Science of Biology
William K. Purves; W. H. Freeman and Company, 1997

A colorfully illustrated, clear, and thorough basic biology text, covering cell and molecular biology, heredity, evolution, the evolution of diversity, the biology of plants and animals, ecology, and biogeography.

SUPPLEMENTS

BIOLOGY AT ABOUT.COM

An excellent and comprehensive collection of Internet resources, categorized by topic. Among these are animal behavior, cell biology, botany, genetics, evolution, virology, zoology, and much more. The site also includes links to biology education for kids of all ages, science-fair projects, virtual dissections, science museums, quizzes, and activities. Web site: biology.about.com.

The Biology Coloring Workbook
Edward I. Alcamo; Princeton Review Press, 1998

Color your way to biological expertise. Background information and to-be-colored diagrams and drawings cover the biology of the cell, basic genetics, DNA and gene expression, evolution, the biology of plants, animals, and humans, and the principles of ecology.

Five Kingdoms: An Illustrated Guide to the Phyla of Life on Earth
Lynn Margulis and Karlene V. Schwartz; W. H. Freeman and Company, 1998

A spectacular illustrated and descriptive tour of the world of living things, with an introductory explanation of taxonomy.

Guide to Microlife
Kenneth G. Rains and Bruce J. Russell; Franklin Watts, 1997

A beautifully illustrated guide to microorganisms, with detailed bibliography. A good supplement for enthusiastic microscopists.

Biology studies should include extensive hands-on experiments and investigations, as well as the use of a varied range of resources, including informational books, biographies of famous biologists, magazines and journals, videos, computer software and Internet sources, and field trips.

1. Structure and function of the cell. Topics to cover include basic cell theory; the structure and function of the cell membrane; enzymes and their functions; prokaryotic cells, eukaryotic cells, and viruses; the concept of the "Central Dogma" of molecular biology: information flow from DNA to RNA to protein; cellular organelles and the process of protein synthesis; the structure and function of chloroplasts and mitochondria; and the processes of photosynthesis and respiration.

2. Principles of inheritance: Mendelian genetics. Topics include the historical background of genetics and inheritance; the studies of Gregor Mendel; basic genetic terminology; the distinction between *genotype* and *phenotype*; autosomal and X-linked characteristics; and methods for calculating probabilities of inheritance from generation to generation.

3. Principles of inheritance: cellular and molecular genetics. Topics include the processes of mitosis and meiosis; chromosomes and genes; crossing over and nondisjunction; recombination frequencies and genetic maps; DNA structure and genetic coding; the processes of transcription, translation, and protein synthesis; and genetic engineering.

4. The theory of evolution. Topics include the historical background of the theory, including the work of Charles Darwin and Alfred Russel Wallace; biological and geological evidence for the theory; mutation and natural selection; Hardy-Weinberg equilibrium; and evolution and diversity.

5. Classification of living things. Topics include the Linnaean system of nomenclature and a survey of the five kingdoms of living things and their characteristics.

6. Human anatomy and physiology. Topics include the structure and functions of the basic body systems and a survey of the immune system.

7. Ecology. Topics include biodiversity, the major components of a biological community, food chains and food webs, the principles of population growth, a survey of the major biomes of the world, and evaluation of the impact of human beings on the environment.

FOREIGN LANGUAGE

Students should demonstrate appropriate mastery of speaking, comprehension of spoken and written material, and grammar and vocabulary.

See resources, pages 47, 268.

ART

A comprehensive art program should include creative hands-on activities and explorations, art theory, art appreciation, and art history. When possible, students should participate in field trips to artists' studios, art galleries, and museums.

1. Apply knowledge of art elements and principles of design to produce a wide range of creative artworks.

See *Drawing With Older Children and Teens,* page 293.

2. Analyze and critique artworks by well-known artists and works from a variety of multicultural sources.

See *A History of Art for Young People,* page 294, *Sister Wendy's Story of Painting,* page 338, and *The Story of Painting: The Essential Guide to the History of Western Art,* page 338.

3. Study art in conjunction with other academic subjects across the curriculum.

In tenth grade, for example, art studies might be correlated with the chronological progression through world history, from A.D. 1000 to the present day. Students should use a range of sources, including fiction and nonfiction books, biographies of famous artists and architects, magazines and journals, videos, computer software and Internet sources, and field trips.

CIVILISATION

A detailed survey of the history of western art on video. The thirteen-part series spans the period from the fall of Rome to the present day, incorporating art, architecture, music, literature, and philosophy. PBS Home Video; (800) 645-4727; www.pbs.org/shop; or Zenger Media; (800) 421-4246; www.zengermedia.com.

MUSIC

A comprehensive music program should include active participation in the form of vocal or instrumental performance, music theory, music appreciation, and music history. Students should use a varied range of resources, including fiction and nonfiction books, biographies of famous musicians and composers, audio and video resources, computer software and Internet sources, and field trips. When possible, they should attend varied musical performances.

1. Use and understand musical concepts studied in previous grades. By this grade level, kids should have a firm grasp of music theory.

See Music Ace 2, page 270, and Music Conservatory, page 340.

2. Recognize and identify the major orchestral families and their individual instruments, keyboard instruments, historical instruments, and ethnic instruments by both sight and sound.

3. Listen and respond to a range of musical pieces by well-known composers and to multicultural selections. Students should be able to identify musical genres, use their knowledge of musical concepts to analyze and critique musical selections, and pair selected compositions with the appropriate composer.

4. Identify and classify musical selections according to historical and cultural context. Students should arrange musical pieces and composers on timelines, associate musical selections with historical periods, and read biographies of representative composers.

See Multimedia History of Music, page 243, and *Bach, Beethoven, and the Boys*, page 313.

5. **Participate in instrumental and vocal performances, group and solo.** Students should continue to hone their instrumental and/or vocal skills.

6. **Create and play original musical compositions.**

7. **Study music in conjunction with other academic subjects across the curriculum.** In tenth grade, for example, music studies might be correlated with world history.

HEALTH AND PHYSICAL EDUCATION

1. **Participate in a range of age-appropriate indoor and outdoor athletic activities designed to provide a well-rounded program of physical fitness.** Homeschooled students might participate in a range of individual, small group, or team sports. Possibilities include gymnastics, dance, tennis, racquetball, skating, jogging, hiking, bicycling, swimming, volleyball, soccer, field hockey, football, baseball, and basketball.

See *Fit Kids!* and *Home School Family Fitness,* page 50.

2. **Participate in a program of drug education.**

3. **Understand the nature of sexually transmitted diseases and the methods of prevention.**

4. **Know the elements of good nutrition and personal hygiene.**

5. **Know common first-aid and safety procedures.**

GRADE ELEVEN

The growth of understanding follows an ascending spiral rather than a straight line.

JOANNA FIELD

LANGUAGE ARTS

For high school options in language arts studies, see page 320.

LITERATURE

INTRODUCTION TO THE GREAT BOOKS PROGRAM

The "Second Series," generally recommended for eleventh-graders, includes "Politics" by Aristotle, "Of Commonwealth" by Thomas Hobbes, "Sorrow-Acre" by Isak Dinesen, "Habit" by William James, and "The Overcoat" by Nikolai Gogol. Each selection is followed by a list of discussion questions intended to promote critical thinking. An excellent resource. Great Books Foundation, 35 E. Wacker Dr., Suite 2300, Chicago, IL 60601-2298; (800) 222-5870; www.greatbooks.org.

Also see CyberGuides, pages 320–321, Learning Links, page 60, Novel Units, page 60, the Writing Company, page 218, and the Shakespeare Catalog, page 217.

1. Read a wide range of age-appropriate fiction and nonfiction materials. Students should supplement literature studies with a varied range of resources, including biographies of well-known writers, audio and video performances, Internet resources, and field trips to theaters, lectures, and prose or poetry readings.

READING SUGGESTIONS FOR ELEVENTH-GRADERS INCLUDE:

As I Lay Dying (William Faulkner; Vintage Books, 1990)
The Bluest Eye (Toni Morrison; Plume Books, 1994)
The Color Purple (Alice Walker; Washington Square Press, 1998)
Emma (Jane Austen; Bantam Classics, 1984)
A Farewell to Arms (Ernest Hemingway; Scribner, 1992)
The Great Gatsby (F. Scott Fitzgerald; Scribner, 1995)
I Know Why the Caged Bird Sings (Maya Angelou; Bantam Books, 1983)
The Moon and Sixpence (W. Somerset Maugham; Viking Press, 1993)
My Antonia (Willa Cather; Houghton Mifflin, 1995)
A Portrait of the Artist as a Young Man (James Joyce; Vintage Books, 1993)
Ragtime (E. L. Doctorow; Plume Books, 1997)
Things Fall Apart (Chinua Achebe; Anchor Books/Doubleday, 1994)
To the Lighthouse (Virginia Woolf; Harcourt Brace, 1990)

See Book Lists, pages 400–402, and On-line Book Lists for Teenagers and *Cicada*, page 322.

2. Evaluate works of literature through discussion, debate, and written critique. Students should read, discuss, and analyze works of fiction and nonfiction, including book-length works, short stories, essays, plays, and poems.

3. Expand upon knowledge of drama, classic and contemporary. Recommendations for this grade level include William Shakespeare's *Othello,* Oliver Goldsmith's *She Stoops to Conquer,*

Sean O'Casey's *Juno and the Paycock*, George Bernard Shaw's *Saint Joan*, Tom Stoppard's *Rosencrantz and Guildenstern Are Dead*, and J. M. Synge's *The Playboy of the Western World*.

4. Read and respond to a variety of poetic forms.

See poetry resources, page 323.

The Classic Hundred
William Harmon, ed.; Columbia University Press, 1990
The 100 most frequently cited poems in English anthologies, with interesting annotations. Number one is William Blake's "The Tyger."

A Poem a Day
Karen McCosker and Nicholas Albery, eds.; Steerforth Press, 1994
A poem for every day of the year, with annotations. Intended to be memorized.

Also see poetry resources, pages 187, 275.

WRITING

For high school options in writing courses, see page 343.

1. Write frequently and for many purposes, producing a range of works including reports, essays, short stories, poems, narratives, journal entries, and business and personal letters. Students should write in all academic disciplines, including math, science, history, and the arts.

Write to Learn
William Zinsser; HarperCollins, 1989
Writing is a highly effective means of learning. Zinsser explains just how, with numerous examples from all branches of the curriculum.

Also see *10,000 Ideas,* page 343, *Models for Writers,* page 343, Researchpaper.com, page 276, and *Merlyn's Pen,* page 323.

2. Be familiar with use of standard writers' reference works. Students should use dictionaries, thesauri, quotation collections, style manuals, and usage handbooks.

3. Use word processing and publishing software.

4. Expand upon knowledge of the history of the English language.

See *The Story of English* and Bethump'd with Words, page 324.

LISTENING AND SPEAKING SKILLS

1. Listen and respond to various forms of oral presentations. Students should attend plays, skits, and poetry and prose readings, speeches, storytelling sessions, and lectures. They should be able to listen critically, analyzing spoken material and evaluating it for bias, propaganda, fallacies, and the like.

2. Participate in group discussions, both as a speaker and a listener.

3. Make well-organized oral presentations to a group.

See public speaking resources, pages 300–301.

4. Analyze historically significant speeches.

See *World's Greatest Speeches*, page 344.

5. Follow multiple-step oral directions.

STUDY SKILLS

1. Obtain information from a wide range of reference sources, including print and electronic sources, interviews, and site visits.

2. Practice effective study techniques. In the fall of eleventh grade, students commonly take the PSAT (Preliminary Scholastic Aptitude Test), which prepares them for the college admissions tests (SAT I and/or ACT) to be taken the following year, either in the spring semester of eleventh grade or the fall semester of twelfth. In view of this, many students find test preparation and practice manuals helpful.

Princeton Review: Cracking the SAT and PSAT
Adam Robinson and John Katzman; Villard Books, 1995
How-tos and sample tests, with accompanying CD-ROM.

For study skills resources and test preparation materials, see the Writing Company, page 218. Also see resources, pages 325, 345.

MATHEMATICS

For an overview of high school options in mathematics, see pages 325–326.

A common recommendation for eleventh-graders is intermediate algebra and trigonometry or a precalculus course that integrates intermediate algebra, geometry, trigonometry, and mathematical analysis.

TEXTS AND PROGRAMS

Advanced Mathematics
John Saxon; Saxon Publishing, 1989
> A course in precalculus mathematics, including algebra, geometry, trigonometry, discrete mathematics, and mathematical analysis. Topics include permutations and combinations; trigonometric identities; inverse trigonometric functions; conic sections; graphs of sinusoids, matrices and determinants; and binomial and rational roots theorems. Saxon Publishers, Inc., 2450 John Saxon Blvd., Norman, OK 73071; (800) 284-7019; www.saxonpub.com.

Algebra and Trigonometry: A View of the World Around Us
David Wells, Lynn Tilson, and Lynn Schmitt; Prentice-Hall, 1997
> The basics of precalculus algebra and trigonometry, incorporating real-world problems and Internet explorations.

Core-Plus Mathematics Project

See pages 326–327.

A Graphical Approach to Precalculus
E. John Hornsby and Margaret L. Lial; Addison-Wesley, 1998
> Precalculus with projects, many practice problems, and tests. The text covers rectangular coordinates, functions, and analysis of linear functions; analysis of graphs of functions; polynomial functions; rational, root, and inverse functions; exponential and logarithmic functions; conic sections and parametric equations; matrices and systems of equations and inequalities; trigonometric functions and their applications; trigonometric identities and equations; and advanced algebra topics. Sample projects: modeling the growth of the world's tallest man; modeling the path of a bouncing ball; and "How Rugged Is Your Coastline?"

Interactive Mathematics Program

IMP Year 3 covers algebra, geometry, probability, and statistics through creative and multifaceted problem-oriented unit studies. Unit titles include "Fireworks," "Orchard Hideout," "Meadows or Malls?" "Small World, Isn't It?" and "Pennant Fever." Key Curriculum Press; (800) 995-MATH; www.keypress.com.

SUPPLEMENTS

AGAINST ALL ODDS: INSIDE STATISTICS

A comprehensive and fascinating introduction to statistics on a thirteen-part video, using many real-life examples, computer animations, and live film footage to explain such concepts as multidimensional data analysis, random variables, sample techniques, and much more. PBS Home Video; (800) 645-4727; www.pbs.org.

Also see *Basic College Mathematics*, page 278, *Mathematics: A Human Endeavor*, page 253, Mathematics for Everyday Life Series, page 347, graphing calculators, page 328, Life by the Numbers, page 348, The Math Forum, page 223, and Mathematics at About.com, page 328.

SOME BASIC TOPICS COVERED IN ADVANCED MATHEMATICS/

PRECALCULUS ARE:

1. Model real-world phenomena using techniques of data analysis. Students should recognize mathematical models of *linear, quadratic, exponential, trigonometric,* and *logarithmic* functions. They should be familiar with the use of *scatter plots* to determine if a given model is appropriate, and with the use of the *linear least squares* method.

2. Create and analyze graphs of functions. Students should be able to sketch graphs of the basic functions, including *constant, linear, quadratic, cubic, square root, absolute value, reciprocal, trigonometric, exponential,* and *logarithmic* functions. They should be able to find the *domain* and estimate the *range* of a function; identify *continuous* and *discontinuous* functions; and graph *transformations* and combinations of transformations for all basic functions. They should also be able to compose two functions and find the domain of the composition; analyze a function by decomposing it into simpler functions; and find the inverse of a function and the domain of the inverse.

3. Graph polynomial and rational functions. Students should be able to find the factors of polynomials algebraically or by using a graphing calculator. They should be able to find the zeros, vertical asymptotes, and horizontal asymptotes of a rational function and sketch the graph of a rational function.

4. Graph, transform, and solve problems with exponential and logarithmic functions.

5. Model nonlinear data from real-world phenomena using techniques of data analysis.

6. Graph and transform trigonometric functions; solve trigonometric equations and inequalities. Students should be able to recognize and graph each of the six trigonometric functions and their transformations and solve trigonometric equations and inequalities algebraically and with a graphing calculator. They should be able to find values of inverse trigonometric functions, evaluate and graph compositions of trigonometric functions and their inverses, and use the laws of sines and cosines to solve problems with triangles and vectors. They should be able to translate degrees to radians and vice versa, convert complex numbers from rectangular to polar form and vice versa, and use DeMoivre's theorem to find roots and powers of complex numbers.

7. Use discrete mathematics concepts to solve problems. Students should be able to follow an algorithm; use operations with matrices and their inverses to solve problems; interpret data in terms of mean, standard deviation, and place on the normal distribution curve; and understand concepts of sequences and series.

HISTORY AND GEOGRAPHY

For high school–level history and geography options, see page 330.

A common choice for eleventh-graders is a survey of American history.

The American Nation
John Arthur Garraty; Addison-Wesley, 1997
> A thorough and fact-laden coverage of United States history in 1,000-plus pages, popular for advance placement American history courses.

American Passages: A History of the United States
Edward L. Ayers, Lewis L. Gould, David M. Oshinsky, Jean R. Sunderland, and David Tatum; Harcourt Brace, 1999
> A comprehensive history of the United States from prehistory to modern times.

These United States
Irwin Unger and Debi Unger; Prentice-Hall, 1995
> A survey of American history from pre-Columbian times to the present, using an "inquiry approach" to historical topics.

SUPPLEMENTS

ANNUAL EDITIONS SERIES
Dushkin/McGraw-Hill
> A large series of themed volumes—titles include *American History, World History, World Politics,* and *Western Civilization*—each a collection of articles selected from magazines, newspapers, and professional journals. Excellent and varied. Updated annually.

Literature Connections to American History: 7–12
Lynda Adamson; Libraries Unlimited, 1997
> Historical fiction, nonfiction, biography, and multimedia resources, categorized by grade level, author, and historical period.

Taking Sides: Clashing Views on Controversial Issues in American History

Volume 1: The Colonial Period to Reconstruction
Volume 2: Reconstruction to the Present
Larry Madaras and James M. Sorelle, eds.; Brown and Benchmark, 1997, 1999
> Students analyze opposing interpretations of history, debating such questions as "Were the English Colonists Guilty of Genocide?"

For greater interest and appeal, American history should be approached with a creative range of resources and methods, rather than relying on a single textbook. Students should study history through hands-on activities, fiction and nonfiction books, biographies of prominent persons, magazines and journals, primary source documents, photographs and newspapers, video and audio resources, computer software and Internet sources, and field trips. They should make frequent use of maps, globes, and timelines, and should integrate history with other academic subjects across the curriculum, including science, literature, and the arts.

See Social Studies School Service, page 197, and Jackdaw Publications, page 284.

1. Prehistory to the Age of Discovery. Topics include the civilizations of pre-Columbian America, the arrival of the European explorers, the first settlements, and the impact of European settlement on the American Indians.

2. The Colonial Period. Topics include the social, political, and economic features of the colonial period; the causes and effects of the French and Indian War; British colonial policies and their implications; the Declaration of Independence; and the Revolutionary War.

LIBERTY! THE AMERICAN REVOLUTION
An excellent overview of the Revolutionary War in a six-video series featuring readings from period letters and diaries and live reenactments. Titles are "The Reluctant Revolutionaries," "Blows Must Decide," "The Times That Try Men's Souls," "Oh, Fatal Ambition," "The World Turned Upside-Down," and "Are We to Be a Nation?" PBS Home Video; (800) 645-4247; www.pbs.org.

3. The new nation. Topics include the Constitution and the Bill of Rights, the organization of the national government, the development of the political party system, the causes and events of the War of 1812, the impact of the Louisiana Purchase, and the Monroe Doctrine.

THE WEST
A nine-part historical documentary by filmmaker Ken Burns, covering the history of the West from the time of the native peoples

and the arrival of the first Europeans to the turn of the twentieth century. PBS Home Video; (800) 645-4247; www.pbs.org.

4. Civil War and Reconstruction. Topics include the historical background and causes of the Civil War, states' rights and secession, major events and leaders of the Civil War, and Reconstruction policies and their impact.

THE CIVIL WAR

Ken Burns's classic Civil War series on video, featuring commentary by noted historians, readings of diaries and letters, period photographs, and a wealth of fascinating stories. Nine tapes cover the conflict from the causes of the war and the firing on Fort Sumter to the surrender at Appomatox Courthouse and the assassination of Lincoln. PBS Home Video; (800) 645-4247; www.pbs.org.

5. The Industrial Revolution. Topics include immigration and its effects, landmark inventors and their inventions, the impact of new technologies in transportation and communication, the effect of industrialization and urbanization on American society, and the late nineteenth-century reform movements.

6. World War I. Topics include the end of the Ottoman Empire and the rise of new Middle Eastern states, the United States and its role as a world power, the causes and major events of World War I, the causes and effects of the Great Depression, and Franklin Delano Roosevelt and the New Deal.

7. World War II. Topics include the rise of totalitarianism in Germany, Italy, and Japan; the causes and major events of World War II; the Holocaust; and the postwar role of the United States in international affairs.

8. Postwar foreign affairs. Topics include the Korean and Vietnam Wars, the causes and effects of the cold war, modern Middle Eastern policies, modern African policies, and the end of the cold war and breakup of the Soviet Union.

9. Postwar domestic affairs. Topics include the impact of the civil rights movement and the contrast between conservative and liberal economic strategies.

SCIENCE

For high school–level science options, see page 333.

A common choice for eleventh-graders is a one-year course in inorganic chemistry.

CHEMISTRY

TEXTS AND PROGRAMS

ChemCom: Chemistry in the Community
American Chemical Society; W. H. Freeman and Company, 2000
A superb one-year basic chemistry course centered around real-world applications of chemistry. Basic principles of chemistry are covered through such issues as air pollution, global warming, acid rain, nuclear fission, solar energy, plastics, drug design, and nutrition. Many fascinating examples.

Chemistry
Antony C. Wilbraham, Dennis D. Staley, Candace J. Simpson, and Michael S. Matta; Addison-Wesley, 1993
A nicely organized and illustrated basic text covering matter and energy, scientific measurement, atomic structure, chemical formulas and reactions, stoichiometry, gases, the periodic table, ionic and covalent bonds, water and aqueous systems, solutions, reaction rates and equilibrium, acids and bases, neutralization and salts, oxidation-reduction reactions, electrochemistry, metals and non-metals, nuclear chemistry, hydrocarbons, and organic reactions.

Introduction to Chemical Principles
H. Stephen Stoker; Prentice-Hall, 1995
A one-year general chemistry course covering atomic structure; chemical nomenclature; chemical bonds; equations; states of matter; the gas laws; solutions, acids and bases; salts, oxidation and reduction reactions; nuclear chemistry; and hydrocarbon compounds. The text also includes capsule biographies of famous scientists and many practice problems and exercises.

CHEMISTRY AT ABOUT.COM

An excellent and enormous compilation of Internet resources, categorized by topic. Among these are acid and bases, periodic tables, atomic structure, inorganic chemistry, organic chemistry, biochemistry, astrochemistry, and the history of chemistry. The site also includes links to K–12 educational resources, books, videos, online tutorials, and message boards. Web site: chemistry.about.com.

Chem Matters

A quarterly magazine for high school students from the American Chemical Society. Fascinating (chemistry-based) articles, hands-on projects, puzzles, and helpful teacher notes. American Chemical Society, Dept. L-0011, Columbus, OH 43268-0011; (800) 333-9511; www.acs.org.

Model Chem Lab

An interactive lab simulation for Windows or Mac on CD-ROM. The program includes an entire curriculum of predesigned experiments for high school chemistry students. Model Science Software; (519) 570-0335; www.modelscience.com.

The Visual Dictionary of Chemistry
Jack Challoner; Dorling Kindersley, 1996

Marvelous color photographs and elaborately labeled diagrams cover the principles and processes of chemistry.

CHEMMYSTERY CENTER

An interactive guide to chemistry for high-school students. Many topics. Web site: library.advanced.org/3659.

CHEMTUTOR

Detailed explanatory text on a long list of chemistry topics. Web site: www.chemtutor.com.

QUIA! CHEMISTRY ACTIVITIES

On-line chemistry games, quizzes, and activities. Web site: www.quia.com/chem.html.

Chemistry studies should include extensive hands-on experiments and investigations, as well as the use of a varied range of resources, including informational books, biographies of famous chemists, magazines and journals, and computer software and Internet sources.

Topics to be covered in an introductory chemistry course include:

1. Principles of chemical investigation. Topics include laboratory techniques and safety procedures; scientific measurement; and concepts of accuracy, precision, and significant figures.

2. Atomic structure and the periodic table. Topics include atomic structure (historical and quantum models) and subatomic particles; the organization and components of the periodic table; concepts of atomic mass, weight, and number; isotopes; and electron configurations and oxidation numbers.

> WEB ELEMENTS
> Click on an element on the periodic table to access a large amount of information, including the history of the element and its compounds; common uses; electronic, physical, and nuclear properties; and related video clips, links, and book suggestions. Web site: www.webelements.com.

3. Chemical formulas and equations. Topics include chemical formulas (molecular, structural, empirical, and Lewis diagrams); balancing chemical equations; ionic and covalent bonds; basic types of reactions; physical and chemical equilibria; and reaction rates and kinetics.

4. Molar relationships. Topics include Avogadro's principle, stoichiometric relationships, the gas laws, and acid/base theory.

5. Kinetic theory. Topics include pressure, temperature, and volume relationships; phase changes; the heats of fusion and vaporization; specific heat capacity; and the properties of solutions.

6. Other areas of chemistry. Topics include organic and biochemistry, electrochemistry, nuclear chemistry, and environmental chemistry.

FOREIGN LANGUAGE

Students should demonstrate appropriate skills in speaking, comprehension of written and spoken material, and grammar and vocabulary.

See resources, pages 47, 268.

ART

A comprehensive art program should include creative hands-on activities and explorations, art appreciation, art theory, and art history. Students should use a wide range of resources, including fiction and nonfiction books, biographies of famous artists, magazines and journals, videos, computer software and Internet sources, and field trips.

1. Apply knowledge of art elements and principles of design to produce a wide range of creative artworks.
See *Drawing With Older Children and Teens,* page 293.

2. Analyze and critique artworks by well-known artists and works from a variety of multicultural art sources.

3. Identify and classify artworks according to historical and cultural context. Students should order artworks and artists on timelines, associate artworks with their proper historical period and/or regional source, and read biographies of representative artists.
See *A History of Art for Young People,* page 294, Sister Wendy's Story of Painting, page 338, and Civilisation, page 356.

4. Study art in conjunction with other academic subjects across the curriculum. In eleventh grade, art studies should be integrated into the study of American history from prehistory to the present day. Kids should study a historical range of artworks, from pre-Columbian artifacts to modern American paintings, sculpture, and architecture.

AMERICAN VISION
The history of the United States through art from the colonial period to modern times in an eight-part video series. PBS Home Video; (800) 645-4727; www.pbs.org/shop.

MUSIC

A comprehensive music program should include active participation in the form of vocal or instrumental performance, music theory, music appreciation, and music history. Students should use a range of resources, including fiction and nonfiction books, biographies of famous musicians and composers, audio and video resources, computer software and Internet sources, and field trips.

1. Use and understand musical concepts acquired in previous grades.
See Music Ace 2, page 270.

2. Recognize and identify the major orchestral families and their individual instruments, keyboard instruments, historical instruments, and ethnic instruments by both sight and sound.

3. Listen and respond to a range of musical pieces by well-known composers and to multicultural selections. Students should be able to identify musical genres, to use their knowledge of musical concepts to analyze and critique musical selections, and to pair selected compositions with the appropriate composer.

4. Identify and classify musical selections according to historical and cultural context. Students should order musical pieces and composers on timelines, associate musical selections with their proper historical periods, and read biographies of representative composers.
See Music Conservatory, page 340, and resources, page 313.

5. Participate in instrumental and/or vocal performances, group and solo. Students should continue to hone their instrumental and/or vocal skills.

6. Create and play original musical compositions.

7. **Study music in conjunction with other academic subjects across the curriculum.** For example, in eleventh grade, music studies might be correlated to American history.

HEALTH AND PHYSICAL EDUCATION

1. **Participate in a range of age-appropriate indoor and outdoor athletic activities designed to provide a well-rounded program of physical fitness.** Possibilities for homeschoolers include individual, small group, or team sports. Students might participate in gymnastics, dance, tennis, racquetball, skating, jogging, hiking, skiing, bicycling, swimming, volleyball, soccer, field hockey, football, baseball, or basketball.
See *Fit Kids!* and *Home School Family Fitness,* page 50.

2. **Participate in a program of drug education.**

3. **Understand the nature of sexually transmitted diseases and the methods of prevention.**

4. **Know the elements of good nutrition and personal hygiene.**

5. **Know common first-aid and safety procedures.**

GRADE TWELVE

The direction in which education starts a man will determine his future life.

PLATO

In twelfth grade, kids ordinarily apply to college or make other plans for the future. Options are legion: In addition to traditional four-year or two-year college programs, homeschooled kids may decide to travel, participate in internships or volunteer programs, tackle a business of their own, and/or embark upon a "homeschool college" experience (see Distance Learning, pages 403–408).

And What About College? How Homeschooling Leads to Admission to the Best Colleges and Universities
Cafi Cohen; Holt Associates, 1997
    A complete guide to college admissions tailored for homeschoolers.

Bears' Guide to Earning College Degrees Nontraditionally
John B. Bear and Mariah P. Bear; C&B Publishing, 1997
    General information on college choices and the application process, and an annotated list of possiblities for nontraditional degree programs.

THE PATH FROM HOMESCHOOL TO COLLEGE

Helpful advice from the College Board. Web site: www.collegeboard.org/features/home/html/intro.html.

Testing the Waters: A Teen's Guide to Career Exploration
Alice N. Culbreath and Saundra K. Neal; JRC Consulting, 1999

Why not try out a career after completing high school? A directory of jobs, internships, volunteer and educational programs, and entrepreneurial ideas for teenagers, with complete descriptions and contact information.

20 WAYS FOR TEENAGERS TO HELP OTHER PEOPLE BY VOLUNTEERING

Suggestions include homeless shelters, Habitat for Humanity, hospitals, libraries, and animal shelters. Web site: www.bygpub.com/books/tg2rw/volunteer.htm.

LANGUAGE ARTS

For an overview of high school options in language arts, see page 320.

LITERATURE

INTRODUCTION TO THE GREAT BOOKS PROGRAM

Selections for twelfth-graders (Third Series) include "On Happiness" by Aristotle, "Habits and Will" by John Dewey, "Crito" by Plato, "On Liberty" by John Stuart Mill, "A Hunger Artist" by Franz Kafka, and "A Room of One's Own" by Virginia Woolf. Each selection is accompanied by discussion questions designed to promote critical thinking. Great Books Foundation, 35 E. Wacker Dr., Suite 2300, Chicago, IL 60601-2298; (800) 222-5870; www.greatbooks.com.

Also see CyberGuides, pages 320–321, Learning Links, page 60, Novel Units, page 60, the Writing Company, page 218, and the Shakespeare Catalog, page 217.

1. **Read a wide range of age-appropriate fiction and nonfiction materials.** Students should supplement their literature studies with a varied range of resources, including biographies of well-known writers, audio and video performances, Internet resources, and field trips to theaters, lectures, and prose or poetry readings.

READING SUGGESTIONS FOR TWELFTH-GRADERS INCLUDE:

All the King's Men (Robert Penn Warren; Harcourt Brace, 1996)

Anna Karenina (Leo Tolstoy; New American Library, 1988)

The Bell Jar (Sylvia Plath; Bantam Books, 1983)

The Brothers Karamazov (Fyodor Dostoyevsky; New American Library, 1999)

The Caine Mutiny (Herman Wouk; Little, Brown, 1992)

The Centaur (John Updike; Ballantine Books, 1996)

David Copperfield (Charles Dickens; W. W. Norton, 1989)

Grendel (John Gardner; Vintage Books, 1989)

The House of the Spirits (Isabel Allende; Bantam Books, 1986)

The Lives of a Cell (Lewis Thomas; Penguin, 1995)

Madame Bovary (Gustave Flaubert; New American Library, 1994)

Metamorphosis (Franz Kafka; Bantam Classics, 1972)

On the Road (Jack Kerouac; Penguin, 1991)

One Day in the Life of Ivan Denisovich (Aleksandr Solzhenitsyn; Signet Classics, 1998)

One Hundred Years of Solitude (Gabriel García Marquez; Harper-Perennial, 1998)

Out of the Silent Planet (C. S. Lewis; Scribner, 1996)

The Sound and the Fury (William Faulkner; Random House, 1990)

The Sun Also Rises (Ernest Hemingway; Macmillan, 1995)

See Book Lists, pages 400–402, On-line Book Lists for Teenagers, page 322, and *Cicada*, page 322.

2. **Evaluate works of literature through discussion, debate, and written critique.** Students should read, discuss, and analyze works of fiction and nonfiction, including book-length works, short stories, essays, plays, and poems.

3. **Expand upon knowledge of drama, classic and contemporary.** Recommendations for twelfth-graders include William

Shakespeare's *Hamlet,* Henrik Ibsen's *A Doll's House,* and *Oedipus* by Sophocles.

4. Read and respond to a varied range of poetic forms.

See poetry resources, pages 187, 323, 360.

WRITING

For high school–level writing options, see page 343.

SOME BASIC COURSE COMPONENTS:

1. Write frequently and for many purposes, producing a range of works including reports, essays, short stories, poems, narratives, journal entries, and business and personal letters.

See *Write to Learn,* page 360, *10,000 Ideas,* page 343, *Models for Writers,* page 343, Researchpaper.com, page 276, and *Merlyn's Pen,* page 323.

2. Be familiar with the use of standard writers' reference works. For example, students should use dictionaries, thesauri, quotation collections, style manuals, and usage handbooks.

3. Use word processing and publishing software.

4. Expand upon knowledge of the history of the English language.

See *The Story of English* and Bethump'd With Words, page 324.

LISTENING AND SPEAKING SKILLS

1. Listen and respond to various forms of oral presentations. Students should attend plays, skits, and poetry and prose readings, speeches, storytelling sessions, and lectures. They should be able to listen critically, analyzing spoken material and evaluating it for bias, propaganda, persuasion, fallacious reasoning, and the like.

2. Participate in group discussions, both as a speaker and a listener.

3. Make well-organized oral presentations to a group.

See public speaking resources, pages 300–301.

4. Analyze historically significant speeches.
See World's Greatest Speeches, page 344.

Study Skills

1. Obtain information from a wide range of reference sources, including print and electronic sources, interviews, and site visits.

2. Practice effective study techniques. In the fall of twelfth grade, students commonly take standardized college admissions tests (SAT I and/or ACT), as well as a battery of optional SAT II tests in specific academic subjects. Some students find test preparation handbooks and practice tests to be helpful.

For a wide assortment of study aids and test preparation materials, see the Writing Company, page 218. Also see resources, pages 325, 345, 361.

MATHEMATICS

For an overview of high school options in mathematics, see pages 325–326.

Mathematics choices for twelfth grade depend upon the individual student's learning pace, career goals, and interests. Some may decide not to pursue math beyond geometry or intermediate algebra; others may study precalculus in twelfth grade rather than eleventh. In some cases, twelfth-graders with a strong interest in mathematics, science, and technology take an introductory course in calculus; in others, introductory calculus is taken as a freshman course in college.

Texts and Programs

Calculus
John Saxon and Frank Wang; Saxon Publishing, 1988
The text, which includes trigonometry and analytic geometry, is a one-year course in advanced placement calculus. Included are review exercises, many practice problems, and real-world links to physics, chemistry, engineering, and business. Saxon Publishers, Inc., 2450 John Saxon Blvd., Norman, OK 73071; (800) 284-7019; www.saxonpub.com.

Calculus with Analytic Geometry
Howard Anton; John Wiley & Sons, 1998

A comprehensive basic calculus text, suitable for advanced secondary-level students and beginning college students.

Interactive Mathematics Program

IMP Year 4 uses interactive problem-centered unit studies to cover concepts in trigonometry, algebra, geometry, and statistics. Unit titles include "High Dive," "As the Cube Turns," Know How," "The World of Functions," and "The Pollster's Dilemma." Key Curriculum Press; (800) 995-MATH; www.keypress.com.

SUPPLEMENTS

GRAPHING CALCULATOR

For calculus courses, students will need a graphing calculator such as the TI-82, the TI-83, or the even more sophisticated TI-85. A range of supplementary books and activities manuals are available to enhance and support calculator activities, including *Calculus With the TI-82 Graphics Calculator* by George W. Best and Sally Fischbeck (Venture Publishing, 1995). For a complete list, see the Texas Instruments home page. Texas Instruments; (800) TI-CARES; www.ti.com.

Also see *Basic College Mathematics*, page 278, *Mathematics: A Human Endeavor*, page 253, Mathematics for Everyday Life Series, page 347, Life by the Numbers, page 348, The Math Forum, page 223, and Mathematics at About.com, page 328.

SOME BASIC TOPICS COVERED IN INTRODUCTORY CALCULUS:

1. Understand and use elementary functions: algebraic, trigonometric, exponential, and logarithmic. For example, students should be able to define a *function* and relate functions to real-world problems and situations. They should be able to find the *domain* and *range* of a function with and without a graphing calculator and to determine the sum, product, and quotient of two functions. They should be able to determine the domain of a composition of two functions and the *absolute value, inverse, periodic-*

ity and *amplitude, symmetry, asymptotes,* and *zeros* of a function. They should be able to find the *limits* of functions and recognize functions that have nonexistent limits.

2. Understand and use the definition of *continuity*.

3. Understand and use concepts of differential calculus. For example, students should be able to find the derivatives of elementary and composite functions, of implicitly defined functions, and of the inverse of a function. They should know and apply the mean value theorem, the relation between differentiability and continuity, and L'Hopital's rule.

4. Understand and apply concepts of a derivative. Students should be able to find the slope of a curve, the tangent line to a curve, and the normal line to a curve. They should be able to use Newton's method to approximate the zeros of a function and find critical points, maximum and minimum points, and points of inflection of a function. They should be able to interpret graphs of the derivative to obtain information about a function and to use derivative concepts to solve problems involving velocity and acceleration.

5. Understand and apply concepts of integral calculus. Students should be able to find *antiderivatives* and solve simple first-order differentiable equations. They should be able to use basic integration formulas, approximate the area under a curve, understand and apply properties of definite integrals, and use the fundamental theorem.

HISTORY AND GEOGRAPHY

For high school–level history and geography options, see page 330.

Depending on school system requirements and individual student interests, some kids may want to complete four years of history/geography courses; others may be satisfied with less.

A common choice for twelfth-graders is a one-year course in civics or American government.

America at Odds: An Introduction to American Government
Edward Sidlow and Beth Henschen; Wadsworth Publishing, 1998

The basics of American government interestingly presented through controversial political points of view. Topics covered include the Constitution, Federalism, civil rights and liberties, the political system, campaigns and elections, government institutions, public policy, and state and local government. Sample controversial questions: "Should the States Take Orders from the National Government?" and "Is Government Bureaucracy Running Amuck?"

Government by the People
James MacGregor Burns, J. W. Peltason, and Thomas E. Cronin; Prentice-Hall, 1997

The text comprises a one-year course in American government, covering constitutional principles, civil rights and liberties, the political process, policy-making institutions, and the politics of national policy.

Practicing American Politics: An Introduction to Government
David V. Edwards and Alessandra Lippucci; Worth Publishing, 1998

An 800-page introductory text covering the philosophy of American democracy; the practice of politics, including the organization of political parties, political campaigns, and the election process; the workings of major governmental institutions; civil liberties and civil rights; and public policy, economic, domestic, and global.

Understanding American Government
Susan Welch, John Gruhl, Michael Steinman, John Comer, and Jan P. Vermeer; West Group, 1997

The text covers all the basics of government through a creative inquiry approach, with included fact boxes and discussions of political solutions to current problems.

Supplements

Taking Sides: Clashing Views on Controversial Political Issues
George McKenna and Stanley Feingold; McGraw-Hill, 1998

Points of View: Readings in American Government and Politics
Robert E. Diclerico and Allan S. Hammock; McGraw-Hill, 1997

Both present opposing points of view on a range of political issues, designed to promote critical thinking, discussion, and debate.

Whatever Happened to Justice?
Richard Maybury; Bluestocking Press, 1993
A fascinating history of law, its evolution in America, and its effect on our economic system, written as a series of letters from Uncle Eric, the author's well-informed alter ego, to a teenage niece/nephew, Chris.

Like earlier history courses, studies of American government should involve a wide range of resources, including informational books, biographies of key persons, magazines and journals, audio-cassettes and videos, computer software and Internet sources, and field trips.

See Social Studies School Service, page 197, Jackdaw Publications, page 284, and Annual Editions Series, page 365.

TOPICS TO COVER IN AMERICAN GOVERNMENT INCLUDE:

1. The United States Constitution. Topics include the historical evolution of democracy; a survey of the principles of democracy as expressed by key political philosophers; political principles expressed in key American documents, such as the Declaration of Independence and the Federalist Papers; the Constitution and its amendments; landmark Supreme Court interpretations of the Constitution; fundamental concepts of democracy; and Federalism.

2. Governmental institutions. Topics include the structure, functions, and powers of executive, legislative, and judicial branches of the federal government; comparisons of federal government, state, and local governments; and the concept of bureaucracy.

3. The political process. Topics include the political party system; the politics of influence: interest groups and the media; political campaigns and the election process; and the responsibilities of citizenship.

4. National policy. Topics include domestic policy, foreign policy, interstate commerce and international trade, governmental regulation, and the comparison of the political and economic systems of the United States to those of other nations.

SCIENCE

For high school–level science options, see page 333.

A common choice for twelfth-grade science students is a one-year course in basic physics.

PHYSICS

TEXTS

Conceptual Physics
Paul G. Hewitt; Addison-Wesley, 1999

A beautifully illustrated introductory physics text for high school students, requiring only a basic knowledge of algebra. Reader-friendly language, many real-world examples, and optional accompanying laboratory manual and problem workbook.

How Things Work: The Physics of Everyday Life
Louis A. Bloomfield; John Wiley & Sons, 1997

A fascinatingly creative (but definitely not lightweight) approach to physics through real-world examples. Topics covered include the laws of motion, simple machines, fluids, heat, thermodynamics, phase transitions, resonance, electricity and magnetism, optics, material science, and nuclear physics—using as examples Frisbees, bicycles, wood stoves, violins, surfboards, fluorescent lamps, and microwave ovens. Chapters include thought-provoking questions, experiments, illustrations, exercises, and problems.

Introductory Physics
Jesse David Wall and Elender Wall; Analog Press, 1997

Intended as a one-semester course for college students as preparation for a more demanding course in general physics. The book includes a conversational text and many illustrations and examples. Students will need a basic knowledge of algebra and trigonometry.

Physics
John H. Saxon Jr.; Saxon Publishers, 1993

A dry, but very thorough, introductory text in 100 detailed lessons, with many practice problems. Topics covered include force and motion, simple machines, gravitational theory, electricity, optics, thermodynamics, and special relativity. Saxon Publishers, Inc., 2450 John Saxon Blvd., Norman, OK 73071; (800) 284-7019; www.saxonpub.com.

SUPPLEMENTS

How to Solve Physics Problems
Robert M. Oman and Daniel M. Oman; McGraw-Hill, 1996
Explanations, step-by-step instructions, and practice problems for all the major topics of basic physics. The book can be used for either calculus-based or noncalculus-based physics courses.

Quantum
A bimonthly magazine for high school physics and advanced math students. Quantum, National Science Teachers Association, 1840 Wilson Blvd., Arlington, VA 22201-3000; (800) 722-NSTA; www.nsta.org.

Why Toast Lands Jelly-side Down
Robert Ehrlich; Princeton University Press, 1997
Hands-on experiments and demonstrations of basic physics principles, with accompanying explanations and equations. Demonstrations cover Newtonian physics, orbital motion and angular momentum, conservation of momentum and energy, fluids, thermodynamics, oscillations and waves, electricity and magnetism, optics, and nuclear physics.

FIZZICS FIZZLE!
An interactive on-line guide to physics, accessible at three levels (upper elementary school to college). Web site: library.advanced. org/16600.

LEARN PHYSICS TODAY!
A physics tutorial for high-school- and college-level students. Web site: library.advanced.org/10796.

PHYSICS AT ABOUT.COM
A comprehensive and enormous collection of Internet resources, categorized by topic. Examples include electricity and magnetism, classical mechanics, particle physics, and optics. The site also

includes links to educational resources, on-line texts and tutorials, physics history, and reference data. Web site: physics.about.com.

A course in physics should include extensive hands-on experiments and investigations, as well as the use of a varied range of resources, including informational books, biographies of famous scientists, magazine and journal articles, videos, computer software, and Internet resources.

TOPICS COVERED IN INTRODUCTORY PHYSICS INCLUDE:

1. **Force and motion.** Topics include Newton's first, second, and third laws, the universal law of gravitation, concepts of circular motion, vectors, and trajectories.

2. **Conservation of momentum and energy.** Topics include the distinctions between kinetic and potential energy, a survey of the kinds of energy (mechanical, radiant, chemical, etc.), elastic and inelastic collisions, and specific heat.

3. **Thermodynamics.** Topics include the laws of thermodynamics, properties of energy transfers, the concept of entropy, and the relationships among heat flow, work, and efficiency.

4. **Oscillations and waves.** Topics include the distinction between transverse and longitudinal waves; concepts of wavelength, frequency, and speed; an overview of the electromagnetic spectrum; basic properties of waves (including interference, diffraction, refraction, polarization, and the Doppler effect); and the wave and photon models of light.

See Virtual Labs: Light, page 266.

5. **Electricity and magnetism.** Topics include an overview of the basic features and concepts of electricity and magnetism; Ohm's law and Coulomb's law, power concepts; properties of resistors, capacitors, and transistors; the relationship between electric current and magnetic field; and the properties of plasmas.

See Virtual Lab: Electricity, page 310.

6. **Nuclear physics.** Topics include atomic structure, radioactivity and half-life, ionization, nuclear fission and fusion, and basic concepts of quantum physics.

FOREIGN LANGUAGE

Students should demonstrate appropriate skills in speaking, comprehension of written and spoken material, and grammar and vocabulary.

See resources, pages 47, 268.

ART

A comprehensive art program should include creative hands-on activities and projects, art appreciation, art theory, and art history. Students should use varied resources, including fiction and nonfiction books, biographies of famous artists, magazine and journal articles, videos, computer software, Internet sources, and field trips. Students should visit artists' studios, museums, and art galleries and exhibits.

1. Apply knowledge of art elements and principles of design to produce a wide range of creative artworks. Homeschooled students often take extracurricular classes from community arts and craft centers. Possible fields of study include painting, drawing, sculpture, printmaking, fiber arts, ceramics and pottery, and photography.

See *Drawing With Older Children and Teens*, page 293.

2. Analyze and critique artworks by well-known artists and works from a variety of multicultural art sources.

3. Identify and classify artworks according to historical and cultural context. Students should order artworks and artists on timelines, associate artworks with their proper historical periods, and read biographies of representative artists.

4. Study art in conjunction with other academic subjects across the curriculum. In conjunction with physics, for example, kids might study kinetic sculptures or the mobiles of Alexander Calder.

Also see *A History of Art for Young People*, page 294, Sister Wendy's Story of Painting, page 338, Civilisation, page 356, and American Vision, page 372.

MUSIC

A comprehensive music program should include active participation in the form of vocal or instrumental performance, music theory, music appreciation, and music history. Students should use varied resources, including fiction and nonfiction books, biographies of famous musicians and composers, audio and video resources, computer software, the Internet, and field trips. If possible, students should attend a variety of musical performances.

1. Know the elements of music theory.
See Music Ace 2, page 270, and Music Conservatory, page 340.

2. Recognize and identify the major orchestral families and their individual instruments, keyboard instruments, historical instruments, and ethnic instruments by both sight and sound.

3. Listen and respond to a range of musical pieces by well-known composers and to multicultural selections. Students should be able to identify musical genres, use the knowledge of musical concepts to analyze and critique selections, and pair selected compositions with the appropriate composer.

4. Identify and classify musical selections according to historical and cultural context. Students should order musical pieces and composers on timelines, associate musical selections with their proper historical periods, and read biographies of representative composers.
See Music Conservatory, page 340, and resources, page 313.

5. Participate in instrumental and/or vocal performances, group and solo. Students should continue to develop their instrumental and/or vocal skills.

6. Create and play original musical compositions.

7. Study music in conjunction with other academic subjects across the curriculum. For example, twelfth-grade physics studies might incorporate elements of music, as kids study sound waves, vibrations, and resonance.

HEALTH AND PHYSICAL EDUCATION

1. Participate in a range of age-appropriate indoor and outdoor athletic activities designed to provide a well-rounded program of physical fitness. There are many possibilities for homeschoolers, including gymnastics, dance, tennis, racquetball, skating, jogging, hiking, skiing, bicycling, swimming, volleyball, soccer, field hockey, football, baseball, and basketball.

See *Fit Kids!* and *Home School Family Fitness*, page 50.

2. Participate in a program of drug education.

3. Understand the nature of sexually transmitted diseases and the methods of prevention.

4. Know the elements of good nutrition and personal hygiene.

5. Know common first-aid and safety procedures.

APPENDIX A

Technology

Computer literacy is a popular phrase these days in educational circles. Computer software, tutorials, and activities are available for kids of all ages, from the moment they're big enough to tap (or pound) upon a keyboard; and parents who lack computer access worry that their children are being left behind, deprived pedestrians lurking on the edges of the Internet highway. The computer, undeniably, is a superb and versatile research tool. Polls show that a stunningly high percentage (over 85 percent) of homeschoolers own one (or more) and use it (or them) intensively for educational purposes.

The computer, in our experience, is an excellent personal tutor. Let a child fool around with it for a few hours and he or she—independently—will master a vast battery of computer interactive skills. Technological education, in my opinion, is a prime example of the efficacy of homeschooling: Enormous numbers of kids have become computer whizzes by teaching themselves. In our household, the kids, without benefit of parental aid, have learned to navigate the Internet, cope with a wide range of software programs, use the word processor, understand programming languages, and design Web sites.

But what if you don't have a computer? Will a computerless early childhood render your kids unfit for life in the Information Age?

Absolutely not. Basic computer literacy can be acquired rapidly by any interested kids; when and if they need it, they'll get it.

Resources for designing a computer literacy curriculum for beginners:

BOOKS

The Computer from A to Z
Bobbie Kalman; Crabtree Publishing, 1998
> An alphabet book of computer terminology, illustrated with color photographs of kids computing. Simple explanations of such terms as *bug, byte, e-mail, font, virtual reality,* and *Web page.*

Computer Guides Series
EDC Publications; 1999
> Brightly illustrated informational guides for kids aged 9–12. Titles in the series include *World Wide Web for Beginners, Internet for Beginners,* and *Build Your Own Website.* Also includes *101 Things to Do on the Internet,* a collection of Internet projects.

Make Your Own Web Page!
Ted Pederson and Francis Moss; Price Stern Sloan, 1998
> A step-by-step approach for kids aged 9–12. Includes readily understandable information on design, HTML programming language, hypertext links, and graphics.

Mousetracks
Peggy L. Steinhauser; Tricycle Press, 1997
> A computer idea book for early elementary–level students. Many projects using word-processing and graphics software, organized by theme. The book includes detailed illustrated instructions.

On-line Kids: A Young Surfer's Guide to Cyberspace
Preston Gralla; John Wiley & Sons, 1999
> Basic information on the nature of cyberspace, Internet safety, search engines, chat groups, and the like, along with reviews of many sites of interest to kids, categorized by topic.

What's a Computer?

What's a Computer Program?

What's the Internet?
Edna Toby; New Tradition Press, 1998

Picture-book introductions to the computer, computer software, and the world of the Internet for kids aged 3–7.

WEB SITES

COMPUTER SKILLS LESSON PLANS K–8

Lessons cover keyboarding, word processing, databases, spreadsheets, and telecomputing. Web site: www.dpi.state.nc.us/curriculum/computer.skills/lssnplns.

EDUCATION AND THE INTERNET

Elementary-level lesson plans that incorporate the Internet, categorized by academic subject. Web site: marauder.millersv.edu/~edfound/intered.html.

HTML WRITER'S GUILD

On-line classes in Web design. Web site: www.hwg.org.

INTERNET LESSON PLANS

Information and activities adaptable for kids over a wide range of ages. Plans cover "What Can the Net Do?" "Guidelines for Net Use," "Electronic Mail," "Web Home Pages," and more. Web site: www.schoolnet.ca/aboriginal/lessons/index e.html.

KIDS AND COMPUTERS WEB SITE

Programming and computer skills lessons for kids in grades 3–9. Web site: www.kidsandcomputers.com.

STUDY WEB COMPUTER SCIENCE

Information and lesson plans on the structure and functions of computer hardware and software, Internet use, and computer programming. Web site: www.studyweb.com.

TEACHING 'N TECHNOLOGY

A database of technology-related lesson plans, searchable by age group from preschool to high school and adult. Web site: twister. coedu.usf/tnt/.

TECHNOLOGY LESSONS

Lessons in a range of computer-related topics categorized by age from early elementary to high school. Web site: www.eecs.umich. edu/~coalition/sciedoutreach/funexperiments/agesubject/ technology.html.

APPENDIX B

Textbooks and Resources

A BEKA BOOK, INC.

Christian textbooks for kids in grades K–12. Box 19100, Pensacola, FL 32523-9100; (877) 223-5226; www.abeka.com.

ADDISON-WESLEY LONGMAN

K–12 texts, materials, and software. One Jacob Way, Reading, MA 01867-3999; (800) 282-0693; www.awl.com.

ALPHA OMEGA

Christian texts and curricula for grades K–12. 300 N. McKenny Ave., Chandler, AZ 85226-2618; (800) 622-3070; www.home-schooling.com.

BEAUTIFUL FEET BOOKS

"History Through Literature" materials for kids of all ages. 139 Main St., Sandwich, MA 02563; (508) 833-8626; www.bfbooks.com.

BROOKS/COLE PUBLISHING COMPANY

Math, science, and technology texts and related Web sites. 511 Forest Lodge Rd., Pacific Grove, CA 93950; (800) 354-9706; www.brookscole.com.

CREATIVE TEACHING PRESS

Books and teaching materials for grades K–8. Box 2723, Huntington Beach, CA 92647-0723; (800) 444-4CTP; www.creativeteaching. com.

DANDY LION PUBLICATIONS

Books and workbooks in all academic subjects for grades K–8. 3563 Sueldo, Suite L, San Luis Obispo, CA 93401; (800) 776-8032; www.dandylionbooks.com.

DUSHKIN/MCGRAW-HILL

High school and college texts for a wide range of subjects, including the Annual Editions Series, continually updated collections of articles from popular and professional periodicals related to specific academic subjects. Sluice Dock, Guilford, CT 06437; (203) 453-4351; www.dushkin.com.

EDC PUBLICATIONS

The American publisher of the Usborne books, a creative and superbly illustrated assortment of books and activity books in a wide range of subjects, including history, science, music, art, language arts, foreign languages, and early childhood skills. Box 470663, Tulsa, OK 74147-0663; (800) 475-4522; www. edcpub.com.

ETA/CUISENAIRE

Creative books, activity books, materials for math and science, grades K–8. 500 Greenview Ct., Vernon Hills, IL 60061; (800) 445-5985; www.etauniverse.com or www.cuisenaire.com.

EVAN-MOOR EDUCATIONAL PUBLISHERS

Books, materials, and thematic units in a wide range of subjects for kids in preK–6. 18 Lower Ragsdale Dr., Monterey, CA 93940-5746; (800) 777-4362; www.evan-moor.com.

GRYPHON HOUSE

Resource and activity books on many academic subjects for preschoolers and early elementary students. Box 207, Beltsville, MD 20704; (800) 638-0928; www.gryphonhouse.com.

HARCOURT SCHOOL PUBLISHERS

Texts and materials for K–12 and high school advanced placement (AP) courses. 6277 Sea Harbor Dr., Orlando, FL 32887; (800) 225-5425; www.harcourt.com.

HOLT, RINEHART, AND WINSTON

Texts and software for language arts, foreign languages, science, health, technology, social studies, and math. 6277 Sea Harbor Dr., Orlando, FL 32887-0001; (800) 544-6678; www.hrw.com.

HOUGHTON MIFFLIN

Elementary-, secondary-, and college-level texts and materials, all subjects. (800) 733-2828; www.hmco.com.

INSTRUCTIONAL FAIR/T. S. DENISON

Activity books, workbooks, and materials in all academic subjects. Searchable by grade level from infant to grade 12. www.edumart.com/ifair

KEY CURRICULUM PRESS

Math texts, workbooks, and programs including the Interactive Mathematics Program and the Key to Series. (800) 995-MATH; www.keypress.com.

PRENTICE HALL

Texts and materials for grades 6–12 covering foreign languages, language arts, math, science and health, social studies, and technology. 4350 Equity Dr., Box 2649, Columbus, OH 43216-2649; (800) 848-9500; www.prenhall.com or www.phschool.com.

SAXON PUBLISHERS

Math texts and supplements for K–12. 2450 John Saxon Blvd., Norman, OK 73071; (800) 284-7019; www.saxonpub.com.

SCOTT FORESMAN-ADDISON WESLEY

Programs, texts, and materials for grades K–6. (800) 552-2259; www.scottforesman.com.

SILVER BURDETT GINN

Literature, math, social studies, and music for grades K–6. (800) 552-2259; www.scottforesman.com.

STECK-VAUGHN

Texts and materials for grades K–12 in all subjects, plus assessment, test preparation, and special education resources. (800) 531-5015; www.steck-vaughn.com.

W. W. NORTON

College texts in a range of subjects. Keystone Industrial Park, Scranton, PA 18512; (800) 233-4830; www.wwnorton.com.

WORTH PUBLISHERS

High school texts for economics, history, psychology, and sociology. Faculty Services, 33 Irving Pl., New York, NY 10003; (800) 446-8923; www.worthpublishers.com.

APPENDIX C

Lesson Plans

BALTIMORE CURRICULUM PROJECT LESSON PLANS

Very detailed lesson plans in all academic subjects for grades K–6 based on the E. D. Hirsch's Core Knowledge Sequence. www.cstone.net/~bcp/BCPIntro2.htm.

BASTROP ISD LESSON PLANS AND REPRODUCIBLES

Many resources and activities for kids categorized by topic. The "Teacher's Toolbox" includes many lesson plan lists for kids of all ages. Categories include math, science, social studies, technology, and thematic units. www.bastrop.isd.tenet.edu.

CEC LESSON PLANS

Lesson plans of all kinds categorized by subject and grade (K–5, 6–8, and 9–12). www.col-ed.org/cur/.

EDUCATOR RESOURCES: LESSON PLANS AND ACTIVITIES

Large, varied lists of lesson plans for arts, language arts, math, science, technology, and social studies. www.mcrel.org/resources/links/hotlinks.asp.

EGGPLANT

A huge selection of math lesson plans for kids in grades K–12. www.eggplant.org/tools/links/lessons.html.

GATEWAY TO EDUCATIONAL MATERIALS

Lesson plans, curriculum units, and resources categorized by age/grade from K–12. www.thegateway.org.

K8AIT LESSON PLANS

Lesson plans, activities, and curriculum bridges to other academic bridges for a range of topics, including mythology, nature, force and motion, aerodynamics, insects, birds, marine life, vehicles, and sports. www.wings.ucdavis.edu/Curriculums.

LANGUAGES ON-LINE

On-line classes, foreign language pen pals, information on grammar, reading and writing, and country studies, quizzes and games, and more. www.eleaston.com.

THE LESSON PLANS PAGE

Hundreds of lesson plans categorized by grade level (preschool–12) and subject. www.lessonplanspage.com.

LESSON STOP

Hundreds of lesson plans categorized by topic and grade level, as well as instructions for writing your own. www.youthline-usa.com/lessonstop.

NWREL'S LIBRARY IN THE SKY

Click on chosen subject for an immense selection of lesson plans, links, and other resources. http://www.nwrel.org/sky/.

ON-LINE LEARNING FOR SCHOOL AND HOME

On-line expeditions and projects, learning activities and games, lesson plans and worksheets. Searchable by grade. www.lightspan.com.

PROTEACHER

Many lesson plans for kids in grades K–6 covering reading, language arts, the humanities, social studies, math, science, technology, and physical education. www.proteacher.com.

SCHOLASTIC TEACHER'S HOMEPAGE

Lesson plans and reproducibles for kids in grades preK–3 or 4–8, plus on-line activities in a range of academic subjects. www.scholastic.com.

SPANISH AND ESL LESSONS

A range of varied lessons categorized by age (K–5, 6–8, 9–12). www.teachspanish.com/lessons.html.

STUDY WEB

Many topics, including lesson plans and curricula. www.studyweb.com.

APPENDIX D

Book Lists

101 OUT-OF-THIS-WORLD BOOKS FOR KIDS AGES 8–13
Categorized by genre. www.als.lib.wi.us/MRList.html.

ATN BOOK LISTS
Many book lists, categorized by academic subject or topic. Examples include "Math in Literature," "Ancient Civilizations," "Ecology," and "Survival Stories." www.rms.concord.k12.nh.us/rl.

BOOK LISTS OF CHILDREN'S LITERATURE
Many annotated readings lists for kids of all ages. www.monroe.lib.in.us/childrens/children_booklists.html.

BOOK SPOT
All kinds of book lists for persons of all ages, including Children's Books, Young Adult Books, Newbery and Caldecott winners, Young Readers' Choices, and more. www.bookspot.com.

BOOKLIST EDITORS' CHOICE
Annotated lists of the best books for kids from the American Library Association, categorized by age (young, middle, and older readers). www.ala.org/booklist.

CARNEGIE LIBRARY CHILDREN'S READING LISTS

Books listed by age group from toddlers and preschoolers through middle school. www.clpgh.org/clp/Childrens/lists/.

CAROL HURST'S LITERATURE SITE

Detailed reviews of children's books by title, author, and genre. Books are also categorized by grade level (preK–9) and curriculum area. www.carolhurst.com.

CHILDREN'S LITERATURE WEB LIST

All kinds of literary resources for kids, including a variety of age- and theme-based book lists. www.acs.ucalgary.ca/~dkbrown.

EAGER READERS

Books for all ages listed by theme and reading level. www.eagerreaders.com.

FAIRROSA CYBER LIBRARY

Many book lists, including thematic lists, special interest lists, and award winners. www.dalton.org/libraries/fairrosa.

GOOD BOOKS FOR GOOD READERS

Books are categorized by genre, including humor, science fiction, math books, historical fiction, and "Long Books and Books With Sequels for Kids Who Read Too Fast." www.members.aol.com/tea73/goodbks/index.htm.

HOAGIE'S KIDS READING LISTS

Excellent lists and related links. Under "Book Lists for Hot Topics," for example, are lists of books for "History Hounds," "Math Nuts," "Physics Fiends," "Programming Prodigies," and many more. www.hoagieskids.org/kidrdlst.htm.

THE INDISPENSABLE CHILDREN'S READING LIST

Books for beginning, intermediate, experienced, and advanced readers. www.watson.org/rivendell/litchildrenlist.html.

NEW YORK PUBLIC LIBRARY RECOMMENDED READING

Lists of "100 Favorites," summer reading lists, and holiday reading lists. www.nypl.org/branch/recread.html.

NOTABLE BOOKS FOR CHILDREN

A long annotated list of the best books for kids, categorized by age (younger, middle, older). www.ala.org/alsc/notable97.html.

READING LISTS FOR GIFTED AND TALENTED CHILDREN

Books for the particularly brilliant, categorized by age. Also includes a list of "must-reads" for parents. www.gtworld.org/gtbook.htm.

RECOMMENDED READING LISTS

Lists of good books by age group from "baby" to "10–12-year-olds." www.readmeabook.com/lists.htm.

SEVENTY-FIVE AUTHORS AND ILLUSTRATORS EVERYONE SHOULD KNOW

Books by the featured authors and illustrators are categorized by age for preschool–K through grades 6–8. www.CBCbooks.org.

YOUNG ADULT LIBRARY SERVICES ASSOCIATION (YALSA) BOOKLISTS

Best books for young adults. www.ala.org/yalsa/booklists/index.html.

YOUTH AND CHILDREN'S SERVICES READING LISTS

Books are listed by genre, including lists of "Read Alikes" for popular favorites. www.stanlylib.org/ycs/jbklists.html.

APPENDIX E

Distance Learning

AMERICAN SCHOOL

Accredited high school correspondence courses. Students can enroll at any time during the school year. 2200 E. 170th St., Lansing, IL 60438; (708) 418-2800; www.iit.edu/~american.

BRIGHAM YOUNG UNIVERSITY INDEPENDENT STUDY

Correspondence and on-line courses for high school students. 206 Harman Bldg., Box 21514, Provo, UT 84602-1514; (800) 914-8931; coned.byu.edu/is/index2.htm

CALIFORNIA VIRTUAL UNIVERSITY

Over 2,000 on-line courses from accredited private and public California universities.www.california.edu.

CALVERT HOME SCHOOL INSTRUCTION DEPARTMENT

Complete curricula by correspondence for grades K–8, with many optional enrichment courses. Students can enroll any time during the year, but must enroll in a complete program. Some individual courses available for grade 8. Calvert School, Dept. 2NET, 105 Tuscany Rd., Baltimore, MD 21210-3098; (410) 243-6030; www.calvertschool.org.

CAMBRIDGE ACADEMY

Over sixty correspondence courses for kids in grades 6–12. 3300 SW 34th Ave., Suite 102, Ocala, FL 34474; (800) 252-3777; www.home-school.com/Mall/Cambridge/CambridgeAcad.html.

CHRISTA MCAULIFFE ACADEMY

On-line courses combined with off-line study for kids in grades K–12. 3601 W. Washington Ave., Yakima, WA 98903; (509) 575-4989; www.cmacademy.org.

CHRYSALIS SCHOOL

Individual courses or full-program enrollment for grades K–12. 14241 NE Woodinville-Duvall Rd., PMB 243, Woodinville, WA 98072; (425) 481-2228; www.chrysalis-school.com.

CITIZENS' HIGH SCHOOL

A correspondence school using standard high school texts adapted for independent study. Box 1929, Orange Park, FL 32067-1929; (904) 276-1700; www.citizenschool.com.

CLONLARA HOME BASED EDUCATION PROGRAM

Their motto is "Educating, not schooling." A home-based education program providing curricula, materials, and support for kids in grades K–12. Many on-line classes for high school students through Clonlara Compuhigh. 1789 Jewett St., Ann Arbor, MI 48104; (734) 769-4511; www.clonlara.org.

DENNISON ACADEMY ON-LINE INTERNET SCHOOL

Individual courses or an integrated program leading to a high school diploma for students in grade 7 and up. Also includes adult education programs. Box 29781, Los Angeles, CA 90029; (818) 371-2001; www.dennisononline.com.

DISTANCE LEARNING RESEARCH NETWORK

Many annotated links to various kinds of distance-learning institutions and programs. www.wested.org/tie/dlrn/k12de.html.

ELECTRONIC HIGH SCHOOL

On-line high school classes. Students can enroll at any time during the year. www.ehs.uen.org.

FLORIDA HIGH SCHOOL

A large selection of on-line courses, available according to semester schedules. 445 W. Amelia St., Educational Leadership Center, Orange County Public Schools, Orlando, FL 32801; (407) 317-3326; fhs.net.

FOUNDATION FOR ON-LINE LEARNING

Free home-educator–taught courses in a range of subjects. www.infinet.com/~ndonald/links/fol.html.

GREENWOOD INSTITUTE

Homeschool support programs for learning-disabled kids, especially those with dyslexia and related problems. R.R. 2, Box 270, Putney, VT 05346; (802) 387-4545; www.greenwoodinstitute.org. or www.greenwoodinstitute.org/homeschool.

HOME STUDY INTERNATIONAL

PreK–12 Christian correspondence courses sponsored by the Seventh Day Adventist Church. Students can enroll for a complete curriculum or for individual subjects. Box 4437, Silver Spring, MD 20914-4437; (301) 680-6570; www.hsi.edu.

ICS HIGH SCHOOL PROGRAM

A complete high school distance learning program. ICS Learning Systems, 925 Oak St., Scranton, PA 18540-9887; (800) 238-9525, ext. 8797; www.icslearn.com/ICS.

INDEPENDENCE HIGH SCHOOL

Kids participate in the design of their own curricula and can receive credit for learning outside the classroom (work, volunteer projects, travel). Alger Learning Center, 121 Alder Dr., Sedro-Woolley, WA 98284; (800) 595-2630; www.independent-learning.com.

INDIANA UNIVERSITY SCHOOL OF CONTINUING STUDIES

A complete high school program. Kids can acquire a diploma and earn college credit. Owen 001/IUB, Bloomington, IN 47405; (800) 334-1011; scs.indiana.edu.

INTERNET HOME SCHOOL

On-line courses and complete academic programs for kids in grades K–12. 915 E. Gurley St. Suite 101, Prescott, AZ 86301; (520) 708-9404; www.internethomeschool.com.

KEYSTONE NATIONAL HIGH SCHOOL

Correspondence or "eSchool" on-line programs. A complete high school curriculum including driver's education and SAT preparation. School House Station, 420 W. Fifth St., Bloomsburg, PA 17815-1564; (800) 255-4937; www.keystonehighschool.com.

KOLBE ACADEMY HOME SCHOOL

Classical Catholic curriculum by correspondence for kids in grades K–12. Includes weekly course plans and quarterly tests. 1600 F St., Napa, CA 94559; (707) 255-6499; www.kolbe.org.

LAUREL SPRINGS SCHOOL

Project-based or textbook-based curricula and on-line courses for kids in grades K–12. Box 1440, Ojai, CA 93024; (805) 646-2473; www.laurelsprings.com.

LOUISIANA STATE UNIVERSITY INDEPENDENT STUDY

Many high school–level correspondence courses. Students can enroll at any time during the year. Office of Independent Study, E106 Pleasant Hall, Louisiana State University, Baton Rouge, LA 70803-1508; (225) 388-3199; www.is.lsu.edu/highschool.

MOORE FOUNDATION ACADEMY

Christian project-focused programs for grades K–12. Box 1, Camas, WA 98607; (800) 891-5255; www.moorefoundation.com.

NEWPROMISE.COM

A database of on-line college courses, searchable by subject or institution. www.mindedge.com.

NORTH DAKOTA DIVISION OF INDEPENDENT STUDY

Print-based or on-line courses for kids in grades 5–12. The program provides study guides, texts, lab kits, and other necessary materials. Tests must be taken through a nonparental supervisor. Box 5036, 1510 12th Ave. N, Fargo, ND 58105-5036; (701) 231-6000; www.dis.dpi.state.nd.us.

SETON HOME STUDY SCHOOL

Classical Catholic curriculum for grades K–12. 1350 Progress Dr., Front Royal, VA 22630; (540) 636-9900; www.setonhome.org.

STANFORD EDUCATION PROGRAM FOR GIFTED YOUTH

Computer-based distance learning for gifted kids from elementary to high school. Classes include math, science, English, and computer science. EPGY, Ventura Hall, Stanford, CA 94305-4115; (650) 329-9920; epgy.stanford.edu.

STUDY WEB

Many useful education-related topics, including a list of correspondence schools. www.studyweb.com/Teaching_Resources.

TEXAS TECH UNIVERSITY

A comprehensive curriculum of on-line and correspondence courses for grades K–12. Outreach and Extended Studies, Texas Tech University, 6901 Quaker Ave., Lubbock, TX 79413; (800)-MYCOURSE; www.dce.ttu.edu.

TUTORNET

On-line virtual classrooms for kids in elementary school through college in a wide range of subjects, including basic math, algebra, geometry, calculus, biology, chemistry, and physics.

Tutornet.com, Inc., 11410 Isaac Newton Square N, Suite 105, Reston, VA 20190; (877) TUTORKIDS; www.tutornet.com.

UNIVERSITY OF MISSOURI INDEPENDENT STUDY

A comprehensive high school curriculum available through correspondence or on-line courses. Enrollment in the diploma program requires written permission from a local school official. University of Missouri, Center for Distance and Independent Study, 136 Clark Hall, Columbia, MO 65211-4200; (800) 609-3727; cdis.missouri.edu.

UNIVERSITY OF NEBRASKA HIGH SCHOOL DIPLOMA PROGRAM

A complete high school curriculum. Students have options for both correspondence and on-line courses. Division of Continuing Studies/Distance Learning, Clifford Hardin Nebraska Center for Continuing Education, Box 839100, Lincoln, NE 68583-9100; (402) 472-2175; dcs.unl.edu/disted.

UNIVERSITY OF NEVADA INDEPENDENT STUDY

A wide selection of correspondence courses for high school students. Division of Continuing Education, University of Nevada, Reno, Box 14429, Reno, NV 89507; (800) 233-8928; www.dce. unr.edu/istudy.

UNIVERSITY OF OKLAHOMA INDEPENDENT STUDY

Over seventy high school correspondence courses, including some lab sciences. Independent Study Department, University of Oklahoma, 1600 S. Jenkins, Rm. 101, Norman, OK 73072-6507; (800) 942-5702; www.occe.ou.edu.

UNIVERSITY OF WISCONSIN LEARNING INNOVATIONS CENTER

High school courses by correspondence. 505 Rosa Rd., Madison, WI 53719-1257; (800) 442-6460; www.learn.wisconsin.edu.

WILLOWAY CYBER SCHOOL

A comprehensive Internet school with daily conferencing, virtual field trips, and collaborative projects for kids in grades 7–12. (610) 678-0214; www.willoway.com.

INDEX

Physical education (*cont.*)
  in Grade Five, 244–45
  in Grade Six, 272
  in Grade Seven, 296
  in Grade Eight, 314
  in Grade Nine, 316, 340
  in Grade Ten, 316, 357
  in Grade Eleven, 317, 373
  in Grade Twelve, 317, 388
  national standards for, 6
  state requirements for, 315
Physical science
  in kindergarten, 42–43
  in Grade One, 93–94
  in Grade Two, 135–37
  in Grade Three, 174–75
  in Grade Four, 206–8
  in Grade Five, 235–38
  in Grade Six, 264–66
  in Grade Seven, 291
  in Grade Eight, 308–11
Physics, 317, 334, 383–85
Preschool education, 7–18
Probability, 193, 224–25, 282, 304
Proportions, in Grade Nine, 330
PSAT (Preliminary Scholastic Aptitude
  Test), 317–18

Ratios, 255–56, 280, 303, 330
Reading
  comprehension, 23–25, 58–61,
    109–10, 317
  in kindergarten, 19–26
  in Grade One, 54–61
  in Grade Two, 107–10
  in Grade Three, 146–49
  in Grade Four, 185–88
  and standardized college admission
    tests, 317

SAT (Scholastic Aptitude Test), 317–18
Science
  in kindergarten, 41–46
  in Grade One, 92–100
  in Grade Two, 134–40
  in Grade Three, 173–80
  in Grade Four, 206–10
  in Grade Five, 235–42
  in Grade Six, 264–67
  in Grade Seven, 290–93
  in Grade Eight, 307–11
  in Grade Nine, 316, 333–37
  in Grade Ten, 316, 334, 352–55
  in Grade Eleven, 316, 334, 368–70

  in Grade Twelve, 317, 334, 383–85
  and standardized college admission
    tests, 317
  state requirements for, 315, 333–34
  See also Biology; Chemistry; Earth/
    space science; Life science; National
    Science Teachers Association;
    Physical science; Physics
Social studies. *See* Civics; Geography;
  History; National Council for the
  Social Studies
Space science. *See* Earth/space science
Speaking skills. *See* Listening and
  speaking skills
Spelling. *See* Writing
Standardized college admission tests,
  317–18
Standards. *See* National standards; State
  requirements; *specific discipline*
State requirements, 3, 4, 315–16
Statistics, 193, 224–25, 282, 304
Study skills
  in kindergarten, 29
  in Grade One, 66–67
  in Grade Two, 114
  in Grade Three, 153–54
  in Grade Four, 190–91
  in Grade Five, 220–21
  in Grade Six, 252
  in Grade Seven, 277–78
  in Grade Eight, 301
  in Grade Nine, 325
  in Grade Ten, 345
  in Grade Eleven, 361
  in Grade Twelve, 378

Technology, 389–92
Textbooks and resources, 318, 383–96
  See also specific grade or discipline
Trigonometry, 325–26, 362–64

U.S. Department of Education, 4

Volunteer work, 316, 318, 374

Web sites
  about high school homelearning, 319
  about technology, 391–92
  for preschool education, 17–18
  *See also specific grade, discipline or
    professional organization*
Word recognition, 20, 58, 108–9
World history
  in kindergarten, 39–41